With its Red for love, and its White for law,
And its Blue for the hope that our fathers saw
Of a larger liberty.

MANUAL OF PATRIOTISM

FOR USE IN THE PUBLIC SCHOOLS
OF THE STATE OF NEW YORK

· · · · · *AUTHORIZED BY ACT OF THE LEGISLATURE* · · · · ·

COMPILED, ARRANGED AND EDITED UNDER THE DIRECTION OF

CHARLES R. SKINNER,

State Superintendent of Public Instruction

... 1900 ...

PRINCETON.N

BRANDOW PRINTING COMPANY
DEPARTMENT PRINTERS
ALBANY, N. Y.

PREFACE.

Patriotism is more than a sentiment; it is a conviction based upon a comprehension of the duties of a citizen and a determination loyally to perform such duties. Patriotism is love of country, born of familiarity with its history, reverence for its institutions and faith in its possibilities, and is evidenced by obedience to its laws and respect for its flag.

American citizenship, safeguarded by the public schools, stands for the best that our institutions can offer to a free and happy people. Believing that our schools should be nurseries of patriotism, it has for many years been my constant purpose to encourage the study of history among the youth of our commonwealth as the strongest inspiration to patriotic citizenship and all that it implies. This book represents the fulfilment of such purpose, and is offered to the teachers of the State in the confident hope that the object sought to be accomplished may find ready and enthusiastic supporters among all educators who are striving for the best results of educational effort.

I have been inspired by the belief that to preserve our free institutions in all their old-time vigor and prestige, our system of public education must more and more lay stress on those civic virtues which develop and ennoble true and patriotic citizenship. This belief has steadily grown under the encouraging sympathy of thoughtful citizens, experienced educators, and patriotic organizations. The legislature of the State has acknowledged the growth of patriotic spirit by providing for the publication of a patriotic manual for use in the public schools of our State, and for its free distribution among them.

The task imposed upon the State Superintendent of Public Instruction by this enactment has not been easy. The limitations to the broad scope of material that could legitimately be made part of such a work were by no means easy to determine. The plan finally adopted and followed in the compilation of this volume was to present

(1)

the choicest literature bearing upon love of country, and upon notable
events and the achievements of proud names in American history, in
the belief that love of country grows best when the youth of the land
have a lively appreciation of what our free institutions have cost in
individual sacrifice, in suffering, and in treasure.

The Manual is now submitted to the teachers and the supervising
officers of the State, and to them is intrusted the important duty of
so using the material provided as to make at least some of its noble
utterances, its vivid pictures of great deeds and patriotic sacrifices,
and its quotations from the sayings of men honored for their clear
patriotic vision, a part of the very souls of the pupils intrusted to their
care.   In this way shall we secure the very result intended by
the legislature in enacting the law which authorized the publication
of this volume.   This can be done successfully only by much repeti-
tion and constant reiteration.   So well established is this fact that I
feel warranted in recommending that a few minutes of the opening
exercises of every public school each day be devoted to observance
based upon the material found in this Manual, or suggested thereby,
and, in addition, that more extended exercises be provided in commemoration of the great days and the great names in our Nation's
history.

I would be glad to have every pupil in our public schools commit
to memory each week some patriotic selection or quotation, no matter
how brief it may be.   Let school be opened by a patriotic song and
a salute to the flag.   This may be followed by a short recitation or
by several brief patriotic quotations from the masterpieces which have
been arranged in this work.   Let pupils choose from among their
number one or more classmates whose duty it shall be to see that the
flag is properly displayed in favorable weather, at other times exhib-
ited in the schoolroom, and all times sacredly cared for.

The task of editing this work was placed in the hands of Professor
William K. Wickes, principal of the high school of Syracuse, to whom
my acknowledgments are due for his loyal and painstaking efforts.   I
also acknowledge my indebtedness to Professor Isaac H. Stout, a
veteran of the civil war associated with me in the educational work of

the State, who suggested and arranged that part of the Manual relating to important dates in American history. I desire especially to acknowledge my obligations to Past-Commanders Albert D. Shaw, Anson S. Wood and Joseph W. Kay, Col. Joseph A. Goulden, chairman of the special committee on instruction in civics and patriotism, and their comrades of the Grand Army of the Republic, Department of New York, without number, for their constant encouragement and earnest co-operation in all matters pertaining to patriotic education, culminating in the publication of this volume.

This Manual is submitted to teachers, school officers, the people, and the legislature in the confident belief that it will be so well used in our school work as to reflect credit on the teaching force, prove the wisdom of the legislature in authorizing its publication, and justify the earnest efforts made in behalf of the law by patriotic citizens and organizations.

Charles R. Skinner

State Superintendent.

Albany, N. Y., *May*, 1900.

EDITOR'S ACKNOWLEDGMENTS.

This Manual is made up from many contributing sources. To all, so far as possible, the editor wishes to make his acknowledgments and pay his meed of thanks. To Statesmen, Orators, Poets — the dead and the living — whose strong and stirring utterances give fresh life and beauty to the thought of Patriotism and its noblest symbol, The Flag. To the following publishers and composers for the crowning grace of music:— the Oliver Ditson Company, for selections from their recent book, "Patriotic Songs for School and Home," filled with gems in an admirable musical setting,— Ginn & Co., whose wide-ranging and inspiring "Academy Song Book" would be a constant joy in any schoolroom,— Silver, Burdett & Co., in whose "Songs of the Nation" may be found a fine epitome of the best in present-day patriotic music,— Houghton, Mifflin & Co., whose "Riverside Song Book" contains in compact form, set to music, the finest patriotic poems of the noblest American poets, and into whose "Riverside Literature Series" have been put illustrations of every possible phase, as it would seem, of American history and life,— the John Church Company for use of the song, "Our Flag,"— Martha Moses Peckham (and her publishers, Clayton F. Summy Company, Chicago), for her unique and rousing song, "Dewey at Manila Bay," — Prof. Hamlin E. Cogswell for his spirit-caught interpretation of "The Liberty Bell" and "The Camp Flag,"— Miss Cornelia A. Moses for the music of the brush in her flag-drawing and initial letters. Above all, to Prof. Ralph W. Thomas for the music of human speech as shown in his many and choice selections of patriotic prose and verse.

THE EDITOR.

INTRODUCTION.

It is well to put in the very forefront of this book, the law in accordance with which this " Manual of Patriotism " has been prepared:

LAWS OF NEW YORK.— By Authority.

CHAP. 481.

AN ACT to provide for the display of the United States flag on the schoolhouses of the State, in connection with the public schools; and to encourage patriotic exercises in such schools.

Became a law April 22, 1898, with the approval of the Governor. Passed, three-fifths being present.

The People of the State of New York, represented in Senate and Assembly, do enact as follows:

SECTION I. It shall be the duty of the school authorities of every public school in the several cities and school districts of the State to purchase a United States flag, flagstaff and the necessary appliances therefor, and to display such flag upon or near the public school building during school hours, and at such other times as such school authorities may direct.

§ 2. The said school authorities shall establish rules and regulations for the proper custody, care and display of the flag, and when the weather will not permit it to be otherwise displayed, it shall be placed conspicuously in the principal room in the schoolhouse.

§ 3. It shall be the duty of the state superintendent of public instruction to prepare, for the use of the public schools of the state, a program providing for a salute to the flag at the opening of each day of school and such other patriotic exercises as may be deemed by him to be expedient, under such regulations and instructions as may best meet the varied requirements of the different grades in such schools. It shall also be his duty to make special provision for the observance in such public schools of Lincoln's birthday, Washington's birthday, Memorial day, and Flag day, and such other legal holidays of like character as may be hereafter designated by law.

§ 4. The State superintendent of public instruction is hereby authorized to provide for the necessary expenses incurred in developing and encouraging such patriotic exercises in the public school.

§ 5. Nothing herein contained shall be construed to authorize military instruction or drill in the public schools during school hours.

§ 6. This act shall take effect immediately.

Reading the foregoing carefully, it will be noted that, law-like, not a word is said as to the intent of the law. But whoever will " read between the lines " cannot fail to see its gracious purpose,— nothing less or other than to awaken in the minds and hearts of the young a strong and abiding regard for the flag and intelligent appreciation of the great men and great deeds that have made it to be, to all American youth, the rallying-cry of patriotism. In other words, the Empire State seeks for its countless host of boys and girls the inculcation of a true spirit of Patriotism and a loving regard for its greatest symbol, the Flag.

Note also in the law the constraint that is put upon the authorities of every public school in the State, to furnish, display, and care for a flag. That means that the State is interested to see that those into whose hands are put all the great interests of the schools — with their large corps of teachers and immense army of pupils — shall make clear the will and mind of the State in respect to the patriotic education of its children.

This good law was put upon the statute-book through efforts made largely by the Department of New York, Grand Army of the Republic. Under " General Orders, No. 6," issued August 9, 1897, a special Committee was appointed " to examine and report to the Department * * * upon the best practical methods of teaching Patriotism and Civics in our public schools." The Committee, having previously been divided into three parts, viz.: on Civics and History; Patriotic Exercises; Public Celebrations,— made its triple report in November, 1897. This report, under the title, " To Promote Patriotic Study in the Public Schools," was published in pamphlet form by the State Superintendent of Public Instruction for general distribution throughout the State. This action greatly influenced the patriotic legislation embodied in the law above quoted. In " General Orders, No. 10," we read: " The comrades feel deeply indebted to Supt.

Skinner for his most helpful and valuable co-operation in this important patriotic work, which lies so close to all their hearts." "Which lies so close to their hearts."—What pathos in those words! The brave men who fought the battles of the Union from '61 to '65 are fast passing away. Not many years hence the last heart will have ceased to beat. But meantime, how active and strenuous they are in all right efforts to vivify and strengthen the sentiment of true patriotism in the hearts of the young! Everywhere they keep Memorial Day,— a constant object lesson to the present generation. But besides this, in some cities, they are the inspiration to a ceremony called the "Transfer of Flags." And a special word of praise is due to Col. A. D. Shaw, Commander-in-Chief of the G. A. R., for his untiring zeal in the sacred cause of patriotism, and for the results he is bringing about in cementing the loyal friend-ship of Blue and Gray. Indeed, in many ways, the veterans of War are showing a profound interest in all that makes for lasting and honorable Peace.

In this work of beneficent patriotism many a Women's Relief Corps is having a large and honorable share. For there are many matters connected with the care of the sick and needy that can be safely and sympathetically entrusted only to women. And thus, through their kind and most unselfish ministrations, patriotism is exalted and made more sacred in the eyes of the young.

But G. A. R. and Women's Relief Corps, though the greatest, are not the only organizations that are helping (each in its own way and sphere) to strengthen the cause of patriotism. Here are a few others: Sons of Veterans, U. S. A., Sons of the Revolution, Sons of the American Revolution, Daughters of the American Revolution, Daughters of the Revolution, Colonial Dames of America, Association of Spanish War Veterans. Let all be welcomed to a part in the work of loyalty-building; let none be found negligent or lukewarm therein!

To no individual, scarcely to any organization, is this Manual so greatly indebted as to Charles R. Skinner, State Superintendent of Public Instruction. The G. A. R. Committee, in acknowledgment of his aid, speaks most gratefully of his "fruitful counsels and sugges-tions." And the editor of the Manual hereby wishes to give his testi-mony to the untiring interest shown by the Superintendent, to his unflagging enthusiasm, his constant wish for the doing of anything, everything, which might increase in youthful hearts the love of the Flag and of Native Land. Let the following letter attest his deep concern for the patriotic welfare of the young:

"ALBANY, *March* 1, 1900.

" *To the Boys and Girls of the Empire State:*

" It is spring by the calendar to-day,— but outside of my windows, the wind is blowing hard and cold and the snow is piling up great drifts in the streets. At such a time how pleasant it would be for me if I could gather you all in one great schoolroom around a big, roaring fire and talk to you about your school. But I cannot do that. There is no room or building on earth large enough to hold you all. So I must talk to you, if at all, with my pen.

" I hope you will all study hard, be obedient to your teachers and kind to your schoolmates. Do not shirk any lessons, no matter how difficult they may be, for if you master your lessons now, you will be better able to conquer many difficulties when you grow to be men and women.

"When you play, I hope you will play as hard as ever you can. It will help you to get strong and keep strong in body, just as hard study will strengthen your minds. Then, in years to come, you will not be in danger of ' breaking down ' when you have much work to do with hands or brain.

" I suppose you have heard it said that ' all work and no play makes Jack a dull boy.' And I believe that all play and no work would be just as bad. Don't you? So I want to tell you how to do something that certainly is not all work and surely is not all play —indeed, most of it is neither work nor play. What to call it I hardly know,— but I am sure that no pupil who does it will be a dull boy or a dull girl.

"When you are tired of work and lessons, and tired, too, of play, just stop your work or your play and think about the Flag of your country. And not only think about it, but read about it, write about it, learn what others have said about it — sing about it. You will find plenty of things to aid you in your thinking, reading, writing and singing, in those programs which your good friend, the editor of the Manual, has prepared for your special use. Now will not that be a pleasant change from work, and far more useful than mere play? I am sure also that it will illumine your work and your play with the ' fine gold' of Patriotism.

" Patriotism, dear children, means love of country. It is something that lives in the heart, and makes one willing to do anything that will be for the good of his country. So you see you cannot learn it from your books, nor get it from your play. But by using the exercises of this book, I think you can find and put away in your hearts that spirit which will make of you all good citizens — true patriots, loving your own land and wishing all nations of the earth to possess that freedom and happiness which you in America so much enjoy. I hope that you will find in this book those symbols of your country which stand for the great principles upon which our government is founded; that you will have your imagination aroused so that you can see, as ' with your eyes shut,' what beautiful lessons in patriotism those symbols teach, lessons that will prove to be like pictures of pleasant things that you may hang on the walls of Memory, never to fade; that in the sweet and strong music of the book you may feel your young spirits strengthened to fight, in years to come, in peace or in war, the noble battles of Patriotism and the Flag.

" Sincerely yours,

" [Signed.]

Charles R. Skinner

SUGGESTIONS TO TEACHERS.

Do not look upon this Manual as a text-book in American history. There are many good books that give the facts, and some that attempt the philosophy of the subject. But this does not pretend to do either. I am of the mind that neither facts nor philosophy alone, nor both combined, can create the sentiment of patriotism, much less foster and strengthen it in the minds and hearts of children. Be yourselves well grounded in the facts, and teach them as may be needful. Seek the philosophy of events, and teach it as far as possible. But when you take this book in your hands, let the light of sentiment and imagination play over facts and theories — tingeing all as with the beautiful Red, White and Blue of the Flag. Put yourselves in the place of the child. When your own mind is thus made responsive to the color-touch in history, try to make your pupils see and feel the illuminating power of great and worthy deeds. Nor of deeds alone. Teach them the wonderful power that abides in great personalities. Hold before their eyes a vision of the commanding figures of our own American history. Inspire them with a sentiment of loyalty and devotion to native land. If so profound a reasoner so wonderful an orator as Webster, constantly wove into the fabric of his most enduring speeches the splendid colors of the imagination, surely we need not hesitate, but rather, should be eager to use as best we can, though in faint degree, that power which he so magnificently wielded. Remember that the imagination is the very heart of all the symbols which are found in this book and are here used to set forth the noblest principles of government, the great underlying truths of our common humanity.

So, it was with intent that pictorial themes were largely chosen for the programs that follow. At the same time, it should be understood that the prefatory matter which caps each program is meant only as a hint or suggestion to be amended or enlarged as any teacher may wish. Keep the Flag ever before the mind's eye. Remember, also, that so far as patriotism finds oral expression it is through music, poetry and prose. They are the gateways beautiful into the mind of the child. Teach them to sing the songs, let them learn " by heart " the poems and prose selections,— for not a strain of music, not a stanza, not a sentence, conveys an unworthy thought. Do not be alarmed at any sentiment for fear it is too profound for children to comprehend. If they learn it not in early years, they will never learn it. But my word for it, the day of a complete understanding of its meaning will come, and then they will remember, with undying thanks, the faithful one who taught them. Do not let them lose sight of the underlying thought of each program, that special quality in pictorial guise, which it is intended to set forth. Perhaps it is sympathy, or freedom or protection — no matter what, in the wide range of patriotism. If the central, rallying word is not given in the preliminary note, let the teacher give it, or better still, let the pupils find it. Let them put it in as clear and compact a " composition " form as possible, or explain it in oral form. Have class exercises frequently; let pupils sing or repeat in concert; borrow the music of other groups or individual programs, if time permits; the selections, poetry or prose, of different groups or single programs, choosing selections from any part of the book. Put in a quotation exercise, now and then, permitting pupils to select for themselves.

Mindful that in school as elsewhere, " time is money," I have made the great majority of the programs so brief that any one may be compassed in ten minutes or less, at the opening or closing of the daily session. All told, the programs number forty, so that a daily exercise may be given through the school year without repeating any one program more than four or five times, just often enough to keep the memory refreshed on the various songs and selections. The programs for Memorial Day, Washington's birthday, Lincoln's birthday, Flag Day, have been made longer than others, as befits their great importance. Each of these four great themes makes a group by itself. The other programs are divided into groups according to the relation they bear to the Flag, the central theme of all the programs. Near the opening of the book a brief history of the flag is given, straightway followed by exercises pertaining to the flag and by the ceremony of " Salutes " and " Pledges of Allegiance." Thus the body of the book has been divided into groups, each distinct and separate, and similarly into programs closely related to " The Flag." Even the abstract subjects, with their wisely-chosen selections, all find their meaning and inspiration in the flag.

It was the first thought of the editor of this Manual to make an extended list of patriotic books for the use of pupils. But that does not fall within the province and scope of the law, and so no such bibliography appears. It is entirely right and commendable, however, for any teacher to point out to his pupils the sources of our history and to give them the knowledge of its facts. For this, any good text in United States History will suffice. Upon the sentiment and romance of our history, the books are almost innumerable. Here again, the teacher's discretion and opportunity must be his guide.

It may be that enthusiastic and progressive teachers will welcome the giving, from time to time, of what may be called a composite program. If so, take any program-subjects, such as liberty bell, sword, dove, shield, flag, let a pupil or pupils tell what each symbolizes, and then show what use any great statesman or statesmen made of these or similar symbols and what the symbols meant to them. Thus, to Abraham Lincoln, and through him to the people of this great nation, the liberty bell meant freedom; the sword, union; the dove, peace with honor; the shield, protection; the flag, loyalty. The possible combinations of such a plan are many, historically interesting, patriotically profitable.

It is greatly to be desired that the ceremony of the " Transfer of Flags " be held in as many schools of the State as possible. Choose a national holiday for the exercise. In cities, let each school be represented by a color-bearer with a flag. Range the delegates in semicircle on the stage. In smaller places, put all the pupils, or as many as possible, upon the stage, accompanied by the flag in the hands of a color-bearer. Alike in cities and smaller places, let the flags to be transferred be those donated by G. A. R. Posts rather than those purchased by the city or district authorities under mandate of the State. Invite veterans, parents, friends. Arrange whatever patriotic exercises seem best, and near the close, let the teacher, or an old soldier, or some adult speaker, give a brief history or eulogy of the flag, exhort each new color-bearer to guard it sacredly, to do nothing that might bring dishonor to its unsullied colors. Then, at the word of command, "Transfer flag!" let the color-bearer who has had the care of the flag for the past year hand it over to another who is to be its custodian for the year to come. It is an inspiring and memorable sight!

For several months, in the scant leisure of a busy life, I have wrought at the plan and making of this book. The task has been, to me, very pleasurable; I hope it may be to others most profitable — to teachers, by strengthening and clarifying their appreciation of the noble history of our common country; to the Young America of the Empire State, by the creation and exaltation of a pure-minded and intelligent patriotism.

And so I drop my pen, with a silent salute and renewed pledge of allegiance to The Flag!

W. K. W.

CONTENTS.

	PAGE.
PREFACE.	iii
INTRODUCTION	v
SUGGESTIONS.	xi

GROUP I. THE FLAG:
Brief History of the Flag; The Stars; The Red, White and Blue; The Half-masted Flag; Saluting the Flag; Patriotic Pledges. Interspersed PATRIOTIC SONGS 1

GROUP II. THE FLAG PROTECTS
The Home; School; Capitol; Restored Union. SONGS 37

GROUP III. THE FLAG WAVES OVER
The Camp; Hospital; Exposition Buildings; Consulate; Land and Sea. SONGS 59

GROUP IV. THE FLAG IS SYMBOLIZED BY
The Liberty Cap; Liberty Bell; Sword and Dove; Eagle; Shield. SONGS. 95

GROUP V. THE FLAG ILLUMINES THE TABLEAUX
Of the Minute Man; Departure and Return of States; March of Flags; Army and Navy; Homage to Columbia 141

    "   —Concluded—THE FLAG GLORIFIES THE PATRIOTIC UTTERANCES
Of Longfellow, Whittier, Holmes, Lowell 152

GROUP VI. THE FLAG RECALLS
Columbus Day; Landing of the Pilgrims; Lexington and Concord; Fourth of July; Yorktown. SONGS 155

THE FLAG HALLOWS MEMORIAL DAY:
Prologue: General Grant and the Civil War; Admiral Dewey and the Spanish-American War; Quotations. SONGS. 185

In Memoriam May 30th. Selections and Songs 227

THE FLAG CONSECRATES THE BIRTHDAY OF GEORGE WASHINGTON:
Selections, Quotations and Songs 241

(xv)

xvi   *CONTENTS.*

THE FLAG BLESSES THE BIRTHDAY OF ABRAHAM LINCOLN :   PAGE.
    Selections, Quotations and Songs................................ 267
FLAG-DAY MAKES SACRED JUNE 14TH:
    Selections, Quotations and Songs................................... 299
SELECTIONS — IN PROSE AND POETRY — ON
    Patriotism.. 329
    Declaration of Independence.. 351
    Constitution of the United States.................................. 353
    Liberty... 355
    Union... 359
    Citizenship... 366
OUR COUNTRY:
    Quotations.. 373
THE NOBILITY OF LABOR... 383
IMPORTANT DATES IN AMERICAN HISTORY................................... 389

MANUAL OF PATRIOTISM.

GROUP I.

THE FLAG.

1. BRIEF HISTORY OF THE FLAG..................Song, *America.*
2. THE STARS...................Song, *The Star-Spangled Banner.*
3. THE RED, WHITE AND BLUE......Song, *The Red, White and Blue.*
4. THE HALF-MASTED FLAG.

5. { SALUTING THE FLAG...............Song, *A Song of the Flag.*
{ PATRIOTIC PLEDGES................Song, *The Waving Flag.*

(1)

AMERICA.

Words by SAMUEL FRANCIS SMITH, D.D.

Moderato.

1. My coun-try! 'tis of thee Sweet land of lib - er - ty, Of thee I sing;
2. My na - tive coun - try, thee— Land of the no - ble free— Thy name I love;
3. Let mu - sic swell the breeze, And ring from all the trees, Sweet free-dom's song;
4. Our fa - ther's God! to Thee, Au - thor of lib - er - ty, To Thee we sing;

Land where my fa - thers died! Land of the Pil - grims' pride!
I love thy rocks and rills, Thy woods and tem - pled hills;
Let mor - tal tongues a - wake; Let all that breathe par - take;
Long may our land be bright With free - dom's ho - ly light;

From ev - 'ry moun - tain side Let free - dom ring!
My heart with rap - ture thrills Like that a - bove.
Let rocks their si - lence break,— The sound pro - long.
Pro - tect us by Thy might, Great God, our King!

A BRIEF HISTORY OF THE FLAG.

HERE were many flags of many kinds in our country in colonial times — long, long ago. The most famous one, perhaps, was that which was raised, for the first time, on January 2, 1776, over the camp of the Continental forces at Cambridge. In mid-May of the same year, a flag of like design floated over the Capitol at Williamsburg. Thus, under similar flags, the great colony of Massachusetts and that of Virginia together marched towards the freedom they so much wished to see.

There is good reason to believe, also, that the famous naval hero, Paul Jones, was the first man in the world to hoist a similar flag upon a regular man-of-war. Nor was it long before a sixteen-gun brig, "The Reprisal," commanded by Capt. Lambert Wickes, sailing from home soon after the adoption of the Declaration of Independence, carried the flag across the seas and unfurled it in the harbors of the Old World.

So, both on land and sea, at home and abroad, waved that Continental Banner which seemed to stretch its folds, like hands of welcome, to greet a new nation.

The first real *American* flag had its origin in the following resolution adopted by the American Congress, June 14, 1777: "*Resolved*, That the flag of the thirteen United States be thirteen stripes alternate red and white; that the union be thirteen stars, white in a blue field, representing a new constellation."

But the flag thus resolved upon could not make *itself*. So, a committee of Congress, accompanied by Washington, sought out the home and services of Mrs. Elizabeth Ross of Philadelphia — better known as " Betsy Ross "— to aid them in the flag-making. Her skillful hands and willing heart soon worked out a plan, and gave to this

(5)

country that red, white and blue banner which is the admiration of all nations and the unfailing joy of every true American.

What a pleasant sight it must have been to see Mistress Betsy Ross, that good dame of Revolutionary days, at work upon that new flag which nowadays we call "the dear *old* flag." Well may we believe that she had a thoughtful yet serene face; that she loved her country with a deep and tender love. For, indeed, it was her country, though not then free from the grasp of King George. Who can tell what a help the sight of the new flag was in gaining that independence which has made our land so great and happy? No wonder that an association has been formed to buy and keep, for patriotic purposes, the home in which was made, by the hands of Betsy Ross, the first real *American* flag.

How old, then, is the flag? Less than a century and a quarter, you see. Yet, curiously enough, it is older than the present banner of Great Britain, adopted in 1801; or Spain's, 1785; or the French tricolor, 1794; or the flag of the Empire of Germany, 1870. Thus the flag seems as old as though it had lived for centuries.

What a history the flag has had since those early days when Washington looked upon it as he stood under the old Elm at Cambridge! The thirteen stars and thirteen stripes were unfurled at the battle of Brandywine, in 1777; they were at Germantown in October of the same year; in the same red-leaved month they sang their song of triumph over defeated Burgoyne at Saratoga; they helped to cheer the hungry and half-clad patriot soldiers at Valley Forge; they saw the surrender of the enemy at Yorktown; they fluttered their "Goodbye" to the British evacuating New York; they made glorious with their sky-born colors the dreary years of the Revolution.

In the War of 1812, the sea breezes blew over no American ship that did not have the flag of the stars and stripes at its fore; its folds seemed to be filled with voices that called aloud the names of gallant seamen — Lawrence, Perry, Hull, Decatur, and many others whose names will never perish.

In the Mexican War, fought in the forties, our flag was carried into foreign territory, and waved over many places of great historic fame. It is true that not all of our citizens approved of that war, but the flag itself was not allowed to suffer harm; on the contrary, it waved triumphant in the very " halls of the Montezumas."

As for the Civil War, what veteran soldier cannot tell of the trials and triumphs of the four memorable years from 1861 to 1865? Then it seemed, again and again, as though the flag would be rent in twain, and the States be severed, never to reunite. Yet to-day we know a grander Union than ever before.

It remained for the Spanish-American War, however, to make this reunion clear and strong — beyond a doubt or shadow. Men of the North and men of the South clasped hands and marched and sailed away, under the same dear flag, to fight on foreign soil for freedom to the down-trodden of earth.

But we must not think that it is only in time of war that the flag has a history. It has a far more cheering and pleasant history in times of peace. There is always something sad about war, even when the flags are raised to celebrate a victory. For the victory has cost a great many brave men their lives, and that always saddens the Nation's heart. But in a time of peace, how proudly the flag floats over our homes and schools; "on land and sea, and in every wind under the whole heavens." Then the people are happy, because there is no loss of life among them by means of war; fathers stay at home and enjoy peace and quiet; their sons are at school or college, in business or working at a trade. On holidays the streets are thronged with happy people, children are at their games or play, or perhaps are in school celebrating the lives and deeds of men and women who have helped to make our country so strong and great among the nations of the world. And this is the peaceful and happy way in which our nation has spent most of its time since the close of the Revolutionary War. During more than a hundred years, the whole time occupied by war has been less than ten years. Those ten years show that we can fight when it is necessary to defend our country, keep our freedom unharmed, our flag unstained; but they also show that we do not fight unless we must for the honor of the flag. They show, also, that we do not go to war merely for the sake of gaining territory from nations that are weak, nor simply to humble the pride of nations that are saucy and strong.

How different is the story of the nations of the Old World, and of the many little countries or republics of South America in the New World! Their citizens seem so fond of killing each other that some of them keep at it most of the time, until their war-offices are filled with blood-stained battle-flags that they have carried with them into war, or have taken from their enemies,— very much as wild Indians might hang up in their wigwams, or fasten at their belts, the scalps they have taken from their victims.

Oh, let us not do anything like that in our dear country. Let us rather set the flag flying, and watch it as it waves over a land of peace and plenty,— a land where the farmer may till the ground, the mechanic work in busy shops, the merchant buy and sell in his store, and thousands of merry boys and girls troop to school — everybody at work, and all in quiet and security because the Red, White and Blue waves triumphant over a happy, peaceful land.

Surely it is well for Young America to honor a flag which has such resistless Power and gives such adequate Protection in time of peace. The flag stands for so much that is worth having and saving; it means so much to every citizen, young or old, that no honor paid to it can be too great. To be good citizens — keeping the laws, obedient to all rightful authority, merciful in the treatment of animals, kind-hearted and sympathetic towards the unfortunate, mindful ever of the good name and fame of our country,— all these things are quiet yet potent ways of doing honor to the flag. Many a veteran, reposing in well-earned quiet after marching and battling, is content to gaze till his eyes brim with tears at the flag that speaks to him so eloquently of days that are gone, of conflicts that are over, of the dearly-bought victories of Peace.

But the eyes of children dance with joy when they see the flag, and they must needs speak and sing and act that joy. And so, it is wise to provide some way by which they may use their young voices and their ever-moving feet and hands.

OUR FLAG.

Fling it from mast and steeple,
  Symbol o'er land and sea
Of the life of a happy people,
  Gallant and strong and free.
Proudly we view its colors,
  Flag of the brave and true,
With the clustered stars and the steadfast bars,
  The red, the white, and the blue.

Flag of the fearless hearted,
  Flag of the broken chain,
Flag in a day-dawn started,
  Never to pale or wane.
Dearly we prize its colors,
  With the heaven-light breaking through,
The clustered stars and the steadfast bars,
  The red, the white, and the blue.

Flag of the sturdy fathers,
  Flag of the loyal sons,
Beneath its folds it gathers
  Earth's best and noblest ones.
Boldly we wave its colors,
  Our veins are thrilled anew;
By the steadfast bars, the clustered stars,
  The red, the white, and the blue.
                    —*Margaret E. Sangster.*

THE FLAG THAT HAS NEVER KNOWN DEFEAT.

On history's crimson pages, high up on the roll of fame,
The story of Old Glory burns, in deathless words of flame.
'Twas cradled in war's blinding smoke, amid the roar of guns,
Its lullabies were battle-cries, the shouts of Freedom's sons;
It is the old red, white, and blue, proud emblem of the free,
It is the flag that floats above our land of liberty.
Then greet it, when you meet it, boys, the flag that waves on high;
And hats off, all along the line, when Freedom's flag goes by.

*   *   *   *   *   *   *   *

All honor to the Stars and Stripes, our glory and our pride,
All honor to the flag for which our fathers fought and died;
On many a blood-stained battle-field, on many a gory sea,
The flag has triumphed; evermore triumphant may it be.
And since again, 'mid shot and shell, its folds must be unfurled,
God grant that we may keep it still unstained before the world.
All hail the flag we love, may it victorious ever fly,
And hats off, all along the line, when Freedom's flag goes by.
     —Charles L. Benjamin and George D. Sutton.

OLD FLAG FOREVER.

She's up there,— Old Glory,— where lightnings are sped;
She dazzles the nations with ripples of red;
And she'll wave for us living, or droop o'er us dead,—
     The flag of our country forever!

She's up there,— Old Glory,— how bright the stars stream!
And the stripes like red signals of liberty gleam!
And we dare for her, living, or dream the last dream,
     'Neath the flag of our country forever!

She's up there,— Old Glory,— no tyrant-dealt scars,
No blur on her brightness, no stain on her stars!
The brave blood of heroes hath crimsoned her bars.
     She's the flag of our country forever!
     —Frank L. Stanton.

THE STARS.

HIRTEEN, and only thirteen stripes,—"alternate red and white," are on every American flag, no matter when made. These stripes tell us of the thirteen colonies that together fought the battles of the Revolution, and afterward entered into an enduring Union under the Constitution. Let us take here the roll-call of that noble band of sister colonies:

Delaware	Maryland
Pennsylvania	South Carolina
New Jersey	New Hampshire
Georgia	Virginia
Connecticut	New York
Massachusetts	North Carolina

Rhode Island.

Yes, the stripes that run their bright bands of color along the length of the flag never number more nor less than thirteen. Not so with the stars,— for each new State, a new star. As the evening of a clear night draws on, have you not watched the stars one by one " peep through the blanket of the dark? " So in our country's sky, State after State, like star after star in the heavens, has flashed upon our sight until, in the closing year of the century, the " blue field " is filled with the radiant splendor of a " constellation " of forty-five States.

This is the order in which they entered the Union: Vermont (1791), Kentucky (1792), Tennessee (1796), Ohio (1802), Louisiana (1812), Indiana (1816), Mississippi (1817), Illinois (1818), Alabama (1819), Maine (1820), Missouri (1821), Arkansas (1836), Michigan (1837), Florida (1845), Texas (1845), Iowa (1846), Wisconsin

(1848), California (1850), Minnesota (1858), Oregon (1859), Kansas (1861), West Virginia (1863), Nevada (1864), Nebraska (1867), Colorado (1876), North Dakota (1889), South Dakota (1889), Montana (1889), Washington (1889), Idaho (1890), Wyoming (1890), Utah (1896).

And here is the list of territories which may yet shine as States: New Mexico, Arizona, Alaska, Indian Territory, Oklahoma,— though perhaps not as States of the first magnitude.

THE STAR-SPANGLED BANNER.

Francis Scott Key. 1814.

Solo or Quartet.

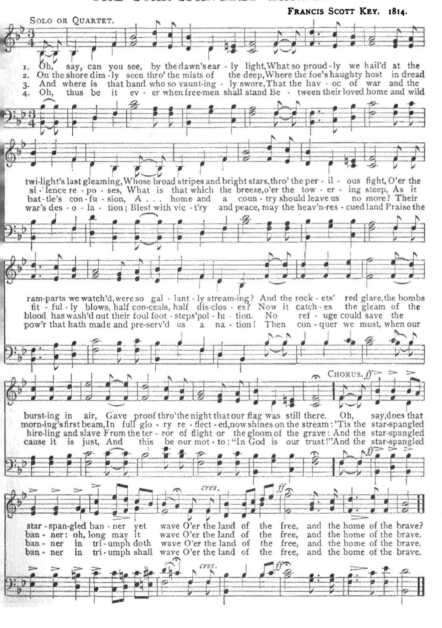

1. Oh, say, can you see, by the dawn's ear - ly light, What so proud-ly we hail'd at the
2. On the shore dim-ly seen thro' the mists of the deep, Where the foe's haughty host in dread
3. And where is that band who so vaunt-ing - ly swore, That the hav - oc of war and the
4. Oh, thus be it ev - er when free-men shall stand Be - tween their loved home and wild

twi-light's last gleaming, Whose broad stripes and bright stars, thro' the per - il - ous fight, O'er the
si - lence re - po - ses, What is that which the breeze, o'er the tow - er - ing steep, As it
bat - tle's con - fu - sion, A . . . home and a coun - try should leave us no more? Their
war's des - o - la - tion; Blest with vic - t'ry and peace, may the heav'n-res - cued land Praise the

ram-parts we watch'd, were so gal - lant - ly stream-ing? And the rock - ets' red glare, the bombs
fit - ful - ly blows, half con-ceals, half dis-clos - es? Now it catch - es the gleam of the
blood has wash'd out their foul foot - steps' pol - lu - tion. No ref - uge could save the
pow'r that hath made and pre-serv'd us a na - tion! Then con - quer we must, when our

Chorus. ff

burst - ing in air, Gave proof thro' the night that our flag was still there. Oh, say, does that
morn-ing's first beam, In full glo - ry re - flect - ed, now shines on the stream: 'Tis the star-spangled
hire-ling and slave From the ter - ror of flight or the gloom of the grave: And the star-spangled
cause it is just, And this be our mot - to: "In God is our trust!" And the star-spangled

cres.   ff

star - span-gled ban - ner yet wave O'er the land of the free, and the home of the brave?
ban - ner: oh, long may it wave O'er the land of the free, and the home of the brave.
ban - ner in tri - umph doth wave O'er the land of the free, and the home of the brave.
ban - ner in tri - umph shall wave O'er the land of the free, and the home of the brave.

cres.   ff

SELECTIONS.

It is the flag of history. Those thirteen stripes tell the story of our colonial struggle, of the days of '76. They speak of the savage wilderness, of old Independence Hall, of Valley Forge and Yorktown. Those stars tell the story of our nation's growth, how it has come from weakness to strength, until its gleam, in the sunrise over the forests of Maine, crimsons the sunset's dying beams on the golden sands of California.— *S. L. Waterbury.*

It is a little thing, perchance, to put the stars and stripes a few miles nearer to the pole than has been put the flag of any other nation; but yet, somehow or other, that fact appeals to us as Americans.— *Adolphus W. Greeley.*

Two years ago, I saw a sight that has ever been present in my memory. As we were going out of the harbor of Newport, about midnight, on a dark night, some of the officers of the torpedo station had prepared for us a beautiful surprise. The flag at the depot station was unseen in the darkness of the night, when suddenly, electric searchlights were turned on it, bathing it in a flood of light. All below the flag was hidden, and it seemed to have no touch with earth, but to hang from the battlements of heaven. It was as if heaven was approving the human liberty and human equality, typified by that flag.— *Benjamin Harrison.*

THE BANNER OF THE STARS.

Hurrah! boys, hurrah! Fling our banner to the breeze!
  Let the enemies of freedom see its folds again unfurled,
And down with the pirates that scorn upon the seas
  Our victorious Yankee banner, sign of freedom to the world!

Chorus: We'll never have a new flag, for ours is the true flag,
      The true flag, the true flag, the red, white, and blue flag.
      Hurrah! boys, hurrah! we will carry to the wars,
      The old flag, the free flag, the banner of the stars.

And what though its white shall be crimsoned with our blood?
  And what though its stripes shall be shredded in the storms?
To the torn flag, the worn flag, we'll keep our promise good,
  And we'll bear the starry blue field, with gallant hearts and arms.
                — *R. W. Raymond.*

A VISION OF THE STARS.

His lonely watch a sentinel was keeping,
　While stars were shining clear;
Within their tents the wearied hosts were sleeping,
　And home in dreams seemed near.

Near by, in peace, the broad Potomac river
　Ran fleetly on and free,
And waves, like shafts from full and silver quiver,
　Shot onward to the sea.

Such was the scene of rare and tranquil beauty,
　That met the soldier's gaze,
And blended with his thoughts of present duty,
　The light of other days.

'Neath roof-tree quiet, far remote, were sleeping
　Those whom he loved so well —
Dreaming perchance of him, or fondly weeping
　At thought of War's dread spell.

Then as he paced, his watchful eyes upturning,
　He saw the arching sky,
Where countless stars in silence clear were burning,
　Bespeaking peace on high.

And gazing thus, he straightway fell to musing
　Upon that wondrous dome,—
And in his wrapt imaginings was losing,
　For once, the thought of home.

To him, that mighty dome the Union seeming,
　The stars were soldiers true
That stood in ranks with watchful eyes a-gleaming,
　And great souls flashing through.

" No hand," he cried, as raptured he stood gazing,
　" Can hurl the Union down,
Or pluck from out that dome of might amazing,
　The stars within its crown."

But as he spake a cloud came blackly drifting
  Across the welkin blue,
And spreading ever, threatening, dense and shifting,
  Hid every star from view.

"Alas," cried he, "is this the war's dread token?
  The stars all swept away.
The dome of Union, lost to man, and broken,
  Forever and for aye?"

Slow grew his step as on he paced,— and musing,
  Sad grew his heart,—
The portent seemed so direful, so confusing,
  The tears began to start!

But lo! once more, through tears, his eyes up-glancing,
  The clouds are passing by!
He sees the dome, and stars with light entrancing,
  Still watching in the sky!

Gone are his fears. Exultant hear him crying,
  "The clouds of War will flee,
And stars of Peace yet chant in chorus vying,
  'Union and Liberty.' "

*   *   *   *   *   *   *   *

Ah, lonely sentinel, let not thy vision,
  Though now fulfilled, e'er cease;
Still point the Nation to the fields Elysian,—
  Thy chosen watchword — Peace.
                    —*W. K. W.*

THE FLAG OF THE CONSTELLATION.

The stars of our morn on our banner borne,
  With the iris of heaven are blended,
The hands of our sires first mingled those fires
  And by us they shall now be defended!
Then hail the true — the Red, White, and Blue,
  The flag of the Constellation;
It sails as it sailed, by our forefathers hailed,
  O'er battles that made us a nation.

What hand so bold to strike from its fold,
  One star or stripe of its bright'ning;
To him be each star a fiery Mars,
  Each stripe a terrible lightning.
Then hail the true,— etc.

Its meteor form shall ride the storm
  Till the fiercest of foes surrender;
The storm gone by, it shall gild the sky,
  As a rainbow of peace and splendor.
Then hail the true,— etc.

Peace, peace to the world — is our motto unfurled,
  Tho' we shun not a field that is gory;
At home or abroad, fearing none but our God,
  We will carve out our pathway to glory!
Then hail the true,— etc.

                                      — *T. Buchanan Read.*

THE RED, WHITE AND BLUE.

WHEN children pick a flower to pieces, just to see how it is made, casting its petals to the ground — *that* destroys both its bright colors and its fragrance. Not so when they first look at the flag, see that it is made up of three colors, and then try to find out with the "mind's eye" what each color stands for. That is a very pleasant and a very profitable exercise. Now, while it would be a good thing for the boys and girls in a school to think out the meaning of the tricolor for themselves, it will do no harm to give them a hint upon which they may work.

Take then the red. Did you ever think how the red tide which we call "blood" courses through the body, and how it supplies the very life-power of the body? So, the red in the flag is the symbol of the *life* of the nation. And again: When you read how the life-blood of men is poured out upon the battle-field, how can you help thinking of the bravery of those men! So, the red of the flag speaks of *Courage*.

That for which white stands, the world over, is purity. So, the white in the flag proclaims that sense of *Honor* which is the safeguard and strength of the nation — that feeling and conscience which keep the citizen from doing anything which will offend against the law or weaken the moral power of the nation.

Who does not know that blue stands for loyalty? Who has not heard the expression "true blue?" So, the blue in the flag means *Patriotism* — that steadfastness of purpose, that devotion to native land, which makes the citizen proud of every noble deed of his countrymen, and willing to undergo any trials for her dear sake.

(19)

SELECTIONS.

THE RIGHT OF THE LINE.

When man with things mortal is through,
  When time shall its sceptre resign,
When follows the final review,
  Who shall hold the right of the line?
The Captain shall make the award,
  Fit place unto each shall assign.
Who, who in Thine army, O Lord,
  Shall be given the right of the line?

*   *   *   *   *   *

The nation which gains the award,
  Which wins by the right that's divine,
Which holds by the will of the Lord,
  Unchallenged, the right of the line;
Shall blazon her banner with stars,
  Stars brighter the sky never knew —
Shall deck it with rainbow-hued bars,
  The Red and the White and the Blue!

Our country! to Liberty true,
  Which ne'er in her service shall fail,
Resisting the rule of the few
  That thus may the many prevail.
Our country! which fights the good fight
  For manhood where'er it may be,
Which stands for the right 'gainst the might,
  Inspiring all lands to be free.

'Tis she who shall be of best cheer
  When summoned to final review;
She'll answer with never a fear —
  No trembling for those that are true;
All hail her! 'neath Heaven's blue arch
  No flag can the Union's outshine,
And they who beneath it shall march
  Will be found at the right of the line.

O goddess of learning, whene'er
  A temple is reared unto thee,
Raised high let our banner appear,
  The beautiful flag of the free;
For know that whene'er 'tis unfurled,
  Thou best canst thy mission pursue,
Thy torch shall illumine the world,
  Beaming bright 'neath the red, white and blue.

O goddess of learning, whene'er
  A temple is reared unto thee,
Raised high let our banner appear,
  The beautiful flag of the free.
Thus they who its splendors behold,
  Shall learn as its fame they recall,
A lesson more precious than gold —
  The duty of each unto all.

As they gaze their souls shall expand,
  Till in ecstacy rises their cry,
" We also at Freedom's command,
  Shall count it all honor to die.
To our sires we swear to be true,
  Whose memory ever shall shine,
And march in the final review,
  With them at the right of the line."
                                    — *Wm. H. McElroy.*

[Read before the Albany High School on the occasion of presentation of flags by the Grand Army of the Republic.]

At Oriskany five British standards were captured, and upon returning to Fort Stanwix they were hoisted and above them an uncouth flag, intended to represent the American stars and stripes.

This rude banner, hastily extemporized out of a white shirt, an old blue coat, and some stripes of red flannel, was the first American flag with stars and stripes ever hoisted in victory.

It was flung to the breeze on the memorable day of Oriskany, August 6, 1777.

The following explanation of the colors and symbolic meaning of the " Stars and Stripes," was written by a member of the old Continental Congress, to whom, with others, was committed the duty of selecting a flag for the infant confederacy:

" The stars of the new flag represent the constellation of States rising in the West. The idea was taken from the constellation Lyra, which in the hand of Orpheus signifies harmony. The blue in the field was taken from the edges of the Covenanter's banner in Scotland, significant of the league covenant of the United Colonies against oppression, involving the virtues of vigilance, perseverance and justice. The stars were in a circle, symbolizing the perpetuity of the Union; the ring, like the circling serpent of the Egyptians, signifying eternity. The thirteen stripes showed with the stars, the number of the United Colonies, and denoted the subordination of the States to the Union, as well as equality among themselves. The whole was the blending of the various flags previous to the Union flag, viz.: The red flag of the armies and the white of floating batteries. The red color, which in the Roman day was the signal of defiance, denotes daring, the blue fidelity, and the white purity."

There is the national flag! He must be cold, indeed, who can look upon its folds rippling in the breeze without pride of country. If he be in a foreign land, the flag is companionship, and country itself, with all its endearments. Who, as he sees it, can think of a State merely? Whose eye, once fastened upon its radiant trophies, can fail to recognize the image of the whole nation?

It has been called a " floating piece of poetry; " and yet, I know not if it have any intrinsic beauty beyond other ensigns. Its highest beauty is in what it symbolizes. It is because it represents all, that all gaze at it with delight and reverence. It is a piece of bunting, lifted in the air; but it speaks sublimely, and every part has a voice. Its stripes of alternate red and white proclaim the original union of thirteen States to maintain the Declaration of Independence. Its stars, white on a field of blue, proclaim that union of States constituting our national constellation, which receives a new star with every new State. The two, together, signify union, past and present. The very colors have a language which was officially recognized by our fathers. White is for purity, red for valor, blue for justice; and all together, bunting, stripes, stars, and colors, blazing in the sky, make the flag of our country, to be cherished by all our hearts, to be upheld by all our hands.— *Charles Sumner.*

THE RED, WHITE, AND BLUE.

D. T. Shaw.

1. Oh, Co-lum-bia, the gem of the o - cean, The home of the brave and the free, The
2. When war wing'd its wide des - o - la - tion, And threaten'd the land to de - form, The
3. The star-spangled ban-ner bring hith-er, O'er Colum-bia's true sons let it wave; May the

shrine of each pa - triot's de - vo - tion, A world of - fers hom-age to thee; Thy
ark then of free-dom's foun-da - tion, Co - lum - bia, rode safe thro' the storm: With the
wreaths they have won nev - er with -er, Nor its stars cease to shine on the brave; May the

man-dates make he - roes as-sem - ble, When Lib - er - ty's form stands in view; Thy
gar - lands of vic - t'ry a-round her, When so proudly she bore her brave crew, With her
ser - vice u - nit - ed ne'er sev - er, But hold to their col - ors so true; The

ban-ners make tyr - an - ny trem-ble, When borne by the red, white and blue, When
flag proud-ly float-ing be - fore her, The boast of the red, white and blue, The
ar - my and na - vy for - ev - er, Three cheers for the red, white and blue, Three

borne by the red, white and blue, When borne by the red, white and blue, Thy
boast of the red, white and blue, The boast of the red, white and blue, With her
cheers for the red, white and blue, Three cheers for the red, white and blue, The

THE RED, WHITE, AND BLUE.

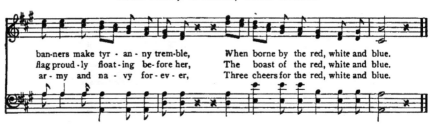

ban-ners make tyr - an - ny trem-ble,   When borne by the red, white and blue.
flag proud - ly float-ing be- fore her,   The   boast of the red, white and blue.
ar - my and na - vy for - ev - er,   Three cheers for the red, white and blue.

THE HALF-MASTED FLAG.

T is well for us to keep in mind not only the birthdays of the men who have done great deeds for their country, but on certain occasions also their deathdays. Thus, the one hundredth anniversary of the death of George Washington was observed on December 14, 1899, in many places, by many people. At such a time, the flag is not raised clear to the top of the pole or "mast," but about half-way,— and so we get the words, "the flag at half-mast," as a symbol of the sorrow of the true patriots for a great soldier and statesman dying long ago (like Washington), or perhaps for one just fallen out from the ranks of the living, like that brave sailor, Lieut. Brumby (died December 17, 1899), the flag lieutenant of Admiral Dewey. This heroic officer and faithful friend of the Admiral stood by him in the great naval fight at Manila. Daring and devoted as he was, why should not the flags throughout his native State of Georgia be placed at half-mast, and his fellow-citizens recall and record his bravery and patriotism?

So it is by keeping in remembrance the brave deeds of those patriots who have died — by telling over again and again the story of their loyalty — by visiting the places made famous by them,— by all these things and in many other ways, that children even may learn many a lesson in true patriotism; and the half-masted flag teaches the lesson.

SELECTIONS.

HOW SLEEP THE BRAVE!

How sleep the brave, who sink to rest,
With all their country's wishes blest!
When Spring, with dewy fingers cold,
Returns to deck their hallowed mould,
She there shall dress a sweeter sod
Than Fancy's feet have ever trod.

(25)

By fairy hands their knell is rung;
By forms unseen their dirge is sung;
There Honor comes, a pilgrim gray
To bless the turf that wraps their clay;
And Freedom shall awhile repair,
To dwell a weeping hermit there.
                    — *William Collins.*

The past rises before me like a dream. Again we are in the great struggle for national life. We hear the sounds of preparation, the music of the boisterous drums, the silvery voices of heroic bugles. We see thousands of assemblages, and hear the appeals of orators; we see the pale cheeks of women, and the flushed faces of men, and in those assemblages we see all the dead whose dust we have covered with flowers. We lose sight of them no more. * * * We see them all as they march proudly away under the flaunting flags, keeping time to the wild, grand music of war, marching down the streets of the great cities, through the towns and across the prairies down to the fields of glory, to do and to die for the eternal right. We go with them one and all. We are by their side on all the gory fields, in all the hospitals of pain, on all the weary marches. We stand guard with them in the wild storm and under the quiet stars. We are with them in ravines running with blood, in the furrows of old fields. We are with them between contending hosts, unable to move, wild with thirst, the life ebbing slowly away among the withered leaves. We see them pierced by balls and torn with shells in the trenches by forts, and in the whirlwind of the charge, where men become iron, with nerves of steel. We are at home when the news comes that they are dead. We see the maiden in the shadow of her first sorrow. We see the silvered head of the old man bowed with the last grief. These heroes are dead. They died for liberty. They died for us. They are at rest. They sleep in the land they made free, under the flag they rendered stainless, under the solemn pines, the sad hemlocks, the tearful willows, and the embracing vines. They sleep beneath the shadows of the clouds, careless alike of sunshine or of storm, each in the windowless palace of rest. Earth may run red with other wars; they are at peace. In the midst of battle, in the roar of conflict, they found the serenity of death. I have one sentiment for the soldiers living and dead: Cheers for the living, and tears for the dead.— *Robert G. Ingersoll.*

THE PHANTOM ARMY.

And I saw a phantom army come,
With never a sound of fife or drum,
But keeping step to a muffled hum
   Of wailing lamentation;
The martyred heroes of Malvern Hill,
Of Gettysburg and Chancellorsville,
The men whose wasted bodies fill
   The patriot graves of the nation.

And there came the unknown dead, the men
Who died in fever-swamp and fen,
The slowly starved of prison pen;
   And marching beside the others,
Came the dusky martyrs of Pillow's fight,
With limbs enfranchised and hearing bright,
I thought — 'twas the pale moonlight —
   . They looked as white as their brothers.

And so all night marched the nation's dead,
With never a banner above them spread,
No sign, save the bare, uncovered head
   Of the silent, grim Reviewer;
With never an arch but the vaulted sky,
With not a flower save those which lie
On distant graves, for love could buy
   No gift that was purer or truer.

So all night long moved the strange array,
So all night long till the break of day
I watched for one who had passed away
   With a reverent awe and wonder;
Till a blue cap waved in the lengthening line,
And I knew that one who was kin of mine
Had come, and I spoke — and lo! that sign
   Wakened me from my slumber.
                       — Bret Harte.

THE BIVOUAC OF THE DEAD.

The muffled drum's sad roll has beat
　　The soldier's last tattoo;
No more on Life's parade shall meet
　　That brave and fallen few.
On Fame's eternal camping ground
　　Their silent tents are spread,
And Glory guards with solemn round,
　　The bivouac of the dead.

　　*　　*　　*　　*　　*　　*　　*

Thus 'neath their parent turf, they rest,
　　Far from the gory field,
Borne to a Spartan mother's breast
　　On many a bloody shield.
The sunshine of their native sky
　　Smiles sadly on them here,
And kindred eyes and hearts watch by
　　The heroes' sepulchre.

Rest on, embalmed and sainted dead;
　　Dear is the blood you gave.
No impious footsteps here shall tread
　　The herbage of your grave.
Nor shall your glory be forgot
　　While Fame her record keeps,
Or Honor points the hallowed spot
　　Where Valor proudly sleeps.

[It was a Southern soldier, Theodore O'Hara, of Kentucky, who wrote the immortal lines above since cast in bronze, and placed in the national cemeteries where lie the soldiers who fell for the Union. This refers to last stanza only.]

DIRGE FOR A SOLDIER.

Close his eyes; his work is done!
　　What to him is friend or foeman,
Rise of moon or set of sun,
　　Hand of man or kiss of woman?

　　　　Lay him low, lay him low,
　　　　In the clover or the snow!
　　　　What cares he? He cannot know;
　　　　Lay him low.

Fold him in his country's stars,
  Roll the drum and fire the volley!
What to him are all our wars?
  What but death-bemocking folly?

Leave him to God's watching eye;
  Trust him to the 'Hand that made him.
Mortal love weeps idly by,
  God alone has power to aid him.
                    — George Henry Boker.

———————

Let them rest where nodding clover
Covers husband, friend and lover,
Where the long cool grass leans over,
  And the stars their watches keep;
Where with drowsy murmurings
Haunts the bees with tireless wings;
Where all night the cricket sings,
  Let them sleep.

———————

Under the guns of the fort on the hill,
Daisies are blossoming, buttercups fill;
Up the grey ramparts the scaling vine flings
High its green ladders, and falters and clings,
    Under the guns,
Under the guns of the fort on the hill.

Under the guns of the fort on the hill,
Once shook the earth with the cannonade's thrill;
Once trod those buttercups feet that, now still,
Lie all at rest, in the trench by the mill,
    Under the guns,
Under the guns of the fort on the hill.

———————

  How they went forth to die!
Pale, earnest thousands, from the busy mills,
And sun-browned thousands from the harvest hills,
Quick, eager thousands from the busy streets,
And storm-tossed thousands from the fishers' fleets,
  How they went forth to die!

A SONG OF THE FLAG.

(Air: Yankee Doodle — each stanza sung to first half of solo.)

Roll a river wide and strong,
Like the tides a-swinging;
Lift the joyful floods of song,
Set the mountains ringing.

Chorus: Run the lovely banner high!
Morning's crimson glory,
Field as blue as God's own sky,
And every star a story.

Drown the guns, outsound the bells,
In the rocking steeple,
While the chorus throbs and swells
Of a happy people.

Chorus: Run the lovely banner, etc.

For our darling flag we sing,
Pride of all the nation,
Flag that never knew a king,
Freedom's constellation.

Chorus: Run the lovely banner, etc.

Blest be God, fraternal wars
Once for all are ended,
And the gashes and the scars
Peace and time have mended.

Chorus: Run the lovely banner, etc.

Massachusetts, Maryland,
Tennessee, Nebraska,
One, Columbia's daughters stand
From Georgia to Alaska.

Chorus: Run the lovely banner, etc.

Staff and masthead swing it forth —
Liberty unblighted,
West and East and South and North
Evermore united!

Chorus: Run the lovely banner, etc.

— *M. Woolsey Stryker.*

SALUTING THE FLAG.

T is well for each boy and girl to own a flag — small and inexpensive,— or for each district to furnish a sufficient number. The flags can be lightly fastened upon the wall, transforming bare and cheerless spots into a bright glow of colors; or, if patriotic pictures are on the walls, the flags may be draped about them with excellent effect. Another plan is to " stack " the flags on the platform or stage, or place them in a rack provided for the purpose.

Now, let us suppose that the day is so fair, the weather so fine, that the flags can be displayed out-of-doors. Good! give the children the blessed tonic of the fresh air. At a given signal, let each pupil take a flag from wall or stack or rack. Marshalling them into line, preceded, if convenient, by a standard-bearer carrying a good-sized flag or the school banner, let them march — singing a patriotic verse or two — till they come to the flagstaff on the school green, or to a spot whence they may see the flag at the roof-peak. Then, at a proper signal from the teacher, let them salute the flag and repeat in unison any one of the five pledge-forms printed below — then march back, " stack arms " and resume seats — ready, if time permits, for any one of the many programs of this book. If the weather is so bad that the flag and the children must both stay in-doors, let the salute and pledge be given as before, and any ten-minute program be taken up,— the only difference between this and the out-door exercise being, that in this the flags are left in their places on platform or walls.

UNCOVER TO THE FLAG

Uncover to the flag; bare head
  Sorts well with heart as, humbly bowed,
We stand in presence of the dead
  Who make the flag their shroud.

Uncover to the flag, for those
  Of Concord and of Bunker Hill,
The first to fire on Freedom's foes,
  With shouts that echo still.

Uncover to the flag, for him
  Who sang the song, the gallant Key,
When in the dawn hour, gray and dim,
  He strained, its stars to see.

Uncover to the flag, for one
  Who scorned to have his colors dip,
And fighting all but flying none,
  Cried, " Don't give up the ship."

Uncover to the flag, for him
  Who stoutly nailed it to the mast,
And dauntlessly, or sink or swim,
  Stood by it to the last.

Uncover to the flag; the land
  It floats above is one anew,—
The North and South, now hand in hand,
  See God's skies, gray and blue.

Uncover to the flag; it flew
  Above the men who manned the Maine,
The pledge that we will mete the due
  Of vengeance out to Spain!

Uncover to the flag; it stands
  For all of bravest, all of best,
In us with flower-laden hands,
  In those who lie at rest.

                    —*E. C. Cheverton.*

THE WAVING FLAG.

W. K. W.

O. R. BARROWS.

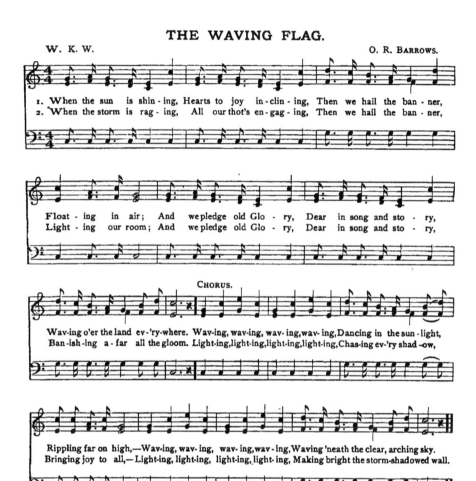

1. When the sun is shin-ing, Hearts to joy in-clin-ing, Then we hail the ban-ner,
2. When the storm is rag-ing, All our thot's en-gag-ing, Then we hail the ban-ner,

Float-ing in air; And we pledge old Glo - ry, Dear in song and sto - ry,
Light-ing our room; And we pledge old Glo - ry, Dear in song and sto - ry,

CHORUS.

Wav-ing o'er the land ev-'ry-where. Wav-ing, wav-ing, wav-ing, wav-ing, Dancing in the sun-light,
Ban-ish-ing a-far all the gloom. Light-ing, light-ing, light-ing, light-ing, Chas-ing ev-'ry shad-ow,

Rippling far on high,—Wav-ing, wav-ing, wav-ing, wav-ing, Waving 'neath the clear, arching sky.
Bringing joy to all,—Light-ing, light-ing, light-ing, light-ing, Making bright the storm-shadowed wall.

PATRIOTIC PLEDGES.

No. 1.

Flag of Freedom! true to thee,
All our Thoughts, Words, Deeds shall be,—
Pledging steadfast Loyalty!

No. 2.

The toil of our Hands,
The thoughts of our Heads,
The love of our Hearts,
We pledge to our Flag!

No. 3.

By the Memories of the Past,
By the Present, flying fast,
By the Future, long to last,
Let the dear Flag wave!

No. 4.

I pledge myself to stand by the Flag that stands for Loyalty, Liberty and Law!

No. 5.

The Youth's Companion " Pledge of Allegiance." (Right hand lifted, palm downward to a line with the forehead and close to it, standing thus, all repeat together slowly:) " I pledge allegiance to my Flag and to the Republic for which it stands; One Nation indivisible, with Liberty and Justice for All." (At the words "to my Flag," the right hand is extended gracefully, palm upward, towards the Flag and remains in this gesture to the end of the affirmation; whereupon all hands immediately drop to the side.)

No. 6.

CIVIC CREED FOR THE BOYS AND GIRLS OF THE GREAT REPUBLIC.

God hath made one blood all nations of men, and we are His children, brothers and sisters all. We are citizens of these United States and we believe our flag stands for self-sacrifice for the good of all the people. We want, therefore, to be true citizens of our great country and will show our love for her by our works. Our country does not ask us to *die* for her welfare only,— she asks us to *live* for her, and so to live and so to act that her government may be pure, her officers honest, and every corner of her territory a place fit to grow the best men and women, who shall rule over her.

SPEECH AT TRANSFER OF FLAGS.

Color-bearers of the public schools: When on the 17th of May last, the flags which you now bear were presented by the two posts of the G. A. R. of this city, you were chosen to represent your schools, because you were thought worthy.

The veterans of the Civil War from whose hands you received them were men who had shown their loyalty upon bloody battle fields. They felt that they were honored in intrusting to you these banners. Young hearts that should beat loyally through the years to come. Young hands that should ever be ready to strike in defense should the time ever demand it.

After carefully guarding these banners for the time they have been in your custody, you are about to surrender them to other hands. They who follow you will in turn be as proud as you. In the years to come all of you will look back to your school days, and feel that the greatest honor bestowed upon you by your school was your selection as color-bearers.

My children, you who are delegates from the various schools, this day and ceremony mean much to you. It is not the flag, with its stripes and stars of red and white, its field of blue, that of itself means anything. The language it speaks is what you should heed, is that which makes it the flag of freedom. Read lessons from its beautiful folds as unfolding in the fresh breezes of the morning they are kissed by the bright sunlight. It tells us that it is not the flag of war, but the flag of peace and good will. Its mission is the friendship of the nations.

But it also tells us that should it ever be necessary to strike against wrong that the blow will be heavy. If ever it is necessary to draw the sword in behalf of wronged or oppressed humanity that that sword will not be sheathed until the wrong is righted, and the hand of the oppressor raised.

Learn that it teaches us to be good citizens, that in all civic affairs we should be upright and not seek office for the sake of pelf. It teaches us that public duty is a trust which should be faithfully performed for the good of our country and not for personal aggrandizement.

Go from here to-day impressed with the thought of being better men and women because you are to be citizens of this great country, and that you will do your best to make it better because you are citizens; then my children you shall best honor the flags, which we intrust to your color-bearers to-day.— *W. H. Scott, G. A. R. veteran.*

MANUAL OF PATRIOTISM.

GROUP II.

THE FLAG PROTECTS

1. HOME...........................Song, *Home, Sweet Home.*
2. SCHOOL..................Song, *The Schoolhouse and the Flag.*
3. CAPITOL........................Song, *The Star of Freedom.*
4. RESTORED UNION..........Song, *O, Starry Flag of Union, Hail!*

HOME, SWEET HOME.

JOHN HOWARD PAYNE.

Sicilian Air.

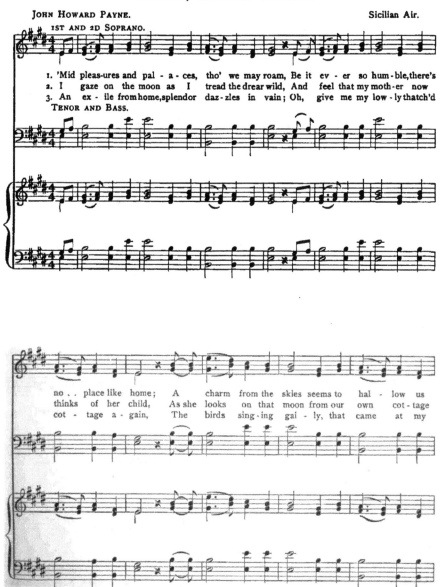

1. 'Mid pleas-ures and pal - a - ces, tho' we may roam, Be it ev - er so hum-ble, there's
2. I gaze on the moon as I tread the drear wild, And feel that my moth-er now
3. An ex - ile from home, splendor daz - zles in vain; Oh, give me my low - ly thatch'd

no .. place like home; A charm from the skies seems to hal - low us
thinks of her child, As she looks on that moon from our own cot - tage
cot - tage a - gain, The birds sing-ing gai - ly, that came at my

HOME, SWEET HOME.

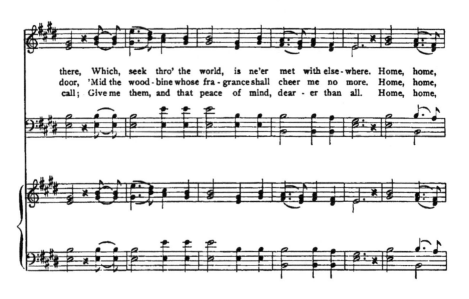

there, Which, seek thro' the world, is ne'er met with else-where. Home, home,
door, 'Mid the wood-bine whose fra-grance shall cheer me no more. Home, home,
call; Give me them, and that peace of mind, dear-er than all. Home, home,

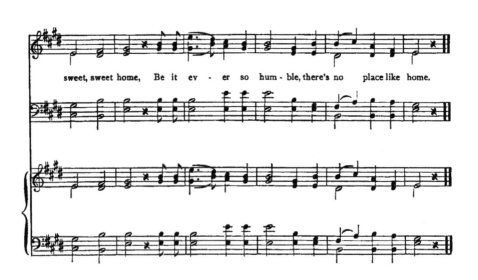

sweet, sweet home, Be it ev-er so hum-ble, there's no place like home.

THE HOME.

O need to ask you, my young friends, whether you love your home. It is, indeed, as the good old song says, " the dearest spot of earth."

And yet, I wonder whether you ever think that it is only because of the shelter which the flag gives you that you have and enjoy your homes! If that flag-shelter were taken away, with it would pass at once the security of home. The flag, like a guardian angel, spreads its folds, like wings, above your dwellings, and guards them with unceasing care, and with all the mighty power of the government. Let the flag, then, fly over your homes. Place it upon the walls of your room, so that when morning carries the flaming torch of Day before your window, touching the red, white and blue with a fresh splendor, you may cry, as once did a famous knight of old, " There's sunshine on the wall."

SELECTIONS.

HOME.

Home's not merely four square walls,
  Though with pictures hung and gilded,—
Home is where affection calls,
  Filled with shrines the heart hath builded.
Home! Go watch the faithful dove
  Sailing 'neath the heaven above us.
Home is where there's one to love;
  Home is where there's one to love us.

Home's not merely roof and room.
  It needs something to endear it.
Home is where the heart can bloom,
  Where there's some kind lip to cheer it.
What is home with none to meet,
  None to welcome, none to greet us?
Home is sweet and only sweet,
  When there's one we love to meet us.

— Charles Swain.

THE HOME, THE NATION'S SAFEGUARD.

A few Sundays ago, I stood on a hill in Washington. My heart thrilled as I looked on the towering marble of my country's Capitol.

*   *   *   *   *   *

A few days later I visited a country home. A modest, quiet house, sheltered by great trees and set in a circle of field and meadow, gracious with the promise of harvest barns and cribs well filled and the old smokehouse odorous with treasure — the fragrance of pink and hollyhock mingling with the aroma of garden and orchard, and resonant with the hum of bees and poultry's busy clucking — inside the house, thrift, comfort, and that cleanliness that is next to godliness, and the old clock that had held its steadfast pace amid the frolic of weddings, and kept company with the watchers of the sick bed, and had ticked the solemn requiem for the dead; and the well-worn Bible that, thumbed by fingers long since stilled, and blurred with tears of eyes long since closed, held the simple annals of the family, and the heart and conscience of the home. Outside stood the master, strong and wholesome and upright; wearing no man's collar; with no mortgage on his roof, and no lien on his ripening harvest; pitching his crops in his own wisdom, and selling them in his own time in his chosen market; master of his lands and master of himself. Near by stood his aged father, happy in the heart and home of his son. And as they started to the house the old man's hands rested on the young man's shoulder, touching it with the knighthood of the fourth commandment, and laying there the unspeakable blessing of an honored and grateful father. As they drew near the door the old mother appeared; the sunset falling on her face, softening its wrinkles and its tenderness, lighting up her patient eyes, and the rich music of her heart trembling on her lips as in simple phrase she welcomed her husband and son to their home. Beyond was the good wife, happy amid her household cares. And the children, strong and sturdy, trooping down the lane with the lowing herd, or weary of simple sport, seeking, as truant birds do, the quiet of the old home nest. And I saw the night descend on that home. And the stars swarmed in the bending skies, and the father, a simple man of God, gathered the family about him, read from the Bible the old, old story of love and faith, and then closed the record of that simple day by calling down the benediction of God on the family and the home!

And as I gazed, the memory of the great Capitol faded from my brain. Forgotten its treasure and its splendor. And I said, " Surely here — here in the homes of the people — is lodged the ark of the covenant of my country. Here is its majesty and its strength. Here the beginning of its power and the end of its responsibility."

The home is the source of our national life. Back of the national Capitol and above it stands the home. Back of the President and above him stands the citizen. What the home is, this and nothing else will the Capitol be. What the citizen wills, this and nothing else will the President be.— *Henry W. Grady.*

MY COUNTRY.

I love my country's pine-clad hills,
Her thousand bright and gushing rills,
  Her sunshine and her storms;
Her rough and rugged rocks that rear
Their hoary heads high in the air
  In wild, fantastic forms.

I love her rivers, deep and wide,
Those mighty streams that seaward glide
  To seek the ocean's breast;
Her smiling fields, her pleasant vales,
Her shady dells, her flowery dales,
  The haunts of peaceful rest.

I love her forests, dark and lone,
For there the wild bird's merry tone
  Is heard from morn till night,
And there are lovelier flowers, I ween,
Than e'er in Eastern lands were seen,
  In varied colors bright.

Her forests and her valleys fair,
Her flowers that scent the morning air,
  Have all their charms for me;
But more I love my country's name,
Those words that echo deathless fame,—
  " The land of liberty."

Oh, give me back my native hills,
My daisied meads, and trouted rills,
  And groves of pine!
Oh, give me, too, the mountain air,—
My youthful days without a care,
When rose for me a mother's prayer,
  In tones divine!

Long years have passed,— and I behold
My father's elms and mansion old,—
  The brook's bright wave;
But, ah! the scenes which fancy drew
Deceived my heart,— the friends I knew
Are sleeping now, beneath the yew,—
  Low in the grave!

The sunny spots I loved so well,
When but a child, seem like a spell
  Flung round the bier!
The ancient wood, the cliff, the glade,
Whose charms, methought, could never fade,
Again I view,— yet shed, unstayed,
  The silent tear!

Here let me kneel, and linger long,
And pour, unheard, my native song,
  And seek relief!
Like ocean's wave, that restless heaves,
My days roll on, yet memory weaves
Her twilight o'er the past, and leaves
  A balm for grief!

Oh, that I could again recall
My early joys, companions, all,
  That cheered my youth!
But, ah, 'tis vain,— how changed am I!
My heart hath learned the bitter sigh!
The pure shall meet beyond the sky,—
  How sweet the truth!

                                        — *Hesperian.*

THE SCHOOLHOUSE AND THE FLAG.

H. Butterworth.

Frank Treat Southwick.

1. Ye who love the Re - pub - lic, re - mem-ber the claim Ye owe to her for-tunes, ye
2. The blue arch a - bove us is Lib - er - ty's dome, The green fields be - neath us E -

owe to her name, To her years of pros-per - i - ty past and in store,— A hun-dred be-
qual - i - ty's home; But the schoolroom to-day is Hu-man - i - ty's friend,—Let the peo - ple the

hind you, a thou-sand be - fore! 'Tis . . the school-house that stands by the flag;
flag and the school-room de - fend!

Let . . the na - tion stand by the school! 'Tis . . the school-bell that

rings for our Lib - er - ty old, 'Tis the school-boy whose bal - lot shall rule.

* Small notes for instrument only.

From Levermore's "Academy Song Book," Ginn and Co., Publishers, by permission.

THE SCHOOL.

ET us all praise and thank the Legislature of our great Empire State for that law which compels every schoolhouse to keep the flag flying during school time. For if home is " the dearest spot," hardly less pleasant should the schoolhouse be. And what can help so much to make it pleasant as the sight of the flag? Faces of the sunniest teachers will sometimes be overcast with clouds; pleasantest voices sometimes be edged with sharpness; sweetest tempers sometimes grow sour, like the richest cream after a thunderstorm; but the flag, ah, the flag! As it floats over the proudest or poorest schoolhouse in the State, it always greets you in the morning with a smile of welcome on its pleasant face, and when you start for home, waves its benediction over you, and shakes out from its folds this cheery voice: " Come again! I'll be here to greet you."

SELECTIONS.

THE SCHOOL — LIBERTY'S SAFEGUARD.

Our glorious Land to-day,
'Neath Education's sway,
  Soars upward still.
Its halls of learning fair,
Whose bounties all may share,
Behold them everywhere
  On vale and hill!

Thy safeguard, Liberty,
The school shall ever be,—
  Our Nation's pride!
No tyrant's hand shall smite,
While with encircling might
All here are taught the Right
  With Truth allied.

(47)

Beneath Heaven's gracious will
The star of Progress still
  Our course doth sway;
In unity sublime
To broader heights we climb,
Triumphant over Time,
  God speeds our way!

Grand birthright of our sires,
Our altars and our fires
  Keep we still pure!
Our starry flag unfurled,
The hope of all the world,
In peace and light impearled,
  God hold secure.
           — Samuel Francis Smith.

THE COMMON SCHOOL.

The sheet-anchor of the Ship of State is the common school. Teach, first and last, Americanism. Let no youth leave the school without being thoroughly grounded in the history, the principles, and the incalculable blessings of American liberty. Let the boys be the trained soldiers of constitutional freedom, the girls the intelligent mothers of freemen. American liberty must be protected.— *Hon. Chauncey M. Depew.*

UNIVERSAL EDUCATION.

The " fine, old conservative policy," as it was called two centuries ago, of " keeping subjects ignorant in order to make them submissive," has happily given place to one which seeks to educate all the people in order to preserve liberty, to enforce law, to develop manhood and womanhood, and to perpetuate the blessings of good government. Free common schools are open to-day all over our broad land. Colleges and universities, high schools, and schools of professional and technical training offer their privileges to all who seek them. Two glorious centuries of educational growth, unmatched in the history of the world! What wondrous changes! What stupendous strides!

Philosophers and statesmen have ever recognized the truth that universal education is the basis of true national prosperity and real greatness. "The fair fabric of Justice raised by Numa," says Plutarch, "passed rapidly away because it was not founded upon education." No truer reason can be given for the decay of everything good in a State. No nation will ever realize its full possibilities which does not build upon the education of the whole people, upon the enlightenment of the masses. Every consideration of public safety points to the wisdom of emancipating the people from the slavery of ignorance. Might alone has made the struggle for greatness and has failed. War, with all its horrors, has proved powerless to make nations great. Rome, great as she was, and leader of the world, fell, not because she lacked brave generals and great rulers, but because her plan of education did not reach to the foundations of her national life and character. In a republic like ours, the system of education, to realize its highest aim, must reach the common people, the "plain people," as Lincoln loved to call them. It is the highest province of the State to determine the character and the quality of the education which will best prepare them for their life work as individuals, and as citizens of the republic.— *Charles R. Skinner*, from the President's Address, delivered before the National Educational Association of the United States, at Milwaukee, Wis., July 6, 1897.

Our fathers, in their wisdom, knew that the foundations of liberty, fraternity and equality must be universal education. The free school, therefore, was conceived the corner-stone of the Republic. Washington and Jefferson recognized that while religious training belongs to the church, and while technical and higher culture may be given by private institutions, the training of citizens in the common knowledge and in the common duties of citizenship belongs irrevocably to the State. We, therefore, uplift the system of free and universal education as the master force which, under God, has been informing each of our generations with the peculiar truths of Americanism.— *Charles R. Skinner*, from address before New York State Teachers' Association, 1897.

4

FREE SCHOOLS INSPIRE LOYALTY TO COUNTRY.

(From the last interview of General Horry with General Marion in 1795.)

Israel of old, you know, was destroyed for lack of knowledge; and all nations, all individuals, have come to naught from the same cause; what signifies then even this government, divine as it is, if it be not known and prized as it deserves? This is best done by free schools.

Men will always fight for their government according to their sense of its value. To value it aright, they must understand it. This they cannot do, without education, and, as a large portion of the citizens are poor, and can never attain that inestimable blessing without the aid of government, it is plainly the first duty of government to bestow it freely upon them. The more perfect the government, the greater the duty to make it well known. * * *

God knows, a good government can hardly be half anxious enough to give its citizens a thorough knowledge of its own excellencies. For as some of the most valuable truths, for lack of careful promulgation, have been lost, so the best government on earth, if not duly known and prized, may be subverted. Ambitious demagogues will rise, and the people, through ignorance and love of change, will follow them.

Look at the people of New England. From Britain their fathers had fled to America for religion's sake. Religion had taught them that God created men to be happy; that to be happy they must have virtue; that virtue is not to be attained without knowledge, nor knowledge without instruction, nor public instruction without free schools, nor free schools without legislative order. Among a free people who fear God, the knowledge of duty is the same as doing it. With minds well informed of their rights, and hearts glowing with love for themselves and posterity, when the war broke out they rose up against the enemy, firm and united, and gave glorious proof how men will fight when they know that their all is at stake.—*Francis Marion.*

THE CAPITOL.

HAVE you ever been in the city of Washington, the capital of your country? If you have, I am sure you never can forget the noble "Capitol" building, at one end of Pennsylvania avenue, while at the other end stands the famous "White House," the home of the President of the United States.

To the Capitol the approach is very beautiful and the first sight of the great building very inspiring. Within its walls the laws which govern our country are made by United States Senators — two from each state in the Union — and Representatives from all the states,— the number from each state being based upon population. Here indeed, from the loftiest peak of the "Capitol," should our dear flag fly. For the flag is the emblem of that justice which the laws of this country must grant to every citizen, no matter how poor or humble he may be. In this building also sit the Justices of the Supreme Court of the United States. It is their duty to see that the laws are right, that justice is done between man and man, and that respect and obedience are shown to these just laws.

Washington is without doubt one of the most beautiful cities in the world. It is in the District of Columbia, so-called. This district is really a territory of the United States, and as such is under the exclusive care and government of Congress. No finer historical program for the Capitol could be devised than to have pupils read about the men and the events that have made Washington, the Capitol, and the District of Columbia, the home of the Capitol—so famous. Then let them mould their reading into short essays, to be read, compared and contrasted as to knowledge of historical perspective shown and real "composing" power.

SELECTIONS.

A few Sundays ago I stood on a hill in Washington. My heart thrilled as I looked on the towering marble of my country's Capitol, and a mist gathered in my eyes as, standing there, I thought of its tremendous significance and the powers there assembled, and the responsibilities there centered — its president, its congress, its courts, its gathered treasure, its army, its navy, and its 60,000,000 of citizens. It seemed to me the best and mightiest sight that the sun could find in its wheeling course — this majestic home of a Republic that has taught the world its best lessons of liberty — and I felt that if wisdom, and justice, and honor abided therein, the world would stand indebted to this temple on which my eyes rested, and in which the ark of my covenant was lodged for its final uplifting and regeneration.— *Henry W. Grady.*

With each succeeding year, new interest is added to this spot. It becomes connected with all the historical associations of our country, with her statesmen and her orators; and alas! its cemetery is annually enriched with the ashes of her chosen sons. Before is the broad and beautiful river, separating two of the original thirteen states, and which a late President, a man of determined purpose and inflexible will, but patriotic heart, desired to span with arches of ever-enduring granite, symbolical of the firmly cemented union of the North and South. On its banks repose the ashes of the Father of His Country; and at our side, by a singular felicity of position, overlooking the city which he designed, and which bears his name, rises to his memory the marble column, sublime in its simple grandeur, and fitly intended to reach a loftier height than any similar structure on the surface of the whole earth. Let the votive offering of his grateful countrymen be freely contributed to carry higher and still higher this monument. May I say, as on another occasion: Let it rise! Let it rise, till it shall meet the sun in his coming. Let the earliest light of the morning gild it, and parting day linger and play on its summit.— *Daniel Webster.*

THE STAR OF FREEDOM.

DONIZETTI.

1. Bright-ly the star of Free-dom shines, Beam-ing with light and glad - ness;
2. O dear Co-lum - bia, glo - rious land! Ev - er we love and bless thee;

Wak-ing to life new scenes of joy, Driv-ing a-way all sad - ness. Hail to our coun-try,
Thy rights we'll ev - er brave de - fend From those who dare oppress thee. Thy laws are just, thy

stout and brave, Land of our deep de - vo - tion; In ev - 'ry clime her flag doth wave,
sons are brave, Sa - cred each loy - al feel - ing; Round our loved flag we firm u - nite,

On ev - 'ry swell - ing o - cean. Bright-ly the star of free-dom shines, Beaming with
Round Freedom's al - tar kneel-ing. Bright-ly the star of free-dom shines, Beaming with

light and glad - ness, Beam-ing with light and glad - ness, Co-lum - bia, brave and free!

THE RESTORED UNION.

"THE Boys in Blue!" When can their glory fade? Have you not heard your fathers tell of the great Civil War — the days from 1861 to 1865? How the flag, so dear to us all in the Northland, was lowered at Fort Sumter on a sorrowful April day? How for four years the conflict raged between the North and the South, with untold loss of life and treasure? Many of you know the story in a far more touching and sacred way than text-books could ever tell it to you.

"The Boys in Gray!" When can their valor fade? Fewer in number than the Northern soldiers, with scantier resources, with the war raging about their very hearthstones and the beautiful Southland filled with lamentation and weeping everywhere, how courageously they fought for the things they held dear! And to-day, thank Heaven, the flag that was lowered at Sumter floats over an undivided land, a united people, a Union restored!

SELECTIONS.

A little while after I came home from the last scene of all [the funeral of Grant], I found that a woman's hand had collected the insignia I had worn in the magnificent, melancholy pageant — the orders assigning me to duty and the funeral scarfs and badges — and had grouped and framed them; unbidden, silently, tenderly; and when I reflected that the hands that did this were those of a loving Southern woman, whose father had fallen on the Confederate side in the battle, I said: "The war indeed is over; let us have peace!" Gentlemen, soldiers, comrades, the silken folds that twine about us here, for all their soft and careless grace, are yet as strong as hooks of steel! They hold together a united people and a great nation; for realizing the truth at last — with no wounds to be healed and no stings of defeat to remember — the South says to the North, as simply and as truly as was said three thousand years ago in that far away meadow upon the margin of the mystic sea: "Whether thou goest, I will go; and where thou lodgest, I will lodge; thy people shall be my people, and thy God, my God."— *Henry Watterson*, at banquet of the Army of the Tennessee in Chicago.

(55)

THE PALMETTO AND THE PINE.

There grows a fair palmetto in the sunny Southern lands;
Upon the stern New England hills a somber pine tree stands,
And each towers like a monument above the perished brave;
A grave 'neath the palmetto — beneath the pine a grave.

The Carolina widow comes this bright May day to spread
Magnolia and jessamine above her soldier dead.
And the Northern mother violets strews upon her son below,—
Her only son, who fell so many weary years ago.

Tears for the gallant Yankee boy — one of Grant's heroes he.
Tears for the stalwart Southern man — the man who marched with Lee.
But love, and only love, between the lonely ones who twine
Their wreaths 'neath the palmetto — their chaplets 'neath the pine.

Oh, tried tree of the Southland! from out whose trunks were wrought
The ramparts of that glorious fort where Sergeant Jasper fought;
Oh, true tree of the Northland! whose pictured form supplied
The emblem for our earliest flag, that waved where Warren died —

Still watch the dead you've watched so long, the dead who died so well;
And matrons mourn, as mourn you must, your lost dear ones who fell;
But joy and peace and hope to all, now North and South combine
In one grand whole, as one soil bears the palmetto and the pine!
— *Manley H. Pike.*

Sectional lines no longer mar the map of the United States. Sectional feeling no longer holds back the love we bear each other. Fraternity is the national anthem, sung by a chorus of forty-five states, and our territories at home and beyond the seas. The Union is once more the common atlas of our love and loyalty, our devotion and sacrifice. The old flag again waves over us in peace, with new glories which your sons and ours have this day added to its sacred folds. * * * What a glorious future awaits us if unitedly, wisely and bravely we face the new problems now pressing upon us, determined to solve them for right and humanity! * * * Re-united! one country again and one country forever! Proclaim it from the press and pulpit! Teach it in the schools! Write it across the skies! — *William McKinley*, on his Southern tour, in 1898.

O STARRY FLAG OF UNION, HAIL!

Words and music by CHARLES W. JOHNSON.

1. O star - ry flag of Un - ion, hail! Now wave thy silk - en folds on high, The
2. Who dares haul down from mast or tow'r, Yon em - blem of Co - lum - bia's pride, His
3. We raise no hand for strife or war, We plead for peace for ev - 'ry land; But

gen - tle breeze that stirs each sail Pro - claims a - broad dear Free - dom nigh.
life holds light in that dread hour, Since brave men for that flag have died.
love we al - way each bright star, Each col - or, stripe, and rain - bow strand.

CHORUS.

Blue - field, thy stars for ev - 'ry State; Thy crim - son stripes, thy peer - less white,

Wave now o'er us, while our cho - rus Swells our watch - word, God and Right!

MANUAL OF PATRIOTISM.

GROUP III.

THE FLAG WAVES OVER

1. THE CAMP............................Song, *The Camp Flag.*
2. THE HOSPITAL.......................Song, *The Good Comrade.*
3. THE EXPOSITION BUILDINGS........Song, *The Centennial Hymn.*
4. THE CONSULATE..............Song, *Many Flags in Many Lands.*
5. { THE LAND......................Song, *Our Own Dear Land.*
   { THE SEA.......................Song, *Ocean-Guarded Flag.*

(59)

THE CAMP.

WHEN your fathers or your brothers enlist to fight for their country, they do not always march for the battle-field. They are sent at first "into camp," as we say. Some of you have seen these camps,— long rows of white tents, with streets stretching between the rows on either side. Here, the brave men stay for a long time, spending their time in drilling, in doing guard duty, and in getting ready for the hardships of a soldier's life. Then, perhaps after months of waiting, the Secretary of War, at Washington, sends word to them to "break camp" and hurry away to the scene of conflict.

Again, a camp is often placed at the very edge of a battle-field, and there the soldiers, in their tents, try to get a little sleep, not knowing but that the bugle may call them "to arms" at any minute. What a joy it is to a soldier, whether in drill-camp or battle-camp, to see floating from the tall staff the banner of the stars and stripes, in whose folds he finds courage for the day of battle!

SELECTIONS.

AN INCIDENT OF THE FRENCH CAMP.

You know, we French stormed Ratisbon;
  A mile or so away,
On a little mound, Napoleon
  Stood on our storming day;
With neck out-thrust, you fancy how,
  Legs wide, arms locked behind,
As if to balance the prone brow,
  Oppressive with its mind.

Just as perhaps, he mused, "My plans,
  That soar, to earth, may fall,
Let once my army leader, Lannes,
  Waver at yonder wall,"

(61)

Out 'twixt the battery-smoke, there flew
  A rider, bound on bound
Full-galloping; nor bridle drew
  Until he reached the mound.

Then off there flung in smiling joy,
  And held himself erect
By just his horse's mane, a boy;
  You hardly could suspect —
(So tight he kept his lips compressed
  Scarce any blood came through)
You looked twice ere you saw his breast
  Was all but shot in two.

"Well," cried he, "Emperor, by God's grace
  We've got you Ratisbon!
The Marshal's in the market place,
  And you'll be there anon
To see your flag-bird flap his vans
  Where I, to heart's desire,
Perched him!" The chief's eye flashed; his plans
  Soared up again like fire.

The chief's eye flashed; but presently
  Softened itself, as sheathes
A film the mother-eagle's eye
  When her bruised eaglet breathes:
"You're wounded!" "Nay," the soldier's pride
  Touched to the quick, he said:
"I'm killed, Sire!" And his chief beside,
  Smiling, the boy fell dead.
                              — *Robert Browning.*

On the morning of July 1st, 1862, five thousand Confederate cavalry advanced upon Booneville, Mo., then held by Col. Philip Sheridan with less than a thousand troopers. The Federal line, being strongly entrenched, was able to hold its ground against this greatly superior force. But Sheridan, fearful of being outflanked, directed a young captain to take a portion of two companies, make a rapid detour, charge the enemy in the rear and throw its line into confusion, thus making possible a simultaneous and successful attack in front. Sheridan said to him: "I expect of your command the quick and desperate work usually imposed upon a forlorn hope," at the same time bidding him what promised to be an eternal farewell. Ninety-two men rode calmly out knowing the supreme moment of their lives had come. What was in their hearts during that silent ride? What lights and shadows flashed across the cameras of their souls? To one pale boy, there came the vision of a quaint old house, a white-haired woman on her knees in prayer, an open Bible by her side, God's peace upon her face. Another memory held a cottage, all imbedded in the shade of sheltering trees and clinging vines; stray bits of sunshine around the open door; within, a fair young mother, crooning lullabies above a baby's crib. And one old grizzled hero seems to see, in mists of un-shed tears, a bush-grown corner of the barnyard fence, and through the rails a blended picture of faded calico, and golden curls, and laughing eyes. And then the little column halted on a bit of rising ground and faced — destiny.

Before them was a brigade of cavalry three thousand strong. That way lay death. Behind them were the open fields, the sheltering woods, safety, and dishonor. Just for a moment every cheek was blanched. A robin sang unheeded in a neighboring limb; clusters of purple daisies bloomed unseen upon the grassy slope; the sweet fresh breath of early summer filled the air, unfelt by all. They only saw the dear old flag of Union overhead; they only knew that foes of country blocked the road in front; they only heard the ringing voice of their gallant leader ordering the charge, and with a yell, the little troop swept on.

> Flashed every sabre bare,
> Flashed as they turned in air,
> Charging an army,
> While all the world wondered.

So sudden and unexpected was the attack, so desperate and irresistible the charge that this handful of men cut their way through the heart of the whole brigade. Then, in prompt obedience to the calm command of their captain they wheeled, re-formed, and charged again. At this opportune moment, while the Confederates were in confusion, Sheridan's whole line dashed forward with mighty cheers, and the day was won. That night, forty of the ninety-two kept their eternal bivouac on the field of battle, their white faces kissed by the silent stars.— *John M. Thurston.*

THE SONG OF THE CAMP.

"Give us a song!" the soldiers cried,
  The outer trenches guarding,
When the heated guns of the camps allied
  Grew weary of bombarding.

The dark Redan, in silent scoff,
  Lay grim and threatening, under;
And the tawny mound of the Malakoff
  No longer belched its thunder.

There was a pause. A guardsman said:
  "We storm the forts to-morrow;
Sing while we may, another day
  Will bring enough of sorrow."

They lay along the battery's side,
  Below the smoking cannon:
Brave hearts from Severn and from Clyde,
  And from the banks of Shannon.

They sang of love, and not of fame;
  Forgot was Britain's glory;
Each heart recalled a different name,
  But all sang "Annie Laurie."

Voice after voice caught up the song,
  Until its tender passion
Rose like an anthem, rich and strong,—
  Their battle-eve confession.

*   *   *   *   *   *   *

Beyond the darkening ocean burned
  The bloody sunset's embers,
While the Crimean valleys learned
  How English love remembers.

And once again, a fiery hell
  Rained on the Russian quarters,
With scream of shot, and burst of shell,
  And bellowing of the mortars.

And Irish Nora's eyes are dim
  For a singer, dumb and gory;
And English Mary mourns for him
  Who sang of "Annie Laurie."

Sleep, soldiers! still in honored rest
  Your youth and valor wearing:
The bravest are the tenderest,—
  The loving are the daring.
                 — Bayard Taylor.

THE FLAG OF FREEDOM.

The flag of Freedom floats in pride
  Above the hills our fathers saved;
It floats as, in the battle tide,
  Above the brave and good it waved.

It wakes the thought of other days,
  When they, who sleep beneath its shade,
Stood foremost in the battle blaze
  And bared for us the patriot blade.

High o'er its stars our spirits leap
  To gratulate their deathless fame,
With them the jubilee to keep,
  And hail our country's honor'd named.

Above the plains, above the rocks,
  Above our fathers' honor'd graves,
Free from a thousand battle shocks,
  Our striped and starry banner waves.

What was the price which bade it ride
  Above our loved and native plains?
And are there men would curb its pride,
  And bind our eagle fast in chains?

5

Spirit of Washington, awake!
  And watch o'er Freedom's chartered land;
The battle peal again may break,
  Again in arms thy children stand!

— *Alonzo Lewis.*

REVEILLE.

The morning is cheery, my boys, arouse!
The dew shines bright on the chestnut boughs,
And the sleepy mist on the river lies,
Though the east is flushing with crimson dyes.
  Awake! awake! awake!
  O'er field and wood and brake,
  With glories newly born,
  Comes on the blushing morn.
    Awake! awake!

You have dreamed of your homes and your friends all night;
You have basked in your sweethearts' smiles so bright;
Come, part with them all for awhile again,—
Be lovers in dreams; when awake, be men.
  Turn out! turn out! turn out!
  You have dreamed full long, I know,
  Turn out! turn out! turn out!
  The east is all aglow.
    Turn out! turn out!

From every valley and hill there come
The clamoring voices of fife and drum;
And out on the fresh, cool morning air
The soldiers are swarming everywhere.
  Fall in! fall in! fall in!
  Every man in his place.
  Fall in! fall in! fall in!
  Each with a cheerful face.
    Fall in! fall in!

— *Michael O'Connor.*

THE CAMP FLAG.

W. K. W.

HAMLIN E. COGSWELL.

Moderato.

1. When the morn-ing dawns in the east-ern skies, And its col-ors
2. When the eve-ning pales in the west-ern skies, And the dy-ing

flame a - far, .. O'er the low-roofed tents there the dear flag flies, And
day is near, .. O'er the low-roofed tents there the dear flag flies, And it

mir - rors each fleet - ing star. .. Now it catch - es the red of a
drives a - way all fear. .. Let the dark - ness fall o'er the

ro - sy cloud As it drifts through the heav - ens bright, And it shakes its
old camp ground, And the night come on a - pace, Still the sen - try

folds when the winds are loud, And its sky - blue breaks on the sight!
smiles on his drear - y round, For he thinks of the Flag's dear face!

THE HOSPITAL.

'AR is a very cruel thing, never to be begun unless the honor or safety of the nation demands it; never to be continued for a single hour beyond that which is needful. For in every war, many brave men are killed and many more are wounded. Now, it is for these poor wounded fellows, as well as for those who are taken sick, that hospitals are needed. Many of them are only large tents, put up outside the line of battle. In these hospital-tents, surgeons and nurses (noble-hearted women) do all they can to relieve the sick and wounded. If they get better, they are often sent to a permanent hospital, or better still to the dear home from which they started for the war.

Nowadays, over every battle-field hospital in all civilized countries is seen the flaming " Red Cross " of the society of that name. That is the pledge that the sick and hurt soldiers will not be attacked by the enemy. And yet, even with that cross of mercy, how dear to the wounded patriot is the sight of that flag for which he is willing to give his life — " the last full measure of devotion."

In hospitals, women are the " ministering angels." What a fine, patriotic exercise children could make up from the services of such immortal names as Florence Nightingale, Harriet Beecher Stowe, and Clara Barton. Theirs is a heroism and patriotism no less grand and self-sacrificing than that of the bravest soldier they ever nursed back to life and health.

(69)

SELECTIONS.

SANTA FILOMENA.

Whene'er a noble deed is wrought,
Whene'er is spoken a noble thought,
   Our hearts in glad surprise,
   To higher levels rise.

The tidal wave of deeper souls
Into our inmost being rolls,
   And lifts us unawares
   Out of all meaner cares.

Honor to those whose words or deeds
Thus help us in our daily needs,
   And by their overflow
   Raise us from what is low!

Thus thought I, as by night I read
Of the great army of the dead,
   The trenches cold and damp,
   The starved and frozen camp,—

The wounded from the battle-plain,
In dreary hospitals of pain,
   The cheerless corridors,
   The cold and stony floors.

Lo! in that house of misery
A lady with a lamp I see
   Pass through the glimmering gloom,
   And flit from room to room.

And slow, as in a dream of bliss,
The speechless sufferer turns to kiss
   Her shadow, as it falls
   Upon the darkening walls.

As if a door in heaven should be
Opened and then closed suddenly,
   The vision came and went,
   The light shone and was spent.

On England's annals through the long
Hereafter of her speech and song,
   That light its rays shall cast
   From portals of the past.

A Lady with a Lamp shall stand
In the great history of the land,
   A noble type of good,
   Heroic womanhood.

Nor even shall be wanting here
The palm, the lily, and the spear,
The symbols that of yore
Saint Filomena bore.

— *H. W. Longfellow.*

AN INCIDENT.

Do you remember, in that disastrous siege in India, when the little Scotch girl raised her head from her pallet in the hospital, and said to the sickening hearts of the English: " I hear the bagpipes; the Campbells are coming!" And they said, " No, Jessie; it is delirium." " No, I know it; I heard it far off." And in an hour, the pibroch burst upon their glad ears, and the banner of St. George floated in triumph over their heads.— *George William Curtis.*

WOMEN OF THE WAR.

(An anonymous poem composed during the Civil War.)

The dim light of the hospital
  Shone on the beds of pain,
And the long night seemed endless,
  When in walked " Betsy Jane."
" My God! is this a woman?"
  Said one poor soldier boy,
And tears rolled down his manly cheeks,
  But they were tears of joy.

And chaos turned to order,
  As Betsy Jane stepped in,
And cleanliness which, we are told,
  " To godliness is kin."
Hard tack and salted bacon
  To chicken broth gave way,
And sanitary stores came in,
  And beef tea won the day.
" Oh, see my soft white pillow!
  My bed is clean once more."
And " some one's darling" smiled upon
  This Woman of the War.

I know not if our " Betsy Jane "
  Was fair to other eyes,
But to her " Boys in Blue " she seemed
  An angel from the skies.
Her apron and her gown of serge
  Each soldier loved to see,
And blessed her footsteps as she brought
  Such " heavenly toast and tea."
All the sweet charities of home
  In plenty there she poured,
And each day's work now brought its own
  " Exceeding great reward! "

It was not in the earthquake,
  Or in the fiery flame,
But in the soothing gentle voice
  That then God's angel came.
And when He comes whose right it is
  Within our hearts to reign,
And reads from out the Book of Life
  The name of " Betsy Jane "—

Oh, in that great Muster Roll
  Before the Judge of all,
When faithful servants of the Lord
  Shall answer to His call,
Perhaps He'll say to some of them:
  " For inasmuch as ye
Have done it to the least of these,
  Ye've done it unto Me."
And then with psalms and tossing palms,
  Like banners waving o'er,
The pearly gates will open wide
  To " Women of the War."

THE GOOD COMRADE.

GERMAN.

Alla marcia.

1. I once had a broth - er sol - dier, A com - rade true and tried; We
2. So swift a ball comes speed - ing, Is it for me or thee? Low
3. No more we'll march, O com - rade, To bat - tle side by side; My

marched at sig - nal giv - en, With step so blithe and e - ven, To
at my feet he's ly - ing, And as I watch him dy - ing, He
hand shall clasp thee nev - er, Yet thou re - main - est ev - er My

bat - tle side by side— To bat - tle side by side.
seems a part of me— He seems a part of me.
com - rade true and tried— My com - rade true and tried.

EXPOSITION BUILDINGS.

N the year 1876 there was a great exposition, or exhibition, at Philadelphia, to celebrate the one hundredth anniversary of our independence as a nation. To that Quaker city gathered people from every part of the globe — many bringing with them strange wares or costly merchandise from across the seas. It was a sight never to be forgotten; it made Americans better acquainted with all the nations of Christendom.

In the year 1893, another and greater exposition was held at Chicago, to celebrate the four hundredth anniversary of the landing of Columbus upon our shores. So many were the buildings, so beautiful even by day, so fairy-like by night when lighted by thousands of dazzling lights, that the millions who saw the sight called it the finest the world had ever known.

But the fairest vision, after all, both at the "Centennial" and the "Columbian Exposition" were the countless flags of red, white and blue that flamed out by night and day — telling of the peace and prosperity of our nation, and inviting the people of every nation to a share in our happiness.

SELECTIONS.

A travelled Frenchman was asked the other day how the buildings of the Columbian World's Fair compared with those of the last exposition in the French capital. After reflecting a moment, he replied: "The buildings at Chicago are what you might have expected at Paris; the buildings in Paris were what you might have expected in Chicago."

No world's exhibition was ever better housed, or more conveniently arranged. As it stood on the day of its formal dedication in October (1892), incomplete, its decoration in progress, with the scaffolding and building stages still marring the architectural effect, in the midst of the debris of ten thousand working-men, driving on the work, night and day, it was already a sufficient answer to the doubt whether the

American genius is equal to the creation of any works except those of
mechanical ingenuity. The distinction of the Columbian Exhibition
is not in its magnitude; it is not that it contains the largest building
ever erected in the world; it is in its beauty, its harmonious grouping,
its splendid landscape and architectural effects. This is best comprehended as a whole in the approach from the lake. The view there,
especially at the coming of evening, when the long rows of classic
columns, the pillars and domes, are in relief against a glowing sunset
sky, is a vision of beauty that will surprise most and will appeal most
to those familiar with the triumphs of man's genius elsewhere. The
little city of the lagoon, reflected in the water as distinctly as it stands
out against the sky, seems like some fairy exhalation on the shore, sug-
gesting the long perspective of columns on the desert of Palmyra, the
approach by the sea of Marmora to Constantinople, and the canals and
palaces of Venice as seen from Lido. In its light and airy grace it is
like a city of the imagination.— *Charles Dudley Warner*, in Harper's
Magazine.

NEW YORK DAY AT THE WORLD'S FAIR.

*   *   *   *   *   *   *

Due honor to the lands
From which we sprung: all hail the ancient fame
Of kindred hearts and hands!
But we began with all that they had won,
A counsel of protection calls us on;
To do no more than they have done were shame.

'Twere better far, I hold,
To see the Iroquois supreme once more
Among the forests old
From hill-girt Hudson's current, broad and slow,
To where 'twixt Erie and Ontario,
Leaps green Niagara with a giant's roar;
To see the paths pursued
By commerce with her flying charioteers
Tangled with solitude.
The Indian trail uncoil among the trees:
The council-runner's torch against the breeze
Its signal fling — " The smoke that disappears."

To have the wigwams rise
By summer-haunted Horicon so fair;
  Fruit blooms and grain-gold dyes
Fade from the shadows in Cayuga's tide,
  The vineyards fail on Keuka's sun-beat side,
The mill-crowned cliffs of Genesee made bare;
  'Twere more to my desire
To see Manhattan's self laid desolate.

*   *   *   *   *   *   *

  But out on dreams of dread!
In him I put my waking faith and trust,
  A king in heart and head
Who masters forces, shapes material things,
  Who loves his kind, whose common sense has wings,
The true American, the kindly just,
  Full prompt in word and deed,
And ready to make good some human hope
  In time of utter need;
To cross at Delaware the ice's gorge,
  Or tread blood-bolted snow at Valley Forge,
Or keep at Gettysburg the gun-shook slope!

*   *   *   *   *   *   *

— *Joseph O'Connor.*

[From poem read at World's Columbian Exposition on New York State Day.]

Jackson Park, the pride to-day of Chicago, upon whose buildings, vast and stately, the majesty of the nation descended this morning in dedicatory services, tells of the resolve to redeem all promises, to realize all hopes. Hither shall be brought the products of labor and art, the treasures of earth and sea, the inventions of this wondrously inventive century, the fruits of learning and genius. The entire globe is astir in preparation to fill to repletion the palaces we have erected. The invitation has gone out to the world in all the fullness and warmth of the heart of this republic, and the nations of the world have harkened to it as they never did before to a voice calling men to an exposition. The best that America can bring, the best the world owns, shall soon be in Jackson Park.

What may be added? I will give reply. What is there more important, more precious than matter and all the forms in which matter

may be invested? Is there not mind? What is there greater than all
the results of the thought — the labor of man? Is there not man
himself, the designer, the maker of his works? Bring hither, then,
mind. Bring men — not merely the millions, anxious to see and to
learn. These do we need; they do not suffice. Bring the men whom
the millions desire to contemplate, and from whom they may receive
valued lessons. Bring the thinkers, the workers, the scholars, the
apostles of action, who have rendered possible or have produced the
marvels which will be housed in Jackson Park, whose dreams make
toward the building up of humanity, whose arms reach out to the
improvement of men along all the lines of human progress. Let
us have the Columbuses of our time. Let us have Parliaments of the
leaders of men convoked from all lands under the sun. In this manner
is your exposition complete in all its parts, truly representative of the
age and truly great. You have matter and men; you have the works
and the workers. In men far more than in matter you have the highest
products of progress. There is progress only when men grow. In
men you have the potent means to determine the progress of the future.
God has made men the agents of progress.— *Right Rev. John Ireland,
D. D.*, at dedication of World's Columbian Exposition.

CENTENNIAL HYMN.

JOHN GREENLEAF WHITTIER.   JOHN KNOWLES PAINE.

Maestoso.

1. Our fa - thers' God, from out whose hand The cen - turies fall like
2. Here, where of old by Thy de - sign, The fa - thers spake that
3. For art and la - bor met in truce, For beau - ty made the
4. Oh, make Thou us, thro' cen - turies long, In peace se - cure, in

grains of sand, We meet to - day, u - nit - ed, free, And
word of Thine Whose ech - o is the glad re - frain Of
bride of use, We thank Thee; but, with - al, we crave The
jus - tice strong; A - round our gift of free - dom, draw The

loy - al to our land and Thee, To thank Thee for the
rend - ed bolt and fall - ing chain, To grace our fes - tal
au - stere vir - tues strong to save, The hon - or proof to
safe - guards of Thy right - eous law; And, cast in some di -

e - ra done, And trust Thee for the o - p'ning one.
time, from all The zones of earth, our guests we call.
place or gold, The man - hood nev - er bought nor sold!
vin - er mould, Let the new cy - cle shame the old!

Words by special arrangement with HOUGHTON, MIFFLIN & Co.
Music used by permission of OLIVER DITSON COMPANY, owners of copyright.

New York has built two houses at the Fair. One is the palatial structure before us, a fitting representation of the dignity and opulence of the Empire State. The other is an humble structure at the opposite end of the park destined to show how a workingman and his family may be enabled to live with due regard to the requirements of sanitation and healthful nutriment. The house in which we stand has been one of the sights of the fair. It has been a matter of pride to every New Yorker visiting Jackson Park that the headquarters of his state were so beautiful, so commodious, and so popular. He has found here the conveniences of a club, the educating influence of a museum, and the rest and refreshment of a summer villa. The true attitude of the people of New York toward this Exposition has nowhere been more fitly represented than in the superb proportions and princely magnificence of this their State house of call. But if this be New York's idea of the regal attire which befits her as a guest at the table of nations, the other edifice — the model workingman's home — is no less typical of her care for the welfare of the lowly, and her sense that the qualities that go to make her great are those which are nourished in the homes of the toilers.— *Roswell P. Flower*, at World's Columbian Exposition, New York State Day.

PROGRESS.

O Progress, with thy restless eyes,
  Sleepless as fate and tireless as the sun,
The mighty mother of the world's emprise —
  Here, where we bring the treasures thou hast won,
Bend thou thine ear and list to our acclaim.
  Stay thy imperial march by land and sea,
While we this temple, vocal with thy name,
  We dedicate to thee!

Whatever here shall show mankind
  That, spite of history's lying page,
Not buried in the years behind,
  But forward lies the golden age;
Whatever here shall worthiest stand,
  The boon of ages yet to be,
Best fruitage of the brain or hand,
  We dedicate to thee.

6

Whatever here shall truest teach
  How round the world may wiser grow
The clearer eye, the wider reach,
  The rule of heaven here below;
Whate'er makes Learning's torch more bright,
  Or wides the boundaries of the free,
The jewels of our empire's might,
  We dedicate to thee!

— William H. McElroy.

[At dedication of New York State Building, World's Columbian Exposition.]

MANY FLAGS IN MANY LANDS.

1. There are man - y flags in man - y lands, There are
2. I know where the pret - ti - est col - ors are, And I'm
3. I would cut a piece from an eve - ning sky, Where the
4. Then I'd want a part of fleec - y cloud, And some
5. We shall al - ways love the "Stars and Stripes," And we

flags of ev - 'ry hue; But there is no flag how -
sure if I on - ly knew How to get them here, I could
stars were shin - ing through, And use it just as it
red from a rain - bow bright; And put them to - geth - er
mean to be ev - er true To this land of ours and the

ev - er grand, Like our own "Red, White and Blue."
make a flag Of glo - rious "Red, White and Blue."
was on high, For my stars and field of blue.
side by side, For my stripes of red and white.
dear old flag, The "Red, the White, and the Blue."

CHORUS.

Then hur - rah for the flag, Our coun - try's flag, It's

stripes and white stars, too; There is no flag in

an - y land Like our own "Red, White and Blue."

THE CONSULATE.

THE word "consulate" is taken from the Latin and, with
Americans, refers to the building in which any man appointed by our government transacts, in any foreign port,
or town or city, such business affairs of the government
as may be entrusted to him. Always, except in very
small places, the office is filled by American citizens, perhaps resid-
ing abroad, but more commonly leaving home for the express purpose of representing our country and its interests in foreign lands. But
the Consul — for by that name is he called — has a more sacred duty
to do — that of protecting any American citizen who may be in danger
in a foreign land. Then the flag flying over the Consulate seems to
demand protection for any and all its citizens seeking its shelter. Even
more,— it often protects men of other nationalities. When a Mr. Poinsett was our Minister to Mexico from 1825 to 1829, the Mexicans, in
a rage, sought the lives of certain European Spaniards. The Spaniards
fled to the Consulate; the Mexicans pursued, and were about to attack the building, when Mr. Poinsett unfurled the Stars and Stripes,
and standing beneath its folds saved his own life and that of the
frightened Spaniards.

SELECTION.

Moral influence is good, but it is also a good thing to have something material behind it. A missionary who recently arrived in this
country, from Turkey in Asia, mentioned the following experience:

" I left," he said, the " town of ——— in the morning. In the
afternoon of that day it was attacked by the Kurds, and several hundred
of the inhabitants were slaughtered. When I reached the seaport, in-
tending to take the steamer on the way to America, I was told by the
local authority that I could not have a permit to embark, for he was
commanded to detain a person answering to my description until fur-

ther orders. I explained to him the necessity of my taking the steamer, and the great inconvenience of delay. He expressed his regret, but declared his inability to allow me to proceed. Presently the steamer sailed without me, and I had to wait another week.

"Day after day passed, bringing only politeness and promises. The Consul telegraphed to Constantinople, but the telegram had to pass through the hands of the Government, and my name was purposely so muddled that the Minister could only telegraph back, 'I have received your communication, but cannot make out to whom it refers.' At last the Consul managed to get word to the commander of the gunboat, which was lying about sixty miles off. Next morning, looking out on the Mediterranean, I saw the smoke of an approaching steamer. As it came nearer, I said to myself, 'Why, that looks like one of the White Squadron.' Presently I saw at her fore-peak the Stars and Stripes. She anchored in the port, and the commander called on the local authority, and said to him, 'I have come to inquire into the case of Mr. ————.' The local magistrate, with great urbanity, said, 'Oh, that is all right. His papers are in order, and he can go at any time.' The commander replied, 'I am very glad of it, for otherwise I should have been compelled to demand him.'"

THE LAND.

HE land, your geographies tell you, makes up a large part of the earth's surface. And I am sure all children know that the extent of land, in this " Country of Ours," as Benjamin Harrison calls it, is very great; very great also the stretches of sea-coast hemming in the land. But the larger the land the worse for the people, unless on every part of it — on every mountain, in every valley — there is enjoyed the order and protection which the flag represents. In olden times beacon-fires on hill-tops were the signals for freemen to rally to their country's aid. Let ours be the better, more inspiring, signal of the waving flag!

SELECTIONS.

I remember reading a short time ago about a Celtic regiment, called the Black Watch, which had been gone from home for many years, and when it landed again upon the shores, the men immediately kneeled down and kissed the sands of Galway. That's the kind of patriotism we want now-a-days; the patriotism that loves the soil upon which we tread, that loves the air that surrounds us here in America, that loves the stars and stripes because they represent this great republic; the kind of patriotism that not only seeks to defend our institutions, but seeks to elevate our manhood and womanhood.— *Anon.*

LOVE OF COUNTRY.

Breathes there the man with soul so dead,
Who never to himself hath said,
  "This is my own, my native land!"
Whose heart hath ne'er within him burned,
As home his footsteps he hath turned,
  From wandering on a foreign strand!
If such there breathe, go, mark him well!
For him no minstrel raptures swell;
High though his titles, proud his name,
Boundless his wealth as wish can claim,
Despite those titles, power, and pelf,
The wretch, concentred all in self,
Living, shall forfeit fair renown,
And, doubly dying, shall go down,
To the vile dust from whence he sprung,
Unwept, unhonored, and unsung.

          — Sir Walter Scott.

OUR OWN DEAR LAND.

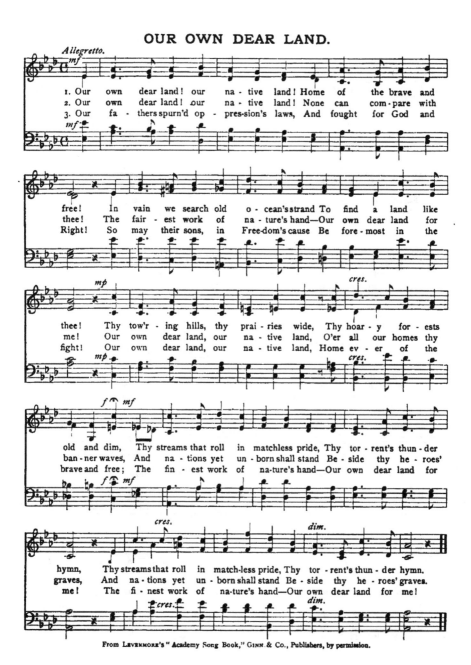

1. Our own dear land! our na - tive land! Home of the brave and free! In vain we search old o - cean's strand To find a land like thee! Thy tow'r - ing hills, thy prai - ries wide, Thy hoar - y for - ests old and dim, Thy streams that roll in matchless pride, Thy tor - rent's thun - der hymn, Thy streams that roll in match-less pride, Thy tor - rent's thun - der hymn.

2. Our own dear land! our na - tive land! None can com - pare with thee! The fair - est work of na - ture's hand—Our own dear land for me! Our own dear land, our na - tive land, O'er all our homes thy ban - ner waves, And na - tions yet un - born shall stand Be - side thy he - roes' graves, And na - tions yet un - born shall stand Be - side thy he - roes' graves,

3. Our fa - thers spurn'd op - pres-sion's laws, And fought for God and Right! So may their sons, in Free-dom's cause Be fore - most in the fight! Our own dear land, our na - tive land, Home ev - er of the brave and free; The fin - est work of na - ture's hand—Our own dear land for me! The fi - nest work of na - ture's hand—Our own dear land for me!

From Livermore's "Academy Song Book," Ginn & Co., Publishers, by permission.

THE OCEAN-GUARDED FLAG.

JAMES RILEY.

L. V. H. CROSBY.
Air, "Dearest Mae."

1. That o - cean-guard-ed flag of light, for - ev - er may it fly! It
2. Tim-bers have crash'd and guns have peal'd be-neath its ar - dent glow; But
3. Its stripes of red, e - ter - nal dyed with heart-streams of all lands; Its

flashed o'er Mon-mouth's blood - y fight, and lit Mc - Hen - ry's sky; It
nev - er did that en - sign yield its hon - or to the foe; Its
white, the snow-capped hills that hide in storm their up - raised hands; Its

bears up - on its folds of flame to earth's re - mot - est wave The
fame shall march with mar - tial tread down a - ges yet to be. . To
blue, the o - cean waves that beat round free-dom's cir - cled shore; Its

names of men whose deeds of fame shall e'er in - spire the brave.
guard those stars that nev - er paled in fight on land or sea.
stars, the prints of an - gels' feet, that shine for ev - er - more.

CHORUS.

For - ev - er may it fly! For - ev - er may it fly! That

o - cean-guard - ed flag of light, For - ev - er may it fly! . .

Words by permission of CASSELL & CO., Limited.

THE SEA.

SEA, with all its perils and shipwrecks, seems to have had little of terror for the hardy seamen of America. In every war in which we have fought, their skill and courage have been shown. And not only ships of war, but ships of trade have run the gauntlet of the waves. But battle-skill and commercial supremacy count for little unless the flag flies from the masthead of every ship and brightens every harbor and haven into which our ships enter. In ancient times, the galley-prows bore figures of heathen gods and heroes. Better far, the adornment of that flag which stands for the living manhood and immortal valor of our sailor lads!

SELECTIONS.

THE SHIP OF STATE.

Thou too, sail on, O ship of state!
Sail on, O Union, strong and great!
Humanity, with all its fears,
With all the hopes of future years,
  Is hanging breathless on thy fate!
We know what Master laid thy keel,
What Workman wrought thy ribs of steel,
  Who made each mast, and sail, and rope,
What anvils rang, what hammers beat,
In what a forge and what a heat,
  Were shaped the anchors of thy hope!
Fear not each sudden sound and shock,
'Tis of the wave and not the rock,
'Tis but the flapping of the sail,
And not a rent made by the gale!

(91)

In spite of rock, and tempest's roar,
In spite of false lights on the shore,
Sail on, nor fear to breast the sea.
Our hearts, our hopes, are all with thee!
Our hearts, our hopes, our prayers, our tears,
Our faith, triumphant o'er our fears,
    Are all with thee — are all with thee!
                    — *Henry Wadsworth Longfellow.*

ADMIRAL FARRAGUT.

During the Civil War it was an easy thing in the North to support the Union, and it was a double disgrace to be against it. But among the highest and loftiest patriots, those who deserved best of the whole country, were the men from the South who possessed such loyalty and heroic courage that they stood by the flag and followed the cause of the whole nation, and the whole people. Among all those who fought in this, the greatest struggle for righteousness, these men stand pre-eminent, and Farragut stands first.

He belongs to that class of commanders who possess in the highest degree the qualities of courage and daring, of readiness to assume great responsibility and to run great risks.

As a boy he had sailed as a midshipman, and he saw the war of 1812, in which, though our frigates and sloops fought some glorious actions, our coasts were blockaded and insulted, and the Capitol at Washington burned, because our statesmen and people had been too short-sighted to build a big fighting navy; and Farragut was able to perform his great feats on the Gulf coast because in the Civil War we had ships as good as any afloat.

No man in a profession as highly technical as the navy can win great success unless he has been specially brought up in and trained for that profession, and has devoted his life to the work. Step by step Farragut rose, but never had an opportunity of distinguishing himself in his profession until, when he was sixty years old, the Civil War broke out. He was made flag-officer of the Gulf squadron; and the first success that the Union forces met with in the southwest was scored when one night he burst the iron chains stretched across the

Mississippi, swept past the forts, sank the rams and gunboats that sought to bar his way, and captured New Orleans.

In the last year of the war he was permitted to attempt the capture of Mobile. All he wanted was a chance to fight. He possessed splendid self-confidence, and utterly refused to be daunted by the rumors of the formidable nature of the defences against which he was to act. " I mean to be whipped or to whip my enemy," he said, " and not to be scared to death."

The attack was made early on the morning of August 5. Every man in every craft was thrilling with excitement. For their foes who fought in sight, for the forts, the gunboats, and the great ironclad ram, they cared nothing; but all, save the very boldest, dreaded the torpedoes — the mines of death — which lay, they knew not where, thickly scattered through the channels. Farragut stood in the port main-rigging of the *Hartford*, close to the main-top, lashed to the mast. As they passed the forts, Farragut heard the explosion of a torpedo and saw the monitor *Tecumseh*, then but five hundred feet from the *Hartford*, reel violently, lurch heavily over, and go down head-foremost. This was the crisis of the fight, and the crisis of Farragut's career. The column was halted in a narrow channel, right under the fire of the forts. A few moments' delay and confusion, and the golden chance would have been past, and the only question would have been as to the magnitude of the disaster. Ahead lay terrible danger, but ahead lay also triumph. The other ships would not obey the signal to go ahead, and the admiral himself resolved to take the lead. Backing hard, he got clear of the others and then went ahead very fast. A warning cry came that there were torpedoes ahead. " Go ahead, full speed," shouted the admiral, and he steamed forward. The cases of torpedoes were heard knocking against the bottom of the ship; but they failed to explode, and the *Hartford* went through the gates of Mobile Bay. Within three hours the Confederate flotilla was destroyed, the bay was won, and the forts around were helpless.

Farragut had proved himself the peer of Nelson, and had added to the annals of the Union the page which tells of the greatest sea-fight in our history.— *Hon. Theodore Roosevelt*, adapted from " Hero Tales."

UNFURL OUR STANDARD HIGH.

Unfurl our standard high!
　Its glorious folds shall wave
Where'er the land looks to the sky,
　Or ocean's surges lave!
And when, beneath its shade, the brave,
　With patriotic ire,
Combat for glory or the grave,
　It shall their hearts inspire
With that chivalric spark which first
Upon our foes in terror burst!

Unfurl the stripes and stars!
　They evermore shall be
Victorious on the field of Mars —
　Triumphant on the sea!
And when th' o'erruling fates decree
　The bolt of war to throw,
Thou, sacred banner of the free,
　Shall daunt the bravest foe;
And never shall thy stars decline
Till circling suns have ceased to shine.
　　　　　　　—Owen Grenliffe Warren.

MANUAL OF PATRIOTISM.

GROUP IV.

THE FLAG IS SYMBOLIZED

BY

1. THE LIBERTY CAP......................Song, *The Liberty Cap.*
2. THE LIBERTY BELL.....................Song, *The Liberty Bell.*
3. { THE SWORD (War)...........Song, *The Sword of Bunker Hill.*
   { THE DOVE (Peace)....................Song, *Angel of Peace.*
4. THE EAGLE.....................Song, *Where the Eagle is King.*
5. THE SHIELD..................Song, *Battle Hymn of the Republic.*

(95)

THE LIBERTY CAP.

Words by Gertrude Sneller.

E. Dora Cogswell.

1. When old moth-er Free-dom a par - ty gave To her sons and her daugh - ters
2. Now Co - lum - bi - a's cap was of red, white, and blue, And be-came her, the dear lit - tle
3. She looked so charm-ing that night at the ball, With the lib - er - ty cap on her

bright, She cautioned them all to look their best When they visited her that night.
elf! There was none oth-er like it in all the world, For Freedom had made it herself.
head, That Dame Freedom kissed her be-fore them all, "You're my favorite child," she said.

THE LIBERTY CAP.

1. 2. "O Co-lum-bi-a fair, O what will you wear? Too poor for a sty-lish
3. Then here is a cheer for the lib-er-ty cap, With its stripes of the red, white, and

poor for a
stripes of the

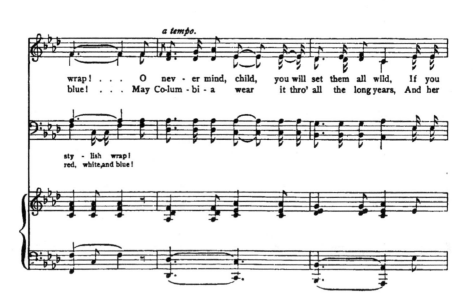

wrap! . . . O nev-er mind, child, you will set them all wild, If you
blue! . . . May Co-lum-bi-a wear it thro' all the long years, And her

sty - lish wrap!
red, white, and blue!

THE LIBERTY CAP.

come in your lib - er - ty cap, If you come, ... if you
chil - dren be loy - al and true! And be true, ... and be

If you come,
And be true,

come, ...
true, ...

come, if you come, If you come in your lib - er - ty cap."
true, and be true, And her chil - dren be loy - al and true!

if you come,
and be true,

THE LIBERTY CAP.

E in America do not often see a liberty cap. That is indeed too bad. For there could not be a prettier emblem to grace the heads of America's boys and girls, whenever they wish to celebrate that Freedom which is the birthright of every American. How straight the cap stands! With what a free and jaunty grace it carries itself! How the ever-beautiful red, white and blue blend in that bewitching headgear! So, may children often

> Don them to wear,
> Doff them to cheer,— for the Flag.

SELECTIONS.

FREEDOM.

Of old sat Freedom on the heights,
  The thunders breaking at her feet;
Above her shook the starry lights,
  She heard the torrents meet.

There in her place she did rejoice,
  Self-gathered in her prophet mind,
But fragments of her mighty voice,
  Came rolling on the wind.

Then stepped she down thro' town and field
  To mingle with the human race,
And part by part to men revealed
  The fullness of her face.

Grave mother of majestic works,
  From her isle altar gazing down,
Who, godlike, grasps the triple forks,
  And kinglike, wears the crown.

Her open eyes desire the truth.
   The wisdom of a thousand years
Is in them. May perpetual youth
   Keep dry their light from tears.

That her fair form may stand and shine,
   Make bright our days and light our dreams,
Turning to scorn with lips divine
   The falsehood of extremes.

— Alfred Tennyson.

All who stand beneath our banner are free. Ours is the only flag
that has in reality written upon it Liberty, Fraternity, Equality, the
three grandest words in all the languages of men. Liberty: give to
every man the fruit of his own labor, the labor of his hand and of his
brain. Fraternity: every man in the right is my brother. Equality:
the rights of all are equal. No race, no color, no previous condition,
can change the rights of men. The Declaration of Independence has at
last been carried out in letter and in spirit. To-day, the black man looks
upon his child, and says: The avenues of distinction are open to you;
upon your brow may fall the civic wreath. We are celebrating the
courage and wisdom of our fathers, and the glad shout of a free people,
the anthem of a grand nation, commencing at the Atlantic, is following the sun to the Pacific, across a continent of happy homes.— *Robert
G. Ingersoll.*

WILLIAM TELL'S ADDRESS TO HIS NATIVE HILLS.

Ye crags and peaks, I'm with you once again!
I hold to you the hands you first beheld,
To show they still are free! Methinks I hear
A spirit in your echoes answer me,
And bid your tenant welcome home again.
   O sacred forms, how fair, how proud you look!
How high you lift your heads into the sky!
How huge you are! how mighty, and how free!
Ye are the things that tower, that shine; whose smile
Makes glad, whose frown is terrible; whose forms,
Robed or unrobed, do all the impress wear
Of awe divine! Ye guards of liberty,

I'm with you once again! I call to you
With all my voice! I hold my hands to you,
To show they still are free! I rush to you
As though I could embrace you!
   Scaling yonder peak,
I saw an eagle wheeling, near its brow,
O'er the abyss. His broad expanded wings
Lay calm and motionless upon the air,
As if he floated there, without their aid,
By the sole act of his unlorded will
That buoyed him proudly up. Instinctively
I bent my bow; yet wheeled he, heeding not
The death that threatened him. I could not shoot.
'Twas liberty! I turned my bow aside,
And let him soar away.
   Oh! with what pride I used
To walk these hills, look up to God,
And bless Him that 'twas free. 'Twas free!
From end to end, from cliff to lake, 'twas free!
Free as our torrents are, that leap our rocks,
And plough our valleys, without asking leave;
Or as our peaks that wear their caps of snow,
In very presence of the regal sun.
How happy was I then! I loved
Its very storms. Yes, I have sat and eyed
The thunder breaking from his cloud, and smiled
To see him shake his lightnings o'er my head;
To think I had no master save his own.
   Ye know the jutting cliff, round which a track
Up hither winds, whose base is but the brow
To such another one, with scanty room
For two abreast to pass? O'ertaken there
By the mountain blast, I've laid me flat along;
The while, gust followed gust more furiously,
As if to sweep me o'er the horrid brink,
And I have thought of other lands, whose storms
Are summer flaws to those of mine, and just
Have wished me there. The thought that mine was free
Has checked that wish, and I have raised my head,
And cried in thraldom to that furious wind,
Blow on! This is a land of liberty!

                —*J. Sheridan Knowles.*

THE VISION OF LIBERTY.

A massive castle, far and high,
　In towering grandeur broke upon my eye.
Proud in its strength and years, the ponderous pile
　　Flung up its time-defying towers;
Its lofty gates seemed scornfully to smile
　　At vain assaults of human powers,
And threats and arms deride.
Its gorgeous carvings of heraldic pride
　　In giant masses graced the walls above;
　　And dungeons yawned below.

　　Bursting on my steadfast gaze,
　　See, within, a sudden blaze!
So small at first, the zephyr's slightest swell,
　　That scarcely stirs the pine-tree top,
　　Nor makes the withered leaf to drop,
The feeble fluttering of that flame would quell.
　　But soon it spread,
　　Waving, rushing, fierce and red,
　　From wall to wall, from town to town,
　　Raging with resistless power;
　　Till every fervent pillar glowed,
　　And every stone seemed burning coal.

Beautiful, fearful, grand,
Silent as death, I saw the fabric stand.
At length a crackling sound began;
From side to side, throughout the pile it ran;
And louder yet and louder grew,
Till now in rattling thunder peals it grew;
Huge, shivered fragments from the pillars broke,
Like fiery sparkles from the anvil's stroke.
The shattered walls were rent and riven,
And piecemeal driven,
Like blazing comets through the troubled sky.
　　'Tis done; what centuries have reared
　　In quick explosion disappeared,
Nor e'en its ruins met my wondering eye.

But in their place,
Bright with more than human grace,
　　Robed in more than mortal seeming,
Radiant glory in her face,
　　And eyes with heaven's own brightness gleaming,

Rose a fair, majestic form,
As the mild rainbow from the storm.
I marked her smile, I knew her eye;
   And when with gesture of command,
   She waved aloft a cap-crowned wand,
My slumber fled 'mid shouts of " Liberty."

Read ye the dream? and know ye not
   How truly it unlocked the world of fate?
Went not the flame from this illustrious spot,
   And spread it not, and burns in every state?
And when their old and cumbrous walls,
   Filled with this spirit, glow intense,
   Vainly they rear their impotent defence:
The fabric falls!
That fervent energy must spread,
   Till despotism's towers be overthrown,
And in their stead
   Liberty stands alone.

Hasten the day, just Heaven!
   Accomplish thy design,
And let the blessings thou hast freely given
   Freely on all men shine,
Till equal rights be equally enjoyed,
And human power for human good employed;
Till law, not man, the sovereign rule sustain,
And peace and virtue undisputed reign.

                  — Henry Ware, Jr.

THE BLACK REGIMENT.

Dark as the clouds of even,
Ranked in the western heaven,
Waiting the breath that lifts
All the dead mass, and drifts
Tempest and falling brand
Over a ruined land;—
So still and orderly,
Arm to arm, knee to knee,
Waiting the great event,
Stands the black regiment.

Down the long, dusky line
Teeth gleam and eyeballs shine;
And the bright bayonet,
Bristling and firmly set,
Flashed with a purpose grand,
Long ere the sharp command
Of the fierce rolling drum
Told them their time had come,
Told them what work was sent
For the black regiment.

"Now," the flag-sergeant cried,
"Though death and hell betide,
Let the whole nation see
If we are fit to be
Free in this land; or bound
Down, like the whining hound —
Bound with red stripes of pain
In our cold chains again!"
Oh! what a shout there went
From the black regiment!

"Charge!" Trump and drum awoke;
Onward the bondmen broke;
Bayonet and sabre-stroke
Vainly opposed their rush.
Through the wild battle's crush,
With but one thought aflush,
Driving their lords like chaff,
In the guns' mouths they laugh;
Or at the slippery brands
Leaping with open hands,
Down they tear man and horse,
Down in their awful course;
Trampling with bloody heel
Over the crashing steel;—
All their eyes forward bent,
Rushed the black regiment.

"Freedom!" their battle-cry —
"Freedom! or leave to die!"
Ah! and they meant the word,
Not as with us 'tis heard,

Not a mere party shout;
They gave their spirits out,
Trusted the end to God,
And on the gory sod
Rolled in triumphant blood;
Glad to strike one free blow,
Whether for weal or woe;
Glad to breathe one free breath,
Though on the lips of death;
Praying — alas! in vain! —
That they might fall again,
So they could once more see
That burst to liberty!
This was what " freedom " lent
To the black regiment.

Hundreds on hundreds fell;
But they are resting well;
Scourges and shackles strong
Never shall do them wrong.
Oh, to the living few,
Soldiers, be just and true!
Hail them as comrades tried;
Fight with them side by side;
Never, in field or tent,
Scorn the black regiment.

—George Henry Boker.

OUR STATE.

The south-land boasts its teeming cane,
The prairied west its heavy grain,
And sunset's radiant gates unfold
On rising marts and sands of gold!

Rough, bleak, and hard, our little State
Is scant of soil, of limits strait;
Her yellow sands are sands alone,
Her only mines are ice and stone!

From autumn frost to April rain,
Too long her winter woods complain;
From budding flower to falling leaf,
Her summer time is all too brief.

Yet, on her rocks, and on her sands,
And wintry hills, the school-house stands;
And what her rugged soil denies
The harvest of the mind supplies.

The riches of the commonwealth
And free, strong minds, and hearts of health;
And, more to her than gold or grain,
The cunning hand and cultured brain.

For well she keeps her ancient stock,
The stubborn strength of Pilgrim Rock;
And still maintains, with milder laws
And clearer light, the good old cause!

Nor heeds the sceptic's puny hands,
While near her school the church-spire stands;
Nor fears the blinded bigot's rule.
While near her church-spire stands the school.

— John Greenleaf Whittier.

THE LIBERTY BELL.

W. K. W.

Music by Hamlin E. Cogswell.

Allegretto.

1. Ring, ring, ring! for Tyr-an-ny is brok-en; Ring, ring, ring the
2. Ring, ring, ring! for Sla-ver-y is brok-en; Ring, ring, ring the

Cho. *Ring, ring, ring! for Tyr-an-ny is brok-en; Ring, ring, ring the*

Bell of Lib-er-ty; Ring, ring, ring for man-date long since spok-en,
Bell of Lib-er-ty; Ring, ring, ring for Lin-coln's word is spok-en,

Bell of Lib-er-ty; Ring, ring, ring for man-date long since spok-en,

meno mosso.   Fine.   *a tempo.*

Mak-ing Our Fa-thers for-ev-er to be free. Long, long they fought with
Grand-ly pro-claim-ing, Ev-'ry Man is Free. Hard was the strife, 'twixt

Mak-ing Our Coun-try for-ev-er to be free.

cour-age all un-daunted; Brave-ly they sought to break oppression's chain! In their proud
gal-lant Blue and Gray; Fierce-ly they fought as on-ly Sax-ons can. Long, long the

D.C. Chorus.

eyes the pow'r of England flaunted; No-bly they fought their free-dom dear to gain.
years that ush-ered Freedom's day, Tell-ing to earth that Ev-'ry Man's a Man.

THE LIBERTY BELL.

HAT boy or girl is there in all this broad land who does not know the story of the wonderful old Liberty Bell; how it rang out the glorious tidings of the adoption of the Declaration of Independence? How this message came down from the steeple as though sent from the skies to the eager and cheering crowds in the streets of Philadelphia? How the bell, now old and cracked, bears upon its surface those words which can never be uttered without stirring the pulse of every patriot, " Proclaim Liberty throughout all the land to all the inhabitants thereof."

SELECTIONS.

INDEPENDENCE BELL, JULY 4, 1776.

There was tumult in the city,
　In the quaint old Quaker's town,—
And the streets were rife with people,
　Pacing, restless, up and down; —
People, gathering at corners,
　Where they whispered, each to each,
And the sweat stood on their temples,
　With the earnestness of speech.

As the bleak Atlantic currents
　Lash the wild Newfoundland shore,
So they beat against the State House,—
　So they surged against the door;
And the mingling of their voices
　Made a harmony profound,
Till the quiet street of Chestnut
　Was all turbulent with sound.

(111)

"Will they do it?" — "Dare they do it?" —
  "Who is speaking?" — "What's the news?" —
"What of Adams?" — "What of Sherman?" —
  "Oh, God grant they won't refuse!" —
"Make some way there!" — "Let me nearer!" —
  "I am stifling!" — "Stifle, then!
When a nation's life's at hazard,
  We've no time to think of men!"

So they beat against the portal,
  Man and woman, maid and child;
And the July sun in heaven
  On the scene looked down and smiled;
The same sun that saw the Spartan
  Shed his patriot blood in vain,
Now beheld the soul of Freedom,
  All unconquered, rise again.

See! See! The dense crowd quivers
  Through all its lengthy line,
As the boy beside the portal
  Looks forth to give the sign!
With his small hands upward lifted,
  Breezes dallying with his hair,
Hark! with deep, clear intonation,
  Breaks his young voice on the air.

Hushed the people's swelling murmur,
  List the boy's strong, joyous cry!
"*Ring!*" he shouts, "Ring! *Grandpa*,
  Ring! Oh, Ring for Liberty!"
And, straightway, at the signal,
  The old bellman lifts his hand,
And sends the good news, making
  Iron music through the land.

How they shouted! What rejoicing!
  How the old bell shook the air,
Till the clang of Freedom ruffled
  The calm, gliding Delaware!
How the bonfires and the torches
  Illumed the night's repose,
And from the flames, like Phoenix,
  Fair Liberty arose!

That old bell now is silent,
  And hushed its iron tongue,
But the spirit it awakened
  Still lives,— forever young.
And, while we greet the sunlight,
  On the fourth of each July,
We'll ne'er forget the bellman,
  Who, 'twixt the earth and sky,
Rung out OUR INDEPENDENCE;
  Which, please God, *shall never die!*

THE BELL.

In some strange land and time,— for so the story runs,— they were about to found a bell for a mighty tower,— a hollow, starless heaven of iron.

It should toll for dead monarchs, "The king is dead;" and it should make glad clamor for the new prince, "Long live the king!" It should proclaim so great a passion, or so grand a pride, that either would be worshipped; or, wanting these, forever hold its peace. Now, this bell was not to be dug out of the cold mountain; it was to be made of something that had been warmed with a human touch, or loved with a human love.

And so the people came like pilgrims to a shrine, and cast their offerings into the furnace.

By and by, the bell was alone in its chamber; and its four windows looked out to the four quarters of heaven. For many a day it hung dumb.

The winds came and went, but they only set it sighing; birds came and sang under its eaves, but it was an iron horizon of dead melody still. All the meaner strifes and passions of men rippled on below it; they out-grouped the ants; they out-wrought the bees; they out-watched the shepherds of Chaldea; but the chamber of the bell was as dumb as the cave of Machpelah.

At last there came a time when men grew grand for Right and Truth, and stood shoulder to shoulder over all the land, and went down like reapers to the harvest of death; looked into the graves of them

8

that slept, and believed there was something grander than living;
glanced on into the far future, and discerned there was something
better than dying; and so, standing between the quick and the dead,
they quitted themselves like men.

Then the bell awoke in its chamber; and the great wave of its
music rolled gloriously out, and broke along the blue walls of the
world like an anthem. Poured into that fiery heat together, the
humblest gifts were blent in one great wealth, and accents feeble as a
sparrow's song grew eloquent and strong; and lo! a people's stately soul
heaved on the waves of a mighty voice.

We thank God, in this our day, for the furnace and the fire; for the
good sword and the true word; for the great triumph and the little
song.

By the memory of the Ramah into which war has turned the land,
for the love of the Rachels now lamenting within it, for the honor of
Heaven and the hope of mankind, let us who stand here, past and
present clasping hands over our heads, the broad age dwindled to a
line under our feet, and ridged with the graves of dead martyrs; let us
declare before God and these witnesses,—" We will finish the Work
that the Fathers began."— *B. F. Taylor.*

THE SWORD.

IT may seem strange to call upon the boys and girls of the Empire State to celebrate the sword — the instrument by which, in days gone by, in our own land, thousands have been slain. For the Sword here stands for muskets, bayonets, guns — small and great — and every sort of weapon by which brave men have lost their lives in battle. In other words, it stands for War, with all its cruelties and horrors. And yet, there come times in the history of every people when they must draw the sword, or perish. Bad as war always is, slavery is worse, the loss of freedom is worse. That is why the American colonists, armed with old-fashioned flint-lock muskets, stood so bravely against the attacks of the British redcoats; that is why

"The farmers gave them ball for ball,
From behind each fence and barnyard wall."

Yes, and more than that: At first the colonists were anxious merely to secure such rights as they thought were fairly theirs under the British government; but soon and fast grew the wish for Independence — the gift of God to all men. Now, was it not worth while to fight in such a cause and to gain such a priceless thing? Let other examples be recalled, and let us not be afraid to rejoice over all true victories won by The Sword.

SELECTIONS.

Americans need to keep in mind the fact that as a nation they have erred far more often in not being willing to fight than in being too willing. Once roused, our countrymen have always been dangerous and hard-fighting foes, but they have been over-difficult to rouse. The educated classes in particular need to be perpetually reminded that, though it is an evil thing to brave a conflict needlessly, or to bully and bluster, it is an even worse thing to flinch from a fight for which there is legitimate provocation.

America is bound scrupulously to respect the rights of the weak, but she is no less bound to make stalwart insistence on her own rights as against the strong.— *Gov. Theodore Roosevelt.*

THE RISING IN 1776.

Out of the North the wild news came,
Far flashing on its wings of flame,
Swift as the boreal light which flies
At midnight through the startled skies.
And there was tumult in the air,
    The fife's shrill note, the drum's loud beat,
And through the wide land everywhere
    The answering tread of hurrying feet;
While the first oath of Freedom's gun
Came on the blast from Lexington;
And Concord roused, no longer tame,
Forgot her old baptismal name,
Made bare her patriot arm of power,
And swelled the discord of the hour.

Within its shade of elm and oak
    The church of Berkeley Manor stood;
There Sunday found the rural folk,
    And some esteemed of gentle blood.
    In vain their feet with loitering tread
Passed 'mid the graves where rank is naught;
All could not read the lesson taught
    In that republic of the dead.

The pastor came; his snowy locks
    Hallowed his brow of thought and care;
And calmly, as shepherds lead their flocks,
    He led into the house of prayer.
The pastor rose; the prayer was strong;
The psalm was warrior David's song;
The text, a few short words of might,
" The Lord of hosts shall arm the right! "

He spoke of wrongs too long endured,
Of sacred rights to be secured;
Then from his patriot tongue of flame
The startling words for freedom came.
The stirring sentences he spake
Compelled the heart to glow or quake;
And, rising on his theme's broad wing,
  And grasping in his nervous hand
  The imaginary battle brand,
In face of death he dared to fling
Defiance to a tyrant king.

Even as he spoke, his frame, renewed
In eloquence of attitude,
Rose, as it seemed, a shoulder higher;
Then swept his kindling glance of fire
From startled pew to breathless choir;
When suddenly his mantle wide
His hands impatient flung aside,
And lo! he met their wondering eyes,
Complete, in all a warrior's guise.

A moment there was awful pause,
When Berkeley cried, " Cease, traitor! cease,
God's temple is the house of peace! "
  The other shouted, " Nay, not so!
When God is with our righteous cause
His holiest places, then, are ours,
His temples are our forts and towers,
  That frown upon the tyrant foe;
In this, the dawn of Freedom's day,
There is a time to fight and pray! "

And now before the open door,
  The warrior priest had ordered so,
The enlisting trumpet's sudden roar
Rang through the chapel o'er and o'er,
  Its long reverberating blow,
So loud and clear, it seemed the ear
Of dusty death must wake and hear.
And there the startling drum and fife
Fired the living with fiercer life;

While overhead, with wild increase,
Forgetting its ancient toll of peace,
  The great bell swung as ne'er before;
It seemed as it would never cease;
And every word its ardor flung
From off its jubilant iron tongue
  Was, " War! War! War! "

"Who dares?" this was the patriot's cry,
  As striding from the desk he came,
  "Come out with me, in Freedom's name,
For her to live, for her to die?"
A hundred hands flung up reply,
A hundred voices answered, " I."

                              — *T. Buchanan Read.*

   Be it in the defense or be it in the assertion of a people's rights, I
hail the sword as a sacred weapon; and if it has sometimes taken too
deep a dye, yet, like the anointed rod of the High Priest, it has at
other times, and as often, blossomed into celestial flowers to deck the
freeman's brow. Abhor the sword? Stigmatize the sword? No! for
in the passes of the Tyrol it cut to pieces the banner of the Bavarian,
and through those craggy defiles struck a path to fame for the peasant
insurrectionist of Innspruck. Abhor the sword? Stigmatize the
sword? No! for it swept the Dutch marauders out of the fine old
towns of Belgium, scourged them back to their own phlegmatic
swamps, and knocked their flag and sceptre, their laws and bayonets
into the sluggish waters of the Scheldt. Abhor the sword? Stigmatize the sword? NO! For at its blow a giant nation started from
the waters of the Atlantic, and by the redeeming magic of the sword,
and in the quivering of its crimson light, the crippled colonies sprang
into the attitude of a proud republic,— prosperous, limitless, invincible.— *Thomas Francis Meagher.*

THE SWORD OF BUNKER HILL.

WILLIAM ROSS WALLACE.   BERNARD COVERT.

1. He lay up-on his dy-ing bed; His eye was grow-ing
2. The sword was brought, the sol-dier's eye Lit with a sud-den
3. "'Twas on that dread, im-mor-tal day, I dared the Brit-on's
4. "O, keep the sword"— his ac-cents broke— A smile— and he was

dim, When with a fee-ble voice he called His
flame; And as he grasped the an-cient blade, He
band, A cap-tain raised this blade on me,— I
dead— But his wrin-kled hand still grasped the blade Up-

weep-ing son to him: "Weep not, my boy!" the vet-'ran said, "I
murmured War-ren's name: Then said, "My boy, I leave you gold— But
tore it from his hand: And while the glo-rious bat-tle raged, It
on that dy-ing bed. The son re-mains; the sword re-mains— Its

THE SWORD OF BUNKER HILL.

ANGEL OF PEACE.

OLIVER WENDELL HOLMES.

MATTHIAS KELLER.

1. An - gel of Peace, thou hast wan - dered too long! Spread thy white wings to the
2. Broth - ers we meet, on this al - tar of thine Ming - ling the gifts we have
3. An - gels of Beth - le - hem, an - swer the strain! Hark! a new birth-song is

sun - shine of love! Come while our voi - ces are blend - ed in song,—
gath - ered for thee, Sweet with the o - dors of myr - tle and pine,
fill - ing the sky!— Loud as the storm-wind that tum - bles the main

ANGEL OF PEACE.

Fly to our ark like the storm-beat-en dove!
Breeze of the prai - rie and breath of the sea,—
Bid the full breath of the or - gan re - ply,—

Fly to our ark on the
Mead - ow and moun-tain and
Let the loud tem - pest of

Fly to our ark like the storm-beat-en dove!
Breeze of the prai - rie and breath of the sea,—
Bid the full breath of the or - gan re - ply,—

Fly to our ark on the
Mead - ow and moun-tain and
Let the loud tem - pest of

wings of the dove,—
for - est and sea!
voi - ces re - ply,—

Speed o'er the far - sounding bil - lows of song,
Sweet is the fra - grance of myr - tle and pine,
Roll its long surge like the earth - shak-ing main!

wings of the dove,—
for - est and sea!
voi - ces re - ply,—

Speed o'er the far - sounding bil - lows of song,
Sweet is the fra - grance of myr - tle and pine,
Roll its long surge like the earth - shak-ing main!

ANGEL OF PEACE.

Crowned with thine ol - ive - leaf gar - land of love,— An - gel of
Sweet - er the in - cense we of - fer to thee,— Broth - ers once
Swell the vast song till it mounts to the sky!— An - gels of

Crowned with thine ol - ive - leaf gar - land of love,— An - gel of
Sweet - er the in - cense we of - fer to thee, Broth - ers once
Swell the vast song till it mounts to the sky!— An - gels of

Peace, thou hast wait - ed too long!
more round this al - tar of thine!
Beth - le - hem, ech - o the strain!

Peace, thou hast wait - ed too long!
more round this al - tar of thine!
Beth - le - hem, ech - o the strain!

PEACE.

THE DOVE.

DOVE is quite a common sight to children living in the country — and a great many boys and girls could write very interesting compositions about its beauty, its quiet ways, and its contented life. They could weave into their thoughts, also, that beautiful story of olden times about the dove that was once sent forth from an ark, at a time when the whole of the Earth's surface was covered with water, to see if she could find a resting place "for the sole of her foot;" and how at first she could find none, but going forth again, after seven days resting in the ark, she returned at evening —"and, lo, in her mouth was an olive leaf pluckt off;" so the people in the ark knew that the waters had abated. Well, ever since that time, almost, the olive leaf, or branch, has meant victory — just as the dry land gained a victory over the water,— and the Dove has been the symbol of Peace — just as peace and happiness came to the dwellers shut up in the storm-tossed ark on the top of the mountain. Now what more pleasant celebration can happy children have, than to read and talk and sing about the glory and prosperity which comes to a nation that is at peace with all the world? Let us talk about the sword and cruel war when we must because our country is in peril; but let the songs of Peace and its praises be ever upon our lips, until

"The war-drums beat no longer,
And the battle-flags are furled
In the Parliament of Man,
The Federation of the World."

(125)

SELECTIONS.

There is a story told
In Eastern tents, when autumn nights grow cold,
And round the fire the Mongol shepherds sit
With grave responses listening unto it;
Once, on the errands of his mercy bent,
Buddha, the holy and benevolent,
Met a fell monster; huge and fierce of look,
Whose awful voice the hills and forests shook.
" O son of Peace!" the giant cried, "thy fate
Is sealed at last, and love shall yield to hate."
The unarmed Buddha looking, with no trace
Of fear or anger, in the monster's face,
    With pity said: " Poor fiend, even thee I love."
Lo! as he spake, the sky-tall terror sank
To hand-breadth size; the huge abhorrence shrank
    Into the form and fashion of a dove;
And where the thunder of its rage was heard,
Brooding above him sweetly sang the bird;
" Hate hath no harm for love," so ran the song,
And peace unweaponed conquers every wrong!"
                                   —*John Greenleaf Whittier.*

It is a beautiful picture in Grecian story, that there was at least one spot, the small island of Delos, dedicated to the gods, and kept at all times sacred from war. No hostile foot ever sought to press this kindly soil; and the citizens of all countries here met, in common worship, beneath the aegis of inviolable peace. So let us dedicate our beloved country; and may the blessed consecration be felt in all its parts, throughout its ample domain! The TEMPLE OF HONOR shall be surrounded here at last, by the Temple of Concord, that it may never more be entered by any portal of war; the horn of abundance shall overflow at its gates; the angel of religion shall be the guide over its steps of flashing adamant; while within its enraptured courts, purged of violence and wrong, JUSTICE, returning to earth from her long exile in the skies, with mighty scales for nations as for men, shall rear her serene and majestic front; and by her side, greatest of all, CHARITY, sublime in meekness, hoping all and enduring all, shall divinely temper every righteous decree and with words of infinite cheer shall inspire those good works that cannot vanish away. And the future chiefs of the Republic, destined to uphold the glories of a new era, unspotted by human blood, shall be " the first in Peace, and the first in the hearts of their countrymen."

But while seeking these blissful glories for ourselves, let us strive to extend them to other lands. Let the bugles sound the *Truce of God* to the whole world forever. Let the selfish boast of the Spartan women become the grand chorus of mankind, that they have never seen the smoke of an enemy's camp. Let the iron belt of martial music, which now encompasses the earth, be exchanged for the golden cestus of Peace, clothing all with celestial beauty.— *Charles Sumner,* from " The True Grandeur of Nations," an oration delivered before the authorities of the city of Boston, July 4, 1845.

THE ARSENAL AT SPRINGFIELD.

This is the arsenal. From floor to ceiling,
　Like a huge organ, rise the burnished arms;
But from their silent pipes no anthem pealing
　Startles the villages with strange alarms.

Ah! what a sound will rise, how wild and dreary,
　When the Death-angel touches these swift keys!
What loud lament and dismal Miserere
　Will mingle with their awful symphonies!

I hear even now the infinite fierce chorus,
　The cries of agony, the endless groan,
Which, through the ages that have gone before us,
　In long reverberations reach our own.

On helm and harness rings the Saxon hammer,
　Through Cimbric forest roars the Norseman's song,
And loud, amid the universal clamor,
　O'er distant deserts sounds the Tartar gong.

I hear the Florentine, who from his palace
  Wheels out his battle-bell with dreadful din,
And Aztec priests upon their teocallis
  Beat the wild war-drums made of serpent's skin.

The tumult of each sacked and burning village;
  The shout that every prayer for mercy drowns;
The soldiers' revels in the midst of pillage;
  The wail of famine in beleaguered towns;

The bursting shell, the gateway wrenched asunder,
  The rattling musketry, the clashing blade;
And ever and anon, in tones of thunder,
  The diapason of the cannonade.

Is it, O man, with such discordant noises,
  With such accursed instruments as these,
Thou drownest Nature's sweet and kindly voices,
  And jarrest the celestial harmonies?

Were half the power that fills the world with terror,
  Were half the wealth bestowed on camps and courts,
Given to redeem the human mind from error,
  There were no need of arsenals or forts:

The warrior's name would be a name abhorred!
  And every nation that should lift again
Its hand against a brother, on its forehead
  Would wear for evermore the curse of Cain!

Down the dark future, through long generations,
  The echoing sounds grow fainter, and then cease;
And like a bell, with solemn, sweet vibrations,
  I hear once more the voice of Christ say, "Peace!"

Peace! and no longer from its brazen portals
  The blast of War's great organ shakes the skies!
But, beautiful as songs of the immortals,
  The holy melodies of love arise.

                              —*H. W. Longfellow.*

THE EAGLE.

THIS, surely, is true: If you have ever seen an Eagle shut up in a cage, deprived of the power to fly, and no scream of triumph ever issuing from his throat, it must have given you a faint idea of the forlorn and unhappy plight of any human being when deprived of liberty, pining away in hopeless captivity.

If you have ever watched that same bird flying high and strong, or have seen him perched upon some tall cliff or crag, rejoicing in the upper air, and gazing with unblinking eyes upon the sun,— you have seen a fine illustration of the joys of Freedom.

SELECTIONS.

THE EAGLE.

Bird of the broad and sweeping wing
  Thy home is high in heaven,
Where wide the storms their banners fling,
  And the tempest clouds are driven.
Thy throne is on the mountain top;
  Thy fields — the boundless air;
And hoary peaks that proudly prop
  The skies, thy dwellings are.

*   *   *   *   *   *   *

And where was then thy fearless flight?
  " O'er the dark, mysterious sea,
To the lands that caught the setting light,
  The cradle of liberty.
There on the silent and lonely shore,
  For ages I watched alone,
And the world, in its darkness, asked no more
  Where the glorious bird had flown.

But then came a bold and hardy few,
  And they breasted the unknown wave;
I caught afar the wandering crew,
  And I knew they were high and brave.

9   (129)

I wheeled around the welcome bark,
    As it sought the desolate shore;
And up to heaven, like a joyous lark,
    My quivering pinions bore.

And now that bold and hardy few
    Are a nation wide and strong;
And danger and doubt I have led them through,
    And they worship me in song;
And over their bright and glancing arms
    On field, and lake, and sea,
With an eye that fires, and a spell that charms,
    I guide them to victory."

                        — *James Gates Percival.*

THE AMERICAN EAGLE.

Bird of Columbia! well art thou
    An emblem of our native land;
With unblenched front and noble brow,
    Among the nations doomed to stand;
Proud, like her mighty mountain woods;
    Like her own rivers wandering free;
And sending forth from hills and floods
    The joyous shout of liberty!
Like thee, majestic bird! like thee,
    She stands in unbought majesty,
With spreading wing, untired and strong,
    That dares a soaring far and long,
That mounts aloft, nor looks below,
    And will not quail, though tempests blow

    The admiration of the earth,
In grand simplicity she stands;
    Like thee, the storms beheld her birth,
And she was nursed by rugged hands;
    But, past the fierce and furious war,
Her rising fame new glory brings,
    For kings and nobles come from far
To seek the shelter of her wings.
And like thee, rider of the cloud,
She mounts the heavens, serene and proud,
Great in a pure and noble fame,
Great in her spotless champion's name,
And destined in her day to be
Mighty as Rome, more nobly free.   — *C. W. Thompson.*

WHERE THE EAGLE IS KING.

Thomas Buchanan Read.

William F. Hartley.

Martial style.

1. Where sweeps round the moun - tains the cloud on the gale, And streams from their
2. I mount the wild horse with no sad - dle or rein, And guide his swift
3. When A - pril is sound - ing his horn o'er the hills, And brook - lets are

foun - tains leap in - to the vale,— As fright-ened deer leap when the storm with his
course with a grasp on his mane: Thro' paths steep and nar - row, and scorn - ing the
bound - ing in joy to the mills,—When warm Au - gust slum - bers a - mong her green

pack Rides o - ver the steep in the wild tor - rent's track,— Ev'n
crag, I chase with my ar - row the flight of the stag; Through
leaves, And har - vest en - cum - bers her gar - ners with sheaves, When the

Words by permission J. B. Lippincott Company; Music, Houghton, Mifflin & Co.

WHERE THE EAGLE IS KING.

there my free home is; there watch I the flocks Wan-der white as the
snow-drifts en-gulf-ing, I fol-low the bear, And face the gaunt
flail of No-vem-ber is swing-ing with might, And the mil-ler De-

foam is on stair-ways of rocks; Se-cure in the gorge there in
wolf when he snarls in his lair, And watch through the gorge there the
cem-ber is man-tled with white,— In field and in forge there the

free-dom we sing, And laugh at King George, where the Ea-gle is king.
red pan-ther spring, And laugh at King George, where the Ea-gle is king.
free-heart-ed sing, And laugh at King George, where the Ea-gle is king.

THE GRAY FOREST EAGLE.

*   *   *   *   *   *   *   *

An emblem of freedom, stern, haughty, and high,
Is the Gray Forest Eagle, that king of the sky.
When his shadows steal black o'er the empires of kings,
Deep terror,— deep, heart-shaking terror,— he brings;
Where wicked oppression is armed for the weak,
There rustles his pinion, there echoes his shriek;
His eye flames with vengeance, he sweeps on his way,
And his talons are bathed in the blood of his prey.

O, that Eagle of Freedom! when cloud upon cloud
Swathed the sky of my own native land with a shroud,
When lightnings gleamed fiercely, and thunderbolts rung,
How proud to the tempest those pinions were flung!
Though the wild blast of battle rushed fierce through the air
With darkness and dread, still the eagle was there;
Unquailing, still speeding his swift flight was on,
Till the rainbow of peace crowned the victory won.

O, that Eagle of Freedom! age dims not his eye,
He has seen earth's mortality spring, bloom, and die!
He has seen the strong nations rise, flourish, and fall,
He mocks at Time's changes, he triumphs o'er all;
He has seen our own land with forests o'erspread,
He sees it with sunshine and joy on its head;
And his presence will bless this his own chosen clime,
Till the Archangel's fiat is set upon time.

              —*Alfred B. Street.*

THE EAGLE.

He clasps the crag with crooked hands;
Close to the sun in lonely lands,
Ring'd with the azure world, he stands.

The wrinkled sea beneath him crawls;
He watches from his mountain walls;
And like a thunderbolt he falls.

              —*Alfred Tennyson.*

Many years ago, a white-headed eagle was taken from its nest when only four months old, and sold to a Wisconsin farmer for a bushel of corn. The bird was very intelligent, and attracted the attention of a gentleman, who purchased and presented him to the Eighth Regiment of Wisconsin, then preparing to go to the front. The eagle was gladly received, and given a place next to the regimental flag. For three years he followed the " Live Eagle Regiment," being near its flag in thirty battles.

This majestic bird was always moved and most demonstrative at the sound of martial music. He shared all the battles of the regiment, but no drop of his blood was ever sacrificed. Vainly did rebel sharp-shooters aim at his dark figure, conspicuously " painted on the crimson sky; " he seemed to bear a charmed life; and his loyal comrades almost looked up to him as their leader, and with pride believed in him as a bird of good omen. He was named " Old Abe," sworn into the service, and proved to be every inch a soldier, listening to and obeying orders, noting time most accurately, always after the first year giving heed to " attention," insisting upon being in the thickest of the fight, and when his comrades, exposed to great danger from the terrible fire of the enemy, were ordered to lie down, he would flatten himself upon the ground with them, rising when they did, and with outspread pinions soar aloft over the carnage and smoke of the battle. When the cannons were pouring forth destruction and death, above the roar and thunder of the artillery rose his wild, shrill, battle-cry of freedom. He was always restless before the march to the encounter, but after the smoke of the battlefield had cleared away he would doff his soldier-like bearing, and with wild screams of delight would manifest his joy at the victory; but if defeat was the result his discomfiture and deep sorrow was manifested by every movement of his stately figure, but drooping head.— Adapted from *M. S. Porter.*

THE SHIELD.

OW great was the reliance of the Roman soldier upon his shield! With it, he warded off the arrows of his enemies aimed at his body; holding it over him, like a roof, he sheltered his head from storms of missiles hurled at him from higher places. But woe be to him, if his shield was not strong enough to withstand the weapons dashed against it!

Recall, also, the command of the Spartan mother to her soldier-son: "My son, return with your shield or upon it." That meant that the soldier was to win the victory if possible; if not, was to give up his life in defense of his country, and be borne home upon his shield as a pall of honor.

So, Our Country is a shield of Law and Justice, giving to every citizen its sure and safe protection. May that shield never be so weak that it cannot withstand the attacks of any and every foe!

On the other hand, every citizen should be as a shield for his country — trying to win right victories for her, or ready, if need be, to die for her, like the Spartan soldier of old.

SELECTIONS.

THE TRUE PATRIOT.

E'en when in hostile fields he bleeds to save her,
'Tis not his blood he loses, 'tis his country's;
He only pays her back a debt he owes.
To her he's bound for birth and education,
Her laws secure him from domestic feuds,
And from the foreign foe her arms protect him.
She lends him honors, dignity, and rank,
His wrong revenges, and his merit pays;
And like a tender and indulgent mother,
Loads him with comforts, and would make his state
As blessed as nature and the gods designed it.

— William Cowper.

I do not know how far the United States of America can inter-
fere in Turkey, but American citizens are suffering in Armenia, and
so far as American citizens are concerned, I would protect them there
at any cost.   We have given no assent to the agreement of European
nations that the Dardanelles should be closed; and if it were necessary
to protect American citizens and their property, I would order United
States ships, in spite of forts, in spite of agreements, to sail up the
Dardanelles, plant themselves before Constantinople, and demand that
American citizens should have the protection to which they are entitled.
I do not love Great Britain particularly; but I think that one of the
grandest things in all the history of Great Britain is that she does
protect her subjects everywhere, anywhere, and under all circumstances.   This incident is a marvellous illustration of the protection
which Great Britain gives to her subjects: The King of Abyssinia took
a British subject, about twenty years ago, carried him up to the fortress
of Magdala, on the heights of a rocky mountain, and put him into a
dungeon, without cause assigned.   It took six months for Great
Britain to find that out.   Then she demanded his immediate release.
King Theobald refused.   In less than ten days after that refusal was
received, ten thousand English soldiers were on board ships of war,
and were sailing down the coast.   When they reached the coast, they
were disembarked, marched across that terrible country, a distance of
seven hundred miles, under a burning sun, up the mountain, up to the
very heights in front of the frowning dungeon; and there they gave
battle, battered down the iron gates of the stone walls, reached down
into the dungeon, and lifted out of it that one British subject.   Then
they carried him down the mountain, across the land, put him on board
a white-winged ship, and sped him home in safety.   That cost Great
Britain twenty-five millions of dollars.   But was it not a great thing
for a great country to do?   A country that can see across the ocean,
across the land, away up to the mountain height, and away down to
the darksome dungeon, one subject of hers, out of thirty-eight millions
of people, and then has an arm strong enough, and long enough to
stretch across the same ocean, across the same lands, up the same
mountain heights, down to the same dungeon, and lift him out and

carry him home to his own country and friends, in God's name, who would not die for a country that will do that? Well, our country will do it, and our country ought to do it; and all that I ask is that our country shall model itself after Great Britain in this one thing: The life of an American citizen must be protected, wherever he may be.— *William P. Frye,* from a speech delivered in the United States Senate, on the Armenian resolutions.

STARS IN MY COUNTRY'S SKY — ARE YE ALL THERE?

Are ye all there? Are ye all there,
  Stars in my country's sky?
Are ye *all* there? *Are ye all there,*
  In your shining homes on high?
"Count us! Count us," was their answer,
  As they dazzled on my view,
In glorious perihelion,
  Amid their field of blue.

I cannot count ye rightly;
  There's a cloud with sable rim;
I cannot make your number out,
  For my eyes with tears are dim.
O bright and blessed angel,
  On white wing floating by,
Help me to count, and not to miss
  One star in my country's sky!

Then the angel touched mine eyelids,
  And touched the frowning cloud;
And its sable rim departed,
  And it fled with murky shroud.
There was no missing Pleiad
  'Mid all that sister race;
The Southern Cross gleamed radiant forth,
  And the Pole Star kept its place.

Then I knew it was the angel
  Who woke the hymning strain
That at our Redeemer's birth
  Pealed out o'er Bethlehem's plain;

And still its heavenly key-stone
  My listening country held,
For all her constellated stars
  The diapason swelled.

— Lydia Huntley Sigourney.

E PLURIBUS UNUM.

Though many and bright are the stars that appear
  In that flag by our country unfurled,
And the stripes that are swelling in majesty there,
  Like a rainbow adorning the world,
Their light is unsullied as those in the sky
  By a deed that our fathers have done,
And they're linked in as true and as holy a tie
  In their motto of "Many in one."

*   *   *   *   *   *   *   *

Then up with our flag! — let it stream on the air;
  Though our fathers are cold in their graves,
They had hands that could strike, they had souls that could dare,
  And their sons were not born to be slaves.
Up, up with that banner! where'er it may call,
  Our millions shall rally around,
And a nation of freemen that moment shall fall
  When its stars shall be trailed on the ground.

— George Washington Cutler.

BATTLE HYMN OF THE REPUBLIC.

NOTE:— This song was inspired by a visit of Mrs. Howe to the "Circling Camps" around Washington, gathered for the defence of the Capital, early in the War of 1861–5.

JULIA WARD HOWE.

Allegretto.

1. Mine eyes have seen the glo - ry of the com - ing of the Lord; He is
2. I have seen Him in the watch-fires of a hun-dred cir - cling camps; They have
3. I have read a fie - ry gos - pel, writ in burnished rows of steel; "As ye
4. He has sound-ed forth the trum - pet that shall nev - er call re - treat; He is
5. In the beau-ty of the lil - ies, Christ was born a - cross the sea, With a

tramp-ling out the vin - tage where the grapes of wrath are stored; He hath
build - ed Him an al - tar in the eve - ning dews and damps; I can
deal with my con - tem - ners, so with you my grace shall deal; Let the
sift - ing out the hearts of men be - fore His judg - ment seat; Oh, be
glo - ry in His bo - som that trans - fig - ures you and me; As He

loosed the fate - ful lightning of His ter - ri - ble swift sword, His truth is marching on.
read His righteous sen - tence by the dim and flar - ing lamps, His day is marching on.
He - ro, born of wo - man, crush the ser - pent with His heel," Since God is marching on.
swift, my soul, to an - swer Him! be ju - bi - lant, my feet! Our God is marching on.
died to make men ho - ly, let us die to make men free, While God is marching on.

FULL CHORUS.

Glo - ry! glo - ry! Hal - le - lu - jah! Glo - ry! glo - ry! Hal - le - lu - jah!

Glo - ry! glo - ry! Hal - le - lu - jah! His truth is march - ing on.

By special arrangement with HOUGHTON, MIFFLIN & CO.

MANUAL OF PATRIOTISM.

GROUP V.

THE FLAG ILLUMINES THE TABLEAUX

OF

1. THE MINUTE MAN,
2. DEPARTURE AND RETURN OF
   STATES,

3. MARCH OF FLAGS,
4. ARMY AND NAVY,
5. HOMAGE TO COLUMBIA,—

AND

THE FLAG GLORIFIES THE PATRIOTIC UTTERANCES

OF

1. LONGFELLOW,
2. WHITTIER,

3. HOLMES,
4. LOWELL.

(141)

TABLEAUX.

THERE is hardly any kind of patriotic exercise in which children give so much pleasure, or from which they receive so much profit, as in the representation, in costume, of a great historical event. It is true that such picture-grouping cannot easily be arranged for an ordinary school-opening. But now and then, on a public occasion in afternoon or evening, there is nothing into which children will so heartily enter as such a pictorial exercise; and there is always some teacher, or children's friend, to be found who has the needful enthusiasm, intelligence and ingenuity to make the matter a success. And let nobody think that great elaboration or expense of costuming is needful. Things simply and inexpensively made, or the use of an old-time coat or dress found in a garret or unused drawer at home, may serve all needful purposes. To all taking part, the meaning of the exercise should be made clear,— and indeed it is well, on printed program, or by oral explanation, to give a preliminary hint to the audience. Several pictorial programs follow, for the benefit of those who believe that novelty induces interest, and interest — in things patriotic as in things financial — begets profit.

NO. I. "THE MINUTE MAN."

The name, "Minute Man" refers to those patriots in the time of the American Revolution, who were ready, "at a minute's notice" to seize their muskets and fight against the British. This was exactly what they did when the "Redcoats" came marching from Boston on through Lexington to Concord. No better idea could be given of the intention of the British than is conveyed by Longfellow's poem of "Paul Revere's Ride." This might be read or recited before the tableau is shown. In the tableau the central figure should be a minute man. A good model of him may be had by studying a photograph of

French's " Minute Man," a finely chiseled bronze statue, standing near the Concord bridge, at a point where the colonial farmers met the British regulars, and sent them, frightened and flying, back towards Boston. About this central figure group thirteen girls, in white, representing the original colonies that stood " shoulder to shoulder " during the Revolution; their arms raised and hands extended as if to bid the rustic soldier " God speed " in his defence of native land. While the tableau is still in view, let a clear-voiced and intelligent pupil repeat the famous ode written and recited by the great American scholar and patriot, Ralph Waldo Emerson. Here it is:

> By the rude bridge that arched the flood,
>   Their flag to April's breeze unfurled,
> Here once the embattled farmers stood,
>   And fired the shot heard round the world.
>
> The foe long since in silence slept;
>   Alike the conqueror silent sleeps;
> And Time the ruined bridge has swept
>   Down the dark stream which seaward creeps.
>
> On this green bank, by this soft stream,
>   We set to-day a votive stone;
> That memory may their deed redeem,
>   When, like our sires, our sons are gone.
>
> Spirit, that made these heroes dare
>   To die, and leave their children free,
> Bid Time and Nature gently spare
>   The shaft we raise to them and thee.

As the poem ends, or even before if the young folks cannot hold their positions, let the curtain fall, and have a good boy speaker declaim " The Minute Man " by another great American, George William Curtis.

THE MINUTE MAN.

The Minute Man of the Revolution! And who was he? He was the husband and father, who left the plough in the furrow, the hammer on the bench, and, kissing wife and children, marched to die or to be free! He was the old, the middle aged, the young. He was Captain Miles, of Acton, who reproved his men for jesting on the march! He was Deacon Josiah Haines, of Sudbury, eighty years old, who marched with his company to South Bridge, at Concord, then joined in that hot pursuit to Lexington, and fell as gloriously as Warren at Bunker Hill. He was James Hayward of Acton, twenty-two years old, foremost in that deadly race from Charlestown to Concord, who raised his piece at the same moment with a British soldier, each exclaiming, " You are a dead man! " The Briton dropped, shot through the heart. Hayward fell, mortally wounded. This was the Minute Man of the Revolution! The rural citizen, trained in the common school, the town meeting, who carried a bayonet that thought, and whose gun, loaded with a principle, brought down, not a man, but a system. With brain and heart and conscience all alive, he opposed every hostile order of British council. The cold Grenville, the brilliant Townsend, the reckless Hillsborough, derided, declaimed, denounced, laid unjust taxes, and sent troops to collect them, and the plain Boston Puritan laid his finger on the vital point of the tremendous controversy, and held to it inexorably. Intrenched in his own honesty, the king's gold could not buy him; enthroned in the love of his fellow-citizens, the king's writ could not take him; and when, on the morning at Lexington, the king's troops marched to seize him, his sublime faith saw, beyond the clouds of the moment, the rising sun of the America we behold, and careless of himself, mindful only of his country, he exultingly exclaimed, " Oh, what a glorious morning! " He felt that a blow would soon be struck that would break the heart of British tyranny. His judgment, his conscience told him the hour had come. Unconsciously, his heart beat time to the music of the slave's epitaph:

> " God wills us free;
> Man wills us slaves;
> I will as God wills:
> God's will be done! "
> — *George William Curtis.*

10

NO. 2. DEPARTURE AND RETURN OF THE STATES.

In the year 1861, as every intelligent boy and girl should know, the following States resolved to sever their connection with the Union, or, as the phrase ran in those days — " to secede " from the Union: South Carolina, Mississippi, Florida, Alabama, Georgia, Louisiana, Texas. Arkansas, North Carolina, Virginia, Tennessee followed. It was a sad day for our country when they decided thus to leave the National roof and the House of the Union that had sheltered them so long! But they seemed to think they were right, and so they marched forth with a very defiant air. Choose, then, seven girls of spirit to represent these departing States. Let South Carolina, bearing a palmetto branch, be the leader,— and all attired in white. Then let the Northern, Eastern, Western States be each represented by a girl,— or if that would make the number too great, let three girls stand, one each, for the North, the East, the West. Let these, in black, take their places in the background, center of the stage or platform, with their eyes downcast, while, to the playing of a piece in a minor key, the procession of the Southern States sweeps by. As they disappear, the North, East, West pass slowly off at the opposite side of the platform. Straightway a sympathetic voice repeats the following poem:

THE BLUE AND THE GRAY.

By the flow of the inland river,
　　Whence the fleets of iron have fled,
Where the blades of the grave-grass quiver,
　　Asleep are the ranks of the dead;
Under the sod and the dew,
　　Waiting the judgment day;
Under the one, the Blue;
　　Under the other, the Gray.

These in the robings of glory,
　　Those in the gloom of defeat;
All with the battle-blood gory,
　　In the dust of eternity meet;
Under the sod and the dew,
　　Waiting the judgment day;
Under the laurel. the Blue;
　　Under the willow, the Gray.

From the silence of sorrowful hours,
　The desolate mourners go,
Lovingly laden with flowers,
　Alike for the friend and the foe;
Under the sod and the dew,
　Waiting the judgment day;
Under the roses, the Blue;
　Under the lilies, the Gray.

So, with an equal splendor,
　The morning sun-rays fall,
With a touch impartially tender,
　On the blossoms blooming for all;
Under the sod and the dew,
　Waiting the judgment day;
Broidered with gold, the Blue;
　Mellowed with gold, the Gray.

So, when the summer calleth,
　On forest and field of grain,
With an equal murmur falleth
　The cooling drip of the rain;
Under the sod and the dew,
　Waiting the judgment day;
Wet with the rain, the Blue;
　Wet with the rain, the Gray.

Sadly, but not with upbraiding,
　The generous deed was done;
In the storm of the years that are fading
　No braver battle was won;
Under the sod and the dew,
　Waiting the judgment day;
Under the blossoms, the Blue;
　Under the garlands, the Gray.

No more shall the war-cry sever,
　Or the winding rivers be red;
They banish our anger forever,
　When they laurel the graves of our dead.
Under the sod and the dew,
　Waiting the judgment day;
Love and tears for the Blue;
　Tears and love for the Gray.

　　　　　　　　　— Francis Miles Finch.

Just as the voice dies away, to a march in major key, the Northern States, in white, march in with flags waving, escorting the Southern States, waving flags also — and all march about the stage singing as only patriotic children can sing, "My Country! 'tis of Thee." After the curtain falls, let the children be seated, or grouped, upon the stage. When the curtain has been raised, let a good speaker declaim the following extract from that great Union Southern citizen, Henry W. Grady; another, the next selection from a great Northern citizen, Robert C. Winthrop.

SELECTIONS.

With consecrated service, what could we not accomplish; what riches we should gather; what glory and prosperity we should render to the Union; what blessings we should gather into the universal harvest of humanity. As I think of it, a vision of surpassing beauty unfolds to my eyes. I see a South, the home of fifty millions of people, who rise up every day to call from blessed cities, vast hives of industry and thrift; her country-sides the treasures from which their resources are drawn; her streams vocal with whirring spindles; her valleys tranquil in the white and gold of the harvest; her mountains showering down the music of bells, as her slow-moving flocks and herds go forth from their folds; her rulers honest and her people loving, and her homes happy and their hearth-stones bright, and their waters still and their pastures green, and her conscience clear; her wealth diffused, and poor-houses empty; her churches earnest and all creeds lost in the gospel. Peace and sobriety walking hand in hand through her borders; honor in her homes; uprightness in her midst; plenty in her fields; straight and simple faith in the hearts of her sons and daughters; her two races walking together in peace and contentment; sunshine everywhere and all the time, and night falling on her gently as from the wings of the unseen dove.

All this, my country, and more, can we do for you. As I look, the vision grows, the splendor deepens, the horizon falls back, the skies open their everlasting gates, and the glory of the Almighty God streams through as He looks down on His people who have given themselves unto Him, and leads them from one triumph to another until they have reached a glory unspeakable, and the whirling stars, as in their courses through Arcturus they run to the Milky Way, shall not look down on a better people or happier land.— *Henry W. Grady*, from an address delivered at Dallas, Texas, October 26, 1887.

We are one, by the memories of our fathers! We are one, by the hopes of our children! We are one, by a Constitution and a Union which have not only survived the shock of foreign and of civil war, but have stood the abeyance of almost all administration, while the whole people were waiting, breathless in alternate hope and fear, for the issues of an execrable crime! We are one, bound together afresh, by the electric chords of sympathy and sorrow, vibrating and thrilling, day by day, of that live-long summer, through every one of our hearts, for our basely wounded and bravely suffering President, bringing us all down on our knees together, in common supplication for his life, and involving us all at last in a common flood of grief at his death! I dare not linger on that great affliction, which has added, indeed, " another hallowed name to the historical inheritance of our Republic," but which has thrown a pall of deepest tragedy upon the falling curtain of our first century. Oh, let not its influence be lost upon us for the century to come, but let us be one, henceforth and always, in mutual regard, conciliation, and affection!

"Go on, hand in hand, O States, never to be disunited! Be the praise and heroic song of all posterity! Join your invincible might to do worthy and godlike deeds!— *Robert C. Winthrop.*

NO. 3. THE MARCH OF THE FLAGS.

In this tableau, an even number of boys and girls — any convenient number, all carrying flags, march upon the stage to the music of "Stars and Stripes Forever," by Sousa. It may be well also to have one additional boy and one girl, with larger flags, round which the rest of the little flag-company may march or wheel. If blue suits for the boys and white for the girls cannot be had, ordinary costumes will do — especially if the boys will wear soldiers' caps, and the girls, sailor or liberty caps. The marching may be very simple or very intricate, according to time and ingenuity. A pleasing effect will be produced if during the march the flags are massed or "stacked" in the center of the stage, leaving the two standard-bearers there as a guard of honor while the rest of the company resume the march around the flags. After a time, the marchers return to the center, each taking a flag from one or other of the standard bearers. Then marching away, but soon returning to the stage-center, they form a tableau, by grouping themselves about the two leaders — the latter standing erect and facing front, while the rest, each holding the flag in the left hand, with the right remove the cap, bowing to and saluting the two central banners on the stage. Then the curtain falls.

NO. 4. THE ARMY AND NAVY.

To the music of familiar tunes, the thirteen colonies, represented by as many girls, march in, in single file, and in the order of the creation of the various colonies as states. They are followed, similarly, by other girls representing the remaining thirty-two states. All march as they may be directed by their teacher-leader, going through, for a little time, with evolutions more or less varied. Finally, as they range into lines at opposite sides of the stage, the boys march in, in single file — the "Army" distinguished by blue coats and soldier caps — the "Navy" by blue blouses and sailor caps. They form a tableau-group in center of stage, with a tall boy as color-sergeant, flag in hand, in the midst of the group. Then the "States" resume their march, circling about the mid-stage soldiers and sailors — and at length all march off the stage in the following order: (1) The Color-Bearer; (2)

The Thirteen Colonies; (3) The Army and Navy; (4) The States. A beautiful color effect will be added to the stage-picture if each girl will carry a short staff with a small " banneret " of red or blue, with the name of colony or state in white letters in the center. Let the soldier-boys carry muskets, easily made — the sailor-boys, cutlasses. One flag will suffice to give distinction to the entire tableau.

NO. 5. HOMAGE TO COLUMBIA.

Columbia should be impersonated by the " Goddess of Liberty " — a girl whose pleasing face and tall figure may come nearest to the ideal of such a character. She should be seated in a chair placed upon a platform or dais. The best costume,— a white dress with the flag draped over it,— or, a flag-dress, such as any skillful and tasty lady teacher can readily make. Upon the head of the Goddess, let a crown, or wreath, or liberty cap be placed; let her right hand carry a spear, surmounted by an eagle. Thus placed and ready, the curtain may be raised. To the sound of march-music the States of the Union, repre-sented by girls, march in,— and following, an equal number of boys, as soldiers and sailors, to stand for the Army and Navy. In single file they pass before the Goddess, each one in turn bowing to her, then passing to form a line at the back of the stage. The march proper may then begin — changing from " ones " to " twos " and " fours," or even wider lines — a boy and girl marching together, well-matched in size and bearing. How to vary the march and execute its " figures," some teacher in every school will well understand. I have tried the plan — and it worked admirably — of having each girl carry a ban-neret of red cloth on which was sewed, in white letters, the name of a state; the soldier boys carrying toy guns; the sailor lads, paper cut-lasses. At the proper time, the Goddess rises — signals for the troop to wheel before her, raise aloft their bannerets and weapons, then bow — as the Goddess extends her spear — bowing lower as the curtain descends.

PATRIOTIC POETS.

1. Henry W. Longfellow, born February 27, 1807.
2. John G. Whittier, born December 17, 1807.
3. Oliver Wendell Holmes, born August 29, 1809.
4. James Russell Lowell, born February 22, 1819.

It would not be possible to estimate the influence which these four poets have had upon our national life and character. They were all born in New England;— yet they all wrote on themes that concerned the whole country. Surely a half-hour, or indeed a half-day, could not be more profitably spent than in reading aloud or reciting a few of the poems of each. So, a few suggestions, easily amplified, are here set down:

1. *Longfellow.*

1. Sketch of Longfellow's Life.
2. Reading from Hiawatha. (Selected.)
3. Recitation, The Ship of State.
4. Recitation, Killed at the Ford.
5. Singing, America.

2. *Whittier.*

1. Essay, The Life of Whittier.
2. Recitation, Barbara Frietchie.
3. Reading, *Laus Deo.*
4. Singing, The Centennial Hymn.
5. Recitation, At Port Royal.

3. *Holmes.*

1. Sketch of the Poet's Life.
2. Recitation, Old Ironsides.
3. Singing, The American Hymn.
4. Reading, A Ballad of the Boston Tea Party.
5. Recitation, Grandfather's Story of Bunker Hill.

4. *Lowell.*

1. Lowell's Life.
2. Reading, Character of Washington.
3. Singing, True Freedom.   (Riverside Song Book.)
4. Recitation, Selection from the Commemoration Ode.
5. Singing, The Fatherland.   (Riverside Song Book.)

MANUAL OF PATRIOTISM.

GROUP VI.

THE FLAG RECALLS

1. COLUMBUS' DAY ....Song, *Columbus.*
2. LANDING OF THE PILGRIMS.Song, *The Breaking Waves Dashed High.*
3. LEXINGTON AND CONCORD...Song, *Three Cheers for the Olden Time.*
4. FOURTH OF JULY....................Song, *Independence Day.*
5. YORKTOWN...................Song, *The Land of Washington.*

(155)

COLUMBUS DAY.

A FEW years ago "this country of ours" made a great celebration in honor of the four hundredth anniversary of the landing of Christopher Columbus on this continent. I suppose all Empire State boys and girls can point out on the map just the spot where the landing was made, the cross planted, and the flag raised. Of course, it was not the dear flag of the stars and stripes. Who can tell what banner it was? I am quite sure you know that,— but perhaps you have forgotten the precise day — October 12, 1492 — when Columbus stepped on shore, saved from the perils of the sea, and from death at the hands of his own crew. Perhaps some of you — the older children — went to Chicago in 1893 and saw the "White City"— a wonderful group of buildings, filled with rare and beautiful things from every part of the earth. And it was all in memory of the great sailor and discoverer, Columbus. But you children cannot celebrate in that way — not even by building palaces of play-blocks. You can recall the great navigator by telling the story of his life,— his birth in far-off Genoa — his longing for the sea — his appearance at the Court of Spain — his reception by Queen Isabella — the sacrifices which, for his sake, she made — his various voyages — his imprisonment and death. It is a wonderful story, is it not? Such a story as boys and girls should cherish because of the lessons of Faith and Perseverance which it teaches,— lessons which may help them to the use of the same noble qualities.

SELECTIONS.

OBSERVATIONS ON THE CHARACTER OF COLUMBUS.

In Columbus were singularly combined the practical and the poetical. His mind had grasped all kinds of knowledge, whether procured by study or observation, which bore upon his theories; impatient of the scanty aliment of the day, his impetuous ardor, as has well been observed, threw him into the study of the fathers of the Church, the Arabian Jews, and the ancient geographers; while his daring, but irregular, genius, bursting from the limits of imperfect science, bore him to conclusions far beyond the intellectual vision of his contemporaries. If some of his conclusions were erroneous, they were at least ingenious and splendid, and their error resulted from the clouds which still hung over his peculiar path of enterprise. His own discoveries enlightened the ignorance of the age, guided conjecture to certainty, and dispelled that very darkness with which he had been obliged to struggle.

In the progress of his discoveries he has been remarked for the extreme sagacity and the admirable justness with which he seized upon the phenomena of the exterior world. The variations, for instance, of terrestrial magnetism, the direction of currents, the grouping of marine plants, fixing one of the grand climacteric divisions of the ocean, the temperatures changing not solely with the distance to the equator, but also with the difference of meridians; these and similar phenomena, as they broke upon him, were discerned with wonderful quickness of perception, and made to contribute important principles to the stock of general knowledge. This lucidity of spirit, this quick convertibility of facts to principles, distinguish him from the dawn to the close of his sublime enterprise, insomuch that with all the sallying ardor of his imagination, his ultimate success has been admirably characterized as a " conquest of reflection."—*Washington Irving.*

COLUMBUS.

Joaquin Miller.   Unknown. (A German Air.)

1. Be - hind him lay the gray A - zores, Be - hind the gates of
2. "My men grow mut' - nous day by day; My men grow ghast - ly
3. They sailed and sailed, as winds might blow, Un - til at last the
4. They sailed, they sailed, then spoke his mate: "This mad sea shows his
5. Then, pale and worn, he kept his deck, And thro' the dark - ness

Her - cu - les; Be - fore him not the ghost of shores, Be - fore him on - ly
wan and weak." The stout mate tho't of home; a spray Of salt wave wash'd his
blanch'd mate said: "Why, now, not e - ven God would know Should I and all my
teeth to-night, He curls his lip, he lies in wait, With lift - ed teeth as
peered that night. Ah, dark - est night! and then a speck— A light! a light! a

shore - less seas. The good mate said: "Now must we pray, For lo! the ver - y
swar - thy cheek." What shall I say, brave Ad - mi - ral, If we sight naught but
men fall dead. These ver - y winds for - get their way, For God from these dread
if to bite! Brave Ad - mi - ral, say but one word; What shall we do when
light! a light! It grew—a star - lit flag nn - furled! It grew to be Time's

stars are gone; Speak, Ad - mi - ral, what shall I say?" "Why say, sail on! and on!"
seas at dawn?" "Why, you shall say, at break of day: 'Sail on! sail on! and on!'"
seas is gone. Now speak, brave Ad - mi - ral, and say"—He said, "Sail on! sail on! and on!"
hope is gone?" The words leaped as a leap - ing sword: "Sail on! sail on! and on!"
burst of dawn; He gained a world! he gave that world Its watchword: "On! and on!"

SELECTIONS.

THE BOY COLUMBUS.

"'Tis a wonderful story," I hear you say,
" How he struggled and worked and plead and prayed,
And faced every danger undismayed,
With a will that would neither break nor bend,
And discovered a new world in the end —
But what does it teach to a boy of to-day?
All the worlds are discovered, you know, of course,
All the rivers are traced to their utmost source:
There is nothing left for a boy to find,
If he had ever so much a mind
  To become a discoverer famous;
And if we'd much rather read a book
About someone else, and the risks he took,
  Why nobody, surely, can blame us."

So you think all the worlds are discovered now;
All the lands have been charted and sailed about,
Their mountains climbed, their secrets found out;
All the seas have been sailed, and their currents known —
To the uttermost isles the winds have blown
They have carried a venturing prow?
Yet there lie all about us new worlds, everywhere,
That await their discoverer's footfall; spread fair
Are electrical worlds that no eye has yet seen,
And mechanical worlds that lie hidden serene
  And await their Columbus securely.
There are new worlds in Science and new worlds in Art,
And the boy who will work with his head and his heart
  Will discover his new world surely.

11

All hail, Columbus, discoverer, dreamer, hero, and apostle! We here, of every race and country, recognize the horizon which bounded his vision, and the infinite scope of his genius. The voice of gratitude and praise for all the blessings which have been showered upon mankind by his adventure is limited to no language, but is uttered in every tongue. Neither marble nor brass can fitly form his statue. Continents are his monument, and unnumbered millions, past, present, and to come, who enjoy in their liberties and their happiness the fruits of his faith, will reverently guard and preserve, from century to century, his name and fame.— *Chauncey Mitchell Depew,* from Dedicatory Oration at World's Columbian Exposition.

THE LANDING OF THE PILGRIMS.

N the year 1620 — some people say on December 21st, others December 22d — a company of Pilgrims, as they are called, landed at a place now known as Plymouth, on the coast of Massachusetts. They were English folk, but came to this country straight from Holland, having been driven from their former home in England by religious persecution. But I need not tell here the story of their sufferings on the slow and stormy voyage across the ocean — nor how cold and cheerless was the landing in the depth of winter. What child has not read it in the history book, or heard the story repeated at the fireside? Yet no matter how often the story may have been read, or told, it is well to keep in mind and to celebrate, at least once a year, the good traits of the Forefathers.

They were not real generous men and women in their treatment of those who differed from them in belief, yet they were mild indeed in comparison with the Puritans, as they were called,— a company of men and women who came to this country much later in the century. But if we cannot celebrate the kindness of the Pilgrims, we certainly may their *faith*. How greatly they needed it in all their troubles on land and tempests on sea, and how grandly they showed it! And so with their *courage*. Was it not a splendid trait in their character? Neither starvation, disease, nor the Indian's tomahawk could make them fear. (Just here might come in a study of " The Indian " in our country's history.) And so, children, study out and tell to your teachers other good things about these early and hardy colonists,— for " they fought a good fight."

THE MEDITATIONS OF COLUMBIA, 1876.

Mayflower, Mayflower, slowly hither flying,
   Trembling westward o'er yon balking sea,
Hearts within, " Farewell, dear England," sighing,
Winds without, " But dear in vain," replying,
Gray-lipped waves, about thee, shouted, crying,
   " No! It shall not be!"

     Jamestown, out of thee;
     Plymouth, thee; thee, Albany.
     Winter cries, " Ye freeze; away!"
     Hunger cries, " Ye starve; away!"
     Vengeance cries, " Your graves shall stay!"

     Then old shapes and masks of things,
     Frames like Faiths, or clothes like kings;
     Ghosts of Goods, once fleshed and fair,
     Grown foul Bads in alien air;
     War, and his most noisy lords,
     Tongued with lithe and poisoned swords,
     Error, Terror, Rage, and Crime,
     All, in a windy night of time,
     Cried to me, from land and sea,—
" No! Thou shalt not be!"

     Now Praise to God's oft-granted grace,
     Now Praise to Man's undaunted face,
     Despite the land, despite the sea,
     I was, I am, and I shall be.
     How long, Good Angel, O, how long?
     Sing me, from heaven, a man's own song!

" Long as thine Art shall love true love,
     Long as thy Science truth shall know,
Long as thy Eagle harms no Dove,
     Long as thy Law by law shall grow,
Long as thy God is God above,
     Thy brother every man below,
So long, dear Land of all my love,
     Thy name shall shine, thy fame shall glow!"

                        — Sidney Lanier.

THE BREAKING WAVES DASHED HIGH.

Felicia Hemans.

Miss Browne, arr.

1. The break-ing waves dash'd high On a stern and rock-bound coast,
2. Not as the con-queror comes, They, the true-heart-ed came;

3. A-mid the storm they sang, The stars heard and the sea!
4. What sought they thus a-far? Bright jew-els of the mine?

The woods a-gainst a storm-y sky Their gi-ant branch-es tossed;
Not with the roll of stir-ring drums, Or trump that sings of fame;

The sound-ing aisles of wood-land rang With an-thems of the free;
The wealth of seas, the spoils of war? They sought a faith's pure shrine!

The heav-y night hung dark, The hills and wa-ters o'er,
Not as the fly-ing come, In si-lence and in fear,

The o-cean ea-gle soared, The roll-ing wave's white foam;
Ay, call it ho-ly ground, The soil where first they trod;

When a band of ex-iles moor'd their bark On wild New Eng-land's shore.
They shook the depths of des-ert's gloom With hymns of loft-y cheer.

The rock-ing pines in for-est roar'd, To bid them wel-come home.
They left un-stained what there they found, Free-dom to wor-ship God.

SELECTIONS.

Here, on this rock, and on this sterile soil,
Began the kingdom, not of kings, but men;
Began the making of the world again.
Here centuries sank, and from the hither brink,
A new world reached and raised an old world link,
 When English hands, by wider vision taught,
And here revived, in spite of sword and stake,
Their ancient freedom of the Wapentake.
 Here struck the seed — the Pilgrims' roofless town,
Where equal rights and equal bonds were set;
Where all the people, equal-franchised, met;
 Where doom was writ of privilege and crown;
 Where human breath blew all the idols down;
Where crests were naught, where vulture flags were furled,
And common men began to own the world!

      — John Boyle O'Reilly.

LANDING OF THE PILGRIMS.

Methinks I see it now, that one solitary, adventurous vessel, the Mayflower of a forlorn hope, freighted with the prospects of a future state, and bound across the unknown sea. I behold it pursuing, with a thousand misgivings, the uncertain, the tedious voyage. Suns rise and set, and weeks and months pass, and winter surprises them on the deep, but brings them not the sight of the wished-for shore. I see them, now, scantily supplied with provisions, crowded almost to suffocation in their ill-stored prison, delayed by calms, pursuing a circuitous route; and now, driven in fury before the raging tempest, in their scarcely seaworthy vessel. The awful voice of the storm howls through the rigging. The laboring masts seem straining from their base; the dismal sound of the pumps is heard; the ship leaps, as it were, madly from billow to billow; the ocean breaks and settles with ingulfing floods over the floating deck, and beats with deadening weight against the staggering vessel. I see them escaped from these perils, pursuing their all but desperate undertaking, and landed at last, after a five months' passage, on the ice-clad rocks of Plymouth, weak and exhausted from the voyage, poorly armed, scantily provisioned, depending on the charity of their ship-master for a draught of beer on board, drinking nothing but water on shore, without shelter, without means, surrounded by hostile tribes.

Shut now the volume of history, and tell me, on any principle of human probability, what shall be the fate of this handful of adventurers? * * * Student of history, compare for me the baffled projects, the deserted settlements, the abandoned adventurers of other times, and find the parallel of this. Was it the winter storm, beating upon the houseless heads of women and children? was it hard labor and spare meals? was it disease? was it the tomahawk? was it the deep malady of a blighted hope, a ruined enterprise, and a broken heart, aching in its last moments at the recollections of the loved and left, beyond the sea? was it some or all of them united that hurried this forsaken company to their melancholy fate? And is it possible that neither of these causes, that not all combined, were able to blast this bud of hope! Is it possible that from a beginning so feeble, so frail, so worthy not so much of admiration as of pity, there has gone forth a progress so steady, a growth so wonderful, a reality so important, a promise yet to be fulfilled so glorious!— *Edward Everett.*

LEXINGTON AND CONCORD.

HESE are memorable places on the map of American history. For the brave stand a few colonial farmers there made against trained British regulars was the opening fight of a Revolution, a struggle for independence, which never ceased nor slackened until England gave up the contest at Yorktown, seven years later.

This fight at Lexington and Concord was fought April 17, 1775. Even yet, that is a great day in New England, and kept with more ceremony and enthusiasm than the Fourth of July. Let me tell you what the boys in Lexington do on that day: Early in the morning they rise up, hurry into their clothes and march away to Concord, over the very ground the soldiers trod a century and a quarter ago. On their march, they pass by many places where now are memorial tablets, telling what was done here and there along the whole line of their journey. Who cannot see what a vividness and sense of reality this early morning march, year by year, must give to these young patriots? But if New York children cannot actually travel on foot from Lexington to Concord, playing soldier, they may, in imagination, walk along the avenue of History, seeing by the roadside the inscriptions and memorials which History herself has put there, that the Nation may keep in mind the dangers and hardships endured by the men of olden time, that they might secure to themselves and their posterity the blessings of independence.

SELECTIONS.

CONCORD HYMN.

By the rude bridge that arched the flood,
   Their flag to April's breeze unfurled,
Here once the embattled farmers stood,
   And fired the shot heard round the world.

The foe long since in silence slept;
   Alike the conqueror silent sleeps;
And Time the ruined bridge has swept
   Down the dark stream which seaward creeps.

On this green bank, by this soft stream,
   We set to-day a votive stone;
That memory may their deed redeem,
   When like our sires, our sons are gone.

Spirit, that made these heroes dare
   To die, and leave their children free,
Bid Time and Nature gently spare
   The shaft we raise to them and thee.

— *Ralph Waldo Emerson.*

THE REVOLUTIONARY ALARM.

Darkness closed upon the country and upon the town, but it was no night for sleep. Heralds on swift relays of horses transmitted the war message from hand to hand, till village repeated to village, the sea to the backwoods, the plains to the highlands, and it was never suffered to droop till it had been borne North and South and East and West, throughout the land. It spread over the bays that receive the Saco and the Penobscot; its loud reveille broke the rest of the trappers of New Hampshire, and, ringing like bugle notes from peak to peak, overleapt the Green Mountains, swept onward to Montreal, and descended the ocean river till the responses were echoed from the cliffs at Quebec. The hills along the Hudson told to one another the tale. As the summons hurried to the South, it was one day at New York, in one more at Philadelphia, the next it lighted a watch-fire at Baltimore, thence it waked an answer at Annapolis. Crossing the Potomac near Mt. Vernon, it was sent forward, without a halt, to Williamsburg. It traversed the Dismal Swamp to Nansemond, along the route of the first emigrants to North Carolina. It moved onward and still onward, through boundless groves of evergreen, to Newbern and to Wilmington.

"For God's sake, forward it by night and day," wrote Cornelius Harnett, by the express which sped for Brunswick. Patriots of South Carolina caught up its tones at the border and despatched it to Charleston, and, through pines and palmettos and moss-clad live-oaks, farther to the South, till it resounded among the New England settlements beyond the Savannah. The Blue Ridge took up the voice and made it heard from one end to the other of the valley of Virginia. The Alleghanies, as they listened, opened their barriers that the "loud call" might pass through to the hardy riflemen on the Holstein, the Watauga and the French Broad. Ever renewing its strength, powerful enough even to create a commonwealth, it breathed its inspiring word to the first settlers of Kentucky, so that hunters who made their halt in the valleys of the Elkhorn commemorated the nineteenth day of April, 1776, by naming their encampment "Lexington." With one impulse the Colonies sprung to arms; with one spirit they pledged themselves to each other, "to be ready for the extreme event." With one heart the continent cried, "Liberty or death!"—*George Bancroft.*

It was a brilliant April night. The winter had been unusually mild, and the spring very forward. The hills were already green; the early grain waved in the fields; and the air was sweet with blossoming orchards. Already the robins whistled, the blue-bird sang, and the benediction of peace rested upon the landscape. Under the cloudless moon, the soldiers silently marched, and Paul Revere swiftly rode, galloping through Medford and West Cambridge, rousing every house as he went, spurring for Lexington, and Hancock, and Adams, and evading the British patrols who had been sent out to stop the news. Stop the news! Already the village church bells were beginning to ring the alarm, as the pulpits beneath them had been ringing for many a year. In the awakening houses lights flashed from window to window. Drums beat faintly far away and on every side. Signal guns flashed and echoed. The watch-dogs barked, the cocks crew. Stop the news! Stop the sunrise! The murmuring night trembled with the summons so earnestly expected, so dreaded, so desired. And as, long ago, the voice rang out at midnight along the Syrian shore, wailing that great Pan was dead, but in the same moment the choiring angels whispered, " Glory to God in the highest, for Christ is born!" so, if the stern alarm of that April night seemed to many a wistful and loyal heart to portend the passing glory of British dominion and the tragical chance of war, it whispered to them with prophetic inspiration, " Good-will to men: America is born!"— *George William Curtis*, from the oration delivered at the centennial celebration of Concord fight.

THREE CHEERS FOR THE OLDEN TIME.

FANNY CROSBY.

1. Three cheers, three cheers, for the old - en time, And the brave that knew no fear, my boys;
2. They dared to look in the flash - ing eye Of the storm-king when he pass'd, my boys;

FINE.

They stood e - rect as the gi - ant oak, And laugh'd when the storm was near, my boys.
A shout went up, and a peal of joy Rang out on the win - 'try blast, my boys.

Like them we'll boast of the land we love, And her proud flag stream-ing high, my boys;
The grass is green where they calm-ly rest, Those vet - 'rans true and brave, my boys;

D.C. al Fine.

We'll sing a - loud from the bright green hills, While the o - cean waves re - ply, my boys.
Their mem - 'ry shines like a ra - diant star, O'er the land they died to save, my boys.

INDEPENDENCE DAY.

BERNHARD KLEIN.

1. Tell me, boys, what mean those voi - ces That are shout - ing in the
2. Near a hun - dred years have float - ed On time's rest - less, chang - ing
3. It was then our youth - ful na - tion Raised its con - se - crat - ed
4. Let us join those hap - py voi - ces That are shout - ing in the

street? Ev - 'ry one I see re - joi - ces; Bands play tunes for march - ing
sea, Since our na - tion rose and vot - ed That the coun - try should be
hand, Sealed with blood the Dec - la - ra - tion Of her In - de - pend - ence
street; Ev - 'ry free - man's heart re - joi - ces; Bright beams ev - 'ry eye we

feet; And the stars and stripes are blow - ing On the o - cean and the shore;
free. Gay the stars and stripes are blow - ing On the o - cean and the shore;
grand. Gay the stars and stripes are blow - ing On the o - cean and the shore;
meet. Gay the stars and stripes are blow - ing On the o - cean and the shore;

SOLI; *repeat in* CHORUS.

All our hearts with thanks o'er - flow - ing, In - de - pend - ence Day once more.

THE FOURTH OF JULY.

T is not likely that boys or girls would consent to go to school on "the glorious Fourth." If they were asked to do so, they probably would read a declaration of independence, all of their own making. And so, it might be asked — "Why suggest any exercise for that day?" Why, because we ought not to forget such a day. True — but are we not in danger of forgetting if we do not call it to mind at least once a year? Alas! it is much to be feared that very many boys think the day was made for the express purpose of setting off firecrackers — small and giant ones — touching off small cannon, skyrockets, Roman candles and lots of other dangerous playthings. With the girls, the Fourth is a great picnic day.

But, really, the day was not made for the sake of powder, picnics and noise. It was set aside as a day in which to recall the signing of the Declaration of Independence — independence from the grasping and greed of England. But such a glorious deed can be celebrated at any convenient time in the calendar of school days. It is always in order to speak of the life and patriotism of Thomas Jefferson, author of the Declaration; always right to read aloud, for the benefit of others, the great truths which the Declaration contains; at any time, interesting to look over the list of signers of the Declaration and to study their lives. Let me commend John Hancock, Roger Sherman, Whipple, of New Hampshire. See, young folks, if you cannot find other names with histories as interesting.

SELECTIONS.

Sink or swim, live or die, survive or perish, I give my hand and my heart to this vote. It is true, indeed, that, at the beginning, we aimed not at independence. But there's a Divinity that shapes our ends. The injustice of England has driven us to arms; and, blinded to her own interest for our good, she has obstinately persisted, till independence is now within our grasp. We have but to reach forth to it, and it is ours. Why, then, should we defer the declaration? * * * Whatever may be our fate, be assured, be assured, that this declaration will stand. It may cost treasure and it may cost blood, but it will stand, and it will richly compensate for both. Through the thick gloom of the present I see the brightness of the future, as the sun in heaven. We shall make this a glorious, an immortal day. When we are in our graves, our children will honor it. They will celebrate it with thanksgiving, with festivity, with bonfires, and illuminations. On its annual return, they will shed tears, copious, gushing tears, not of subjection and slavery, not of agony and distress, but of exultation, of gratitude, and of joy. Sir, before God, I believe the hour has come. My judgment approves this measure, and my whole heart is in it. All that I have, and all that I am, and all that I hope in this life, I am now ready here to stake upon it; and I leave off as I began, that live or die, survive or perish, I am for the declaration. It is my living sentiment, and, by the blessing of God, it shall be my dying sentiment; independence, *now;* and INDEPENDENCE FOREVER! — *Daniel Webster,* from supposed speech of John Adams.

Through the chances and changes of vanished years,
   Our thoughts go back to the olden time,—
That day when the people resolved to be free,
   And, resolving, knew that the thing was done.
What booted the struggle yet to be,
   When the hearts of all men beat as one,
And hand clasped hand, and eyes met eyes,
And lives were ready to sacrifice?

The years since then have come and sped,
And the heroes of those old days are dead;
   But their spirit lives in to-day's young men;
And never in vain would our country plead
For sons that were ready to die at her need.

           — *Louise Chandler Moulton.*

The United States is the only country with a known birthday. All the rest began, they know not when, and grew into power, they knew not how. If there had been no Independence Day, England and America combined would not be so great as each actually is. There is no " Republican," no " Democrat " on the Fourth of July,— all are Americans. All feel that their country is greater than party.— *James G. Blaine.*

On the Fourth of July, 1776, the representatives of the United States of America, in Congress assembled, declared that these united colonies are, and of right ought to be, free and independent states. This declaration, made by most patriotic and resolute men, trusting in the justice of their cause, and the protection of Providence, and yet not without deep solicitude and anxiety, has stood for seventy-five years, and still stands. It was sealed in blood. It has met dangers and overcome them. It has had enemies and it has conquered them. It has had detractors, and it has abashed them all. It has had doubting friends, but it has cleared all doubts away. And now, to-day, raising its august form higher than the clouds, twenty millions of people contemplate it with hallowed love, and the world beholds it, and the consequences which have followed, with profound admiration.— *Daniel Webster.*

You have all read the Declaration of Independence; you have it by heart; you have heard it read to-day. A hundred years ago, it was a revelation, startling, with new terror, kings on their thrones, and bidding serfs in their poor huts rise and take heart, and look up with new hope of deliverance. It asserted that all men, kings and peasants, master and servant, rich and poor, were born equal, with equal rights, inheritors of equal claim to protection before the law; that governments derived their just powers, not from conquest or force, but from the consent of the governed, and existed only for their protection and to make them happy. These were the truths, eternal, but long unspoken; truths that few dared to utter, which, Providence ordained, should be revealed here in America, to be the political creed of the people, all over the earth. Like a trumpet blast in the night, it pealed through the dark abodes of misery, and roused men to thought, and hope and action.— *Richard O'Gorman.*

12

LIBERTY'S LATEST DAUGHTER.

Foreseen in the vision of sages,
   Foretold when martyrs bled,
She was born of the longing ages,
   By the truth of the noble dead
   And the faith of the living, fed!
No blood in her lightest veins
Frets at remembered chains,
Nor shame of bondage has bowed her head.
   In her form and features, still,
   The unblenching Puritan will,
Cavalier honor, Huguenot grace,
   The Quaker truth and sweetness,
And the strength of the danger-girdled race
   Of Holland, blend in a proud completeness.
From the home of all, where her being began,
She took what she gave to man: —
Justice that knew no station,
   Belief as soul decreed,
Free air for aspiration,
   Free force for independent deed.
She takes, but to give again,
As the sea returns the rivers in rain;
And gather the chosen of her seed
From the hunted of every crown and creed.
Her Germany dwells by a gentler Rhine;
Her Ireland sees the old sunburst shine;
Her France pursues some dream divine;
Her Norway keeps his mountain pine;
Her Italy waits by the western brine;
And, broad-based, under all
   Is planted England's oaken-hearted mood,
   As rich in fortitude
As e'er went world-ward from the island wall.
   Fused by her candid light,
   To one strong race all races here unite;
Tongues melt in hers; hereditary foemen
   Forget their sword and slogan, kith and clan.
'Twas glory once to be a Roman;
   She makes it glory now to be a man.

                — *Bayard Taylor.*

THE BATTLE OF YORKTOWN.

THIS great battle — great for the time and great in its consequences — was fought October 19, 1781. There was scattered fighting for a year or two after that day between
America and England,— but the Revolution really ended
with that memorable struggle. It will prove of great
interest to the young folks in school to trace the history of our
seven years' Revolutionary War from Lexington to Yorktown.
Let them not think of naming every battle, just when, just where
it was fought,— but picking out here and there a great event,
let them follow the long road, now sunlighted, now deeply shad-
owed, from colonial dependence to independent statehood. Knowledge of this sort, thus gained, will make of the children in years to
come more intelligent, more patriotic citizens, than they could possibly be without such training. And on that long road they should
be able to pick up, as one might pluck a flower by the wayside, many
a pleasant story of the times whose fragrance and memory may be
lasting and sweet. Take, for instance, the story of Dolly Madison
for the girls; for the boys, that of the Boston lads who went to General
Gage and made their demands upon him, like the saucy little Yankees
they were!

And when they have reached the end of the long road, let them
stop and see the Yorktown battle by sea and land; note the help of
the French and the gallantry of La Fayette; watch the daring of the
Americans and the bravery of Washington. Will it not indeed pay us
to remember Yorktown?

SELECTIONS.

THE YORKTOWN LESSON.

(Closing passage from Centennial address, October 18, 1881.)

"You are the advance guard of the human race; you have the future of the world," said Madame de Stael to a distinguished American, recalling with pride what France had done for us at Yorktown. Let us lift ourselves to a full sense of such responsibility for the progress of freedom, in other lands as well as in our own. * * *

We cannot escape from the great responsibilities of this great intervention of American example; and it involves nothing less than the hope or the despair of the Ages! Let us strive, then, to aid and advance the liberty of the world, in the only legitimate way in our power, by patriotic fidelity and devotion in upholding, illustrating, and adorning our own free institutions. We have nothing to fear except from ourselves. We are one by the configuration of nature and by the strong impress of art,— inextricably intwined by the lay of our land, the run of our rivers, the chain of our lakes, and the iron network of our crossing and recrossing and ever multiplying and still advancing tracks of trade and travel. We are one by the memories of our fathers. We are one by the hopes of our children. We are one by a Constitution and a Union which have not only survived the shock of foreign and civil war, but have stood the abeyance of almost all administrations, while the whole people were waiting breathless, in alternate hope and fear, for the issues of an execrable crime. With the surrender to each other of all our old sectional animosities and prejudices, let us be one, henceforth and always, in mutual regard, conciliation, and affection!

"Go on, hand in hand, O States, never to be disunited! Be the praise and heroic song of all posterity!" On this auspicious day let me invoke, as I devoutly and fervently do, the choicest and richest blessings of Heaven on those who shall do most, in all time to come, to preserve our beloved country in Unity, Peace, and Concord.— *Robert Charles Winthrop.*

THE LAND OF WASHINGTON.

Note.—"The melody of this song was called the "Drum and Fife March," by the Provincial army, and was a great favorite of the American troops, especially as it was played by them at the Battle of Yorktown. As the publisher is desirous of rescuing from oblivion a spirit-stirring melody, once so familiar in the American camp, it is here given anew."

Words by GEO. P. MORRIS.

Music adapted by F. H. BROWN.

1. I love the pa-triot sa - ges, Who in the days of yore, In combat met the foe - men, And
2. I love the loft-y spir - it That impell'd our sires to rise And found a mighty na - tion Be-

drove them from our shore; Who in the days of yore, .. In combat met the
neath the western skies; Impell'd our sires to rise .. And found a mighty

foe - men, And drove them from our shore. Who flung our banner's starry field, In triumph to the breeze,
na - tion Beneath the west-ern skies. No clime so bright and beautiful As that where sets the sun;

THE LAND OF WASHINGTON.

SELECTIONS.

The Marquis de Rochambeau, at the Centennial Anniversary of Yorktown, said:

" Citizens of the United States: You have invited us to celebrate with you a great achievement of arms, and we did not hesitate to brave the terrors of the ocean to say to you that what our fathers did in 1781 we, their sons, would be willing to do to-day, and attest our constant friendship, and further show that we cherish the same sentiments as our fathers in those glorious days we now celebrate. In the name of my companions, who represent here the men who fought, permit me to hope that the attachment formed in these days around this monument which is about to be erected will be renewed in one hundred years, and will again celebrate the victory which joined our fathers in comradeship and alliance."

President Arthur's address, at the Centennial Anniversary of Yorktown:

" Upon this soil one hundred years ago our forefathers brought to a successful issue their heroic struggle for independence. Here and then was established, and, as we trust, made secure upon this continent for ages yet to come, that principle of government which is the very fibre of our political system — the sovereignty of the people. The resentments which attended and for a time survived the clash of arms have long since ceased to animate our hearts. It is with no feeling of exultation over a defeated foe that to-day we summon up a remembrance of those events which have made holy ground where we tread. Surely no such unworthy sentiment could find harbor in our hearts, so profoundly thrilled with that expression of sorrow and sympathy which our national bereavement has evolved from the people of England and their august sovereign; but it is altogether fitting that we should gather here to refresh our souls with the contemplation of the unfaltering patriotism, the sturdy zeal and the sublime faith with which were achieved the results we now commemorate. For so, if we learn aright the lesson of the hour, shall we be incited to transmit to the generation

which shall follow the precious legacy which our fathers left to us —
the love of liberty protected by law.

" Of that historic scene which we here celebrate, no feature is more
prominent and none more touching than the participation of our gallant allies from across the sea.   It was their presence which gave fresh
and vigorous impulse to the hopes of our countrymen when well-nigh
disheartened by a long series of disasters.   It was their noble and
generous aid, extended in the darkest period of that struggle, which
sped the coming of our triumph and made capitulation at Yorktown
possible, a century ago.   To their descendants and representatives who
are here present as honored guests of the nation, it is my glad duty
to offer a cordial welcome.   You have a right to share with us the
associations which cluster about the day when your fathers fought
side by side with our fathers in the cause which was here crowned
with success, and none of the memories awakened by this anniversary
are more grateful to us all than the reflection that the national friend-
ships here so closely cemented have outlasted the mutations of a
changeful century.   God grant, my countrymen, that they may ever
remain unshaken, and that henceforth, with ourselves and with all
nations of the earth, we may be at peace."

MANUAL OF PATRIOTISM.

THE FLAG HALLOWS
MEMORIAL DAY.

PROLOGUE.

GENERAL GRANT AND THE CIVIL WAR.
Song, *See, the Conqu'ring Hero Comes.*
ADMIRAL DEWEY AND THE SPANISH WAR.
Song, *Dewey at Manila Bay.*

IN MEMORIAM — MAY 30TH.

SELECTIONS . Song, *Song for Memorial Day.*
SELECTIONS . . . Song, *The Heroes' Greeting.*
SELECTIONS . . . . . . Song. *In Memoriam.*
SELECTIONS . . . . Song, *Remembered.*

MANUAL OF PATRIOTISM.

THE FLAG HALLOWS MEMORIAL DAY.

Prologue.

GENERAL GRANT AND THE CIVIL WAR,
> Song, *See, the Conqu'ring Hero Comes.*

ADMIRAL DEWEY AND THE SPANISH WAR,
> Song, *Dewey at Manila Bay.*

In Memoriam — May 30th.

SELECTIONS.......................Song, *Song for Memorial Day.*
SELECTIONS.........................Song, *The Heroes' Greeting.*
SELECTIONS..............................Song, *In Memoriam.*
SELECTIONS................................Song, *Remembered.*

(185)

GENERAL GRANT AND THE CIVIL WAR.

THE name of Ulysses S. Grant is forever linked in history with the Civil War, waged between the North and the South from 1861 to 1865. Many a general and officer and thousands upon thousands of private soldiers, on both sides, fought with indescribable bravery. But it remained for General Grant to bring the war to an end by the surrender of Robert E. Lee, commander-in-chief of the Southern army, at Appomattox Courthouse, April 9, 1865. Grant was often charged with cruelty and even with indifference as to the number of his soldiers killed in battle. But this is not true. The sacrifice of human life in the fierce battles that he fought was great, but it was necessary. And when the "cruel war" was over and peace really came to a sorrowing land, sore-stricken in every part, no man in all the nation was kinder than he to the conquered foe, as they surrendered on the last battlefield of the war, nor more compassionate afterwards to the whole people of the desolated and impoverished South. To show such kindness and compassion he had indeed a rare opportunity, as President of the United States for two terms. In this great office he was vexed, perplexed and troubled by many problems of Reconstruction such as no other President had ever known; but throughout all he was patient, though firm, and loyal to the last degree to what he believed to be the good of the whole people. No wonder that New York, the greatest city of the Empire State, and the metropolis of the land, asked that the hero and statesman might repose within its borders. And so was built the "Tomb of General Grant" at Riverside, in Greater New York. (If time permits, a sketch of Grant's boyhood and youth, stories from his Autobiography, and a description of the famous "Tomb" would prove of very great interest, conveying much information on heroic patriotism.)

SELECTIONS.

"HIS FIRST AND LAST SURRENDER."

Toll! bells of the nation, toll!
　For Grant, our brave defender,
The hero true, who made to Death
　"His first and last surrender;"
　　Toll! O bells, to-day,
　　And let your echoes roll
　　Solemnly, mournfully
　　O'er all the land
　　From strand to strand;
Toll! bells of the nation, toll!
　For Liberty's defender.

Rise! sons of the nation, rise!
　And love's true homage render
To him who grandly made to Death
　"His first and last surrender;"
　　Lament, O world, to-day,
　　And let the earth and skies
　　Silently, mournfully
　　Be witness to their grief
　　Who mourn an honored chief;
Mourn, sons of the nation, mourn,
　For Grant, our brave defender.

It was on Decoration Day, in the city of New York, the last one he ever saw on earth. That morning, the members of the Grand Army of the Republic, the veterans in that vicinity, rose earlier than was their wont. They seemed to spend more time that morning in unfurling the old battle-flags, in burnishing the medals of honor which decorated their breasts, for on that day they had determined to march by the house of their dying commander, to give him a last marching salute. In the streets, the columns were formed; inside the house, on that bed from which he never was to rise again, lay the stricken chief. The hand which had seized the surrendered sword of countless thousands could scarcely return the pressure of the friendly grasp.

That voice that had cheered on to triumphant victory the allegiance of America's manhood, could no longer call for the cooling draught which slaked the thirst of a fevered tongue, and prostrate on that bed of anguish lay the form which, in the New World, had ridden at the head of the conquering column — which, in the Old World, had been deemed worthy to stand with head covered and with feet sandaled in the presence of princes, kings and emperors. In the street his ear caught the sound of martial music. Bands were playing the same strains which had echoed his guns at Vicksburg, the same quick-steps to which his men sped in hot haste when pursuing Lee through Virginia. And then came the heavy, measured step of moving columns, a step which can be acquired only by years of service in the field. He recognized it all now. It was the tread of his old veterans. With his little remaining strength, he arose, and dragged himself to the window. He gazed upon those battle-flags dipped to him in salute, those precious standards, bullet-riddled, battle-stained, but remnants of their former service, with scarcely enough left of them on which to print the names of the battles. They had seen his eyes once more light with the flames that had enkindled them at Shiloh, at the heights of Chattanooga, amid the glories of Appomattox, and as those war-scarred veterans looked, with uncovered heads and upturned faces, for the last time upon the pallid features of their old chief, the cheeks which had been bronzed with Southern suns, and begrimed with powder, were bathed in the tears of manly grief. Soon they saw rising the hand which had so often pointed out to them the path of victory. He raised it slowly and painfully to his head in recognition of their salutation. When the column had passed, the hand fell heavily by his side. It was his last military salute.— *Horace Porter.*

ULYSSES SIMPSON GRANT.

When his work was done, this man of blood was as tender toward his late adversaries as a woman towards a son! He imposed no humiliating conditions, spared the feelings of his antagonists, sent home the disbanded Southern men with food and horses for working their crops, and when a revengeful spirit in the executive chair showed itself and threatened the chief Southern generals, Grant, with a holy indignation, interposed himself, and compelled his superior to relinquish his rash purpose.

A man he was, without vices, with an absolute hatred of lies, and an eradicable love of truth, of a perfect loyalty to friendship, neither envious of others nor selfish of himself. With a zeal for the public good unfeigned, he has left to memory only such weaknesses as connect him with humanity, and such virtues as will rank him among heroes.

The tidings of his death, long expected, gave a shock to the whole world. Governments, rulers, eminent statesmen, and scholars from all civilized nations, gave sincere tokens of sympathy. For the hour, sympathy rolled as a wave over the whole land. It closed the last furrow of war; it extinguished the last prejudice; it effaced the last vestige of hatred; and cursed be the hand that shall bring them back!

Johnston and Buckner on one side of his bier, and Sherman and Sheridan upon the other, he has come to his tomb,— a silent symbol that liberty had conqured slavery, and peace war.

He rests in peace! No drum nor cannon shall disturb his slumber!

Sleep, hero, sleep, until another trumpet shall shake the heavens and the earth! Then come forth to glory and immortality.— *Henry Ward Beecher.*

SEE! THE CONQUERING HERO COMES.

W. K. W.

G. F. HANDEL.

1. "See! the con-qu'ring he - - - ro comes, Sound .... the
2. Great our he - ro, fierce ..... in fight, Clear .... in
3. Grand our he - ro, mild ..... in peace, Bid - - ding

trum - pets, beat ... the drums; Hearts .... pre - pare, the
coun - cil, full ... of might; Greet .... the sol - dier,
pas - sion, dis - - cord cease; Greet ..... the states - man

lau - - rel bring; Songs ..... of tri - umph
prais - - es bring; Songs ..... of tri - umph
prais - - es bring; Songs ..... of tri - umph

to .... him sing. Hearts pre - pare, the

lau - - rel bring; Songs ... of tri - umph to .... him sing."

SELECTIONS.

GRANT.

When the shuddering earth foretold
Ruin, and war's thunder rolled,
  Who was honest as the soil,
Natural, simple, free of cant,
  Patient as the oxen toil?
    Grant.

While the earthquake rent the land,
Brothers battling hand to hand,
  Who looked never toward the rear,
Let the politicians rant,
  Void of selfishness and fear?
    Grant.

Oh, the need of one, could do
Work for twenty! stanch and true,
  Taciturn through praise and blame —
One, disaster could not daunt,
  Firm, decided as the name,
    Grant!

When our leaders weakened, then
Who was master over men?
  While dismay the Nation smote,
Thoughtful, wise, of anger scant,
  Greatest who, in plainest coat?
    Grant.

Silent battler, manly judge,
Weighing chiefs without a grudge,
  When the gun-smoke parted, foes
Shielded from revenge and taunt,
  Shared your heart who bore your blows,
    Grant.

Faithful to the falsest friends,
Duped by rogues for paltry ends,
  You were like the wholesome earth,
Home for oak and poison-plant!
  Fair and foul but raised your worth,
    Grant!

13

Red and black usurp the white;
Fear of death is fear of night:
   Redder, blacker moments far,
Fenced about with spectres gaunt,
   You have passed in hateful war,
       Grant.

Though the last dark field you plow,
Fearless then, no fear is now,
   Great our General! What is night?
Shades that o'er the landscape slant —
   All beyond them, glorious Light,
      Grant!

Fame for you for aye shall run
Even as all-victorious Sun,
   For like him you cannot die.
Dawns your lofty deeds will chant,
   Hark! the coming aeons cry —
      " Grant, Grant! "
               — C. De Kay.

(New York, March 30, 1885.)

VANQUISHED.

Not by the ball or brand
Sped by a mortal hand,
Not by the lightning stroke
When fiery tempests broke,—
Not 'mid the ranks of war
Fell the great Conqueror.

Unmoved, undismayed,
In the crash and carnage of the cannonade,—
Eye that dimmed not, hand that failed not,
Brain that swerved not, heart that quailed not,
Steel nerve, iron form,—
The dauntless spirit that o'erruled the storm.

While the Hero peaceful slept
A foeman to his chamber crept,
Lightly to the slumberer came,
Touched his brow and breathed his name;
O'er the stricken form there passed
Suddenly an icy blast.

The Hero woke; rose undismayed;
Saluted Death — and sheathed his blade.

The Conqueror of a hundred fields
To a mightier Conqueror yields;
No mortal foeman's blow
Laid the great Soldier low.
Victor in his latest breath —
Vanquished but by Death.

                    — *Francis F. Browne.*

General Sheridan, in reply to a request for his opinion of General Grant as a commander, recently said: " He was a far greater man than people thought him to be. He was able, no matter how situated, to do more than was expected of him. That has always been my opinion of General Grant. I have the greatest admiration for him, both as a man and as a commander."

WHY THEY CALLED HIM LEADER.

General Sherman, having been asked why he and Sheridan always acknowledged the leadership of Grant, replied: " Because, while I could map out a dozen plans for a campaign, every one of which Sheridan would declare he could fight out to victory, neither he nor I could tell which of the plans was the best one; but Grant, who simply sat and listened and smoked while we had been talking over the maps, would, at the end of our talking, tell us which was the best plan, and, in a dozen or two words, the reason of his decision, and then it would all be so clear to us that he was right that Sheridan and I would look at each other and wonder why we hadn't seen the advantage of it ourselves. I tell you, Grant is not appreciated yet. The military critics of Europe are too ignorant of American geography to appreciate the conditions of his campaigns. I have seen Grant plan campaigns for 500,000 troops along a front line 2,500 miles in length, and send them marching to their objective points, through sections where the surveyor's chain was never drawn, and where the commissariat necessities alone would have broken down any transportation system of Europe; and three months later I have seen those armies standing where he said they should be, and what he planned accomplished; and I give it as my military opinion that General Grant is the greatest commander of modern times, and with him only three others can stand — Napoleon, Wellington and Moltke."

ADMIRAL DEWEY AND THE SPANISH-AMERICAN WAR.

THE name of George Dewey, in every part of our country, is " a household word." He stands forth as the best-known American who fought in what is known as " The Spanish-American War." There may be a great many young pupils in our common schools who do not know just what that war was, or just why it was fought,— but it would be difficult to find one, beyond the primary grades, who has not heard of Admiral Dewey, the great sailor, and how he sailed with his ships over mines and torpedoes and sunken vessels, straight into the harbor of Manila, and on May 1, 1898, without the loss of a man or a gun or a ship, won the greatest naval victory, in many respects, ever achieved by man. And when, in the autumn of 1899, the famous sailor came to this country, he received no warmer welcome, no finer tribute to his glory, than that given him by the school children of Greater New York, a welcome that was renewed and prolonged by the boys and girls of Vermont when the Admiral returned, after many years of sea-life, to his birth-place and boyhood's home in the " Green Mountain State." Is it not right, then, for all the boys and girls of the Empire State to have a part in the celebration which their school-fellows in Greater New York began? Yes, surely. But the wise teacher will not fail to seize the opportunity to give to his school — to each and every pupil — the best idea possible of the cause of the brief war,— of the valor of our soldiers and sailors — of the fight at Santiago — the battle at San Juan and the bravery there displayed by regulars and volunteers, and by the " Rough Riders " under the leader-ship of the patriot and soldier who is now the Governor of New York, Theodore Roosevelt — the meaning of the " Dewey Arch " erected in Greater New York,— and, above all, to make clear and strong the les-son taught Spain by this country, that oppression and tyranny, as that of Cuba by Spain, must cease,— that Freedom is the privilege of all mankind.

SELECTIONS.

Sure of the right, keeping free from all offense ourselves, actuated only by upright and patriotic considerations, moved neither by passion nor selfishness, the Government will continue its watchful care over the rights and property of American citizens, and will abate none of its efforts to bring about by peaceful agencies a peace which shall be honorable and enduring. If it shall hereafter appear to be a duty imposed by our obligations to ourselves, to civilization and humanity, to intervene with force, it shall be without fault on our part, and only because the necessity for such action will be so clear as to command the support and approval of the civilized world.— *President McKinley,* from Message to Congress, December, 1897.

THE MAINE.

On the morning of February 16th came the news that on the previous evening the battle-ship Maine had been blown up and totally destroyed in the harbor of Havana. This gigantic murder of sleeping men, in the fancied security of a friendly harbor, was the direct outcome and the perfect expression of Spanish rule, and the appropriate action of a corrupt system struggling in its last agony. At last the unsettled question had come home to the United States, and it spoke in awful tones, which rang loud and could not be silenced. A wave of swift, fierce wrath swept over the American people. But a word was needed, and war would have come then in response to this foul and treacherous act of war, for such, in truth, it was. But the words of Captain Sigsbee, the commander of the Maine, whose coolness, self-restraint, and high courage were beyond praise, asking, even in the midst of the slaughter, that judgment should be suspended, were heeded alike by government and people.— *Henry Cabot Lodge.*

The long trial has proved that the object for which Spain has waged the war cannot be attained. The fire of insurrection may flame or may smoulder with varying seasons, but it has not been and it is plain that it cannot be extinguished by present methods. The only hope of relief and repose from a condition which can no longer be endured is the enforced pacification of Cuba. In the name of humanity, in the name of civilization, in behalf of endangered American interests, which give us the right and the duty to speak and to act, the war in Cuba must stop. The issue is now with the Congress. It is a solemn responsibility. I have exhausted every effort to relieve the intolerable condition of affairs which is at our doors. Prepared to execute every obligation imposed upon me by the constitution and the law, I await your action.— *President McKinley*, from Message to Congress, April 11, 1898.

On the 24th of April, I directed the Secretary of the Navy to telegraph orders to Commodore George Dewey, of the United States Navy, commanding the Asiatic Squadron, then lying in the port of Hong Kong, to proceed forthwith to the Philippine Islands, there to commence operations and engage the assembled Spanish fleet. Promptly obeying that order, the United States squadron entered the harbor of Manila at daybreak on the 1st of May and immediately engaged the entire Spanish fleet of eleven ships, which were under the protection of the fire of the land forts. After a stubborn fight, in which the enemy suffered great loss, their vessels were destroyed or completely disabled, and the water battery at Cavite silenced. Of our brave officers and men, not one was lost, and only eight injured, and those slightly. All of our ships escaped any serious damage. * * * The magnitude of this victory can hardly be measured by the ordinary standards of naval warfare. Outweighing any material advantage is the moral effect of this initial success. At this unsurpassed achievement, the great heart of our nation throbs, not with boasting or with greed of conquest, but with deep gratitude that this triumph has come in a just cause, and that by the grace of God an effective step has thus been taken toward the attainment of the wished-for peace. To those whose skill, courage, and devotion have won the fight, to the gallant commander, and the brave officers and men who aided him, our country owes an incalculable debt.— *President McKinley*, from Message to Congress, May 9, 1898.

THE SAILING OF THE FLEET.

Two fleets have sailed from Spain. The one would seek
  What lands uncharted ocean might conceal.
Despised, condemned, and pitifully weak,
  It found a world for Leon and Castile.

Another, mighty, arrogant, and vain,
  Sought to subdue a people who were free.
  Ask of the storm-gods where its galleons be,—
Whelmed 'neath the billows of the northern main!

A third is threatened. On the westward track,
  Once gloriously traced, its vessels speed,
With gold and crimson battle-flags unfurled.
On Colon's course, but to Sidonia's wrack,
  Sure fated, if so need shall come to need,
For sons of Drake are lords of Colon's world.

                    — The New York Tribune.

DEWEY'S VICTORY — May 1, 1898.

" Capture or destroy the Spanish fleet at Manila." Such was the
purport of President McKinley's order to Commodore George Dewey,
commanding the American squadron in Asiatic waters; and right nobly
did he carry out his instructions. Anchored in the harbor of a friendly
power, he was informed that by the laws of neutrality he must put
to sea. Six thousand miles from home, with no base of supplies, there
were but two things for the intrepid commander to do: He must seek
in flight the safety of our own shores, or he must fight against over-
whelming odds. He did not hesitate; but chose the latter alternative
as if there were no other.

How the haughty Spaniards sneered at his pretensions! Why
should they, with a fleet superior in numbers, protected by the great
guns of their forts, fear the " Yankee pigs "? — the commercials who
could not fight? They were soon to learn another lesson. On the
evening of April 30, the order to advance to action was given. And,
under cover of the darkness, our majestic ships, with lights extinguished, crept slowly, like tigers of the jungle, through the mine-pro-

tected channel, past the forts up to the very teeth of the Spaniards. When the morning of the first of May broke over the peaceful Oriental sea, it saw the despised American in the very fangs of her proud enemy.

What a charming scene! The great ships heaving on the bosom of the placid bay, like graceful swans. The sleeping city, quiet in the distant haze. The gaily plumaged tropical bird calling to its mate in a neighboring palm. The pennants of the forts lazily flapping on their supporting poles.

The scene changes, and the heavenly peace of nature gives place to the hell of war! The great guns of our ships belch forth their wrath of fire and steel. The Spanish ships and forts reply. Soon, chaos and destruction reign. Shells shriek through the quivering air. The peaceful sea has become a volcano from seething shot and bursting shell! The startled Spaniards had not expected such an onslaught. Surely this foe can fight!

The Spanish flag-ship is on fire! The flag is bravely transferred to another; but that too is soon disabled. Frantically the iron hail is poured from fort and ship; but it glances from our steel sides or falls harmlessly into the sea. Slowly our great ships move on, firing with unerring aim as if at target practice. Three times they move around the deadly curve and the last Spanish ship is burned or sunk; the forts on shore are a mass of ruins. The victory is won, and not an American has been killed, not a ship seriously injured. Does our hero exult? Not he. He sends a message to the Spanish admiral commending his bravery and offering to care for his wounded sailors.

Days of suspense follow. There are rumors that Dewey has been victorious, followed by others of a less reassuring nature. Spanish dispatches claim a victory; but singularly omit to mention American losses. Then comes a report that Dewey has been trapped; and the whole nation is anxious; but not a word of censure is heard. Those who know Commander Dewey say, " Do not fear, he is a quiet man; but when he fights, he fights hard."

At last authentic news is received; and all the world wonders. Men recall to mind the achievements of Nelson, when he defeated the combined fleets of France and Spain ninety-three years ago.

The authorities at Washington promptly make him an admiral and vote him a sword.

A new star is added to the already brilliant galaxy of American naval heroes; and to the names of Paul Jones, Decatur, Hull, Lawrence, Perry, and Farragut, is added George Dewey. The civilized world is amazed. Men recall the great feats of the past; but history reveals nothing like this. A whole fleet, supported by shore batteries, destroyed without the loss of a single man on the victorious squadron.

The new warships have been tried, and the product of modern thought has triumphed.

The nations awake to the fact that a new power has risen with which they must reckon. This young giant has struck his first blow in the very cradle of the race, in the stronghold of despotism and tyranny; and that blow was struck in the name of liberty. Hope revives in the hearts of the down-trodden millions. Liberty is no longer a dream, a sentiment. It has a champion who makes it an assured fact.

And with the dawning of the new century come prophetic murmurings, never heard before, that the great race, speaking one tongue, that has carried light to the dark places of tne earth, shall be united, and carry law, and liberty, and justice to all the world.—*John D. Wilson.*

Youngest descendant of a glorious line,—
  Jones, Perry, Hull, Decatur, heroes bold,
    Who fought this nation's brave sea-fights of old,
And Farragut, whose great deeds on the brine
Through our wild civil strife with fierce glow shine,—
  Dewey, all hail! With theirs is now enrolled
    Thy name; with theirs thy story shall be told;
Thy country's praise and gratitude are thine;
Thy daring sally in Manila Bay
  Has stirred the whole world's pulse, and well begun
The war for human rights we wage to-day
  With consecrated sword. Hero, well done!
The fleet was heaven-directed in that fray —
  No grander battle e'er yet fought and won.

       — *Virginia Vaughan.*

DEWEY AT MANILA BAY.

Lilian Budington.

Martha Moses Peckham.

INTRODUCTION.

1. Night came down o'er Ma - ni - la's Bay, Where Span - ish ships at an - chor lay; And
2. Shot and shell on Ma - ni - la's Bay Wrought well God's work that first of May; And

Span - ish mines be - neath the wave To Span - ish hearts bold cour - age gave. A
Span - ish ty - rants on the wave Learn'd right is might with A - meri - ca's brave.

rit. a tempo.

mist roll'd in o'er Ma - ni - la's Bay, And A - meri - can ships sailed in to stay, Where
Night came down o'er Ma - ni - la's Bay, Where A - meri - can ships at an - chor lay; And A -

a tempo.

rit.

DEWEY AT MANILA BAY.

MEMORIAL DAY.

THIS national holiday was at first called "Decoration Day"—because of the custom of decorating the graves of Union soldiers on that day. But now it bears the sweeter and more sacred name of Memorial Day,—because of the calling to remembrance then, in a special and public way, the brave men and brave deeds of the terrible Civil War of 1861. We Americans ought to regard the thirtieth of May, each year, as an Holy Day, rather than a mere amusement holiday. Alas! it is fast becoming a day for sports and games and out-door spectacles. And yet, it can never become wholly that, as long as there remains on earth a single soldier of the Grand Army of the Republic. For to him will be present on each Sabbath Day of the Nation the thought of the mighty conflict, with its patriotic spirit, its heroic deeds, its loyal "Boys in Blue,"—all indeed that made that conflict so memorable; and his trembling hands will still seek to strew flowers of remembrance upon the graves of his former companions-in-arms. So, let a like spirit of loyalty and patriotism animate the soul of every one of the thousands of G. A. R. Veterans still living. Let every teacher, in his or her place, seek to instill into the mind of every pupil a knowledge of the great events and actors in the war-drama; better still, an idea of the meaning of the war, its triumphant issue in a restored Union and an emancipated race — and best of all, a sentiment in every youthful heart of ever-enkindling, ever-growing love for this dear "Country of Ours!"

Probably there is not a school district in the State in which there is not at least one veteran of the Civil War. And the one best way to keep Memorial Day in school will be to invite him, as the guest of honor, to tell his story of the war. If a G. A. R. "post" is in the neighborhood, summon its members to your memorial service and let some of them speak for all. If any soldier or sailor of the recent war with Spain is nigh at hand, ask him to be present and speak. He will be heard giving the meed of praise and honor to the men of '61 for their unparalleled devotion to the Union,— and they, The Fathers, will testify in turn to the patriotic spirit which led The Sons to beat down tyranny and lift the Cuban to the joys of Freedom. Do not fear that such a service will celebrate the glories of war, and so create a warlike spirit in youthful hearts; no, for it commemorates, rather, the sorrowful and heart-aching phases of strife. Nor fear that the keeping of such a day will stir up a spirit of bitterness against the conquered South; no, that has died away by the healing effects of time, by the thought of a common origin and common destiny of all the states in the Union. The South as well as the North keeps its Memorial Day — for sorrow for the dead, as Washington Irving has told us, is the only sorrow from which we refuse to be separated. But in recent years — on platforms, in burial-grounds, wherever and however Memorial Day has been kept,— the "Boys in Blue" and the "Boys in Gray" have met and each borne testimony to the valor and honor of the other. If the teacher of a school cannot arrange for an exercise in the school, at least see to it that the boys and girls have a part in any commemoration arranged by a G. A. R. post or committee. And whether in school, in public hall or assembly, at a cemetery — wherever Memorial Day is kept,— let it be understood and impressed that it is always the mission of Right and Duty to declare and carry on war, whenever the Union is in peril, or the cause of Freedom demands the sacrifice.

SONG FOR MEMORIAL DAY.

Slow March.

FRIEDRICH SILCHER.

1. We vis - it the graves of our sol - diers to - day, While
2. Though stran - gers with com - rades lie min - gled in sleep, The
3. Now an - thems of praise and thanks - giv - ing we sing, While

na - ture is robed with the beau - ty of May; We'll car - ry of flow - ers the
soil where they rest we will sa - cred - ly keep; For in the great con - flict they
gar - lands and wreaths in pro - fu - sion we bring; And thou - sands will bless, from each

bright - est with care, Of ten - der af - fec - tion the
stood side by side, To - geth - er they fought and to -
sta - tion in life, The gal - lant and no - ble who

em - blems so fair, Of ten - der af - fec - tion the em - blems so fair.
geth - er they died, To - geth - er they fought and to - geth - er they died.
fell in the strife, The gal - lant and no - ble who fell in the strife.

QUOTATIONS.

Mid the flower-wreathed tombs I stand
Bearing lilies in my hand.
　　　　　　— Thomas Wentworth Higginson.

The light that shines from a patriot's grave is a pure and holy light.*— Homer Everett.*

Proudly do I give
A song to you who kept the banner old,
The dearest flag o'er any country blowing.
　　　　　　— Maurice F. Thompson.

Let us scatter over their graves the brightest beauties of life — the glad tokens of a blessed immortality.*— George S. Mitchell.*

Wherever Honor's sword is drawn,
And Justice rears her head,
Where heroes fall and martyrs bleed,
There rest our Country's dead.
　　　　　　— Cornelia M. Jordan.

There is a shrine in the temple of ages where lies, forever embalmed, the memories of such as have deserved well of their country and their race.*— John Mason Brown.*

Foes we were in the years long past,
Now friends in Union true;
And the tie that binds our loyal love
Is the Red, the White and Blue.
　　　　　　— Anon.

So long as the glorious flag for which they died waves over our reunited country, will each recurring spring see fresh laurels on the graves of our country's dead.*— Anon.*

* * * fallen in manhood's fairest noon,—
We will remember, mid our sighs,
He never yields his life too soon,
For country and for right who dies.
　　　　　　— Atlantic Monthly.

Our Country's Gallant Dead— Our country's soil gives them all sepulture. They sleep beneath the Stripes and Stars.*— Joseph H. Twitchell.*

14

> The Northern Lights are blending
>   With the rays of the Southern Cross,
> And the gulf is bridged between them
>   By a common sense of loss.
>   — *Susan J. Adams.*

They have not died in vain. The great hope that inspired and armed them has been realized how gloriously! They saved their country — they and such as they.— *George Putnam* (adapted).

> They throng the silence of the heart,
>   We see them as of yore;
> The kind, the true, the brave, the sweet,
>   Who talk with us no more.
>   — *Anon.*

Invoke all to heed well the lesson of Decoration Day, to weave each year a fresh garland for the grave of some hero and to rebuke any and all who talk of civil war, save as the "last dread tribunal of kings and peoples."— *Gen. William T. Sherman* (adapted).

> Their names resplendent on the roll of fame,
>   Their monument each flag that floats on high:
> Why should we weep? No, no, they are not dead;
>   A grateful country will not let them die.
>   — *Thomas F. Power.*

In the field of Gettysburg, as we now behold it, the blue and the gray blending in happy harmony, like the mingling hues of the summer landscape, we may see the radiant symbol of the triumphant America of our pride, our hope and our joy.— *George William Curtis.*

> Sleep, comrades, sleep in calm repose,
>   Upon Columbia's breast;
> For thee with love her bosom glows
>   Rest ye, brave heroes, rest!
>   —*J. Henry Dwyer.*

Every act of noble sacrifice to the country, every instance of patriotic devotion to her cause has its beneficial influence. A nation's character is the sum of its splendid deeds; they constitute our common patrimony, the nation's inheritance.— *Henry Clay.*

```
*   *   *  in the great review
    When crowns and uniforms shall never fade,
Heroes, receive your honors due
                On grand parade.
```
> *— John A. Murphy.*

All the great and good shall live in the heart of ages, while marble and bronze shall endure, and when marble and bronze have perished, they shall "still live" in memory so long as men shall reverence law and honor patriotism and love liberty.— *Edward Everett.*

```
            Glorious and meet
        To honor thus the dead,
        Who chose the better part
        And for their country bled.
```
> *— Richard Watson Gilder.*

"Dead on the field of honor!" This is the record of thousands of unnamed men, whose influence upon other generations is associated with no personal distinction, but whose sacrifice will lend undying lustre to the nation's archives, and richer capacity to the national life.— *E. A. Chapin.*

```
        Soft stream the sunshine overhead,
            Green grow the grasses on your graves;
        Heaven will remember you, though dead,
            Ungarlanded, immortal braves.
```
> *— Harper's Magazine.*

Those who fought against us, are now of us and with us reverently acknowledge that above all the desires of men move the majestic laws of God, evolving alike from victory or defeat of nations, a substantial good for all His children.— *Gen. George A. Sheridan.*

```
        Sleep soldiers! still in honored rest
            Your truth and valor wearing;
        The bravest are the tenderest,—
            The loving are the daring.
```
> *— Bayard Taylor.*

We join you in setting apart this land as an undying monument of peace, brotherhood, and perpetual Union. We unite in the solemn consecration of these hallowed hills as a holy, eternal pledge of fidelity to the life, freedom and unity of this cherished Republic.— *Gen. John B. Gordon*, Address on behalf of Confederate veterans, Gettysburg, Pa., July 3, 1888.

A debt we ne'er can pay
  To them is justly due,
And, to the Nation's latest day,
Our children's children still shall say,
  " They died for me and you."
                              — Anon.

By the homely traditions of the fireside, by the headstones in the churchyard consecrated to those whose forms repose far off in rude graves, or sleep beneath the sea, embalmed in the memory of succeeding generations of parents and children, the heroic dead will live on in immortal youth.— *Governor Andrew,* of Massachusetts.

So close the Blue and Gray have fought,
  So near they lowly lie,
God grant, that now their life-work wrought,
  Their arms be linked on high

        *   *   *   *   *   *   *

Peace blesses all our happy land,
  One flag from lake to sea.
Great God! each loyal heart and hand,
  And voice is praising Thee.
                              —D. H. Kent.

To-day it is the highest duty of all, no matter on what side they were, but above all of those who have struggled for the preservation of the Union, to strive that it become one of generous confidence in which all the States shall, as of old, stand shoulder to shoulder, if need be, against the world in arms.— *Ex-Attorney-General Charles Devens.*

SELECTIONS.

Your marches, sieges, and battles, in distance, duration, resolution, and brilliancy of results, dim the luster of the world's past military achievements, and will be the patriot's precedent in defense of liberty and right in all time to come. In obedience to your country's call, you left your homes and families, and volunteered in her defense. Victory has crowned your valor, and secured the purpose of your patriotic hearts; and with the gratitude of your countrymen, and the highest honors a great and free nation can accord, you will soon be permitted to return to your homes and families, conscious of having discharged the highest duties of American citizens.— *Ulysses S. Grant* (from his farewell to the Union Army).

The soldiers of the Republic were not seekers after vulgar glory. They were not animated by the hope of plunder or the love of conquest. They fought to preserve the blessings of liberty and that their children might have peace. They were the defenders of humanity, the destroyers of prejudice, the breakers of chains, and in the name of the future they slew the monster of their time. All honor to the Brave! They kept our country on the map of the world, and our flag in heaven. The soldiers of the Republic finished what the soldiers of the Revolution commenced. They relighted the torch that fell from their august hands and filled the world again with light.— *Robert G. Ingersoll.*

Grander than the Greek, nobler than the Roman, the soldiers of the Republic, with patriotism as taintless as the air, battled for the rights of others; for the nobility of labor; fought that mothers might own their babes; that arrogant idleness should not scar the back of patient toil; and that our country should not be a many-headed monster made of warring states, but a nation, sovereign, grand, and free. Blood was water, money, leaves, and life was common air until one flag floated over a Republic, without a master and without a slave. The soldiers of the Union saved the South as well as the North. They made us a nation. Their victory made us free and rendered tyranny in every other land as insecure as snow upon volcano lips. They rolled the stone from the sepulchre of progress, and found therein two angels clad in shining garments — Nationality and Liberty.— *Robert G. Ingersoll.*

I share with you all the pleasure and gratitude which Americans should feel on this anniversary (July 4). But I must dissent from one remark to the effect that I saved the country during the war. If our country could be saved or ruined by the efforts of one man, we should not have a country. If I had never held command, if I had fallen, if all our generals had fallen, there were ten thousand behind who would have done our work just as well, and who would have followed the contest to the end and never surrendered the Union. We should have been unworthy of our country and of the American name if we had not made every sacrifice to save the Union.— *Ulysses S. Grant.*

Sometimes in passing along the street, I meet a man who, in the left lapel of his coat, wears a little, plain, modest, unassuming bronze button. The coat is often old and rusty; the face above, seamed and furrowed by the toil and suffering of adverse years; perhaps beside it hangs an empty sleeve, and below it stumps a wooden peg. But when I meet the man who wears that button, I doff my hat and stand uncovered in his presence — yea! to me the very dust his weary feet has pressed is holy ground; for I know that man, in the dark hour of the nation's peril, bared his breast to the hell of battle to keep the flag of our country in the Union sky.

May be at Donelson, he reached the inner trench; at Shiloh, held the broken line; at Chattanooga, climbed the flame-swept hill; or stormed the clouds on Lookout Heights. He was not born or bred to soldier life. His country's summons called him from the plow, the bench, the forge, the loom, the mine, the store, the office, the college, the sanctuary. He did not fight for greed of gold, to find adventure, or to win renown. He loved the peace of quiet ways; and yet he broke the clasp of clinging arms, turned from the witching glance of tender eyes, left good-bye kisses on tiny lips, to look death in the face on desperate fields. And when the war was over, he quietly took up the broken threads of love and life as best he could, a better citizen for having been so good a soldier.— *John H. Thurston.*

The Minute Man of the Revolution! And who was he? He was the husband and father, who left the plough in the furrow, the hammer on the bench, and kissing his wife and children, marched to die or to be free. The Minute Man of the Revolution! He was the old, the middle-aged, the young. He was Captain Miles of Acton, who reproved his men for jesting on the march! He was Deacon Josiah Haines, of Sudbury, eighty years old, who marched with his company to South Bridge, at Concord, then joined in that hot pursuit to Lexington, and fell as gloriously as Warren at Bunker Hill. This was the Minute Man of the Revolution! The rural citizen, trained in the common school, the town-meeting, who carried a bayonet that thought, and whose gun, loaded with a principle, brought down, not a man, but a system. Intrenched in his own honesty, the king's gold could not buy him; enthroned in the love of his fellow-citizens, the king's writ could not take him; and when, on the morning at Lexington, the king's troops marched to seize him, his sublime faith saw, beyond the clouds of the moment, the rising sun of the America we behold, and careless of himself, mindful only of his country, he exultingly exclaimed: " Oh! What a glorious morning! " — *George William Curtis.*

All honor to the Army of the United States. Truly is its muster roll shorter than the list of its achievements. Yet amid all strictures, cavil, and carping it has a place well earned and warm in the heart of this people, for its generals have never sought to be dictators, nor its regiments pretorian guards, and with them the safety of the country and the liberties of the people are secure. And long, long may it be so! — *William E. Furness.*

Every mountain and hill shall have its treasured name, every river shall keep some solemn title, every valley and every lake shall cherish its honored register; and till the mountains are worn out and the rivers forget to flow, till the clouds are weary of replenishing springs, and the springs forget to gush, and the rills to sing, shall their names be kept fresh with reverent honors which are inscribed upon the book of National Remembrance.— *H. W. Beecher.*

> Thank God for deeds of valor done!
> Thank God for victories hardly won!
> That such as you need never know
> The anguish of those days of woe;
> For time and peace old wounds have healed,
> And flowers now strew the battle-field.
>   But ah! the graves that no man names or knows,
> Uncounted graves, which never can be found;
> Graves of the precious " missing " where no sound
>   Of tender weeping will be heard, where goes
> No loving step of kindred.
> But nature knows her wilderness,

There are no "missing" in her numbered ways,
In her great heart is no forgetfulness,
Each grave she keeps, she will adorn, caress;
We cannot lay such wreaths as Summer lays,
And all her days are Decoration Days.

        — Helen Hunt.

  The muffled drum's sad roll has beat
   The soldier's last tattoo;
  No more on Life's parade shall meet
   That brave and fallen few.
  On Fame's eternal camping ground
   Their silent tents are spread,
  And Glory guards, with solemn round,
   The bivouac of the dead.

  * * * * * * *

  Rest on, embalmed and sainted dead!
   Dear as the blood ye gave,
  No impious footsteps here shall tread
   The herbage of your grave.
  Nor shall your story be forgot
   While Fame her record keeps,
  Or Honor points the hallowed spot .
   Where Valor proudly sleeps.

  * * * * * * *

        — Theodore O'Hara.

THE HEROES' GREETING.

CHARLES E. BOYD.

Allegro moderato.

1. In tri - umph ad - vanc - ing, our he - roes ap - pear,
2. Let flow'rs strew their path - way, let pæ - ans break forth;
3. Where can - non were thun - d'ring, and sa - bres drank blood,

Who left us in hope, now in glo - ry are here.
We greet them re - joic - ing, with mu - sic and mirth;
With death all a - round them, un - daunt - ed they stood,

We hail them re - joic - ing, o - va - tions pre - pare,
Brave sol - diers of free - dom, de - fend - ers of right;
Or rushed on the foe - men, re - sist - less in might,

From " Cecilian Series," published by SILVER, BURDETT & Co.

THE HEROES' GREETING.

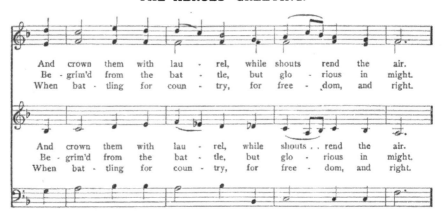

And crown them with lau - rel, while shouts rend the air.
Be - grim'd from the bat - tle, but glo - rious in might.
When bat - tling for coun - try, for free - dom, and right.

And crown them with lau - rel, while shouts . . rend the air.
Be - grim'd from the bat - tle, but glo - rious in might.
When bat - tling for coun - try, for free - dom, and right.

CHORUS, 1, 2, 3.

In tri - umph ad - vanc - ing, our he - roes ap - pear, Then

our he - roes ap - pear, Then

greet them tri - um - phant with cheer . . . up - on cheer.

greet them tri - um - phant with cheer . . . up - on cheer.

SELECTIONS.

BUGLES OF GETTYSBURG.

Sound, bugles! sound again!
Rouse them to life again,
   Awake them all!
Here, where the Blue and Gray
Struggled in fierce array,
Wake them in peace to-day;
   God bless them all!

Sound bugles! sound again!
Sound o'er these hills again,
   Where gather all;
Those who are left to-day,
Left of the battle's fray,
Left of the Blue and Gray;
   God bless them all!

Sound bugles! sound again!
Bid all unite again,
   Like brothers all;
Here, clasping hands, to-day,
With love for Blue and Gray,
Dead is all hate to-day;
   God bless them all!
              — Wellesley Bradshaw.

No nobler emotion can fill the breast of any man than that which prompts him to utter honest praise of an adversary whose convictions and opinions are at war with his own; and where is there a Confederate soldier in our land who has not felt a thrill of generous admiration and applause for the pre-eminent heroism of the gallant Federal admiral who lashed himself to the mainmast, while the tattered sails and frayed cordage of his vessel were being shot away by piecemeal above his head, and slowly but surely picked his way through sunken reefs of torpedoes, whose destructive powers consigned many of his luckless comrades to watery graves? The fame of such men as Farragut, Stanley, Hood, and Lee, and the hundreds of private soldiers, who were the true heroes of the war, belongs to no clime or section, but is the common property of mankind. They were all cast in the same grand mould of self-sacrificing patriotism, and I intend to teach my children to revere their names as long as the love of country is respected as a noble sentiment in the human breast.— *Lawrence Sullivan Ross.*

THE BLUE AND THE GRAY.

By the flow of the inland river,
　Whence the fleets of iron have fled,
Where the blades of the grave-grass quiver,
　Asleep are the ranks of the dead;
Under the sod and the dew,
　Waiting the judgment-day;
Under the one, the Blue;
　Under the other, the Gray.

These in the robings of glory,
　Those in the gloom of defeat;
All with the battle-blood gory,
　In the dusk of eternity meet;
Under the sod and the dew,
　Waiting the judgment day;
Under the laurel, the Blue;
　Under the willow, the Gray.

From the silence of sorrowful hours,
　The desolate mourners go,
Lovingly laden with flowers,
　Alike for the friends and the foe.
Under the sod and the dew,
　Waiting the judgment day;
Under the roses, the Blue;
　Under the lilies, the Gray.

So, with an equal splendor,
　The morning sun-rays fall,
With a touch impartially tender,
　On the blossoms blooming for all.
Under the sod and the dew,
　Waiting the judgment day;
Broidered with gold, the Blue;
　Mellowed with gold, the Gray.

So, when the summer calleth,
  On forest and field of grain,
With an equal murmur falleth
  The cooling drip of the rain;
Under the sod and the dew,
  Waiting the judgment day;
Wet with the rain, the Blue;
  Wet with the rain, the Gray.

Sadly, but not with upbraiding,
  The generous deed was done;
In the storm of the years that are fading
  No braver battle was won.
Under the sod and the dew,
  Waiting the judgment day;
Under the blossoms, the Blue;
  Under the garlands, the Gray.

No more shall the war-cry sever,
  Or the winding rivers be red;
They banish our anger forever
  When they laurel the graves of our dead.
Under the sod and the dew,
  Waiting the judgment day;
Love and tears for the Blue;
  Tears and love for the Gray.
                              —*Francis M. Finch.*

As to the kind of preparation which sound policy dictates, the navy, most certainly, in any point of view, occupies the first place. It is the safest, most effectual, and cheapest mode of defense. If the force be the safest and most efficient, which is at the same time the cheapest, on that should be our principal reliance. We have heard much of the danger of standing armies to our liberties. The objection cannot be made to the navy. Generals, it must be acknowledged, have often advanced at the head of armies to imperial rank; but in what instance has an admiral usurped the liberties of his country? Put our strength in the navy for foreign defense and we shall certainly escape the whole catalogue of possible evils painted by gentlemen on the other side.

*　　*　　*　　*　　*　　*

If anything can preserve the country in its most imminent dangers from abroad, it is this species of armament. If we desire to be free from future wars (as I hope we may be), this is the only way to effect it. We shall have peace then, and, what is of still higher moment, peace with perfect security.— *John C. Calhoun.*

CONCORD HYMN.

By the rude bridge that arched the flood,
　Their flag to April's breeze unfurled,
Here once the embattled farmers stood,
　And fired the shot heard round the world.

The foe long since in silence slept;
　Alike the conqueror silent sleeps;
And Time the ruined bridge has swept
　Down the dark stream which seaward creeps.

On this green bank, by this soft stream,
　We set to-day a votive stone;
That memory may their dead redeem,
　When, like our sires, our sons are gone.

Spirit, that made those heroes dare
　To die, and leave their children free,
Bid Time and Nature gently spare
　The shaft we raise to them and thee.
　　　　　　　　　　　— *Ralph Waldo Emerson.*

No praise can be too great for the American volunteers, who passed through days of battle, enduring fatigue without a murmur, always in the right place at the right time, and emerging from the fiery ordeal a compact body of veterans, equal to any task that brave and disciplined men can be called upon to undertake.— *Gen. George McClellan.*

General Grant said: " We did our work as well as we could, and so did thousands of others. What saved the Union was the coming forward of the young men of the nation. They came from their homes and fields, as they did in the time of the Revolution. The humblest soldier who carried a musket is entitled to as much credit as those who were in command. So long as our young men are animated by this spirit, there will be no fear for the Union."

THE SOLDIER BOY.

The man who wears the shoulder straps
  And has his sword in hand,
Who proudly strides along in front,
  Looks good, and brave, and grand;
But, back there in the ranks somewhere,—
  Just which I cannot see,—
With his gun upon his shoulder, is
  The soldier boy for me!

The man who wears the shoulder straps
  Is handsome, brave, and true,
But there are other handsome boys,
  And other brave ones, too!
When there are heights that must be won
  While bullets fill the air,
'Tis not the officer alone
  Who braves the dangers there.

The man who wears the shoulder straps
  Is cheered along the way,
And public honor dulls his dread
  Of falling in the fray;
But there behind him in the ranks,
  And moving like a part
Of some machine, is many a man
  With just as brave a heart.

The man who wears the shoulder straps
  Deserves the people's praise;
I honor and applaud him for
  The noble part he plays;
But, back there in the ranks somewhere,
  Stout-hearted, is he,—
Prepared to do, and nerved to dare,—
  The soldier boy for me!

                — S. E. Kiser.

THE MEN BEHIND THE GUNS.

A cheer and salute for the admiral, and here's to the captain bold,
And never forget the commodore's debt when the deeds of might are told!
They stand to the deck thro' the battle's wreck, when the great shells roar and
 screech,—
And never they fear when the foe is near to practise what they preach;
But off with your hat, and three times three for Columbia's true-blue sons,—
The men below, who batter the foe,— the men behind the guns!

The steel decks rock with the lightning shock, and shake with the great recoil,
And the sea grows red with the blood of the dead and reaches for its spoil,—
But not till the foe has gone below, or turns his prow and runs,
Shall the voice of peace bring sweet release to the men behind the guns!

—*John James Rooney.*

At Grant's tomb, when speaking of the perils, the services, and
the heroism of the men who made up the Union armies, President Mc-
Kinley put the matter none too strongly when he said: "What is
true patriotism? It is an absolute consecration to country. It is an
abandonment of business; it is turning away from cherished plans,
which have been fondly formed for a life's career; it is the surrendering
of bright prospects and the giving up of ambition in a chosen work;
it is the sundering of ties of blood and family and almost snapping of
the heartstrings which bind us to those we love; it is the surrendering
of ourselves absolutely to the demands of country; it may mean disease; it may mean imprisonment, insanity or death; it may mean hunger,
thirst, and starvation. In our Civil War it meant all these."

The captains and the armies who brought to a close the Civil War
have left us more than a reunited realm. The material effect of what
they did is shown in the fact that the same flag flies from the Great
Lakes to the Rio Grande, and all the people of the United States are
richer because they are one people and not many, because they belong
to one great nation, and not to a contemptible knot of struggling
nationalities. But beside this, beside the material results of the Civil
War, we are all, North and South, incalculably richer for its memories.

We are the richer for each grim campaign, for each hard-fought battle. We are the richer for valor displayed by those who fought so valiantly for the right, and by those who, no less valiantly, fought for what they deemed the right. We have in us nobler capacities for what is great and good, because of the infinite woe and suffering, and because of the splendid ultimate triumph.— *Theodore Roosevelt*, in " American Ideals."

THE NEW MEMORIAL DAY.

Oh, the roses we plucked for the blue
 And the lilies we twined for the gray,
We have bound in a wreath,
And in silence beneath
 Slumber our heroes to-day.

- Over the new-turned sod
 The sons of our fathers stand,
And the fierce old fight
Slips out of sight
 In the clasp of a brother's hand.

For the old blood left a stain
 That the new has washed away,
And the sons of those
That have faced as foes
 Are marching together to-day.

Oh, the blood that our fathers gave!
 Oh, the tide of our mothers' tears!
And the flow of red,
And the tears they shed,
 Embittered a sea of years.

But the roses we plucked for the blue,
 And the lilies we twined for the gray,
We have bound in a wreath,
And in glory beneath
 Slumber our heroes to-day.

           — *Albert Bigelow Paine.*

15

OUR STANDING ARMY.

We have no standing army?
  Nay, look around, and see!
The man who ploughs the furrow
  The man who fells the tree,
The statesman and the scholar,
  At the first word of fear
Turn to their country, breathing,
  " My mother, I am here!"

Not of a dumb, blind people
  Is this, our army, made;
Where schoolhouse and where steeple
  Have cast their friendly shade
Our army grows in knowledge,
  As it to manhood grows,
And, trained in school and college,
  Stands ready for its foes.

The brawny arms of gunners
  Serve minds alert and keen;
The sailor's thought has travelled
  To lands he has not seen.
Not for the joy of killing,
  Not for the lust of strife,
Have these come forth with gladness
  To offer up their life.

Behold our standing army —
  Not, as in other lands,
An army standing idle,
  With empty minds and hands.
But each one in his station;
  And peaceful victory
Is training for the nation
  Heroes of land and sea.

                          —*Margaret Vandegrift.*

IN MEMORIAM.

By special permission SILVER, BURDETT & Co.

If those who win battles and save civilization are dear to the hearts of men, how cherished will be the memory of the tenacious soldier whom nothing could shake off from success.

Breaking up on the Rapidan in early May, Grant forced his fiery way through the Wilderness and was called a butcher. By one of the most masterly and daring of military movements, he forced the enemy within their capital and was called incapable. " He'll do no more," shouted the exultant friends of the rebellion. They did not know the man. Undismayed by delay, holding Richmond in both hands, he ordered Thomas to annihilate Hood, and he did it; he ordered Terry to take Fort Fisher, and he took it; he ordered Sheridan to sweep the Shenandoah, and he swept it clean. The terror of Sherman's presence, one hundred miles away, emptied Charleston of troops. Across Georgia, across South Carolina into North Carolina, he moved, scourging the land with fire. Then the genius of the great commander, by the tireless valor of his soldiers, lighted all along the line, burst over the enemy's works, crushed his ranks, forced his retreat, and overwhelmed Lee and his army.— *George William Curtis.*

By the sacrifice of the Union soldiers, some questions were settled, never to be reopened, over which politicians, and statesmen, and philosophers had wrangled a hundred years. No man will ever after this claim that in politics a part is greater than the whole, or a state greater than a nation, nor will any have the rashness to maintain that " E Pluribus Unum " means many out of one.

The graves of 300,000 patriots are our witness to-day, that henceforth, from the pine forests of our cold northern border to the orange groves of the gulf, from the great Atlantic metropolis of the Empire State to the golden gates of the Pacific, the stars and stripes will brook no rival. On every headstone of the graves decorated to-day may be read, albeit in invisible characters, yet unfading as though written by the hand of fate, " Liberty, Union, Equality;" " One Flag and One Country." Such was their contribution to their country, to humanity, to posterity. Do we not justly enroll their names among earth's benefactors, and garland their graves as those of heroes and martyrs? — *Oscar D. Robinson.*

At the battle of Mission Ridge, General Thomas was watching a body of troops painfully pushing their way up a steep hill against a withering fire. Victory seemed impossible, and the General, even he, that rock of valor and patriotism, exclaimed, " They can't do it! They will never reach the top." His chief of staff, watching the struggle with equal earnestness, said softly, " Time, time, General; give them time;" and presently the moist eyes of the brave leader saw his soldiers victorious upon the summit. They were American soldiers — so are we. They were fighting an American battle — so are we. They were climbing a height — so are we. Give us time, and we, too, shall triumph.— *George William Curtis.*

" Did you hear that fearful scream? " asked a Union soldier of his comrade in the early days of the Civil War, as they pressed on in the deadly assault up the bloody slope. " Yes; what is it? " " It is the Rebel yell. Does it frighten you? " " Frighten me! " said the young soldier, as he pressed more eagerly forward, " Frighten me! " it is the music to which I march! " And they planted the starry flag of victory upon the enemy's rampart.

When the enemy's yell is the music to which the soldier marches, he marches to victory. Patience then, and forward.— *George William Curtis.*

IN THE TIME OF STRIFE.

We may not know
How red the lilies of the spring shall grow;
What silver flood,
Sea streaming, take the crimson tints of blood.

We may not know
If victory shall make the bugles blow;
If still shall wave
The flag above our freedom or our grave.
We only know
One heart, one hand, one country, meet the foe;
On land and sea
Her liegemen in the battle of the free.

— *Frank L. Stanton.*

The shot which the embattled farmers fired at Lexington echoed "round the world," and produced most of those revolutions in all lands by which power has fallen from the throne and been gained by the people. It was the echo of that shot which in 1861 aroused the national spirit to the protection of the national life, and while Lexington founded the Republic, the memory of Lexington preserved it.— *Chauncey Mitchell Depew.*

HOW SLEEP THE BRAVE!

How sleep the brave, who sink to rest,
By all their country's wishes blest!
When Spring, with dewy fingers cold,
Returns to deck their hallowed mould,
She there shall dress a sweeter sod
Than Fancy's feet have ever trod.

By fairy hands their knell is rung;
By forms unseen their dirge is sung;
There Honor comes, a pilgrim gray,
To bless the turf that wraps their clay;
And Freedom shall awhile repair,
To dwell a weeping hermit there.
— *William Collins.*

The great Civil War was remarkable for the inventive mechanical genius and the resolute daring shown by the combatants. This was especially true of the navy. The torpedo boat managed by W. B. Cushing against the Confederate ram, Albemarle, was an open launch, with a spar rigged out in front, the torpedo being placed at the end. The crew consisted of fifteen men. Cushing not only guided his craft, but himself handled the torpedo by means of two small ropes, one of which put it in place, while the other exploded it. Cushing possessed reckless courage, presence of mind, and high ability. On the night of October 27, 1864, he left the Federal fleet, steamed a dozen miles up river, where the great ram lay under the guns of the fort, with a regiment of guns to defend her. He was almost upon her before he was discovered. The rifle balls were singing about him, and he heard the noise of the great guns as they got ready. Still erect in his little craft, he brought the torpedo full against the side of the huge ram and exploded it just as the pivot gun of the ram was fired at him not ten yards off. At once the ram settled, the launch sinking at the same time, while Cushing and his men swam for their lives.— Adapted from *Theodore Roosevelt.*

Tears for the slave, when Nature's gift
   Of all that man can be
Wastes, like the scattered spars that drift
   Upon the unknown sea.
Tears when the craven sinks at last,
   No deed of valor done;
But no tears for the soul that passed
   When Honor's fight was won.

He takes the hand of heavenly fate
   Who lives and dies for truth.
For him the holy angels wait,
   In realms of endless youth.
The grass upon his grave is green
   With everlasting bloom;
And love and glory make the sheen
   Of glory round his tomb.
                       — William Winter.

The American Republic was established by the united valor and wisdom of the lovers of liberty from all lands. The Frenchman, with his gay disregard of danger, the German with his steady courage, the Pole with his high enthusiasm, and the Irishman with all these qualities combined, were here in the long and bloody struggle for independence. Lafayette, the beloved of Washington; Hamilton, who rode by his side, and assisted to organize the government; Pulaski, Montgomery, Steuben, all were born under alien skies, and came to the banquet of battle and of death because of their love for human freedom At every subsequent period of American history the foreign-born citizen, in council and in the field, has been faithful to the common cause of liberty.— *Daniel W. Voorhees.*

EIGHT VOLUNTEERS.

Eight volunteers! on an errand of death!
  Eight men! Who speaks?
Eight men to go where the cannon's hot breath
  Burns black the cheeks.
Eight men to man the old Merrimac's hulk;
Eight men to sink the old steamer's black bulk,
Blockade the channel where Spanish ships skulk —
  Eight men! Who speaks?

"Eight volunteers!" said the Admiral's flags!
  Eight men! Who speaks?
Who will sail under El Morro's black crags —
  Sure death he seeks?
Who is there willing to offer his life?
Willing to march to this music of strife —
Cannon for drum and torpedo for fife?
  Eight men! Who speaks?

Eight volunteers! on an errand of death!
  Eight men! Who speaks?
Was there a man who in fear held his breath?
  With fear-paled cheeks?
From ev'ry warship ascended a cheer!
From ev'ry sailor's lips burst the word "Here!"
Four thousand heroes their lives volunteer!
  Eight men! Who speaks?

                                    — Lansing C. Bailey.

In the midst of other cares, however important, we must not lose
sight of the fact that the war power is still our main reliance. Our
chiefest care must still be directed to the army and navy, who have
thus far borne their harder part so nobly and well. And it may be
esteemed fortunate that, in giving the greatest efficiency to these indispensable arms, we do also honorably recognize the gallant men, from
commander to sentinel, who compose them, and to whom, more than
to others, the world must stand indebted for the home of freedom,
disenthralled, regenerated, enlarged, and perpetuated.— *Abraham Lin-*
coln.

TRUE FAME.

The heart so leal and the hand of steel
   Are palsied aye for strife,
But the noble deed, and the patriot's meed
   Are left of the soldier's life.

The bugle call and the battle ball
   Again shall rouse him never;
He fought and fell, he served us well;
   His furlough lasts forever.
                      — Samuel P. Merrill.

"We bring, O brothers of the North, the message of fellowship and love. This message comes from consecrated ground. All around my native home are the hills down which the gray flag fluttered to defeat, and through which the American soldiers from both sides charged like demi-gods. I could not bring a false message from those old hills, witnesses to-day, in their peace and tranquility, of the imperishable union of the American States, and the indestructible brotherhood of the American people."— *Henry W. Grady*, in New York.

At Gettysburg, the world witnessed a battle-field disfigured by no littleness and spoiled by no treachery. So long as the world lasts men will differ about the best strategy in war, and concerning the wisdom of commanders and the quality of their generalship. But no criticism, however clever, can at all belittle the supreme glory of this day and field. Here the world saw a great army confronted with a great crisis, and dealing with it in a great way. Here all lesser jealousies and rivalries disappeared in the one supreme rivalry how each one should best serve his country, and, if need be, die for her.— *Henry C. Potter.*

To be cold and breathless, to feel not and speak not; this is not the end of existence to the men who have breathed their spirits into the institutions of their country, who have stamped their characters on the pillars of the age, who have poured their heart's blood into the channels of the public prosperity. Tell me, ye who tread the sods of yon sacred height, is Warren dead? Can you not still see him, not pale and prostrate, the blood of his gallant heart pouring out of his ghastly wound, but moving resplendent over the field of honor, with the rose of heaven upon his cheek, and the fire of liberty in his eye? Tell me, ye who make your pious pilgrimage to the shades of Vernon, is Washington indeed shut up in that cold and narrow house? That which made these men, and men like these, cannot die. The hand that traced the charter of independence is, indeed, motionless; the eloquent lips that sustained it are hushed; but the lofty spirits that conceived, resolved, and maintained it, and which alone, to such men " make it life to live," these cannot expire:

> These shall resist the empire of decay,
> When time is o'er, and worlds have passed away;
> Cold in the dust the perished heart may lie,
> But that which warmed it once can never die.
>
> — *Edward Everett.*

Whiter, for the fires that strove to blacken and blast its fame; purer, for the blood that watered its base; stronger, for the tramp of armed men around its assaulted portals,— we, now and here, rejoice in the rescued temple of our liberties. The credit and glory of the undesecrated walls of that temple and of its unmoved foundations are due to the work and hardships of the American soldier. It was their service which made us to-day fellow-citizens enjoying the same rights, the same chances, the same incalculable career, whether we hail from the East or from the West, from the North or from the South. Honor then to the American soldier now and ever! Honor him in sermon and speech! Honor him in sonnet, stanza, and epic! Honor him in the unwasting forms by which art seeks to prolong his well-earned fame! Honor the volunteer soldier, who, when his work of devastation and death was ended, put aside his armor, melting into the sea of citizenship, making no ripple of disturbance upon its surface! Honor the citizen soldier of America, who never knew the feeling of vindictiveness or revenge! — *John L. Swift.*

To-day the nation looks back and thanks God that, in a great crisis, the children whom it had nurtured in peace and prosperity suddenly showed the stuff of heroes; they were not afraid to dare and to die when the bugle rang clear across the quiet fields. Whenever and however duty called, they answered with their lives. Let the nation thank God that it still breeds the men who make life great by service and sacrifice; that time and work and pleasure and wealth have not sapped the sources of its inward strength; that it still knows how to dare all and do all in that hour when manhood alone counts and achieves.— *The Outlook.*

On a beautiful May Day more than thirty years ago, there gathered beneath the overhanging boughs of a fruit-bearing tree, beside an open grave, the friends and kinsmen of one who, though a mere boy, had smelled the smoke of battle, felt the sting of rebel lead and won for himself the golden crown of martyrdom in the military service of his country. There were also gathered there a few of his old companions in arms — bronzed veterans — survivors of the dreadful carnage at Malvern Hill and the awful slaughter of Gettysburg, who had come to drop a tear at a comrade's grave and breathe a prayer for the safety of his soul. Just as the solemn rites of burial were over and the last shovelful of earth had been heaped upon his last resting-place, God's breath shook the overhanging boughs and sweet and beautiful apple blossoms came gently down and decorated that young hero's grave; and ever since, when the pleasant days and fragrant flowers of spring come, the loyal people of this country gladly follow the example Heaven so graciously set and see to it that no veteran's grave is neglected.— From a Memorial Day address of *Col. Anson S. Wood,* Commander Department of New York, Grand Army of the Republic.

Look to your history, — that part of it which the world knows by heart, and you will find on its brightest page the glorious achievements of the American sailor. Whatever his country has done to disgrace him and break his spirit, he has never disgraced her. Man for man, he asks no odds and he cares for no odds when the cause of humanity or the glory of his country calls him to the fight.

Who, in the darkest days of our Revolution, carried your flag into the very chops of the British Channel, bearded the lion in his den, and awoke the echo of old Albion's hills by the thunder of his cannon, and the shouts of his triumph? It was the American sailor; and the names of John Paul Jones and the Bon Homme Richard will go down the annals of time forever.

* * * * * * * * * *

Who struck the first blow that humbled the Barbary flag, — which, for a hundred years, had been the terror of Christendom, — drove it from the Mediterranean, and put an end to the infamous tribute it had been accustomed to exact? It was the American sailor; and the names of Decatur and his gallant companions will be as lasting as monumental brass.

* * * * * * * * * *

In your War of 1812, when your arms on shore were covered by disaster, when Winchester had been defeated, when the army of the Northwest had surrendered, and when the gloom of despondency hung like a cloud over the land, who first relit the fires of national glory, and made the welkin ring with the shouts of victory? It was the American sailor; and the names of Hull and the " Constitution " will be remembered as long as we have a country to love.

That one event was worth more to the Republic than all the money which has ever been expended for a navy. Since that day the navy has had no stain upon its national escutcheon, but has been cherished as your pride and glory; and the American sailor has established a reputation throughout the world, in peace and in war, in storm and in battle, for a heroism and prowess unsurpassed.—*Commodore Stockton*, from speech against whipping in the navy.

MANILA BAY.

The first great fight of the war is fought!
    And who is the victor,— say,—
Is there aught of the lesson now left untaught
    By the fight of Manila Bay?

Two by two were the Spanish ships
    Formed in their battle line;
Their flags at the taffrail peak and fore,
And batteries ready upon the shore,
    Silently biding their time.

Into their presence sailed our fleet,—
    The harbor was fully mined,—
With shotted guns and open ports
Up to their ships,— ay,— up to their forts;
    For Dewey is danger blind.

Signalled the flagship, "Open fire,"
    And the guns belched forth their death.
"At closer·range," was the order shown;
Then each ship sprang to claim her own,
    And to lick her fiery breath.

Served were our squadron's heavy guns
    With gunners stripped to the waist,
And the blinding, swirling, sulph'rous smoke
Enveloped the ships, as each gun spoke,
    In its furious, fearful haste.

Sunk and destroyed were the Spanish ships,
    Hulled by our heavy shot,
For the Yankee spirit is just the same,
And the Yankee grit, and the Yankee aim,
    And their courage, which faileth not.

                                        —H. E. W., Jr.

REMEMBERED.

W. K. W.

KOSCHAT.

1. Re - mem - bered, re - mem - bered, re - mem - bered are they, Who for
2. Re - mem - bered, re - mem - bered, re - mem - bered for aye Is the
3. For - got - ten, for - got - ten, for - got - ten the strife, In the

love of the na - tion their lives gave a - way; For their deeds shine for -
band of our he - roes who lin - ger to - day; For though halt - ing their
love of our coun - try, our na - tion's dear life! For the Northland and

ev - er in mem - o - ry's light, And their chil - dren sing ev - er, "They
foot - steps, and fail - ing their sight, Yet their chil - dren sing ev - er, "You
South - land are one in their might, And their chil - dren sing ev - er, "We'll

fought a good fight!" And their chil - dren sing ev - er, "They fought a good fight!"
fought a good fight!" Yet their chil - dren sing ev - er, "You fought a good fight!"
fight the good fight!" And their chil - dren sing ev - er, "We'll fight the good fight!"

FIRST PRESIDENT OF THE UNITED STATES.

MANUAL OF PATRIOTISM.

THE FLAG CONSECRATES

THE

BIRTHDAY OF GEORGE WASHINGTON.

(February 22, 1732).

SELECTIONS..................Song, *Ode for Washington's Birthday.*
SELECTIONS.........................Song, *God Speed the Right.*

THE BIRTHDAY OF WASHINGTON.

THE twenty-second of February — the day on which George Washington was born (1732) is a national holiday. When it comes on any one of the five school-days of the week, the children are freed from their books, and may stay at home or spend the time as they please. But in some schools the pupils are called together, their parents and friends invited in, and a patriotic exercise is given in which the character and career of Washington and the stormy yet glorious days of the American Revolution are made the subject of song, composition, and the "speaking of pieces." This is better far than for children to be idle at home or roaming the streets, — and it is greatly to be wished that the custom of the few schools become the custom of all. But until that sensible plan is adopted, the next best thing seems to be to devote an hour or more of the previous day's session to the exercise. Now, it is clear to see that the pupils of any particular school will appreciate such an exercise just in proportion to their knowledge of the man and the times. If, then, the scholars are old enough and their historical study or reading has been wide enough, let the program be correspondingly strong; if not, let the teacher take pains to explain and inform, infusing as much of the historical as possible under the guise of the romantic — so making appeal to the imagination and that sense of admiration for adventure and bravery innate in the minds of children. A long program is herewith given, with the thought of choice among the selections, if the time is very brief.

QUOTATIONS.

Oh, Washington! thou hero, patriot, sage,
Friend of all climes and pride of every age!

— Thomas Paine.

Washington is the mightiest name of earth.— *Abraham Lincoln.*

One of the greatest captains of the age.— *Benjamin Franklin.*

The voice of mankind shall ascend in acclaim,
And the watchword of nations be Washington's name.

—James G. Brooks.

Washington is to my mind the purest figure in history.— *William Ewart Gladstone.*

Of all great men he was the most virtuous and most fortunate.— *Guizot.*

Columbia's darling son,
The good, the great, the matchless Washington.

— William Leggett.

Washington — the greatest man of our own or of any age.— *Edward Everett.*

He was invested with a glory that shed a lustre on all around him.— *Archbishop John Carroll.*

Washington hath left
His awful memory
A light for after times.

— Robert Southey.

Washington — the ideal type of civic virtue to succeeding generations.— *James Bryce.*

The greatest man of modern times.— *Sir Henry Grattan.*

The mighty name of Washington
Is the grand synonym of all we prize
Of great and good in this wide western world.

—Christopher P. Cranch.

No nobler figure ever stood in the forefront of a nation's life.— *John Richard Green.*

In this world the seal is now put on his greatness.— *Alexander Hamilton.*

> Freedom's first and favorite son —
> He whose patriotic valor universal homage won —
> He who gave the world the Union — the immortal Washington!
> > — *Francis DeHass Janvier.*

He had every title at command, but his first victory was over himself.— *Gouverneur Morris.*

The want of the age is an European Washington.— *Lamartine.*

> The grandest, purest, best,
> Of heroes, earth has known,
> That man who for his country's sake,
> Spurned from him crown and throne.
> > — *C. G. Rosenburg.*

First in war, first in peace, first in the hearts of his countrymen.— *Henry Lee.*

I am not surprised at what George has done, for he was always a good boy.— *Mary Washington, his mother.*

> For truth and wisdom, foremost of the brave;
> Him glory's idle glances dazzled not;
> Twas his ambition, generous and great,
> A life to life's great end to consecrate.
> > — *Percy Bysshe Shelley.*

A pure and high-minded gentleman, of dauntless courage and stainless honor, simple and stately of manner, kind and generous of heart.— *Henry Cabot Lodge.*

Here indeed is a character to admire and revere; a life without a stain, a fame without a flaw.— *William Makepeace Thackeray.*

> His work well done, the leader stepped aside,
> Spurning a crown with more than kingly pride,
> Content to wear the higher crown of worth,
> While time endures, " First Citizen of Earth."
> > — *James J. Roche.*

George Washington — the highest human personification of justice and benevolence.— *William H. Seward.*

He was great as he was good; he was great because he was good.— *Edward Everett.*

The good, the brave,
Whose mighty dust in glory sleeps,
Where broad Potomac swells and sweeps,
And mourns and murmurs past his grave.
— *Abraham Coles.*

The universal consent of mankind accords to Washington the highest place among the great men of the race.— *George F. Hoar.*

Among a world of dreamers he was the only one whose vision in the slightest degree approached the great realities of the future.— *Edward Everett Hale.*

He lives, ever lives in the hearts of the free,
The wings of his fame spread across the broad sea;
He lives where the banner of freedom 's unfurled,
The pride of his country, the wealth of the world.
— *Alfred Tennyson.*

His example is complete; and it will teach wisdom and virtue to magistrates, citizens and men, not only in the present age but in future generations.— *John Adams.*

Washington — a fixed star in the firmament of great names, shining without twinkling or obscuration, with clear, steady, beneficent light.— *Daniel Webster.*

* * *   though often told,
The story of thy deeds can ne'er grow old,
Till no young breast remains to be inspired,
And virtue, valor, greatness have expired.
— *Hannah Gould.*

The fame of Washington stands apart from every other in history, shining with a truer lustre and more benignant glory.— *Washington Irving.*

His memory will be cherished by the wise and good of every nation, and truth will transmit his character to posterity in all its genuine lustre.— *John Jay.*

Shortest month of all, we greet thee;
Bring us clouds or bring us sun,
Surely all will bid thee welcome,
Month that gave us Washington!
— *Emma C. Dowd.*

When the storm of battle blows darkest and rages highest, the memory of Washington shall nerve every American arm and cheer every American breast.— *Rufus Choate.*

The anniversary of his birthday does not come round too often for us to devote some hour of it, whenever it returns, to meditation upon him and to gratitude for his spirit and his work.— *Thomas Starr King.*

> Virginia gave us this imperial man,
>   Cast in the massive mold
>   Of those high-statured ages old
> Which into grander forms our metal ran;
> She gave us this unblemished gentleman.
>   — *James Russell Lowell.*

The more clearly Washington's teaching and example are understood, the more faithfully they are followed, the purer, the stronger, the more glorious will this Republic become.— *Carl Schurz.*

Sincerely honoring him, we cannot become indifferent to those great principles of human freedom, consecrated by his life, and by the solemn act of his last will and testament.— *Charles Sumner.*

> For tho' the years their golden round
>   O'er all the lavish region roll,
>   And realm on realm, from pole to pole,
> In one beneath thy Stars be bound,
> The far-off centuries as they flow,
> No whiter name than this shall know!
>   — *Francis T. Palgrave.*

The filial love of Washington for his mother is an attribute of American manhood, a badge which invites our trust and confidence and an indispensable element of American greatness.— *Grover Cleveland* (adapted).

The majesty of that life — whether told in the pages of Marshall or Sparks, of Irving or Bancroft, or through the eloquent utterances of Webster, or Everett, or Winthrop, or the matchless poetry of Lowell, or the verse of Byron — never grows old.— *Melville Fuller, Chief Justice United States Supreme Court.*

SELECTIONS.

GEORGE WASHINGTON.

Washington was the only man in the United States who possessed the confidence of all. There was no other man who was considered as anything more than a party leader. The whole of his character was in its mass perfect, in nothing bad, in a few points indifferent. And it may be truly said that never did nature and fortune combine more perfectly to make a man great, and to place him in the same constellation with whatever worthies have merited from man an everlasting remembrance.— *Thomas Jefferson.*

If we look over the catalogue of the first magistrates of nations, whether they have been denominated Presidents, or Consuls, Kings or Princes, where shall we find one whose commanding talents and virtues, whose overruling good fortune, have so completely united all hearts and voices in his favor? who enjoyed the esteem and admiration of foreign nations, and fellow-citizens, with equal unanimity? Qualities so uncommon are no common blessing to the country that possesses them. By these great qualities, and their benign effects, has Providence marked out the head of this nation, with a hand so distinctly visible as to have been seen by all men, and mistaken by none.— *John Adams.*

In the war of the Revolution, when it was thought the cause was lost, men became inspired at the very mention of the name of George Washington. In 1812, when we succeeded once more against the mother country, men were looking for a hero, and there arose before them that rugged, grim, independent old hero, Andrew Jackson. In the last, and greatest of all wars, an independent and tender-hearted man was raised up by Providence to guide the helm of state through that great crisis, and men confidingly placed the destinies of this great land in the hands of Abraham Lincoln. In the annals of our country, we find no man whose training had been so peaceful, whose heart was so gentle, whose nature was so tender, and yet who was called upon to marshal the hosts of the masses of the people during four years of remorseless and bloody and unrelenting fratricidal war.— *Horace Porter.*

Nor must it be supposed that Washington owed his greatness to the peculiar crisis which called out his virtues. His more than Roman virtues, his consummate prudence, his powerful intellect, and his dauntless decision and dignity of character, would have made him illustrious in any age. The crisis would have done nothing for him, had not his character stood ready to match it. Acquire his character, and fear not the recurrence of a crisis to show forth its glory.— *William Wirt.*

The name of Washington is intimately blended with whatever belongs most essentially to the prosperity, the liberty, the free institutions, and the renown of our country. That name was of power to rally a nation, in the hour of thick-thronging public disasters and calamities; that name shone, amid the storm of war, a beacon light to cheer and guide the country's friends; it flamed, too, like a meteor to repel her foes. That name, in the days of peace, was a loadstone, attracting to itself a whole people's confidence, a whole people's love, and the whole world's respect; that name, descending with all time, spreading over the whole earth, and uttered in all the languages belonging to the tribes and races of men, will forever be pronounced with affectionate gratitude by every one, in whose breast there shall arise an aspiration for human rights and human liberty.— *Daniel Webster.*

It is the peculiar good fortune of this country to have given birth to a citizen whose name everywhere produces a sentiment of regard for his country itself. In other countries, whenever and wherever this is spoken of to be praised, and with the highest praise, it is called the country of Washington. Half a century and more has now passed away since he came upon the stage and his fame first broke upon the world; for it broke like the blaze of day from the rising sun, almost as sudden and seemingly as universal. The eventful period since that era has teemed with great men, who have crossed the scene and passed off. Some of them have arrested great attention. Still

Washington retains his pre-eminent place in the minds of men, still his peerless name is cherished by them in the same freshness of delight as in the morn of its glory.— *Asher Robbins.*

Washington served us chiefly by his sublime moral qualities. To him belonged the proud distinction of being the leader in a revolution, without awakening one doubt or solicitude as to the spotless purity of his purpose. His was the glory of being the brightest manifestation of the spirit which reigned in this country, and in this way he became a source of energy, a bond of union, the center of an enlightened people's confidence.

By an instinct which is unerring, we call WASHINGTON, with grateful reverence, THE FATHER OF HIS COUNTRY, but not its saviour. A people which wants a saviour, which does not possess an earnest and pledge of freedom in its own heart, is not yet ready to be free.— *William E. Channing.*

Jefferson said of Washington: " His integrity was the most pure, his justice the most inflexible I have ever known, no motives of interest, or consanguinity, or hatred being able to bias his decision. He was, in every sense of the words, a wise, a good, and a great man."

As the ocean washes every shore, and, with all-embracing arms, clasps every land, while on its heaving bosom it bears the products of various climes, so peace surrounds, protects and upholds all other blessings. Without it, commerce is vain, the ardor of industry is restrained, justice is arrested, happiness is blasted, virtue sickens and dies. And peace has its own peculiar victories, in comparison with which Marathon and Bannockburn and Bunker Hill, fields sacred in the history of human freedom, shall lose their lustre. Our own Washington rises to a truly heavenly stature, not when we follow him over the ice of the Delaware to the capture of Trenton, not when we behold him victorious over Cornwallis at Yorktown, but when we regard him, in noble deference to justice, refusing the kingly crown which a faithless soldiery proffered, and, at a later day, upholding the peaceful neutrality of the country while he received unmoved the clamor of the people wickedly crying for war.— *Charles Sumner.*

I see in Washington a great soldier who fought a trying war to a successful end, impossible without him; a great statesman, who did more than all other men to lay the foundations of a republic which has endured in prosperity for more than a century. I find in him a marvellous judgment which was never at fault, a penetrating vision which beheld the future of America when it was dim to other eyes, a great intellectual force, a will of iron, an unyielding grasp of facts, and an unequalled strength of patriotic purpose. I see in him, too, a pure and high-minded gentleman of dauntless courage and stainless honor, simple and stately of manner, kind and generous of heart. Such he was in truth. The historian and the biographer may fail to do him justice, but the instinct of mankind will not fail. The real hero needs not books to give him worshipers. George Washington will always receive the love and reverence of men, because they see embodied in him the noblest possibilities of humanity.— *Henry Cabot Lodge.*

To us, citizens of America, it belongs, above all others, to show respect to the memory of Washington, by the practical deference which we pay to those sober maxims of public policy which he has left us,— a last testament of affection in his Farewell Address. Of all the exhortations which it contains, I scarce need say to you that none are so emphatically uttered, none so anxiously repeated, as those that enjoin the preservation of the union of these states. No one can read the Farewell Address without feeling that this was the thought, and this the care which lay nearest and heaviest upon that noble heart; and if, which Heaven forbid, the day shall ever arrive when his parting counsels on that head shall be forgotten, on that day, come it soon or come it late, it may as mournfully as truly be said that "Washington has lived in vain." Then the vessels, as they ascend and descend the Potomac, may toll their bells with new significance as they pass Mount Vernon; they will strike the requiem of constitutional liberty for us,— for all nations.— *Edward Everett*, Oration on Washington.

A great and venerated character like that of Washington, which commands the respect of an entire population, however divided on other questions, is not an isolated fact in history to be regarded with barren admiration; it is a dispensation of Providence for good.

It was well said by Mr. Jefferson, in 1792, writing to Washington to dissuade him from declining a renomination: " North and South will hang together while they have you to hang to."

Washington in the flesh is taken from us; we shall never behold him as our Fathers did; but his memory remains, and I say, let us hang to his memory. Let us make a national festival and holiday of his birthday; and ever, as the 22d of February returns, let us remember that, while with these solemn and joyous rites of observance we celebrate the great anniversary, our fellow-citizens on the Hudson, on the Potomac, from the Southern plains to the Western lakes, are engaged in the same offices of gratitude and love.— *Edward Everett,* Oration on Washington.

We are met to celebrate the one hundred and tenth anniversary of the birthday of Washington.

Washington is the mightiest name on earth, long since mightiest in the cause of civil liberty, still mightiest in moral reformation.

On that name a eulogy is expected. It cannot be. To add brightness to the sun or glory to the name of Washington is alike impossible. Let none attempt it.

In solemn awe pronounce the name, and, in its naked, deathless splendor, leave it shining on.— *Abraham Lincoln.*

If Washington had one passion more strong than any other, it was love of country. The purity and ardor of his patriotism were commensurate with the greatness of its object. Love of country in him was invested with the sacred obligations of a duty, and from the faithful discharge of this duty he never swerved for a moment, either in thought or deed, throughout the whole period of his eventful career. — *Jared Sparks.*

It has been said Washington was not a great soldier; but certainly he created an army out of the roughest materials, outgeneralled all that Britain could send against him, and, in the midst of poverty and distress, organized victory. He was not brilliant and rapid. He was slow, defensive, and victorious. He made " an empty bag stand upright," which, Franklin says, is "hard." Some men command the world, or hold its admiration, by their ideas or by their intellect. Washington had neither original ideas nor a deeply-cultured mind. He commanded by his integrity, by his justice. He loved power by instinct, and strong government by reflective choice. Twice he was made Dictator, with absolute power, and never abused the awful and despotic trust. The monarchic soldiers and civilians would make him king. He trampled on their offer, and went back to his fields of corn and tobacco at Mount Vernon. The grandest act of his public life was to give up his power; the most magnanimous deed of his private life was to liberate his slaves. Cromwell is the greatest Anglo-Saxon who was ever a ruler on a large scale. In intellect he was immensely superior to Washington; in integrity, immeasurably below him. For one thousand years no king in Christendom has shown such greatness, or gives us so high a type of manly virtue. He never dissembled. He sought nothing for himself. In him there was no unsound spot, nothing little or mean in his character. The whole was clean and presentable. We think better of mankind because he lived, adorning the earth with a life so noble.— *Theodore Parker.*

In the production of Washington it does really appear as if Nature was endeavoring to improve upon herself, and that all the virtues of the ancient world were but so many studies preparatory to the patriot of the new. Individual instances, no doubt, there were: splendid exemplifications of some single qualification. Caesar was merciful, Scipio was continent, Hannibal was patient; but it was reserved for Washington to blend them all in one, and, like the lovely masterpiece of the Grecian artist, to exhibit in one glow of associated beauty the pride of every model and the perfection of every master. As a general, he marshalled the peasant into a veteran and supplied by discipline the absence of experience. As a statesman he enlarged the policy of the cabinet into the most comprehensive system of general advantage; and such was the wisdom of his views and the philosophy of his counsels that to the soldier and the statesman he almost added the character of the sage. A conqueror, he was untainted with the crime of blood; a revolutionist, he was free from any stain of treason, for aggression commenced the contest, and a country called him to the command; liberty unsheathed his sword, necessity stained, victory returned it. If he had paused here history might doubt what station to assign him, whether at the head of her citizens or her soldiers, her heroes or her patriots. But the last glorious act crowned his career and banishes hesitation. Who, like Washington, after having freed a country, resigned her crown and retired to a cottage rather than reign in a capitol! Immortal man! He took from the battle its crime, and from the conquest its chains; he left the victorious the glory of his self-denial, and turned upon the vanquished only the retribution of his mercy. Happy, proud America! The lightnings of heaven yielded to your philosophy! The temptations of earth could not seduce your patriotism.— *Charles Phillips.*

ODE FOR WASHINGTON'S BIRTHDAY.

Oliver Wendell Holmes.

Ludwig van Beethoven.
From the Ninth or Choral Symphony.

1. Wel-come to the day re-turn-ing, Dear-er still as a-ges flow;
2. Hear the tale of youth-ful glo-ry, While of Brit-ain's res-cued band,
3. Look! the shad-ow on the di-al Marks the hour of dead-lier strife;
4. Vain is em-pire's mad temp-ta-tion! Not for him an earth-ly crown!
5. "By the name that you in-her-it, By the suf-f'rings you re-call,
6. Fa-ther! we whose ears have tin-gled With the dis-cord notes of shame,—

While the torch of faith is burn-ing, Long as free-dom's al-tars glow!
Friend and foe re-peat the sto-ry, Spread his fame o'er sea and land,
Days of ter-ror, years of tri-al, Scourge a na-tion in-to life.
He whose sword has freed a na-tion Strikes the of-fered scep-tre down.
Cher-ish the fra-ter-nal spir-it; Love your coun-try first of all!
We, whose sires their blood have min-gled In the bat-tle's thun-der flame,—

See the he-ro whom it gave us Slumb'ring on a moth-er's breast,
Where the red cross fond-ly stream-ing, Flaps a-bove the frig-ate's deck,
Lo, the youth be-came her lead-er! All her baf-fled ty-rants yield;
See the throne-less con-queror seat-ed, Rul-er by a peo-ple's choice;
Lis-ten not to i-dle ques-tions If its bands may be un-tied;
Gath'ring while this ho-ly morn-ing Lights the land from sea to sea,

For the arm he stretched to save us, Be its morn for-ev-er blest.
Where the gold-en lil-ies, gleam-ing, Star the watchtow'rs of Que-bec.
Through his arm the Lord hath freed her; Crown him on the tent-ed field!
See the pa-triot's task com-plet-ed; Hear the fa-ther's dy-ing voice!
Doubt the pa-triot whose sug-ges-tions Strive a na-tion to di-vide!"
Hear thy coun-sel, heed thy warn-ing; Trust us, while we hon-or thee!

By special arrangement with Houghton, Mifflin & Co.

SELECTIONS.

Just honor to Washington can only be rendered by observing his precepts and imitating his example. He has built his own monument. We, and those who come after us, in successive generations, are its appointed, its privileged guardians. The widespread republic is the future monument to Washington. Maintain its independence. Uphold its constitution. Preserve its union. Defend its liberty. Let it stand before the world in all its original strength and beauty, securing peace, order, equality, and freedom to all within its boundaries; and shedding light, and hope, and joy upon the pathway of human liberty throughout the world; and Washington needs no other monument. Other structures may fully testify our veneration for him: this, this alone, can adequately illustrate his services to mankind. Nor does he need even this. The republic may perish, the wide arch of our ranged Union may fall, star by star its glories may expire, stone by stone its columns and its capitol may moulder and crumble, all other names which adorn its annals may be forgotten, but as long as human hearts shall anywhere pant, or human tongues anywhere plead, for a true, rational, constitutional liberty, those hearts shall enshrine the memory, and those tongues prolong the fame, of GEORGE WASH-INGTON.— *Robert C. Winthrop.*

American youth know that Washington captured Cornwallis, made a brilliant retreat after the battle of Long Island and worried and fretted the British armies into exhaustion during a seven years' war. They also know that he was President twice and declined to become President a third time. There are not many who know that the only time tears were seen in his eyes was at the close of the war, when his army, encamped upon the banks of the Hudson, was about to be disbanded. There were men in his army who were fearful that the ambitions and jealousies of some of those who had been of influence during the Revolution would attempt to gain great personal power. There were others who believed that there would be established in America a constitutional monarchy, modeled after that of Great Britain. The nation, as we now know it, was a government yet to be created.

17

So a company of officers — men having influence — having talked this matter over, agreed to go to Washington, ask him to accept the crown of empire and to promise him the support of the army in thus establishing a personal throne. When they approached Washington, he thought that as friends they had come to him for counsel. He was in a happy frame of mind that morning. The war had ended victoriously, and he had already been in consultation with Hamilton respecting the form of civil government which the now free colonies should undertake.

They offered him the crown in but a single sentence. A few years before, across the river, Washington, being seated at breakfast, had been approached by an officer, who told him that Benedict Arnold had fled after an attempt to betray West Point into the hands of the British. The news was appalling, for he had admired Arnold's splendid courage and loved the man. Yet so great was his self-command, so superb his capacity for controlling emotion, so thoroughly had he schooled himself to face adversity with calmness, that those about him only saw a look of sad sternness come to his countenance as he uttered the now historic words, " Whom can we trust? "

But when these officers proposed to him the empire, and tried to put the sceptre in his hand, Washington broke down. There was sorrow and there was anger in his countenance and in his manner. Tears came to his eyes, and, when he dismissed them with a sad gesture and only a brief word, these men realized that Washington had been shocked and grieved that it could have entered their hearts that he could for one moment have regarded an empire as possible, or could have fought through those seven years that he might himself attain the throne. In his action Washington not only revealed his moral greatness, but made it impossible that a monarchy could ever be established in the United States.

> Fame was too earnest in her joy,
> Too proud of such a son
> To let a robe and title
> Mask our noble Washington.

The fame of Washington stands apart from every other in history, shining with a truer lustre and a more benignant glory. With us his memory remains a national property, where all sympathies meet in unison. Under all dissensions and amid all storms of party, his precepts and examples speak to us from the grave with a paternal appeal; and his name — by all revered — forms a universal tie of brotherhood,— a watchword of our Union.— *John Fiske.*

No nobler figure ever stood in the forefront of a nation's life. Washington was grave and courteous in address; his manners were simple and unpretending; his silence and the serene calmness of his temper spoke of perfect self-mastery; but there was little in his outward bearing to reveal the grandeur of soul which lifts his figure, with all the simple majesty of an ancient statue, out of the smaller passions, the meaner impulses of the world around him. It was only as the weary fight went on that the colonists learned, little by little, the greatness of their leader, his clear judgment, his heroic endurance, his silence under difficulties, his calmness in the hour of danger or defeat, the patience with which he waited, the quickness and hardness with which he struck, the lofty and serene sense of duty that never swerved from its task through resentment or jealousy, that never, through war or peace, felt the touch of a meaner ambition, that knew no aim save that of guarding the freedom of his fellow-countrymen, and no personal longing save that of returning to his own fireside when their freedom was secured.— *Green's* " Short History of the English People."

Washington, from first to last, inspired every one with the idea that he could be trusted. No one ever suspected him for a moment, as Caesar, as Frederick, as Napoleon were with reason suspected,— with a design to use the power committed to him for the furtherance of his own ambition. Here was a man who thought only of his duty, who resigned power with far more alacrity than he assumed it, and who paid the bond of patriotism in full.— *Henry M. Towle.*

Of all the great men in history, Washington was the most invariably judicious. Those who knew him well noticed that he had keen sensibilities and strong passions; but his power of self-command never failed him, and no act of his public life can be traced to personal caprice, ambition, or resentment.   In the despondency of long-continued failure, in the elation of sudden success, at times when his soldiers were deserting by hundreds, and when malignant plots were formed against his reputation, amid the constant quarrels, rivalries, and jealousies of his subordinates, in the dark hour of national ingratitude, and in the midst of the most universal and intoxicating flattery, he was always the same calm, wise, just, and single-minded man, pursuing the course which he believed to be right, without fear, or favor, or fanaticism; equally free from the passions that spring from interest and from the passions that spring from imagination.   Washington never acted on the impulse of an absorbing or uncalculating enthusiasm, and he valued very highly fortune, position, and reputation, but at the command of duty he was ready to risk and sacrifice them all.   He was, in the highest sense of the words, a gentleman and a man of honor, and he carried into public life the severest standard of private morals.— *William E. H. Lecky,* from " The History of England in the Eighteenth Century."

Arise! 'tis the day of our Washington's glory;
  The garlands uplift for our liberties won.
O! sing in your gladness his echoing story,
  Whose sword swept for freedom the fields of the sun.

Not with gold, nor with gems, but with evergreens vernal,
  And the banner of stars that the continent span,
Crown, crown we the chief of the heroes eternal,
  Who lifted his sword for the birthright of man.
          — *Hezekiah Butterworth.*

When the storm of battle blows darkest and rages highest, the memory of Washington shall nerve every American arm, and cheer every American heart.— *Rufus Choate.*

It was not character that fought the Trenton campaign and carried the revolution to victory.   It was military genius.   It was not character that read the future of America and created our foreign policy.   It was statesmanship of the highest order.   Without the great moral qualities that Washington possessed his career would not have been possible; but it would have been quite as impossible if the intellect had not equalled the character.

There is no need to argue the truism that Washington was a great man, for that is universally admitted. But it is very needful that his genius should be rightly understood, and the right understanding of it is by no means universal.

His character has been exalted at the expense of his intellect, and his goodness has been so much insisted upon both by admirers and critics that we are in danger of forgetting that he had a great mind as well as high moral worth.— *Henry Cabot Lodge.*

With the sure sagacity of a leader of men, Washington at once selected, for the highest and most responsible stations, the three chief Americans who represented the three forces in the nation which alone could command success in the institution of the government. Hamilton was the head, Jefferson was the heart, and John Jay was the conscience. Washington's just and serene ascendancy was the lambent flame in which these beneficent powers were fused, and nothing less than that ascendancy could have ridden the whirlwind and directed the storm that burst around him.— *George William Curtis.*

Washington's appointments, when President, were made with a view to destroy party and not to create it, his object being to gather all the talent of the country in support of the national government; and he bore many things which were personally disagreeable in an endeavor to do this.— *Paul Leicester Ford.*

Men are beginning to feel that Washington stands out, not only as the leading American, but as the leading man of the race. Of men not named in Sacred Scripture, more human beings this day know and honor the name of George Washington than that of any other of the sons of men.— *Charles F. Deems.*

An Englishman by race and lineage, Washington incarnated in his own person and character every best trait and attribute that have made the Anglo-Saxon name a glory to its children and a terror to its enemies throughout the world. But he was not so much an

Englishman that, when the time came for him to be so, he was not even more an American; and in all that he was and did, a patriot so exalted, and a leader so wise and great, that what men called him when he came to be inaugurated as the first President of the United States the civilized world has not since then ceased to call him — *the Father of his Country.*— *Right Rev. Henry C. Potter.*

There is Franklin, with his first proposal of Continental union. There is James Otis, with his great argument against Writs of Assistance, and Samuel Adams, with his inexorable demand for the removal of the British regiments from Boston. There is Quincy, and there is Warren, the protomartyr of Bunker Hill. There is Jefferson, with the Declaration of Independence fresh from his pen, and John Adams close at his side. There are Hamilton and Madison and Jay bringing forward the Constitution; but, towering above them all is Washington, the consummate commander, the incomparable President, the world-renowned patriot.— *Robert C. Winthrop.*

CARMEN BELLICOSUM.

In their ragged regimentals
Stood the old Continentals,
    Yielding not,
When the grenadiers were lunging,
And like hail fell the plunging
    Cannon-shot;
    When the files
    Of the isles,
From the smoky night encampment, bore the banner of the rampant
    Unicorn,
And grummer, grummer, grummer rolled the roll of the drummer,
    Through the morn!

Then with eyes to the front all,
And with guns horizontal,
    Stood our sires;
And the balls whistled deadly,
And in streams flashing redly
    Blazed the fires;
    As the roar
    On the shore,

Swept the strong battle-breakers o'er the green-sodded acres
    Of the plain;
And louder, louder, louder cracked the black gunpowder,
    Cracked amain!

Now like smiths at their forges
Worked the red St. George's
    Cannoniers;
And the " villainous saltpetre "
Rung a fierce, discordant metre
    Round their ears;
    As the swift
    Storm-drift,
With hot sweeping anger, came the Horse Guard's clangor
    On our flanks.
Then higher, higher, higher burned the old-fashioned fire
    Through the ranks!

Then the old-fashioned colonel
Galloped through the white infernal
    Powder-cloud;
And his broadsword was swinging,
And his brazen throat was ringing
    Trumpet loud.
    Then the blue
    Bullets flew,
And the trooper jackets redden at the touch of the leaden
    Rifle-breath;
And rounder, rounder, rounder, roared the iron six-pounder.
    Hurling death!

                     —Guy Humphrey McMaster.
(This stirring poem was written when the author was only nineteen years old.)

GOD SPEED THE RIGHT.

W. E. Hickson.

German Air.

Maestoso.

1. Now to heav'n our pray'r as-cend-ing, God speed the right;
2. Be that pray'r a-gain re-peat-ed, God speed the right;
3. Pa-tient, firm, and per-se-ver-ing, God speed the right;

In a no-ble cause con-tend-ing, God speed the right.
Ne'er de-spair-ing, tho' de-feat-ed, God speed the right.
Ne'er th'e-vent nor dan-ger fear-ing, God speed the right.

Be our zeal in heav'n re-cord-ed, With suc-cess on
Like the good and great in sto-ry, If we fail we
Pains, nor toils, nor tri-als heed-ing, In the strength of

earth re-ward-ed, God speed the right, God speed the right.
fail with glo-ry, God speed the right, God speed the right.
heav'n suc-ceed-ing, God speed the right, God speed the right.

SIXTEENTH PRESIDENT OF THE UNITED STATES.

MANUAL OF PATRIOTISM.

THE FLAG BLESSES

THE

BIRTHDAY OF ABRAHAM LINCOLN.

(Feb. 12, 1809.)

QUOTATIONS.............................. In *Prose and Poetry.*
SELECTIONS.......................... Song, *The Man for Me.*
SELECTIONS............................... Song, *Laus Deo.*

(267)

THE BIRTHDAY OF ABRAHAM LINCOLN.

T is indeed necessary that children, in so far as they are capable, should know the theory of our government, and the great events that, like milestones, have marked its course. But, after all, theories and abstract facts never can take such hold upon the minds of children — upon memory and imagination — nor stir them to such a sense of their country's worth — as can the history, the life, of a great man. It will be difficult to make the little folks understand the causes, direct or indirect, which led to the Civil War of '61. Indeed, who of us who are older and trained to teach are competent to tell all the influences that ended in that terrible struggle? But what child can fail to know and feel the real greatness of the personality and life of Abraham Lincoln? He was what we may call *a boy's man* — having that sense of humor, that spirit of fun which appeals so irresistibly to boys,— yes, even to "boys of larger growth." Let much be made, therefore, in any celebration of Lincoln's birthday, of those incidents, so strange, so fascinating, which marked his early boyhood in his cabin home — of the trials which beset his youth-time, his wonderful skill in political debate — his perilous journey to the city of Washington, there to be inaugurated President of the United States — his care for the soldiers in the field and the poor black men in slavery in the South,— and, at length, his martyr death. (Just here might come in a study of " The Negro " in our history.) Fear not to blend with all, the stories which made him as well known as his statesmanship — indeed, which were, many of them, illustrations of the very spirit and philosophy of statesmanship.

(269)

QUOTATIONS.

A man born for his time.— *Morrison R. Waite.*

Abraham Lincoln was the genius of common sense.— *Charles Dudley Warner.*

His constant thought was his country and how to serve it.— *Charles Sumner.*

> A name that shall live through all coming time,
> Unbounded by country, by language, or clime.
> —*C. P. Corliss.*

Washington was the father, and Lincoln the savior of his country.— *Henry L. Dawes.*

The typical American, pure and simple.— *Asa Gray.*

The plain, honest, prudent man,— safe in council, wise in action, pure in purpose.— *John C. New.*

> Patriot, who made the pageantries of kings
> Like shadows seem, and unsubstantial things.
> —*R. W. Dale.*

Lincoln was the purest, the most generous, the most magnanimous of men.— *Gen. W. T. Sherman.*

His career closed at a moment when its dramatic unity was complete.— *Governor Andrew, of Massachusetts.*

Abraham Lincoln was worthy to be trusted and to be loved by all his countrymen.— *Gen. Howard.*

> He lives in endless fame,
> All honor to his patriot name.
> —*H. C. Ballard.*

He stands before us and will so stand in history as the Moses of this Israel of ours.— *Charles Lowe.*

A man of great ability, pure patriotism, unselfish nature, full of forgiveness for his enemies.— *Ulysses Simpson Grant.*

Kind, unpretending, patient, laborious, brave, wise, great and good, such was Abraham Lincoln.— *Theodore Frelinghuysen.*

> Long centuries hence thy name shall shine as one
> No blame can cloud — our second Washington.
> > — *Henry Peterson.*

Freedom's great high-priest, who set apart his life, while others sought but gold or bread.— *T. C. Pease.*

His career teaches young men that every position of eminence is open before the diligent and worthy.— *Bishop Matthew Simpson.*

The purity of his patriotism inspired him with the wisdom of a statesman and the courage of a martyr.— *Stanley Matthews.*

> * * * so true and tender,
> The patriot's stay, the people's trust,
> The shield of the offender.
> > — *Oliver Wendell Holmes.*

Such a life and character will be treasured forever as the sacred possession of the American people and of mankind.— *James A. Garfield.*

A great man, tender of heart, strong of nerve, of boundless patience and broadest sympathy, with no motive apart from his country.— *Frederick Douglass.*

The purest of men, the wisest of statesmen, the most sincere and devoted patriot, the loveliest character of American statesmen.— *Hon. Charles Foster.*

> His country saved, his work achieved,
> He boasted not of what he'd done,
> But rather in his goodness, grieved
> For all sad hearts beneath the sun,
> > — *G. Martin.*

Under the providence of God, he was, next to Washington, the greatest instrument for the preservation of the Union and the integrity of our country.— *Peter Cooper.*

Of all the men I ever met he seemed to possess more of the elements of greatness combined with goodness than any other.— *Gen. W. T. Sherman.*

Lincoln, the honest man, who, without personal ambition, always supported by a strong perception of his duties, deserved to be called emphatically a great citizen.— *Louis Phillipe, Duc D'Orleans.*

> All the kindly grace,
> The tender love, the loyalty to truth,
> That flow and mingle in the gentlest blood,
> Were met together in his blameless life.
>
> *— Mary A. Ripley.*

The past century has not, the century to come will not have, a figure so grand as that of Abraham Lincoln.— *Emilio Castelar (Spain).*

The life of Abraham Lincoln is written in imperishable characters in the history of the great American Republic.— *John Bright (England).*

By his fidelity to the True, the Right, the Good, he gained not only favor and applause, but what is better than all, love.— *W. D. Howells.*

> The form is vanished and the footsteps still,
> But from the silence Lincoln's answers thrill;
> "Peace, charity and love!" in all the world's best needs
> The master stands transfigured in his deeds.
>
> *— Kate M. B. Sherwood.*

He was a true believer in the divinity of the rights of man as man, the civil as well as the religious hope of the race.— *Sidney Dyer.*

In Lincoln there was always some quality that fastened him to the people and taught them to keep time to the music of his heart.— *David Swing.*

"You will find the whole of my early life," said Lincoln to a friend, "in a single line of Gray's Elegy"

> "The short and simple annals of the poor."
>
> *— Anon.*

> Heroic soul, in homely garb half hid,
> Sincere, sagacious, melancholy, quaint;
> What he endured, no less than what he did,
> Has reared his monument and crowned him saint.
>
> *— J. T. Trowbridge.*

He was one whom responsibility educated, and he showed himself more and more nearly equal to duty as year after year laid on him ever fresh burdens. God-given and God-led and sustained we must ever believe him.—*Wendell Phillips.*

He was warm-hearted; he was generous; he was magnanimous; he was most truly, as he afterward said on a memorable occasion, " with malice toward none, with charity for all."—*Alexander H. Stephens.*

It is the great boon of such characters as Mr. Lincoln's that they reunite what God has joined together and man has put asunder. In him was vindicated the greatness of real goodness and the goodness of real greatness.—*Bishop Phillips Brooks.*

> We rest in peace, where his sad eyes
>   Saw peril, strife and pain;
> His was the awful sacrifice,
>   And ours the priceless gain.
>
> —*John G. Whittier.*

SELECTIONS.

Let me endeavor to give those in this audience who never saw Mr. Lincoln some idea of his personal appearance. He was a very tall man — 6 feet 4 inches. His complexion was dark, his eyes and hair black; and though he was of lean, spare habit, I should suppose he must have weighed about 180 pounds. He was a man of fine fibre, and thus a brain of superior power was contained in a small, but rather elongated, skull. * * * His movements were rather angular, but never awkward; and he was never burdened with that frequent curse of unfortunate genius, the dreadful oppression of petty self-consciousness. It was a most remarkable character, that of Abraham Lincoln. He had the most comprehensive, the most judicial mind; he was the least faulty in his conclusions of any man that I have ever known.— *Charles A. Dana,* Lecture on " Lincoln and His Cabinet," at New Haven, March 10, 1896.

Mr. Lincoln was not what you would call an educated man. The college that he had attended was that which a man attends who gets up at daylight to hoe the corn, and sits up at night to read the best book he can find, by the side of a burning pine knot. What education he had, he picked up in that way. He had read a great many books; and all the books that he had read, he knew. He had a tenacious mem-

18

ory, just as he had the ability to see the essential thing. He never took an unimportant point and went off upon that; but he always laid hold of the real thing, of the real question, and attended to that without attending to the others any more than was indispensably necessary. — *Charles A. Dana*, Lecture, " Lincoln and His Cabinet."

There, by his courage, his justice, his even temper, his fertile counsel, his humanity (Abraham Lincoln) stood a heroic figure in the centre of a heroic epoch. He is the true history of the American people in his time. Step by step he walked before them; slow with their slowness, quickening his march by theirs, the true representative of this continent; an entirely public man; father of his country, the pulse of twenty millions throbbing in his heart, the thought of their minds articulated by his tongue.— *Ralph Waldo Emerson.*

We can still count as one of ourselves, with his honor and his sadness, with his greatness and his everyday homeliness, with his wit and his logic, with his gentle chivalry that made him equal to the best born knight, and his awkward and ungainly way that made him one of the plain people, our martyred President, our leader of the plain people, Abraham Lincoln. * * * Beyond the rulers of every age, Lincoln was the leader of the people,— of what he called the plain people. * * * He knew, as no other man did, as cabinets and congresses did not know, the sentiments and feelings of the plain people of the Northern States. He knew that they loved, beyond everything else, the Union, and he would move only so fast as, over the electric currents which connected his heart and brain with every fireside in the land, came the tidings to him that they were ready for another advance along the lines of revolutionary action which would preserve the Union.— *Chauncey M. Depew*, Speech at Lincoln Dinner.

I have often contemplated and described (Lincoln's) life. Born in a cabin of Kentucky, of parents who could hardly read; born a new Moses in the solitude of the desert, where are forged all great and obstinate thoughts, monotonous, like the desert, and, like the desert, sublime; growing up among those primeval forests, which, with their fragrance, send a cloud of incense, and, with their murmurs, a cloud of prayers, to heaven; a boatman at eight years, in the impetuous cur- rent of the Ohio, and at seventeen in the vast and tranquil waters of the Mississippi; later, a woodman, with axe and arm felling the imme- morial trees, to open a way to unexplored regions for his tribe of wandering workers; reading no other book than the Bible, the book of great sorrows and great hopes, dictated often by prophets to the sound of fetters they dragged through Nineveh and Babylon; a child of nature, in a word, by one of those miracles only comprehensible among free peoples, he fought for the country, and was raised by his fellow-citizens to the Congress at Washington, and by the nation to the presidency of the Republic; and, after emancipating three million slaves, that nothing might be wanting, he dies in the very moment of victory,— like Christ, like Socrates, like all redeemers, at the foot of his work. His work! Sublime achievement! over which humanity shall eternally shed its tears, and God His benedictions.— *Emilio Castelar (Spanish orator).*

From the union of the colonists, Puritans and Cavaliers, from the straightening of their purposes and the crossing of their blood, slow perfecting through a century, came he who stands as the first typical American, the first who comprehended within himself all the strength and gentleness, all the majesty and grace of this republic — Abraham Lincoln. He was the sum of Puritan and Cavalier, for in his ardent nature were fused the virtues of both, and in the depths of his great soul the faults of both were lost. He was greater than Puritan, greater than Cavalier, in that he was American, and that in his honest form were first gathered the vast and thrilling forces of his ideal government — charging it with such a tremendous meaning and so elevating it above human suffering, that martyrdom, though infamously aimed, came as a fitting crown to a life consecrated from the cradle to human liberty. Let us build with reverent hands to the type of this simple, but sublime life, in which all types are honored.— *Henry W. Grady,* of Georgia, from the speech at the New England Club, in New York city, December 21, 1886.

If ever the face of a man writing solemn words glowed with holy joy, it must have been the face of Abraham Lincoln as he bent over the Emancipation Proclamation.   Here was an act in which his whole soul could rejoice, an act that crowned his life.   All the past, the free boyhood in the woods, the free youth upon the farm, the free manhood in the honorable citizen's employment — all his freedom gathered and completed in this.   And is it any wonder that among the swarthy multitudes, ragged, and tired, and hungry, and ignorant, but free forever from anything but the memorial scars of the fetters and the whips,— is it any wonder there grew up in camps and hovels a superstition, which saw in Lincoln the image of one who was more than man, and whom with one voice they loved to call " Father Abraham? " — *Phillips Brooks.*

The nation's debt to these men (Washington and Lincoln) is not confined to what it owes them for its material well-being, incalculable though this debt is.   Beyond the fact that we are an independent and united people, with half a continent as our heritage, lies the fact that every American is richer by the noble deeds and noble words of Washington and of Lincoln.   Each of us who reads the Gettysburg speech or the second inaugural address of the greatest American of the nineteenth century, or who studies the long campaigns and lofty statesmanship of that other American who was even greater, cannot but feel within him that lift toward things higher and nobler which can never be bestowed by the enjoyment of mere material prosperity.— From " American Ideals," *Theodore Roosevelt.*

On the day of his death, this simple Western attorney, who, according to one party, was a vulgar joker, and whom some of his own supporters accused of wanting every element of statesmanship, was the most absolute ruler in Christendom, and this solely by the hold his good-humored sagacity had laid on the hearts and understandings of his countrymen.   Nor was this all, for it appeared that he had drawn the great majority, not only of his fellow-citizens, but of mankind also, to his side.   So strong and persuasive is honest manliness, without a single quality of romance or unreal sentiment to help it!   A civilian during times of the most captivating military achievements, awkward, with no skill in the lower technicalities of manners, he left behind him a fame beyond that of any conqueror, the memory of a grace higher than that of outward person, and of gentlemanliness deeper than mere breeding. Never before that startled April morning did such multitudes of men shed tears for the death of one they had never seen, as if with him a friendly presence had been taken away from their lives, leaving them colder and darker. Never was funeral panegyric so eloquent as the silent look of sympathy which strangers exchanged when they met on that day. Their common manhood had lost a kinsman.— *James Russell Lowell.*

To Horace Greeley, the greatest of American editors, his party associate and a stinging thorn in his flesh, Lincoln wrote: " If there be those who would not save the Union unless they could at the same time save slavery, I do not agree with them." " If there be those who would not save the Union unless they could at the same time destroy slavery, I do not agree with them."

" *My paramount object is to save the Union, and not either to save or destroy slavery.*" " If I could save the Union without freeing any slave, I would do it —if I could do it by freeing all the slaves, I would do it — and if I could do it by freeing some and leaving others alone, I would also do that." " What I do about slavery and the colored race, I do because I believe it helps to save the Union, and what I forbear, I forbear because I do not believe it would help to save the Union."

From the hour of that touching farewell speech to his neighbors in the Springfield depot, down to the fatal night in Ford's Theatre, his life was consecrated to the restoration of a disseevered country.

Walking in the busy streets of the city of Atlanta, not long since, I came upon a fine statue of Henry W. Grady. Beneath the bronze figure of the young orator, whose early death has been so widely regretted, was the legend: " He died while literally loving a nation into peace."

Even more suggestive than his cheering words was the act of the Southern masses, which placed this monument in their busiest thoroughfare, a witness of their satisfaction at the sentiments which had distinguished him. No traveler in the South can doubt that there is a " New South." The industries are growing and the schools are multiplying. There is a healthier sentiment upon sociological and economic questions, because the slave system is no longer there to throttle it. * * * The South has a new feeling towards the North. As we understand each other better, we love each other more. The roads are being broken out. Beaten paths are being made. Commercial intercourse has commenced and fraternal regard is grow- ing. The Ohio river no longer separates two opposing peoples, who merely sustain diplomatic relations with each other; there is a chemical affinity in progress; we are amalgamating. The bitterness of a century of controversy is well-nigh gone. The wounds torn by the rough hoof of war have almost healed. The soldiers of the two armies, and the young men and women of the new generation, who " look forward and not back," have attained this magnificent result. The Union is stronger, safer, because it stood the shock of battle. The people are more homogeneous because more free. A hundred millions of united, industrious, frugal, educated Christian people, under a free flag, stand in a place so high among the nations that they can command anything that is right by the force and dignity of their position, and without resort to war. And the work of Abraham Lincoln is accomplished.— *President Andrew S. Draper*, University of Illinois, Lincoln's Birthday, 1896.

While we say that Mr. Lincoln was an uneducated man, unedu- cated in the sense that we recognize in any college town, he yet had a singularly perfect education in regard to everything that concerns the practical affairs of life. His judgment was excellent, and his informa- tion was always accurate. He knew what the thing was. He was a man of genius, and, contrasted with men of education, genius will always carry the day. I remember very well going into Mr. Stanton's room in the War Department on the day of the Gettysburg celebration, and he said: " Have you seen these Gettysburg speeches? " " No," said I, " I didn't know you had them." He said: " Yes; and the people will be delighted with them. Edward Everett has made a speech that will make three columns in the newspapers, and Mr. Lincoln has made a speech of perhaps forty or fifty lines. Everett's is the speech of a scholar, polished to the last possibility. It is eloquent and it is learned; but Lincoln's speech will be read by a thousand men where one reads Everett's, and will be remembered as long as anybody's speeches are remembered who speaks in the English language."

That was the truth. If you will take those two speeches now, you will get an idea how superior genius is to education; how superior that intellectual faculty is which sees the vitality of a question and knows how to state it; how superior that intellectual faculty is which regards everything with the fire of earnestness in the soul, with the relentless purpose of a heart devoted to objects beyond literature.— *Charles A. Dana*, Lecture on " Lincoln and His Cabinet."

Another interesting fact about Abraham Lincoln was that he developed into a great military man, that is to say, a man of supreme military judgment. I do not risk anything in saying that if you will study the records of the war and study the writings relating to it, you will agree with me that the greatest general we had, greater than Grant or Thomas, was Abraham Lincoln. It was not so at the beginning; but after three or four years of constant practice in the science and art of war, he arrived at this extraordinary knowledge of it, so that Von Moltke was not a better general or an abler planner or expounder of a campaign than President Lincoln was. He was, to sum it up, a born leader of men. He knew human nature; he knew what chord to strike, and he was never afraid to strike it when he believed that the time had arrived.— *Charles A. Dana*, Lecture on " Lincoln and His Cabinet."

Another remarkable peculiarity of Mr. Lincoln's was that he seemed to have no illusions. He had no freakish notions that things were so or might be so, when they were not so. All his thinking and all his reasoning, all his mind, in short, was based continually on actual facts, and upon facts of which, as I said, he saw the essence. I never heard him say anything that was not so. I never heard him foretell things. He told what they were. But I never heard him intimate that such and such consequences were likely to happen, without the consequences following. I should say, perhaps, that his greatest quality was wisdom. And that is something superior to talent, superior to education. I do not think it can be acquired. He had it. He was wise; he was not mistaken; he saw things as they were. All the advice that he gave was wise; it was judicious; and it was always timely. This wisdom, it is scarcely necessary to add, had its animating philosophy in his own famous words: "With charity toward all; with malice toward none."—*Charles A. Dana*, Lecture on "Lincoln and His Cabinet."

Not long since, as I sat in a crowded courtroom, there came to the witness stand a venerable, white-haired negro. Born a slave, he had stood upon the auction block and been sold to the highest bidder. Now, he came into a court of Justice to settle, by the testimony of his black lips, a controversy between white men. When asked his age, he drew himself proudly up, and said: "For fifty years I was a chattel. On the first day of January, 1863, Uncle Abe Lincoln made me a man."

The act which set that old man free was the crowning glory of Lincoln's life, for by it he not only saved his country, but emancipated a race. We of the Anglo-Saxon tongue are justly proud of the Magna Charta. We are justly proud of the Declaration of Independence, of the right of government by the people. True it is that the genesis of American Liberty was in the Declaration of Independence, but the gospel of its new testament was written by Abraham Lincoln in the Emancipation Proclamation.— *John M. Thurston*, New York, Lincoln's Birthday, 1895.

Mr. Lincoln had many amiable and lovable personal qualities, but the great thing was the fact *that he succeeded;* that the Civil War was ended under his rule. He succeeded, with the forces of the anti-slavery states, in putting down a rebellion in which twelve millions of people were concerned, determined people, educated people, fighting for their ideas and their property, fighting to the last, fighting to the death. I don't think there is anything else in history to compare with that achievement. How did he do it?

In the first place, he never was in haste. As I said, he never took a step too soon, and also he never took a step too late. When the whole northern country seemed to be clamoring for him to issue a proclamation abolishing slavery, he didn't do it. Deputation after deputation went to Washington. I remember once, a hundred gentlemen came, dressed in black coats, mostly clergymen, from Massachusetts. They appealed to him to proclaim the abolition of slavery. But he didn't do it. He allowed Mr. Cameron and General Butler to execute their great idea of treating slaves as contraband of war, and of protecting those who had got into our lines against being recaptured by their Southern owners. But he would not prematurely make the proclamation that was so much desired. Finally the time came; and of that he was the judge. Nobody else decided it; nobody commanded it; the proclamation was issued as he thought best; and it was efficacious. The people of the North, who during the long contest over slavery had always stood strenuously by the compromises of the Constitution, might themselves have become half rebels if this proclamation had been issued too soon. They at last were tired of waiting, tired of endeavoring to preserve even a show of regard for what were called the compromises of the Constitution, when they believed that the Constitution itself was in danger. Thus public opinion was ripe when the proclamation came, and that was the beginning of the end. This unerring judgment, this patience which waited and which knew when the right time had arrived — those were intellectual qualities, which I do not find exercised upon any such scale by any other man in history, and with such unerring precision. This proves Abraham Lincoln to have been intellectually one of the greatest of rulers.— *Charles A. Dana*, Lecture on " Lincoln and His Cabinet."

Abraham Lincoln was the grandest figure of the nineteenth century. With a giant intellect, a boundless love of his kind, and an irrevocable determination that right should triumph, he stood before the people of the world, and so conducted himself that all criticism was disarmed, and all oppressors put to shame. Sensitive as a child, firm as a rock, he lifted up the lowly, restrained the arrogant, and, with a foresight that was almost inspiration, made possible and certain the union of the states. He was neither appalled by disaster nor elated by the grandest successes. Devoid of self-esteem, unconscious of his mighty ability, he aimed at and attained results because he believed eternal justice demanded them. With the growth of centuries, the name of Abraham Lincoln will be more highly honored, and the value of his work more fully appreciated.— *George W. Ray.*

Abraham Lincoln cannot be compared with any man. He stands alone. More and more, as time goes on, does his work impress itself upon the world. His genius was fitted exactly to the circumstances under which he lived and labored. He is the conspicuous example of the truth that an all-wise Providence provides the man for the emergency. And then what an inspiration he has become to every ambitious, struggling young American! By his sterling integrity to thought and conviction, by untiring industry, and by his large common sense, he rose from obscurity to the first place in the nation, and has become the priceless heritage of every American.— *James S. Sherman.*

The chief characteristics of Lincoln were his integrity and common sense. Many of his contemporaries excelled him in eloquence, in learning, and in culture, but in the quality that is stronger and higher than either, the quality that inspires confidence and courage in times of crisis, he surpassed them all. He was fortunate in his career while living, and fortunate in his sad and tragic death. Hardly in the history of the human race has a ruler died whose loss seemed to the people so near a personal grief, and the power of his name increases steadily. He was neither orator, soldier nor scholar, but a leader, trusted and loved as few had ever been. In the historic struggle in which his is the great name, his countrymen felt that other leaders might be right, but he was sure to be right.— *Frank S. Black.*

The glory of Abraham Lincoln is a masterful mind forever loyal to the majesty and power of a great thought. That great thought was the supremacy of the Constitution of the United States, loyalty to which is the first and last duty of an American citizen, higher than all personal considerations, and superior to all sectional interests. Like a heavenly enchantment it allured him to duty, and like a perennial inspiration it was his courage in danger, fortitude in adversity, and faith in the certainty of the future.

*   *   *   *   *   *   *   *   *   *

From earliest manhood, he had been the patient student of this great instrument of our political economy (the Constitution), and to maintain the supreme authority thereof over every citizen and over every inch of our national domain was the larger purpose of all his state papers, of every act of his administration, and of the war measures he approved. Himself the gentlest of souls and the sincerest of men, he loved peace but he loved the Union more, and called upon his country-men to die with him for the right. He hated slavery, but he hated rebellion more, and he would suppress rebellion with slavery or without slavery; and, when the time came to suppress the one by the destruction of the other, the sword of Grant and the pen of Lincoln were the chosen instruments of Providence to scatter the rebels and emancipate the slaves. — *John P. Newman.*

It is not difficult to place a correct estimate upon the character of Lincoln. He was the greatest man of his time, especially approved of God for the work He gave him to do. History abundantly approves his superiority as a leader, and establishes his constant reliance upon a higher power for guidance and support. The tendency of this age is to exaggeration, but of Lincoln, certainly none have spoken more highly than those who knew him best.

A distinguished orator of to-day has said: "Lincoln surpassed all orators in eloquence; all diplomatists in wisdom; all statesmen in foresight; and the most ambitious in fame."

This is in accord with the estimate of Stanton, who pronounced him "the most perfect ruler of men the world had ever seen."

Seward, too, declared Lincoln "a man of destiny, with character made and moulded by Divine power to save a nation from perdition."

Ralph Waldo Emerson characterized him as "the true represen-tative of this continent; an entirely public man; father of his country; the pulse of twenty millions throbbing in his heart, the thought of their minds articulated by his tongue."

Bancroft wisely observed: " Lincoln thought always of mankind as well as of his own country, and served human nature itself; he finished a work which all time cannot overthrow."

Sumner said that in Lincoln " the West spoke to the East, pleading for human rights as declared by our fathers."

Horace Greeley, in speaking of the events which led up to and embraced the Rebellion, declared: " Other men were helpful and nobly did their part; yet, looking back through the lifting mists of those seven eventful, tragic, trying, glorious years, I clearly discern the one providential leader, the indispensable hero of the great drama, Abraham Lincoln."

James Russell Lowell was quick to perceive and proclaim Lincoln's greatness. In December, 1863, in a review of the " President's Policy," in the Atlantic Monthly, he said: " Perhaps none of our presidents since Washington has stood so firm in the confidence of the people as Lincoln, after three years' stormy administration. * * * A profound common sense is the best genius for statesmanship. Hitherto the wisdom of the President's measures have been justified by the fact that they have always resulted in more firmly uniting public opinion." — *William McKinley*, at Albany, N. Y., Lincoln's Birthday, 1895.

What were the traits of character that made him leader and master, without a rival in the greatest crisis in our history? What gave him such mighty power? Lincoln had sublime faith in the people. He walked with and among them. He recognized the importance and power of an enlightened public sentiment and was guided by it. Even amid the vicissitudes of war, he concealed little from public inspection. In all that he did, he invited rather than evaded public examination and criticism. He submitted his plans and purposes, as far as practicable, to public consideration with perfect frankness and sincerity. There was such homely simplicity in his character, that it could not be hedged in by the pomp of place, nor the ceremonials of high official station. He was so accessible to the public that he seemed to take the whole people into his confidence. Here, perhaps, was one secret of his power. Bancroft, the historian, alluding to this characteristic, which was never so conspicuously manifested as during the darkest hours of the war, beautifully illustrated it in these memorable words: " As a child in a dark night, on a rugged way, catches hold of the hand of its father for guidance and support, Lincoln clung fast to the hand of the people, and moved calmly through the gloom." — *William McKinley*, at Albany, N. Y., Lincoln's Birthday, 1895.

Lincoln was an orator. We hear in these days that the power of the orator has passed; that the spoken word will soon be a thing of the past. The people can read all that the orator can tell them, and that soon the orator will be among the things that are the history of a country. Abraham Lincoln became President of the United States, not because he served in the legislature — he was a nobody there; not because he served in Congress — for he was unknown there; not because he was a lawyer, for he had only a state reputation. He became President because of the stump and the platform. He never left them without leaving the impression that a great soul, a great mind, had made itself known, and that a man who ought to be a leader of the people had spoken to them — a man who it was intended should carry the torch.— *Chauncey M. Depew*, Albany, N. Y., Lincoln's Birthday, 1893.

During the whole of the struggle, he was a tower of strength to the Union. Whether in defeat or victory, he kept right on, dismayed at nothing, and never to be diverted from the pathway of duty. Always cool and determined, all learned to gain renewed courage, calmness, and wisdom from him, and to lean upon his strong arm for support. The proud designation of "Father of his Country" was not more appropriately bestowed upon Washington than the affectionate title, "Father Abraham," was given to Lincoln by the soldiers and loyal people of the North.

The crowning glory of Lincoln's administration, and the greatest executive act in American history, was his immortal Proclamation of Emancipation. Perhaps more clearly than any one else, Lincoln had realized, years before he was called to the Presidency, that the country could not continue half slave and half free. He declared it before Seward declared the "Irrepressible conflict." The contest between freedom and slavery was inevitable; it was written in the stars. The nation must either be all slave or all free. Lincoln, with almost super- natural prescience, foresaw it. His prophetic vision is manifested through all his utterances, notably in the great debate between him- self and Douglass. To him was given the duty and responsibility of making that great classic of liberty, the Declaration of Independence, no longer an empty promise, but a glorious fulfillment.— *William McKin- ley*, at Albany, N. Y., Lincoln's Birthday, 1895.

A man of great ability, pure patriotism, unselfish nature, full of forgiveness to his enemies, bearing malice toward none, he proved to be the man above all others for the struggle through which the nation had to pass to place itself among the greatest in the family of nations. His fame will grow brighter as time passes and his great work is better understood.— *U. S. Grant.*

Lincoln was a man of moderation. He was neither an autocrat nor a tyrant. If he moved slowly sometimes, it was because it was better to move slowly, and he was only waiting for his reserves to come up. Possessing almost unlimited power, he yet carried himself like one of the humblest of men. He weighed every subject. He considered and reflected upon every phase of public duty. He got the average judgment of the plain people. He had a high sense of justice, a clear understanding of the rights of others, and never heedlessly inflicted an injury upon any man. He always taught and enforced the doctrine of mercy and charity on every occasion. Even in the excess of rejoic- ing, he said to a party who came to serenade him a few nights after the Presidential election in November, 1864: " Now that the election is over, may not all having a common interest re-unite in common effort to save our country? So long as I have been here, I have not willingly planted a thorn in any man's bosom. While I am deeply sensible to the high compliment of a re-election, and duly grateful, as I trust, to Almighty God, for having directed my countrymen to a right con- clusion, as I think, for their own good, it adds nothing to my satisfac- tion that any other man may be disappointed or pained by the result." — *William McKinley*, at Albany, N. Y., Lincoln's Birthday, 1895.

The South was shocked inexpressibly by the foul assassination of Mr. Lincoln. The world has never held the South responsible for the act of the madman. Yet, horrified as they were, and stirred as were their generous sympathies at the cruel fate of their greatest antagonist, the Southern people knew not how much of hope for them, how much of love, how much of helpfulness in their hour of sorest need, lay buried in the coffin of Abraham Lincoln. As he had been the mainstay of the Union, he could have gone further than any other man in the North would have dared to do in the way of kindness and forgiveness to his foes. As he was truly great, he knew the constraining power of such magnanimity. As he was truly good, its exercise would have been to him the sweetest guerdon of his great endeavors and triumph. Yet fate decreed otherwise. The curse of his assassination was added to the calamity of defeat in the full cup of bitterness which was commended to the lips of the South during the long and humiliating years of reconstruction. Year by year she is learning to know Lincoln as he was, and not as she has pictured him. She is learning to realize that his devotion to the Union and his advocacy of emancipation were as natural to him as the contrary views entertained by her own people. She is learning, above all, to realize that, strong and true to his convictions as he was, he was struck down at the very hour when he would have proved himself her friend, and that, whether viewed as a friend or as a foe, candor must class him among the wisest, truest, simplest and greatest men that America ever produced.— *Ex-Governor George D. Wise*, of Virginia.

Lincoln was an immense personality — firm but not obstinate. Obstinacy is egotism — firmness, heroism. He influenced others without effort — unconsciously; and they submitted to him as men submit to nature — unconsciously. He was severe with himself, and for that reason lenient with others.

He appeared to apologize for being kinder than his fellows.

He did merciful things as stealthily as others committed crimes.

Almost ashamed of tenderness, he said and did the noblest words and deeds with that charming confusion, that awkwardness, that is the perfect grace of modesty.

He wore no official robes either on his body or his soul. He never pretended to be more or less, or other, or different, from what he really was.

He was neither tyrant nor slave. He neither knelt nor scorned.

With him men were neither great nor small — they were right or wrong.

Through manners, clothes, titles, rags and race he saw the real — that which is. Beyond accident, policy, compromise and war he saw the end.

He was patient as Destiny, whose undecipherable hieroglyphs were so deeply graven on his sad and tragic face.— *Robert G. Ingersoll*, at Dinner on Lincoln's Birthday.

It is the glory of Lincoln that, having almost absolute power, he never abused it, except on the side of mercy.

Wealth could not purchase, power could not awe, this divine, this loving man.   .

He knew no fear except the fear of doing wrong. Hating slavery, pitying the master — seeking to conquer, not persons, but prejudices — he was the embodiment of self-denial, the courage, the hope, and the nobility of a Nation.

He spoke not to inflame, not to upbraid, but to convince.

He raised his hands, not to strike, but in benediction.

He loved to see the pearls of joy on the cheeks of a wife whose husband he had rescued from death.

Lincoln was the grandest figure of the fiercest Civil War. He is the gentlest memory of our world.— *Robert G. Ingersoll*, at Dinner on Lincoln's Birthday.

THE MAN FOR ME.

Air, "The Rose that All are Praising."

1. Oh, he is not the man for me, Who buys or sells a slave; Nor
2. He sure is not the man for me, Whose spir - it will suc - cumb, When
3. No, no, he's not the man for me, Whose voice o'er hill and plain Breaks

he who will not set him free, But sends him to his grave. But
men en - dowed with lib - er - ty Lie bleed - ing, bound and dumb. But
forth for glo - rious lib - er - ty, But binds him - self the chain! The

he whose no - ble heart beats warm For all men's life and lib - er - ty; Who
he whose faith - ful words of might Ring through the land from shore to sea, For
might - iest of the no - ble band Who prays and toils the world to free, With

loves a - like each hu - man form— Oh, that's the man for me, . . . Oh,
man's e - ter - nal e - qual right, Oh, that's the man for me, . . . Oh,
head, and heart, and voice, and vote— Oh, that's the man for me, . . . Oh,

that's the man for me, . . Oh, that's the man for me. . . . .

O CAPTAIN! MY CAPTAIN!

*   *   *   *   *   *   *

O Captain! My Captain! Our fearful trip is done,
The ship has weathered every rack, the prize we sought is won;
The port is near, the bells I hear, the people all exulting,
While follow eyes, the steady keel, the vessel grim and daring;
     But, O heart! heart! heart!
       O the bleeding drops of red,
        Where on the deck my Captain lies
         Fallen, cold and dead.

O Captain! My Captain! rise up and hear the bells;
Rise up — for you the flag is flung — for you the bugle trills —
For you bouquets and ribboned wreaths — for you the shores a-crowding;
For you they call, the swaying mass, their eager faces turning;
       Here, Captain! dear father!
        This arm beneath your head!
        It is some dream that, on the deck,
         You've fallen cold and dead!

My Captain does not answer, his lips are pale and still;
My father does not feel my arm, he has no pulse nor will;
The ship is anchored safe and sound, its voyage closed and done;
From fearful trip, the victor ship comes in, with object won;
       Exult, O shores! and ring, O bells!
        But I, with mournful tread,
        Walk the deck my Captain lies
         Fallen, cold, and dead.

                — *Walt Whitman.*

This man whose homely face you look upon,
    Was one of Nature's masterful, great men;
Born with strong arms that unfought victories won,
    Direct of speech and cunning with the pen,
Chosen for large designs, he had the art
    Of winning with his humor, and he went
Straight to his mark, which was the human heart;
    Wise, too, for what he could not break, he bent.
Upon his back, a more than Atlas' load,
    The burden of the Commonwealth was laid:
He stooped, and rose up with it, though the road
    Shot suddenly downwards, not a whit dismayed.
Hold, warriors, councilors, kings! All now give place
    To this dead Benefactor of the Race!

                — *Richard Henry Stoddard.*

Here was a type of the true elder race,
One of Plutarch's men talked with us face to face;
I praise him not; it were too late;
And some innative weakness there must be
In him who condescends to victory
Such as the present gives, and cannot wait,
Safe in himself as in a fate.

    So always, firmly, he;
      He knew to bide his time,
    And can his fame abide,
      Still patient in his simple faith sublime,
    Till the wise years decide.
      Great captains, with their guns and drums,
    Disturb our judgment for the hour,
    But at last silence comes.

These are all gone, and, standing like a tower,
    Our children shall behold his fame,
The kindly, earnest, brave, foreseeing man,
    Sagacious, patient, dreading praise, not blame,
New birth of our new soil, the first American.
                      —James Russell Lowell.

He was the North, the South, the East, the West,
    The thrall, the master, all of us in one;
There was no section that he held the best;
    His love shone as impartial as the sun;
And so, Revenge appealed to him in vain,
    He smiled at it, as at a thing forlorn,
And gently put it from him, rose and stood
      A moment's space in pain,
    Remembering the prairies and the corn
And the glad voices of the field and wood.
    And then when Peace set wing upon the wind
And, northward flying, fanned the clouds away,
    He passed as martyrs pass. Ah, who shall find
The chord to sound the pathos of that day!
    Mid-April blowing sweet across the land,
New bloom of freedom opening to the world,
    Loud paeans of the homeward-looking host,
      The salutations grand
From grimy guns, the tattered flags unfurled;
    But he must sleep, to all the glory lost!
                    —Maurice Thompson.

All days which are notable should be remembered. The world does well to mark its sense of the importance of such days, for one of the most fatal diseases of the mind is indifference, and hence everything which tends to rouse men out of their indifference is beneficial. The life of Lincoln should never be passed by in silence by young or old. He touched the log cabin and it became the palace in which greatness was nurtured. He touched the forest and it became to him a church in which the purest and noblest worship of God was observed. His occupation has become associated in our minds with the integrity of the life he lived. In Lincoln there was always some quality that fastened him to the people, and taught them to keep time to the music of his heart. Instances are given of his honesty, but there are tens of thousands of men as honest as he. The difference is that they are not able to concentrate the ideal of honor as he did. He reveals to us the beauty of plain backwoods honesty. He grew up away from the ethics of the colleges, but he acquired a sense of honesty as high and noble as the most refined of the teachers of ethics could comprehend.— *David Swing.*

Of Mr. Lincoln's general character I need not speak. He was warm-hearted; he was generous; he was magnanimous; he was most truly, as he afterwards said on a memorable occasion, " with malice toward none, with charity for all." He had a native genius far above his fellows. Every fountain of his heart was overflowing with the " milk of human kindness." From my attachment to him, so much deeper was the pang in my own breast, as well as of millions, at the horrible manner of his " taking off." This was the climax of our troubles, and the spring from which came unnumbered woes. But of those events, no more, now. Let not history confuse events. Emancipation was not the chief object of Mr. Lincoln in issuing the Proclamation. His chief object, the ideal to which his whole soul was devoted, was the preservation of the Union. Pregnant as it was with coming events, initiative as it was of ultimate emancipation, it still originated, in point of fact, more from what was deemed the necessities of war, than from any purely humanitarian view of the matter. Life is all a mist, and in the dark our fortunes meet us! This was evidently the case

with Mr. Lincoln.   He, in my opinion, was, like all the rest of us, an
instrument in the hands of that Providence above us, that " Divinity
which shapes our ends, rough-hew them how we will."— *Alexander
Hamilton Stephens*, of Georgia.

The month of February contains two great days, — days that commemorate the two most thrilling and imperial figures in our American
history.   There could not possibly be two more opposite and dissimilar
types; the one with all the advantages of high station, culture and fine
breeding, refinement and gracious surroundings; unspoiled, as gracious
as the humblest among us all.

And, then, that other; that singular and incomparable character,
of whom, when anybody tells something more about his young life, you
get a sense of how fine and high, amid all his poverty and hardship, it
was; how truly noble that other was — our own Lincoln.

What was it that made these two men great; one with inheritances
to make greatness of an external kind; the other with only the simple
ruggedness of a great character?   What but this: That each one held
himself, first of all, as a servant of the Power above him, and, sitting in
the high chair of state, sat there remembering always that he was a
servant of the people, and only that because he was the servant of
God.— *Right Rev. Henry C. Potter.*

An anecdote, showing Lincoln's merciful nature in a touching
light, and related by Mr. L. E. Chittenden in his " Recollections of
President Lincoln and His Administration," from authentic sources, is
the one of the sleeping sentinel, William Scott, the Vermont boy, whose
life Lincoln saved after he had been condemned to be shot.   Lincoln
personally saw Scott and talked with him a long time.   Scott would
not talk to his comrades of the interview afterward until one night,
when he had received a letter from home, he finally opened his heart to
a friend in this wise:

" The President was the kindest man I had ever seen.   I was scared
at first, for I had never before talked with a great man.   But Mr. Lincoln was so easy with me, so gentle, that I soon forgot my fright.
* * * He stood up, and he says to me, ' My boy, stand up here and

look me in the face.' I did as he bade me. 'My boy,' he said, 'you are not going to be shot to-morrow. I am going to trust you and send you back to your regiment. I have come up here from Washington, where I have a great deal to do, and what I want to know is how you are going to pay my bill.' There was a big lump in my throat. I could scarcely speak. But I got it crowded down and managed to say: 'There is some way to pay you, and I will find it after a little. There is the bounty in the savings bank. I guess we could borrow some money on a mortgage on the farm.' I was sure the boys would help, so I thought we could raise it, if it wasn't more than $500 or $600. 'But it is a great deal more than $500 or $600,' he said. Then I said I didn't see how, but I was sure I would find some way — if I lived. Then Mr. Lincoln put his hands on my shoulders and looked into my face as if he were sorry, and said: 'My boy, my bill is a very large one. Your friends cannot pay it, nor your bounty, nor your farm, nor all your comrades. There is only one man in all the world who can pay it, and his name is William Scott. If from this day William Scott does his duty, so that if I was there when he comes to die he can look me in the face as he does now, and can say: " I have kept my promise and I have done my duty as a soldier!" then my debt will be paid. Will you make that promise and try to keep it?' I said I would make the promise and with God's help I would keep it. He went away out of my sight forever. I know I shall never see him again, but may God forget me if I ever forget his kind words or my promise."— *Washington Star.*

Years pass away, but Freedom does not pass;
    Thrones crumble, but man's birthright crumbles not;
And, like the wind across the prairie grass
    A whole world's aspirations fan this spot
With ceaseless pantings after liberty,
    One breath of which would make even Russia fair,
    And blow sweet summer through the exile's care
And set the exile free;
    For which I pray, here, in the open air
Of Freedom's·morning-tide, by Lincoln's grave.
                                        — *Maurice Thompson.*

We all recognize two characters in the annals of American history that will ever be inseparably associated with the great War of the Rebellion, with the heroic age of the country — Abraham Lincoln and Ulysses S. Grant. One the Commander-in-Chief, the other the General-in-Chief of that immortal Union Army, baptized in blood, consecrated in tears, hallowed in prayers, an army whose memory will remain green in the hearts of a grateful people as long as manly courage is talked of or heroic deeds are honored. Both possessed in a remarkable degree that most uncommon of all virtues, common sense. With them there was no posing for effect; no indulgence in mock heroics; no mawkish sentimentality — possessions of the heart of the demagogue. Each was possessed of as brilliant an intellect as ever wore the mantle of mortality. The mind of each was one great storehouse of useful information. Neither laid any claim to knowledge he did not possess. Each seemed to feel that vaunted learning is, like hypocrisy, a form of knowledge without the power of it. Even where their characteristics were unlike, they only served to supplement each other, but added to that united power wielded for the welfare and safety of a republic. Both entered public life from the same great state; both were elected for a second time to the highest office in the gift of the people. One fell a victim to an assassin's bullet, the other to the most dreaded form of fell disease, so that both may be crowned with the sublimity of martyrdom.— *General Horace Porter*, Albany, N. Y., Lincoln's Birthday, 1895.

LINCOLN.

His towering figure, sharp and spare,
　Was with such nervous tension strung,
　As if on each strained sinew swung
The burden of a people's care.

His changing face what pen can draw?
　Pathetic, kindly, droll, or stern;
　And with a glance so quick to learn
The inmost truth of all he saw.

　　　　　　　— Charles G. Halpine.

LAUS DEO!

John Greenleaf Whittier. Arranged from Jonathan Battishill.

1. It is done! Clang of bells and roar of gun
2. Ring, O bells! Every stroke exulting tells
3. It is done! In the circuit of the sun
4. Ring and swing, Bells of joy! On morning's wing

Send the tidings up . . . . . and down;
Of the burial hour . . . . of crime;
Shall the sound there of . . . . go forth;
Send the song of praise . . . a - broad!

How the belfries rock and reel!
Loud and long that all may hear,
It shall bid the sad re - joice,
With a sound of bro - ken chains

How the great guns, peal on peal, Fling the joy from town . . to town!
Ring for every listening ear of e - ter - ni - ty . . . and time!
It shall give the dumb a voice, It shall belt with joy . . . the earth!
Tell the nations that He reigns, Who a - lone is Lord . . and God!

By special arrangement with Houghton, Mifflin & Co.

MANUAL OF PATRIOTISM.

FLAG-DAY

MAKES SACRED

JUNE 14TH.

QUOTATIONS..........................Song, *The American Flag.*

SELECTIONS................................Song, *Our Flag.*

SELECTIONS.............................Song, *Flag of the Free.*

SELECTIONS................................Song, *America.*

FLAG-DAY.

THIS day, June fourteenth, — more cheerful always in its associations than Memorial Day, even as the weather is fairer in mid-June than at the last of May, — more widespread in its significance than "the glorious Fourth," or the birthday of Washington or Lincoln, since the flag is the symbol of every great deed or event of patriotism, and not of any one man or fact alone, — is not yet generally observed as a national holiday. But the signs are many that the time will come when the jubilee of the flag will be kept with a display of waving colors — the blending of the matchless Red, White and Blue — such as will gladden the eyes of every American, young and old, and fan to a brighter flame the fire of patriotism in every heart. In this deepening and extending honor to the flag it is natural and possible for children to take the lead. And wherever and whenever they lead the way, the rest of us will fall into line. When the G. A. R. held its annual reunion in Buffalo a few years ago, there was no sight "half so fine," so "never-to-be-forgotten" as the "Living Shield" of red, white and blue, composed of school children, several thousand in number, suitably arranged. When Syracuse kept the semi-centennial of its life as a city there was nothing that so drew and held the gaze of the thronging crowds as the sight of four hundred high-school girls arranged in the semblance and colors of a "Living Flag" — the boys meanwhile making the streets alive with color, as they marched in procession with waving banners. But of course it is not always possible, never necessary, to use such elaborate means in celebrating. At slight expense, let each boy and girl in a school be provided with a flag, and there is nothing rhythmic in speech or song for which they cannot easily supply an accompaniment of waving flags; no march whose movement they cannot "time" with moving banners. And out of each Flag-day exercise, whether annual or oftener, there should come a better appreciation of the worth of the flag and the meaning of true patriotism. Moreover, the exercises may be greatly varied by the use of any number among the forty programs which this book contains — for all the forty subjects, like a chorus of voices, "Rally 'Round the Flag."

QUOTATIONS.

Our glory's path by stars it shows,
And crimson stripes for Freedom's foes.

— Henry P. Beck.

God bless each precious fold,
Made sacred by the patriot hands that now are still and cold.

— Jennie Gould.

Let all the ends thou aim'st at be thy Country's,
Thy God's and Truth's.

— William Shakespeare.

One flag, one land, one heart, one hand,
One nation, evermore.

— Oliver Wendell Holmes.

Bear that banner proudly up, young warriors of the land,
With hearts of love, and arms of faith and more than iron hand.

—Thomas Williams.

Waves from sea to mountain crag,
Freedom's starry Union flag.

— Frederic Dennison.

Let it float undimmed above,
Till over all our vales shall bloom
The sacred colors that we love.

— Phoebe Cary.

THE AMERICAN FLAG.

JOSEPH RODMAN DRAKE.   JOHN W. TUFTS.

IN UNISON OR IN PARTS.

1. When Freedom from her mountain height Unfurled her standard to the air, She tore the az - ure
2. Flag of the free heart's hope and home, By an - gel hands to val - or given, Thy stars have lit the

3. Forever float that standard sheet! Where breathes the foe but falls before us, With Freedom's soil be -

robe of night, And set the stars of glo - ry there— And set the stars of glo - ry there—
wel - kin dome, And all thy hues were born in heaven— And all thy hues were born in heaven.

neath our feet, And Freedom's banner streaming o'er us—And Freedom's banner streaming o'er us.

SELECTIONS.

It was no holiday flag, emblazoned for gayety, or for vanity. It was a solemn national signal. When that banner first unrolled to the sun, it was the symbol of all those holy truths and purposes which brought together the Colonial American Congress! Our flag means, then, all that our fathers meant in the Revolutionary War; it means all that the Declaration of Independence meant; it means all that the Constitution of our people, organizing for justice, for liberty, and for happiness, meant. Our flag carries American ideas, American history, and American feelings. Beginning with the colonies, and coming down to our time, in its sacred heraldry, in its glorious insignia, it has gathered and stored chiefly this supreme idea — *divine right of liberty in man.* Every color means liberty; every thread means liberty; every form of star and beam or stripe of light means liberty; not lawlessness, not license; but organized institutional liberty, — liberty through law, and laws for liberty.— *Henry Ward Beecher.*

Behold it! Listen to it! Every star has a tongue; every stripe is articulate. "There is no language or speech where their voices are not heard." There is magic in the web of it. It has an answer for every question of duty. It has a solution for every doubt and perplexity. It has a word of good cheer for every hour of gloom or of despondency. Behold it! Listen to it! It speaks of earlier and of later struggles. It speaks of victories, and sometimes of reverses, on the sea and on the land. It speaks of patriots and heroes among the living and the dead. But before all and above all other associations and memories, whether of glorious men, or glorious deeds, or glorious places, its voice is ever of Union and Liberty, of the Constitution and the Laws.— *Robert C. Winthrop.*

All hail to our glorious ensign! Courage to the heart, and strength to the hand to which, in all time, it shall be entrusted! May it ever wave in honor, in unsullied glory, and patriotic hope, on the dome of the capitol, on the dome of the country's stronghold, on the tented plain,

20

on the wave-rocked topmast.   Wherever, on the earth's surface, the
eye of the American shall behold it, may he have reason to bless it!   On
whatsoever spot it is planted, there may freedom have a foothold,
humanity a brave champion, and religion an altar.   Though stained
with blood in a righteous cause, may it never, in any cause, be stained
with shame.   Alike, when its gorgeous folds shall wanton in lazy holiday
triumphs on the summer breeze, and its tattered fragments be dimly
seen through the clouds of war, may it be the joy and the pride of the
American heart.   First raised in the cause of right and liberty, in that
cause alone. may it forever spread its streaming blazonry to the battle
and the storm.   Having been borne victoriously across the continent,
and on every sea, may virtue, and freedom, and peace forever follow
where it leads the way.— *Edward Everett.*

For myself, in our Federal relations, I know but one section, one
union, one flag, one government.   That section embraces every state;
that union is the union sealed with blood and consecrated by the tears
of the Revolutionary struggle; that flag is the flag known and honored
on every sea under heaven; which has borne off glorious victory from
many a bloody battlefield, and yet stirs with warmer and quicker pulsa-
tions the heart's blood of every true American when he looks upon
the stars and stripes.   I will sustain that flag wherever it waves — over
the sea or over the land.   And when it shall be despoiled and disfigured, I will rally around it still, as the star-spangled banner of my
fathers and my country; and, so long as a single stripe can be discovered,
or a single star shall glimmer from the surrounding darkness, I will
cheer it as the emblem of a nation's glory and a nation's hope.— *Daniel
S. Dickinson.*

There is the national flag!   He must be cold, indeed, who can
look upon its folds, rippling in the breeze, without pride of country.
If he be in a foreign land, the flag is companionship, and country itself,
with all its endearments.   Who, as he sees it, can think of a state
merely?   Whose eye, once fastened on its radiant trophies, can fail to
recognize the image of the whole nation?   It has been called a "float-
ing piece of poetry;" and yet I know not if it has any intrinsic beauty

beyond other ensigns.   Its highest beauty is in what it symbolizes.   It is because it represents all, that all gaze at it with delight and reverence. It is a piece of bunting lifted in the air; but it speaks sublimely, and every part has a voice.   Its stripes, of alternate red and white, proclaim the original union of thirteen States to maintain the Declaration of Independence.   Its stars, white on a field of blue, proclaim that union of States, constituting our national constellation, which receives a new star with every new State.   The two, together, signify union, past and present.   The very colors have a language, which was officially recognized by our fathers.   White is for purity, red for valor, blue for justice; and all together,— bunting, stripes, stars, and colors blazing in the sky,— make the flag of our country, to be cherished by all of our hearts, to be upheld by all our hands.— *Charles Sumner.*

I have recently returned from an extended tour of the States, and nothing so impressed and so refreshed me as the universal display of this banner of beauty and glory.   It waved over the schoolhouses; it was in the hands of the school children.   As we speeded across the sandy wastes, at some solitary place a man, a woman, a child would come to the door and wave it in loyal greeting.   Two years ago, I saw a sight that has ever been present in my memory.   As we were going out of the harbor of Newport, about midnight on a dark night, some of the officers of the torpedo station had prepared for us a beautiful surprise.   The flag at the depot station was unseen in the darkness of the night, when suddenly electric searchlights were turned on it, bathing it in a flood of light.   All below the flag was hidden, and it seemed to have no touch with earth, but to hang from the battlements of heaven.   It was as if heaven was approving the human liberty and human equality typified by that flag.— *Benjamin Harrison.*

It is on such an occasion as this that we can reason together — reaffirm our devotion to the country and the principles of the Declaration of Independence.   Let us make up our mind that when we do put a new star upon our banner it shall be a fixed one, never to be dimmed by the horrors of war, but brightened by the contentment and prosperity of peace.   Let us go on to extend the area of our usefulness, add star upon star, until their light shall shine upon five hundred millions of a free and happy people.— *Abraham Lincoln*, on raising a new flag over Independence Hall, Philadelphia, February 22, 1861.

THE STRIPES AND THE STARS.

O Star Spangled Banner! The flag of our pride!
Though trampled by traitors and basely defied,
Fling out to the glad winds your red, white and blue,
For the heart of the Northland is beating for you!
And her strong arm is nerving to strike with a will,
Till the foe and his boastings are humbled and still!
Here's welcome to wounding and combat and scars
And the glory of death, for the Stripes and the Stars!

From prairie, O ploughman! speed boldly away,
There's seed to be sown in God's furrows to-day!
Row landward, lone fisher! stout woodman, come home!
Let smith leave his anvil, and weaver his loom,
And hamlet and city ring loud with the cry:
"For God and our country we'll fight till we die!
Here's welcome to wounding and combat and scars
And the glory of death, for the Stripes and the Stars!"

Invincible banner! the flag of the free,
Oh, where treads the foot that would falter for thee?
Or the hands to be folded till triumph is won
And the eagle looks proud, as of old, to the sun?
Give tears for the parting, a murmur of prayer,
Then forward! the fame of our standard to share!
With welcome to wounding and combat and scars
And the glory of death, for the Stripes and the Stars!

O God of our fathers! this banner must shine
Where battle is hottest, in warfare divine!
The cannon has thundered, the bugle has blown,
We fear not the summons, we fight not alone!
O lead us, till wide from the gulf to the sea
The land shall be sacred to freedom and Thee!
With love for oppression; with blessing for scars,
One Country, one Banner, the Stripes and the Stars!

— *Edna Dean Proctor.*

In the ceremonies at Philadelphia, I was, for the first time, allowed the privilege of standing in old Independence Hall. * * * My friends there had provided a magnificent flag of the country. They had arranged it so that I was given the honor of raising it to the head of its staff. And when it went up, I was pleased that it went up to its place by the strength of my own feeble arm. When, according to the arrangement, the cord was pulled, and it floated gloriously to the wind without an accident, in the light, glowing sunshine of the morning, I could not help hoping that there was in the entire success of that beautiful ceremony at least something of an omen of what is to come. How could I help feeling then, as I often have felt, in the whole of that proceeding I was a very humble instrument?

I had not provided the flag; I had not made the arrangements for elevating it to its place. I had applied but a very small portion of my feeble strength in raising it. In the whole transaction, I was in the hands of the people who had arranged it. And, if I can have the same generous co-operation of the people of the nation, I think the flag of our country may still be kept flaunting gloriously.— *Abraham Lincoln*, Address to the Legislature, Harrisburg, February 22, 1861.

OUR COUNTRY AND FLAG.

Hail, brightest banner that floats on the gale!
Flag of the country of Washington, hail!
Red are thy stripes with the blood of the brave;
Bright are thy stars as the sun on the wave;
Wrapt in thy folds are the hopes of the free.
Banner of Washington! blessings on thee!

*   *   *   *   *   *

Traitors shall perish, and treason shall fail:
Kingdoms and thrones in thy glory grow pale!
Thou shalt live on, and thy people shall own
Loyalty's sweet, when each heart is thy throne:
Union and Freedom thine heritage be.
Country of Washington! blessings on thee!

—William E. Robinson.

OUR FLAG IS THERE!

Our flag is there, our flag is there,
  We'll hail it with three loud huzzas.
Our flag is there, our flag is there,
  Behold the glorious Stripes and Stars.
Stout hearts have fought for that bright flag,
  Strong hands sustained it mast-head high,
And, oh, to see how proud it waves,
  Brings tears of joy in every eye.

That flag has stood the battle's roar,
  With foemen stout, with foemen brave;
Strong hands have sought that flag to lower,
  And found a speedy watery grave.
That flag is known on every shore,
  The standard of a gallant band:
Alike unstained in peace or war,
  It floats o'er Freedom's happy land.

             —American Naval Officer, 1812.

OUR FLAG.

WM. A. MONTGOMERY.

HAMLIN E. COGSWELL.

With animation.

SOLO OR DUET.

1. Oh, flag of a res - o - lute na - tion, Oh, flag of the strong and free, The cher - ished of true - heart - ed mil - lions, We hal - low thy col - ors three; Three proud, float-ing em - blems of

2. Thy red is the deep crim-son life - stream, Which flowed on the bat - tle - plain, Re - deem - ing our land from op - pres - sion, And leav - ing no ser - vile stain. Thy white is a proud peo-ple's

3. Thy blue is the na - tion's en - dur - ance, And points to the blue a - bove; The lim - it - less, meas - ure - less az - ure, A type of our Fa - ther's love. Thy stars are God's wit - ness of

OUR FLAG.

glo - ry, Our guide for the com - ing time; The
hon - or, Kept spot - less and clear as light; A
bless - ing, And smile at the foe - man's frown; They

red, white and blue, in their beau - ty, Love gives them a mean-ing sub - lime.
pledge of un - fal - ter - ing jus - tice, A sym - bol of truth and right.
spar - kle and gleam in their splen - dor, Bright gems in the great world's crown.

CHORUS.

Oh, flag of a res - o - lute na - tion, Oh, flag of the strong and the free;

The cher - ished of true heart - ed mil - lions, We hal - low thy col - ors three.

THE FLAG.

Let it idly droop, or sway
  To the wind's light will:
Furl its stars, or float in day,
  Flutter, or be still!
It has held its colors bright,
  Through the war-smoke dun:
Spotless emblem of the right,
  Whence success was won.

*   *   *   *

In the gathering hosts of hope,
  In the march of man,
Open for it place and scope,
  Bid it lead the van.
Till beneath the searching skies
  Martyr-blood be found,
Purer than our sacrifice,
  Crying from the ground.

Till a flag with some new light
  Out of Freedom's sky,
Kindles through the gulfs of night
  Holier blazonry.
Let it glow, the darkness drown!
  Give our banner sway,
Till its joyful stars go down
  In undreamed-of Day!

— *Lucy Larcom.*

COLUMBIA, THE GEM OF THE OCEAN.

O Columbia, the gem of the ocean,
  The home of the brave and the free,
The shrine of each patriot's devotion,
  A world offers homage to thee.
Thy mandates make heroes assemble,
  When Liberty's form stands in view;
Thy banners make tyranny tremble,
  When borne by the Red, White and Blue.

CHORUS: When borne by the Red, White, and Blue,
When borne by the Red, White, and Blue,
  Thy banners make tyranny tremble
When borne by the Red, White, and Blue.

MANUAL OF PATRIOTISM.

When war winged its wide desolation,
  And threatened the land to deform,
The ark then of Freedom's foundation,
  Columbia, rode safe through the storm,
With the garlands of victory around her,
  When so proudly she bore her brave crew,
With her flag proudly floating before her,
  The boast of the Red, White, and Blue.

— David T. Shaw.

O'er the high and o'er the lowly
Floats that banner bright and holy,
  In the rays of Freedom's sun,
In the nation's heart imbedded,
O'er our Union newly wedded,
  One in all, and all in one.

Let that banner wave forever,
May its lustrous stars fade never,
  Till the stars shall pale on high:
While there's right the wrong defeating,
While there's hope in true hearts beating,
  Truth and freedom shall not die.

As it floated long before us,
Be it ever floating o'er us,
  O'er our land from shore to shore:
There are freemen yet to wave it,
Millions who would die to save it,
  Wave it, save it, evermore!

— Dexter Smith.

All nature sings wildly the song of the free,
The Red, White, and Blue float o'er land and o'er sea:
The White, in each billow that breaks on the shore,
The Blue, in the arching that canopies o'er
The land of our birth in its glory outspread,
And sunset dyes deepen and glow into red:
Day fades into night and the red stripe retires,
But stars o'er the blue light their sentinel fires;
And though night be gloomy, with clouds overspread,
Each star holds its place in the field overhead.
When scatter the clouds and the tempest is through,
We count every star in the field of the blue.

— Anonymous.

It is the flag of history. Those thirteen stripes tell the story of our colonial struggle, of the days of '76. They speak of the savage wilderness, of old Independence Hall, of Valley Forge, and Yorktown. Those stars tell the story of our nation's growth, how it has come from weakness to strength, until its gleam, in the sunrise over the forests of Maine, crimsons the sunset's dying beams on the golden sands of California.— *S. L. Waterbury.*

The stars of our morn on our banner borne,
  With the iris of Heaven are blended,
The hands of our sires first mingled those fires,
  By us they shall be defended!
Then hail the true, the Red, White, and Blue,
  The flag of the " Constellation:"
It sails as it sailed, by our forefathers hailed,
  O'er battles that made us a nation.

    *   *   *   *   *   *

Peace, peace to the world, is our motto unfurled,
  Tho' we shun not a field that is gory:
At home or abroad, fearing none but our God;
  We will carve out our pathway to glory!
                              — *Thomas Buchanan Read.*

In radiance heavenly fair,
  Floats on the peaceful air
That flag that never stooped from victory's pride:
  Those stars that softly gleam,
  Those stripes that o'er us stream,
In war's grand agony were sanctified:
  A holy standard, pure and free
To light the home of peace, or blaze in victory.
                              —*F. Marion Crawford.*

Washed in the blood of the brave and the blooming,
  Snatched from the altars of insolent foes,
Burning with star fires, but never consuming,
  Flash its broad ribbons of lily and rose.

    *   *   *   *   *

God bless the flag and its loyal defenders,
  While its broad folds over the battle-field wave,
Till the dim star-wreath rekindle its splendors,
  Washed from its stains in the blood of the brave!
                              —*Oliver Wendell Holmes.*

THE AMERICAN FLAG.

When Freedom, from her mountain height,
  Unfurled her standard to the air,
She tore the azure robe of Night,
  And set the stars of glory there.
She mingled with its gorgeous dyes
The milky baldric of the skies,
And striped its pure, celestial white,
With streakings of the morning light:
Then, from his mansion in the sun,
She called her eagle bearer down,
And gave into his mighty hand
The symbol of her chosen land.

*　　*　　*　　*　　*　　*　　*

Flag of the free heart's hope and home!
  By angel hands to valor given!
Thy stars have lit the welkin dome,
  And all thy hues were born in Heaven.
Forever float that standard sheet!
  Where breathes the foe but falls before us,
With Freedom's soil beneath our feet,
  And Freedom's banner streaming o'er us?
                              — *J. Rodman Drake.*

Thou lofty ensign of the free,
  May every land thy glory know,
And every freeman cling to thee,
  While breezes 'mid thy folds shall flow.
May hand, and heart, and hopes, and zeal,
  Be ever by thy form inspired,
And, should it shake the commonweal,
  May every soul by thee be fired,
Each patriot heart discern amid thy form,
A beacon star in the battle storm.
                              — *I. C. Pray, Jr.*

FLAG OF THE FREE.

From "Lohengrin."

Steady time.

1. Flag of the free, fair - est to see! Borne thro' the strife and the
2. Flag of the brave! long may it wave, Cho - sen of God while His

thun - der of war; Ban - ner so bright with star - ry light,
might we a - dore; In lib - er - ty's van for man - hood of man,

D.S. *While thro' the sky loud rings the cry,*

Fine.

Float ev - er proud - ly from moun - tain to shore. Em - blem of free - dom,
Sym - bol of right thro' the years pass - ing o'er! Pride of our coun - try,

Un - ion and lib - er - ty! One ev - er - more!

D.S.

hope to the slave, Spread thy fair folds but to shield and to save,
hon - or'd a - far, Scat - ter each cloud that would dark - en a star,

From Levermore's "Academy Song Book." Published by Ginn & Co. By permission.

Every nation has its flag. Every ship in foreign waters is known by the colors she shows at her peak. When we were colonies of England, we sailed and fought under her flag. We finally rebelled; it was nothing less; and to England our George Washington was merely a leading rebel. We were thirteen little States, fringed along on the Atlantic coast, with the unbroken forest behind us, and among the great family of nations we had neither place nor name. We had to fight to obtain due respect from all the great old nations who were looking on. Of course, we had no flag; we had to earn that too. Our army at Cambridge celebrated New Year's Day, January 1, 1776, by unfurling for the first time in an American camp the flag of thirteen stripes. On the 14th of June, 1776, Congress, which met then in Philadelphia, settled upon our style of flag. " It shall have," said they, " thirteen stripes, alternate red and white; and the union of the States shall be indicated by thirteen stars, white, in a blue field, representing a new constellation." They followed up the adoption of a flag by a Declaration of Independence; and then we went to fighting harder than ever, and France acknowledged our independence, and helped us to make England acknowledge it. Afterward it was decided to add another star for every new State as it joined the Union. So that the constellation, as it is now, with forty-five stars in it, has grown a good deal from the original thirteen. But the stripes still remain the same in number, to remind us of the first little band of States " who fought it out " against Great Britain.— *Kate Foote.*

Stream, Old Glory, bear your stars
 High among the seven;
Stream a watchfire on the dark,
 And make a sign in Heaven!
Out upon the four winds blow,
 Tell the world your story:
Thrice in heart's blood dipped before
 They called your name Old Glory!

When from sky to sky you float,
 Far in wide savannas,
Vast horizons lost in light
 Answer with hosannas.

Symbol of unmeasured power,
  Blessed promise sealing,
All your hills are hills of God,
  And all your founts are healing.

Still to those, the wronged of earth,
  Sanctuary render:
For hope, and home, and Heaven they see
  Within your sacred splendor!
Stream, Old Glory, bear your stars
  High among the seven:
Stream a watchfire on the dark,
  And make a sign in Heaven!

              — Harriet Prescott Spofford.

THE STAR SPANGLED BANNER.

Oh, say, can you see by the dawn's early light
  What so proudly we hailed at the twilight's last gleaming,
Whose broad stripes and bright stars, through the perilous fight,
  O'er the ramparts we watched were so gallantly streaming?
And the rocket's red glare, the bombs bursting in air,
Gave proof through the night that our flag was still there:
Oh, say, does that star-spangled banner yet wave
O'er the land of the free, and the home of the brave?

On that shore, dimly seen through the mists of the deep,
  Where the foe's haughty host in dread silence reposes,
What is that which the breeze, o'er the towering steep,
  As it fitfully blows, now conceals, now discloses?
Now it catches the gleam of the morning's first beam,
In full glory reflected, now shines on the stream:
'Tis the star-spangled banner — Oh, long may it wave
O'er the land of the free and the home of the brave!

   *   *   *   *   *   *   *

Oh, thus be it ever, when freemen shall stand
  Between their loved homes and the war's desolation!
Blest with victory and peace, may the heaven-rescued land
  Praise the Power that hath made and preserved us a nation.
Then conquer we must, when our cause it is just;
And this be our motto: " In God is our trust; "
And the star-spangled banner in triumph shall wave
O'er the land of the free, and the home of the brave!

                  — Francis Scott Key.

SALUTE THE FLAG.

Off with your hat as the flag goes by!
  And let the heart have its say:
You're man enough for a tear in your eye
  That you will not wipe away.

You're man enough for a thrill that goes
  To your very finger tips —
Ay! the lump just then in your throat that rose,
  Spoke more than your parted lips.

Lift up your boy on your shoulder high,
  And show him the faded shred;
Those stripes would be red as the sunset sky
  If death could have dyed them red.

Off with your hat as the flag goes by!
  Uncover the youngster's head;
Teach him to hold it holy and high
  For the sake of its sacred dead.
                              —*H. C. Bunner.*

OLD FLAG FOREVER.

She's up there,— Old Glory,— where lightnings are sped;
She dazzles the nations with ripples of red;
And she'll wave for us living, or droop o'er us dead,—
  The flag of our country forever!
She's up there,— Old Glory,— how bright the stars stream!
And the stripes, like red signals of liberty, gleam!
And we dare for her, living, or dream the last dream,
  'Neath the flag of our country forever!
She's up there,— Old Glory,— no tyrant-dealt scars,
No blur on her brightness, no stain on her stars!
The brave blood of heroes hath crimsoned her bars.
  She's the flag of our country forever.
                              —*Frank L. Stanton.*

THE BANNER OF THE STARS.

We'll never have a new flag, for ours is the true flag,
The true flag, the true flag, the Red, White, and Blue flag.
Hurrah! boys, hurrah! we will carry to the wars
The old flag, the free flag, the Banner of the stars!
And what tho' its white shall be crimsoned with our blood?
  And what tho' its stripes shall be shredded in the storms?
To the torn flag, the worn flag, we'll keep our promise good,
  And we'll bear the starry blue flag with gallant hearts and arms.
21   —*R. W. Raymond.*

The flag of a nation is the sign of its sovereignty. The American flag is but the historic parallel of older nations, and yet it stands alone in this — that from the day it was first unfurled in the breeze it has stood for manly independence and a people's government. It has never been sullied by ignoble conquests, and it has been glorified by the proudest possible service in the cause of human freedom.

And it is a curious fact that it is the oldest flag among the great nations of the world in its characteristic present form. Most of the older nations have modified the design of their flags within a hundred years, while ours remains unchanged.

What splendid memories cluster about this beautiful flag! What heroic deeds have made immortal the gallant volunteer heroes who have defended it through all its perils and triumphs of over 120 years, as it has floated in the van of the march of American progress and civilization on this continent!— *Albert D. Shaw*, Commander-in-Chief (1899–1900) G. A. R.

The history of our country is grandly illustrated in our Stars and Stripes. New stars have been added to its field of blue as new States have been admitted into our Union. It had its origin in the era of Washington, when our republic was established, and it had its greatest trial in the epoch of Lincoln, when the mightiest civil war of the world tested its power and vindicated its supreme control and command over the discordant elements arrayed in deadly and brave attempt to destroy it. To-day this flag stands for no one party or section, but floats over the whole country, one and undivided, without sectional hates, united in the bonds of universal liberty and in the sentiments of an inspiring American civilization. It is the proud sign of peace among ourselves and with all the world.— *Albert D. Shaw.*

Our beautiful flag is surrounded by touching memories and associations. Its bright stripes and fair stars are perishable, but the sentiments it teaches, like the spirit of liberty, can never die. " These shall resist the Empire of decay, when time is o'er and worlds have passed away." Let it be treasured as one of the greatest inspiring factors in the blessed work of science and art here devoted to the uplifting of the youth of our land along the plane of peace and happiness, and may it inspire coming generations to

Stand by the flag! Its folds have streamed in glory,
To foes a fear, to friends a festal robe;
And spread in rhythmic lines the sacred story,
Of Freedom's triumphs over all the globe.

Stand by the flag! On land and ocean billow,
By it our fathers stood, unmoved and true;
Living, defended; dying, for their pillow,
With their last blessing, passed it on to you.

Stand by the flag! All doubt and treason scorning,
Believe, with courage firm and faith sublime,
That it will float until the eternal morning
Pales in its glories all the lights of time.

— Extract from address presenting flag to the Brooklyn Institute of Arts and Sciences, from *Albert D. Shaw.*

HATS OFF!

Hats off!
Along the street there comes
A blare of bugles, a ruffle of drums,
  A flash of color beneath the sky:
Hats off!
  The flag is passing by!

Blue and crimson and white it shines,
Over the steel-tipped, ordered lines.
Hats off!
The colors before us fly;
But more than the flag is passing by.

Sea-fights and land-fights, grim and great,
Fought to make and to save the State;
Weary marches and sinking ships;
Cheers of victory on dying lips;

Days of plenty and years of peace,
March of a strong land's swift increase:
Equal justice, right and law,
Stately honor and reverent awe;

Sign of a nation, great and strong
To ward her people from foreign wrong;
Pride and glory and honor, all
Live in the colors to stand or fall.

Hats off!
Along the street there comes
A blare of bugles, a ruffle of drums;
  And loyal hearts are beating high:
Hats off!
  The flag is passing by!

               —H. H. Bennett.

MONTEREY.

We were not many, we who stood
 Before the iron sleet that day;
Yet many a gallant spirit would
Give half his years if but he could
  Have been with us at Monterey.

Now here, now there, the shot it hailed
 In deadly drifts of fiery spray,
Yet not a single soldier quailed
When wounded comrades round them wailed
  Their dying shout at Monterey.

And on, still on our column kept
  Through walls of flame its withering way;
Where fell the dead, the living stept,
Still charging on the guns which swept
  The slippery streets of Monterey.

The foe himself recoiled aghast,
  When, striking where he strongest lay,
We swooped his flanking batteries past,
And braving full their murderous blast,
  Stormed home the towers of Monterey.

Our banners on those turrets wave,
  And there our evening bugles play;
Where orange-boughs above their grave,
Keep green the memory of the brave
  Who fought and fell at Monterey.

We are not many, we who pressed
  Beside the brave who fell that day;
But who of us has not confessed
He'd rather share their warrior rest
  Than not have been at Monterey?
            — *Charles Fenno Hoffman.*

THE TWO FLAGS.

On leaving England a few years ago Miss Willard saw from the hansom in which she was riding along Piccadilly the London omnibus, with its English flag at the front, whereupon there came into her mind the words: " With its red for love, and its white for law, and its blue for the hope that our fathers saw of a larger liberty." This was penciled at the moment, and on the train en route for Southampton to take the steamship for New York, Miss Willard wrote the accompanying lines, leaving them as a goodbye tribute in the hand of her friend, Lady Henry Somerset:

The eyes that follow thee, old flag, are fond,
  A Western heart leaps up thy folds to greet,
A Saxon's eyes confess the sacred bond
  As England's standard flutters down the street,
With its red for love, and its white for law,
  And its blue for the hope that our fathers saw
    Of a larger liberty.

Thou art the mother flag of destiny,
  Our banner of the spangled stars is trine;
Cromwell was sire of Washington and we
  Claim the same cross that blazons thy ensign,
With its red for love, and its white for law,
  And its blue for the hope that our fathers saw
    Of a larger liberty.

O, holy flags, bright with one household glow,
  Together light the highway of our God
Till the dear cross of Christ to men shall show
  That stripes and stars both mark the path he trod,
With their red for love, and their white for law,
  And their blue for the hope that our fathers saw
    Of a larger liberty.

The long march of the nations shall be led
  By these two flags — till war and tumult cease
Along the happy highway where shall tread
  The brotherhood of labor and of peace,
With their red for love, and their white for law,
  And their blue for the hope that our fathers saw
    Of a larger liberty.

— Miss Frances E. Willard.

Wherever civilization dwells, or the name of Washington is known, it bears on its folds the concentrated power of armies and navies, and surrounds the votaries with a defense more impregnable than a battlement of wall or tower. Wherever on earth's surface an American citizen may wander, called by pleasure, business, or caprice, it is a shield, securing him against wrong and outrage.— *Galusha A. Grow.*

MY COUNTRY, 'TIS OF THEE.

SAMUEL FRANCIS SMITH.

Unknown.
Air, "God Save the King."

Moderato.

1. My coun - try, 'tis of thee, Sweet land of lib - er - ty,
2. My na - tive coun - try, thee— Land of the no - ble free—
3. Let mu - sic swell the breeze, And ring from all the trees
4. Our fa - thers' God, to Thee, Au - thor of lib - er - ty,

Of thee I sing; Land where my fa - thers died, Land of the
Thy name I love; I love thy rocks and rills, Thy woods and
Sweet free - dom's song; Let mor - tal tongues a - wake; Let all that
To Thee we sing; Long may our land be bright With free - dom's

Pil - grim's pride; From ev - 'ry moun - tain side, Let free - dom ring.
tem - pled hills; My heart with rap - ture thrills, Like that a - bove.
breathe par - take; Let rocks their si - lence break— The sound pro - long.
ho - ly light; Pro - tect us by Thy might, Great God, our King.

F. N. GILSON COMPANY, MUSIC TYPOGRAPHERS, BOSTON, U. S. A.

MANUAL OF PATRIOTISM.

SELECTIONS

IN

PROSE AND POETRY

ON

PATRIOTISM.

DECLARATION OF INDEPENDENCE.

CONSTITUTION OF THE UNITED STATES.

LIBERTY.

UNION.

CITIZENSHIP.

THE NOBILITY OF LABOR.

(329)

PATRIOTISM.

NO efforts to cultivate the spirit of loyalty and patriotism can, we believe, be more beneficial in their influence or lasting in their results than those which are directed towards the rising generation which is preparing for the duties of citizenship. Whatever can be done to create in the minds of the young an enthusiastic devotion to their country will contribute much to the well-being of the republic. We believe that the cultivation of this spirit should form a necessary part of every system of education. But it seems especially fitting that efforts of this kind should be made in connection with that part of our educational system which is supported by the public. Our public schools are an essential part of the American system. In them are being trained the reserve forces of our country; and they afford the best field, not only for diffusing an intelligent knowledge of our institutions, but also for cultivating that deep, patriotic impulse without which no nation can long exist.— *From Report of Committee, New York Department, G. A. R., on "The Teachings of Civics and History."— Prof. W. C. Morey, Chairman.*

The one who would appreciate the greatness and true significance of American civilization must understand the sources of its development, the conditions of its growth, and the process of its evolution. He must imbibe the spirit of liberty, which in great measure prompted the colonization of this land. He must study the foundations of our local governments as they were laid by the early colonists, and follow these pioneers of the new world through the vicissitudes of their industrial, religious and political life. He must understand the nature of those constitutional rights to which they tenaciously clung and from which arose the majestic fabric of our free institutions. He must be translated to the days of 1776 and comprehend the great questions involved in the War of Independence.   He must enter into the struggles which attended the formation of the Constitution.   He must understand the terrific issues which culminated in the Civil War, and the political principles which by that war became established.   He must, in fine, see in the successive stages of our history the progressive growth of a great republic, stretching from ocean to ocean, which is at once democratic, representative and federative, " an indissoluble Union of indestructible States."   To eliminate emotion from the study of our country's history would be as difficult as to repress the feeling of awe when contemplating the grandeur of its natural scenery.   There are elements of greatness and sublimity in the expanding life of our nation which cannot fail to touch the soul of any sympathetic student. — *Report, G. A. R.,* as above.

The kind of patriotism which we, as survivors of the Civil War, would seek to promote and foster in the young is not a spirit born of discord and strife, but a sentiment inspired by the love of our common country, and a desire that all its citizens may be bound together by the possession of common rights and the recognition of common duties.   It was for the preservation of the Union and the integrity of American institutions that we once fought, and it is for the same objects that we would still continue to labor.   We are proud of the records of the war for the Union, but we are more proud of the Union which that war made perpetual.   Not in the humiliation of the men who were defeated, but in the vindication of the principles which were triumphant, do we most sincerely rejoice.   " With malice towards none, but with charity for all," we would maintain the unity and the honor of our great republic, the supremacy of its laws, and the spirit of absolute loyalty which must everywhere form an element of the truest citizenship.   With all due respect for the bonds of local interest and the obligation of party ties, we believe in a patriotism which is not confined to any section or to any party, but which is as broad as the boundaries of our great nation, and which comprehends in its scope the highest welfare of the whole American people.— *Report, G. A. R.,* as above.

The power that guided our fathers across the water and planted their feet on Plymouth Rock; the power that gave victory against the mother country, and assured our independence; the power that kept our Union from being torn asunder in civil strife, and freed the slave, and made us in fact, as in name, a nation; the power that gave us Manila Bay and Santiago Harbor, and the fertile island of Porto Rico, with loss of life so small that the story seems like the record of a miracle in the far Judean age: that selfsame power will keep and guide our flag in its goings across the Pacific seas, if we go, not for conquest, but for humanity, for civilization, and for liberty.— *Stewart L. Woodford*, Speech at New England Dinner, in New York.

We cannot honor our country with too deep a reverence; we cannot love her with an affection too pure and fervent; we cannot serve her with an energy of purpose or a faithfulness of zeal too steadfast and ardent. And what is our country? It is not the East, with her hills and her valleys, with her countless sails, and the rocky ramparts of her shore. It is not the North, with her thousand villages, and her harvest-home, with her frontiers of the lake and the ocean. It is not the West, with her forest-sea and her inland isles, with her luxuriant expanses, clothed in the verdant corn, with her beautiful Ohio, and her majestic Missouri. Nor is it yet the South, opulent in the mimic snow of the cotton, in the rich plantations of the rustling cane, and in the golden robes of the rice-field. What are these but the sister families of one greater, better, holier family, our country? Be assured that we cannot, as patriot scholars, think too highly of that country, or sacrifice too much for her.— *Thomas S. Grimke.*

With malice toward none, with charity for all, with firmness in the right, as God gives us to see the right, let us strive on to finish the work we are in, to bind up the nation's wounds, to care for him who shall have borne the battle, and for his widow and his orphans — to do all which may achieve and cherish a just and lasting peace among ourselves and with all nations.— *Abraham Lincoln.*

A man's country is not a certain area of land, but it is a principle, and patriotism is loyalty to that principle. So, with passionate heroism of which tradition is never weary of tenderly telling, Arnold von Winkelried gathers into his bosom the sheaf of foreign spears. So Nathan Hale, disdaining no service his country demands, perishes untimely, with no other friend than God and a satisfied sense of duty. So George Washington, at once comprehending the scope of the destiny to which his country was devoted, with one hand puts aside the crown, and with the other sets his slaves free. So, through all history, from the beginning, a noble army of martyrs has fought fiercely, and fallen bravely for that unseen mistress, their country. So, through all history to the end, as long as men believe in God, that army must still march, and fight and fall,— recruited only from the flower of mankind, cheered only by their own hope of humanity, strong only in their confidence in their cause.— *George William Curtis.*

Observe good faith and justice toward all nations; cultivate peace and harmony with all. Religion and morality enjoin this conduct; and can it be that good policy does not equally enjoin it? It will be worthy of a free, enlightened, and, at no distant period, a great nation, to give to mankind the magnanimous and too novel example of a people always guided by exalted justice and benevolence. Who can doubt that, in the course of time and things, the fruits of such a plan would richly repay any temporary advantages which might be lost by a steady adherence to it? Can it be that Providence has not connected the permanent felicity of a nation with its virtue? The experiment, at least, is recommended by every sentiment which ennobles human nature.— *George Washington.*

Is patriotism a narrow affection for the spot where a man was born? Are the very clods where we tread entitled to this ardent preference because they are greener? No, this is not the character of the virtue, and it soars higher for its object. It is an extended self-love, mingling with all the enjoyments of life, and twisting itself with the minutest filaments of the heart. It is thus we obey the laws of society, because they are the laws of virtue.   In their authority we see, not the array of force and terror, but the venerable image of our country's honor.   Every good citizen makes that honor his own, and cherishes it, not only as precious but as sacred.   He is willing to risk his life in its defense, and is conscious that he gains protection while he gives it.— *Fisher Ames.*

What is it to be an American?   Putting aside all the outer shows of dress and manners, social customs and physical peculiarities, is it not to believe in America, and in the American people?   Is it not to have an abiding and moving faith in the future and in the destiny of America? — something above and beyond the patriotism and love which every man whose soul is not dead within him feels toward the land of his birth?   Is it not to be national, and not sectional, independent, and not colonial?   Is it not to have a high conception of what this great new country should be, and to follow out that ideal with loyalty and truth?— *Henry Cabot Lodge.*

And how is the spirit of a free people to be formed and animated and cheered, but out of the storehouse of its historic recollections? Are we to be eternally ringing the changes upon Marathon and Thermopylae; and going back to read in obscure texts of Greek and Latin of the exemplars of patriotic virtue?   I thank God that we can find them nearer home, in our own country, on our own soil; that strains of the noblest sentiment that ever swelled in the breast of man are breathing to us out of every page of our country's history, in the native eloquence of our native tongue; that the colonial and provincial councils of America exhibit to us models of the spirit and character which gave Greece and Rome their name and their praise among nations. Here we may go for our instruction; the lesson is plain, it is clear, it is applicable.— *Edward Everett.*

Have we not learned that not stocks nor bonds nor stately houses nor lands nor the product of the mill is our country?   It is a spiritual thought that is in our minds.   It is the flag and what it stands for.

It is its glorious history. It is the fireside and the home. It is the high thoughts that are in the heart, born of the inspiration which comes by the stories of their fathers, the martyrs to liberty; it is the graveyards into which our careful country has gathered the unconscious dust of those who have died. Here, in these things, is that which we love and call our country, rather than in anything that can be touched or handled.— *Benjamin Harrison.*

I was born an American; I live an American; I shall die an American; and I intend to perform the duties incumbent upon me in that character to the end of my career. I mean to do this with absolute disregard of personal consequences. What are personal consequences? What is the individual man, with all the good or evil that may betide him, in comparison with the good or evil which may befall a great country, and in the midst of great transactions which concern that country's fate? Let the consequences be what they will, I am careless. No man can suffer too much, and no man can fall too soon, if he suffer, or if he fall, in the defense of the liberties and constitution of his country.— *Daniel Webster.*

I have seen my countrymen, and I have been with them, a fellow-wanderer, in other lands; and little did I see or feel to warrant the apprehension, sometimes expressed, that foreign travel would weaken our patriotic attachments. One sigh for home — home, arose from all hearts. And why, from palaces and courts, why, from galleries of the arts, where the marble softened into life, and painting shed an almost living presence of beauty around it, why, from the mountain's awful brow, and the lonely valleys and lakes touched with the sunset hues of old romance, why, from those venerable and touching ruins to which our very heart grows, why, from all these scenes, were they looking beyond the swellings of the Atlantic wave, to a dearer and holier spot on earth,— their own country? Doubtless, it was, in part, because it is their country! But it was also, as everyone's experience will testify, because they knew that *there* was no oppression, no pitiful exaction of petty tyranny; because that *there* they knew was no accredited and irresistible religious domination; because that *there* they knew they should not meet the odious soldier at every corner, nor swarms of imploring beggars, the victims of misrule; that *there* no curse causeless did fall, and no blight worse than plague and pestilence did descend amidst the pure dews of heaven; because, in fine, that there they knew was liberty — upon all the green hills and amidst all the peaceful villages — liberty, the wall of fire around the humblest home; the crown of glory, studded with her ever-blazing stars, upon the proudest mansion.— *Orville Dewey.*

Here in this sylvan seclusion, amid the sunshine and the singing of birds, we raise the statue of the Pilgrim, that in this changeless form the long procession of the generations which shall follow us may see what manner of man he was to the outward eye, whom history and tradition have so often flouted and traduced, but who walked undismayed the solitary heights of duty and of everlasting service to mankind. Here let him stand, the soldier of a free church, calmly defying the hierarchy, the builder of a free state serenely confronting the continent which he shall settle and subdue. The unspeaking lips shall chide our unworthiness, the lofty mien exalt our littleness, the unblenching eye invigorate our weakness, and the whole poised and firmly planted form reveal the unconquerable moral energy — the master force of American civilization. So stood the sentinel on Sabbath morning, guarding the plain house of prayer while wife and child and neighbor worshipped within. So mused the Pilgrim in the rapt sunset hour on the New England shore, his soul caught up into the dazzling vision of the future, beholding the glory of the nation that should be. And so may that nation stand, forever and forever, the mighty guardian of human liberty, of godlike justice, of Christlike brotherhood.— *George William Curtis*, from oration on " The Pilgrim."

Fourscore and seven years ago, our fathers brought forth on this continent a new nation, conceived in liberty, and dedicated to the proposition that all men are created equal. Now we are engaged in a great civil war, testing whether that nation or any nation so con-

22

ceived and so dedicated can long endure. We are met on a great battlefield of that war. We have come to dedicate a portion of that field as a final resting-place for those who here gave their lives that that nation might live. It is altogether fitting and proper that we should do this. But, in a larger sense, we cannot dedicate, we cannot consecrate, we cannot hallow this ground. The brave men, living and dead, who struggled here, have consecrated it, far above our poor power to add or detract. The world will little note, nor long remember, what we say here, but it can never forget what they did here. It is for us, the living, rather, to be dedicated here to the unfinished work which they who fought here have thus far so nobly advanced. It is rather for us to be here dedicated to the great task remaining before us, that from these honored dead we take increased devotion to that cause for which they gave the last full measure of devotion; that we here highly resolve that these dead shall not have died in vain, that this nation, under God, shall have a new birth of freedom, and that government of the people, by the people, for the people, shall not perish from the earth.— *Abraham Lincoln*, Speech at Gettysburg.

Believe in your country,— be Americans. Give what you can of your time and thought to your country's service. Give as much as you can, but in any event take an interest in public affairs and do something. Whether partisan or independent, strive to be just, and to see things as they are. The men who are doing the work of the world are not perfect, and their work is not perfect, but it is under their impulse that the world moves.

Live the life of your time, and take your share in its battles. You will be made, thereby, not only more effective, but more manly and more generous.— *Henry Cabot Lodge.*

I believe in that old-fashioned patriotism which places America before all the world beside. I believe that the man who is the best father of a family is the best citizen, that a man who is the best patriot does the best service to his fellow-man.

I remember reading, a short time ago, a little story about a Celtic regiment called the " Black Watch," which had been gone from home for many years, and when it landed upon the shores again the men sprang from the boats and immediately kneeled down and kissed the sands of Galway. That's the kind of patriotism we want nowadays. The patriotism that loves the soil upon which we tread, that loves the air that surrounds us here in America, that loves the Stars and Stripes because they represent this great republic. The patriotism that not only seeks to defend our institutions, but which seeks to elevate our manhood and womanhood. The institutions under which we live are, after all, but men. Our institutions are but the hearts, intelligence and conscience of the American people, and their permanence depends upon the quality of American manhood.— *Hon. Charles T. Saxton,* Lieutenant-Governor of the State of New York, Albany, N. Y., Lincoln's Birthday, 1895.

Patriotism has come rather generally to be interpreted as a willingness to fight and die for one's country and its institutions. That answers very well for a definition of patriotism during times of war, but is generally deficient in that it allows no room for patriotism in times of peace.

If a man loves his country, and is true to her institutions, and affectionately concerned for their quality and permanence, there will be something which he will be all the time doing in her behalf. Shooting our national enemies is only a small and accidental part of the matter. What our country needs most is men who will live for her rather than die for her, but live for her while there is no shooting to be done.— *Rev. Charles H. Parkhurst.*

And for your country, boy, and for that flag, never dream but of serving her as she bids you. No matter what happens to you, no matter who flatters you or abuses you, never look at another flag, never let a night pass but you pray God to bless that flag. Remember, that behind all these men you have to do with, behind officers, and government, and people even, there is the Country Herself, your Country, and that you belong to Her as you do belong to your own mother. Stand by her as you would stand by your own mother.— *Edward Everett Hale,* in "The Man without a Country."

FROM THE " COMMEMORATION ODE."

O beautiful, my country! Ours once more!
Smoothing thy gold of war-dishevelled hair,
O'er such sweet brows as never other wore,
   And letting thy set lips,
   Freed from wrath's pale eclipse,
The rosy edges of thy smile lay bare.
What words divine of lover or of poet
Could tell our love and make thee know it,
Among the nations bright beyond compare?
What were our lives without thee?
What all our lives to save thee?
We reck not what we gave thee;
We will not dare to doubt thee;
But ask whatever else, and we will dare.
          —James Russell Lowell.

Patriotism is not only a legitimate sentiment, but a duty. There are countless reasons why, as Americans, we should love our native land. We may feel no scruples as Christians in welcoming and nourishing a peculiar affection for its winds and soil, its coast and hills, its memories and its flag. We cannot more efficiently labor for the good of all men than by pledging heart, brain, and hands to the service of keeping our country true to its mission, obedient to its idea. Our patriotism must draw its nutriment and derive its impulse from knowledge and love of the ideal America, as yet but partially reflected in our institutions, or in the general mind of the Republic. Thus quickened it will be both pure and practical.— *T. Starr King.*

THE PATRIOT'S ELYSIUM.

There is a land, of every land the pride,
Beloved by Heaven o'er all the world beside;
Where brighter suns dispense serener light,
And milder moons emparadise the night.
There is a spot of earth supremely blest,
A dearer, sweeter spot than all the rest:
Where man, creation's tyrant, casts aside
His sword and scepter, pageantry and pride,
While in his softened looks benignly blend
The sire, the son, the husband, brother, friend.
"Where shall that *land*, that *spot of earth*, be found?"
Art thou a man? a patriot? look around!
Oh, thou shalt find, howe'er thy footsteps roam,
That land thy country, and that spot thy home!
          —James Montgomery.

In this extraordinary war, extraordinary developments have manifested themselves, such as have not been seen in former wars; and, among these manifestations, nothing has been more remarkable than these fairs for the relief of suffering soldiers and their families, and the chief agents in these fairs are the women of America!

I am not accustomed to the use of language of eulogy. I have never studied the art of paying compliments to women; but I must say that, if all that has been said by orators and poets since the creation of the world in praise of women were applied to the women of America, it would not do them justice for their conduct during the war.

I will close by saying, God bless the women of America! — *Abraham Lincoln.*

MY COUNTRY, 'TIS OF THEE.

My country, 'tis of thee,
Sweet land of liberty,
  Of thee I sing:
Land where my fathers died,
Land of the pilgrim's pride,
From every mountain side
  Let freedom ring.

My native country, thee,
Land of the noble, free;
  Thy name I love.
I love thy rocks and rills,
Thy woods and templed hills;
My heart with rapture thrills
  Like that above.

Let music swell the breeze,
And ring from all the trees
  Sweet freedom's song.
Let mortal tongues awake,
Let all that breathe partake,
Let rocks their silence break,
  The sound prolong.

Our fathers' God, to Thee,
Author of liberty,
  To Thee we sing.
Long may our land be bright
With freedom's holy light:
Protect us by Thy might,
  Great God, our King!

— *Samuel Francis Smith.*

Breathes there a man with soul so dead,
Who never to himself hath said:
  "This is my own, my native land!"
Whose heart hath ne'er within him burned,
As home his footsteps he hath turned
  From wandering on a foreign strand?
If such there breathes, go, mark him well —
For him no minstrel raptures swell:
High though his titles, proud his name,
Boundless his wealth as wish can claim:
Despite those titles, power and pelf,
The wretch concentred all in self,
Living, shall forfeit all renown,
And, doubly dying, shall go down
To the vile dust, from whence he sprung,
Unwept, unhonored, and unsung.

— *Sir Walter Scott.*

God bless our native land!
Firm may she ever stand,
  Through storm and night!
When the wild tempests rave,
Ruler of wind and wave,
Do Thou our country save
  By Thy great might.

For her our prayer shall rise
To God above the skies:
  On Him we wait.
Thou, who art ever nigh,
Guarding with watchful eye,
To Thee aloud we cry,
  God save the State.

—*John Sullivan Dwight.*

A man's country is not merely that of his birth, so often a matter of chance, but the land of his happiness. Born in one quarter of the globe, without attachment for its associations, he may become so bound up and identified with that of his adoption as to hold it in every respect as his own true native land. In this light do very many of our citizens consider America. It has afforded shelter and refuge; it has recognized the liberty that is theirs through a common humanity. In no other land is there like freedom in matters of conscience, such recognition and appreciation of the great principles of religion, and the universal obligation of all men to seek the highest happiness of all.— *Raphael Lasker.*

The first two words of the national motto are as much a part of it as the last. They have never been changed since their use began. They have been borne in every battle and on every march, by land or sea, in defeat as in victory. They are still blazoned on our escutcheon, and copied in every seal of office. May that motto never be mutilated or disowned. It should be written on the walls of the Capitol and on every statehouse. Its three words contain a faithful history; may they abide for ages, pledges of the future, as they are witnesses of the past.— *David Dudley Field.*

THE BRAVE AT HOME.

The maid who binds her warrior's sash
  With smile that well her pain dissembles,
The while beneath her drooping lash
  One starry tear-drop hangs and trembles;
Though Heaven alone records the tear,
  And Fame shall never know her story,
Her heart has shed a drop as dear
  As e'er bedewed the field of glory!

The wife who girds her husband's sword,
  'Mid little ones who weep or wonder,
And bravely speaks the cheering word,
  What though her heart be rent asunder;
Doomed nightly in her dreams to hear
  The bolts of death around him rattle,
Hath shed as sacred blood as e'er
  Was poured upon the field of battle!

The mother who conceals her grief
  While to her breast her son she presses,
Then breathes a few brave words and brief,
  Kissing the patriot brow she blesses —
With no one but her secret God
  To know the pain that weighs upon her,
Sheds holy blood as e'er the sod
  Received on Freedom's field of honor!

                              — *Thomas Buchanan Read.*

Give us but a part of that devotion which glowed in the heart of
the younger Pitt and of our own elder Adams, who, in the midst of
their agonies, forgot not the countries they had lived for, but mingled
with the spasms of their dying hour a last and imploring appeal to
the Parent of all mercies that He would remember, in eternal blessings,
the land of their birth. Give us their devotion, give us that of the
young enthusiast of Paris, who, listening to Mirabeau in one of his
surpassing vindications of human rights, and, seeing him falling from
his stand, dying, as a physician proclaimed, for the want of blood,
rushed to the spot, and, as he bent over the expiring man, bared his
arm for the lancet, and cried again and again, with impassioned voice,
"Here, take it, oh! take it from me! let me die so that Mirabeau and
the liberties of my country may not perish!" Give us something only
of such a love of country, and we are safe, forever safe; the troubles
which shadow over and oppress us now will pass away like a summer
cloud. Give us this and we can thank God and say, "These, these, are
my brethren, and OH! THIS, THIS TOO, IS MY COUNTRY!"— *J. McDowell.*

The peace we have won is not a selfish truce of arms, but one
whose conditions presage good to humanity. At Bunker Hill liberty
was at stake, at Gettysburg the Union was the issue, before Manila
and Santiago our armies fought, not for gain or revenge, but for
human rights. They contended for the freedom of the oppressed, for
whose welfare the United States has never failed to lend a hand to
establish and uphold, and, I believe, never will. The glories of the
war cannot be dimmed, but the result will be incomplete and unworthy

of us unless supplemented by civil victories harder possibly to win, in their way not less indispensable. We will have our difficulties and our embarrassments. They follow all victories and accompany all great responsibilities. They are inseparable from every great movement of reform. But American capacity has triumphed over all in the past. Doubts have in the end vanished. Apparent dangers have been averted or avoided, and our own history shows that progress has come so naturally and steadily on the heels of new and grave responsibilities that, as we look back upon the acquisition of territory by our fathers, we are filled with wonder that any doubt could have existed, or any apprehension could have been felt of the wisdom of their action or their capacity to grapple with the then untried and mighty problems. The Republic is to-day larger, stronger, and better prepared than ever before for wise and profitable developments. Forever in the right, following the best impulses and clinging to high purposes, using properly and within right limits our power and opportunities, honorable reward must inevitably follow.— *William McKinley.*

CENTENNIAL HYMN.

Our fathers' God, from out whose hand
The centuries fall like grains of sand,
We meet to-day, united, free,
And loyal to our land and Thee,
To thank Thee for the era done,
And trust thee for the opening one.

*   *   *   *   *

Oh! make Thou us through centuries long,
In Peace secure, in Justice strong:
Around our gift of Freedom, draw
The safeguards of Thy righteous law;
And, cast in some diviner mould,
Let the new cycle shame the old.

— *John Greenleaf Whittier.*

Let me say a word for a little more patriotism in the schools. We have little in our every-day life to arouse patriotic ardor. We have no frequent or great exhibitions of power; no army to stand in awe of; no royalty to worship; no emblems or ribbons to dazzle the eye; and .

but few national airs. We have elections so frequently, and then say such terribly hard things of each other, and about the management of government, that I imagine the children wonder what kind of a country this is that they have been born into. There is no such inculcation of patriotism among our children as among the children of some other lands. If I had my way, I would hang the flag in every schoolroom, and I would spend an occasional hour in singing our best patriotic songs, in declaiming the masterpieces of our national oratory, and in rehearsing the proud story of our national life.— *Andrew S. Draper.*

In the van of the progressive movement of civilization, our country alike greets the most ancient of nations, and the social fabric whose many centuries know no change. Further, she has garnered within her borders all colors, creeds, and minds. Providence has bidden America to train, educate, uplift, blend in fraternity, eastern and western, northern and southern humanity. Here, in these United States, is the grandest school of the brotherhood of man! Here, the conscience and religion are free! Here, the Fatherhood of God is best illustrated in church, in government, and in the human institutions which interpret Him! In the old countries, the people are feared and despised; here, the people are trusted, made responsible, allowed to govern themselves. Here, in marvellous harmony, local forms of freedom are blended with central power.— *William E. Griffis.*

Bereft of Patriotism, the heart of a nation will be cold and cramped and sordid; the arts will have no enduring impulse, and commerce no invigorating soul; society will degenerate and the mean and vicious triumph. Patriotism is not a wild and glittering passion, but a glorious reality. The virtue that gave to Paganism its dazzling lustre, to Barbarism its redeeming trait, to Christianity its heroic form, is not dead. It still lives to console, to sanctify humanity. It has its altar in every clime; its worship and festivities.— *Thomas F. Meagher.*

The name of Republic is inscribed upon the most imperishable monuments of the species, and it is probable that it will continue to be associated, as it has been in all past ages, with whatever is heroic in character, sublime in genius, and elegant and brilliant in the cultivation of art and letters. What land has ever been visited with the influence of liberty that did not flourish like the spring? What people has ever worshipped at her altars without kindling with a loftier spirit, and putting forth more noble energies? Where has she ever acted that her deeds have not been heroic? Where has she ever spoken that her eloquence has not been triumphant and sublime? — *Hugh S. Legare.*

The sheet anchor of the ship of state is the common school. Teach, first and last, Americanism. Let no youth leave the school without being thoroughly grounded in the history, the principles, and the incalculable blessings of American liberty. Let the boys be the trained soldiers of constitutional freedom, the girls the intelligent lovers of freemen.— *Chauncey M. Depew.*

No phrase ever embodied more truth than the oft-repeated one that "Eternal vigilance is the price of liberty," and our work as patriots is no less binding to-day than in the days when we wore the army blue. Let it be our lofty aim to emulate the patriotism of those who gave their lives that Government of the People, by the People, and for the People, might not perish from the earth.— *Oscar D. Robinson.*

Patriotism is one of the positive lessons to be taught in every school. Everything learned should be flavored with a genuine love of country. Every glorious fact in the nation's history should be emphasized, and lovingly dwelt upon. The names of her illustrious citizens should be treasured in the memory. Every child should feel that he is entitled to a share, not only in the blessings conferred by a free government, but also in the rich memories and glorious achievements of his country.— *Richard Edwards.*

A man's country is not a certain area of land, of mountains, rivers, and woods, but it is principle; and patriotism is loyalty to that principle. In poetic minds and in popular enthusiasm, this feeling becomes closely associated with the soil and the symbols of the country. But the secret sanctification of the soil and the symbol is the idea which they represent; and this idea the patriot worships, through the name and the symbol, as a lover kisses with rapture the glove of his mistress and wears a lock of her hair upon his heart.— *George W. Curtis.*

I am no pessimist as to this Republic. I always bet on sunshine in America. I know that my country has reached the point of perilous greatness, and that strange forces, not to be measured or comprehended, are hurrying her to heights that dazzle and blind all mortal eyes, but I know that beyond the uttermost glory is enthroned the Lord God Almighty, and that when the hour of her trial has come He will lift up his everlasting gates and bend down above her in mercy and in love. For with her He has surely lodged the ark of His covenant with the sons of men. And the Republic will endure. Centralism will be checked, and liberty saved — plutocracy overthrown and equality restored. The struggle for human rights never goes backward among English-speaking people. The trend of the times is with us.— *Henry W. Grady.*

THE SHIP OF STATE.

Thou, too, sail on, O Ship of State!
Sail on, O Union strong and great!
Humanity, with all its fears,
With all its hopes of future years,
Is hanging breathless on thy fate!
We know what master laid Thy keel,
What workmen wrought thy ribs of steel,
    Who made each mast, and sail, and rope,
What anvils rang, what anvils beat,
In what a forge and what a heat,
    Were shaped the anchors of thy hope!
Fear not each sudden sound and shock,
'Tis of the wave, and not the rock;
'Tis but the flapping of the sail,
And not a rent made by the gale;
In spite of rock and tempest roar,
In spite of false lights on the shore,
Sail on, nor fear to breast the sea!
Our hearts, our hopes are all with thee:
Our hearts, our hopes, our prayers, our tears,
Our faith triumphant o'er our fears,
    Are all with thee, are all with thee.

— *Henry Wadsworth Longfellow.*

The time has come when the history of our own country should stand among the fundamental studies to be pursued in our schools. In the teaching of history, we need not attach first importance to the dates of battles, the number of men engaged upon each side, or the number killed and wounded. These are but incidents in history. We should teach causes and results. We need not teach that the soldiers on one side were braver than the soldiers on the other. The " boys in gray " who stood up against you at Gettysburg and a hundred other battle-fields were as brave as you were. We know that they were mistaken, but they were brave, and they were Americans. They have done their share in making American history, and one happy result of the war with Spain is that sectional lines have been wiped out and no longer is there any North and South in the consideration of American bravery. We need not spend any time in demonstrating the bravery of the American people. It has been thoroughly tested and the whole world knows it. I believe that we should teach these things to our children. — *Hon. Charles R. Skinner*, Speech before G. A. R. Committee.

One of the definitions of patriotism is " love of country." If we do not teach our boys and girls to love their country, how can we teach them to be patriotic? Patriotism is sometimes misunderstood. Patriotism is not an impulse or a sentiment, but a conviction. Where the heart is right, there you will find true patriotism. I want a patriot-ism that does not wait for the firing of a gun on a national holiday to manifest itself. I want a patriotism which is good every day in the year, and which means an understanding of public duty and a determi-nation to perform that duty.— *Hon. Charles R. Skinner,* Speech before G. A. R. Committee.

Here, at last, is its sacred secret revealed! It is in the patriotic instinct which has brought to this field the army of Northern Virginia and the army of the Potomac. It lies in the manly emotion with which the generous soldier sees only the sincerity and courage of his ancient foe and scorns suspicion of a lingering enmity. It lies in the perfect freedom of speech, and perfect fraternity of spirit, which now for three

days have glowed in these heroic hearts, and echoed in this enchanted
air. These are the forces that assure the future of our beloved country!
May they go before us on our mighty march, a pillar of cloud by day,
of fire by night! Happy for us, happy for mankind, if we and our
children shall comprehend that they are the fundamental conditions of
the life of the Republic! Then, long after, when, in a country whose
vast population, covering the continent with the glory of a civilization
which the imagination cannot forecast, the completed century of the
great battle shall be celebrated, the generation which shall gather here,
in our places, will rise up and call us blessed! Then, indeed, the fleeting
angel of this hour will have yielded his most precious benediction; and
in the field of Gettysburg, as we now behold it, the blue and the gray
blending in happy harmony, like the mingling hues of the summer
landscape, we may see the radiant symbol of the triumphant America
of our pride, our hope, and our joy! — *George William Curtis.*

THE DECLARATION OF INDEPENDENCE.

"WE hold these truths to be self-evident, that all men are created equal; that they are endowed by their Creator with certain inalienable rights; that among these are life, liberty, and the pursuit of happiness; that to secure these rights, governments are instituted among men, deriving their just powers from the consent of the governed." There is the origin of Popular Sovereignty. Who, then, shall come in at this day and claim that he invented it? That is the electric cord in the Declaration that links the hearts of patriotic and liberty-loving men together; that will link those patriotic hearts as long as the love of freedom exists in the minds of men throughout the world.— *Abraham Lincoln.*

It is in vain for demagogism to raise its short arms against the truth of history. The Declaration of Independence stands there. No candid man ever read it without seeing and feeling that every word of it was dictated by deep and earnest thought, and that every sentence of it bears the stamp of philosophic generality. It is the summing up of the results of the philosophical development of the age; the practical embodiment of the progressive ideas which, far from being confined to the narrow limits of the English colonies, pervaded the atmosphere of all civilized nations.— *Carl Schurz.*

I have never had a feeling, politically, that did not spring from the sentiments embodied in the Declaration of Independence. I have often pondered over the dangers which were incurred by the men who assembled here and framed and adopted the Declaration of Independence. I have pondered over the toils that were endured by the officers and soldiers of the army who achieved that independence. I have often inquired of myself what great principle or idea it was that kept this confederacy so long together. It was not the mere matter of the separation of the colonies from the motherland, but that sentiment in the Declaration of Independence which gave liberty, not alone to the people of this country, but, I hope, to the world for all future time. It was that which you promised, that in due time the weight would be lifted from the shoulders of all men. This is the sentiment embodied in the Declaration of Independence.— *Abraham Lincoln.*

On the fourth of July, 1776, the representatives of the United States of America, in Congress assembled, declared that these United Colonies are, and of right ought to be, free and independent states. This Declaration, made by most patriotic and resolute men, trusting in the justice of their cause and the protection of Providence — and yet not without deep solicitude and anxiety — has stood for seventy-five years, and still stands. It was sealed in blood. It has met dangers and overcome them; it has had enemies and it has conquered them; it has had detractors and it has abashed them all; it has had doubting friends, but it has cleared all doubts away; and, now, to-day, raising its august form higher than the clouds, twenty millions of people contemplate it with hallowed love, and the world beholds it, and the consequences which have followed, with profound admiration.— *Daniel Webster.*

The Declaration of Independence is the grandest, the bravest, and the profoundest political document that was ever signed by the representatives of the people. It is the embodiment of physical and moral courage and of political wisdom. I say physical courage because it was a declaration of war against the most powerful nation then on the globe; a declaration of war by thirteen weak, unorganized colonies; a declaration of war by a few people, without military stores, without wealth, without strength, against the most powerful kingdom on the earth; a declaration of war made when the British navy, at that day the mistress of every sea, was hovering along the coast of America, looking after defenceless towns and villages to ravage and destroy. It was made when thousands of English soldiers were upon our soil, and when the principal cities of America were in the substantial possession of the enemy. And so I say, all things considered, it was the bravest political document ever signed by man.—*Robert G. Ingersoll.*

THE CONSTITUTION OF THE UNITED STATES.

E can give up everything but our Constitution, which is the sun of our system. As the natural sun dispels fogs, heats the air, and vivifies and illumines the world, even so does the Constitution, in days of adversity and gloom, come out for our rescue and our enlightening. If the luminary which now sheds its light upon us and invigorates our sphere should sink forever in his ocean bed, clouds, cold, and perpetual death would environ us; and if we suffer our other sun, the Constitution, to be turned from us, if we neglect or disregard its benefits, if its beams disappear but once in the west, anarchy and chaos will have come again, and we shall grope out in darkness and despair the remainder of a miserable existence.— *Daniel Webster.*

In order to understand the theory of the American Government, the most serious, calm, persistent study should be given to the Constitution of the United States. I don't mean learning it by heart, committing it to memory. What you want is to understand it; to know the principles at the bottom of it; to feel the impulse of it; to feel the heart-beat that thrills through the whole American people. That is the vitality that is worth knowing; that is the sort of politics that excels all the mysteries of ward elections, and lifts you up into a view where you can see the clear skies, the unknown expanse of the future.— *Charles A. Dana.*

Every free government is necessarily complicated, because all such governments establish restraints, as well on the power of government itself as on that of individuals. If we will abolish the distinction of branches and have but one branch; if we will abolish jury trials, and leave all to the judge; and if we place the executive power in the same hands, we may readily simplify government. We may easily bring it to the simplest of all possible forms, — a pure despotism. But a separation of departments, so far as practicable, and the preservation of clear lines of division between them, is the fundamental idea in the creation of all our constitutions; and, doubtless, the continuance of regulated liberty depends on maintaining these boundaries.— *Daniel Webster.*

There never existed an example before of a free community spreading over such an extent of territory; and the ablest and profoundest thinkers, at the time, believed it to be utterly impracticable that there should be. Yet this difficult problem was solved — successfully solved — by the wise and sagacious men who framed our Constitution. No; it was above unaided human wisdom — above the sagacity of the most enlightened. It was the result of a fortunate combination of circumstances co-operating and leading the way to its formation, directed by that kind Providence which has so often and so signally disposed events in our favor.— *John C. Calhoun.*

The Constitution of the United States, the nearest approach of mortal to perfect political wisdom, was the work of men who purchased liberty with their blood, but who found that, without organization, freedom was not a blessing. They formed it, and the people, in their intelligence, adopted it. And what has been its history? Has it trodden down any man's rights? Has it circumscribed the liberty of the press? Has it stopped the mouth of any man? Has it held us up as objects of disgrace abroad? How much the reverse! It has given us character abroad; and when, with Washington at its head, it went forth to the world, this young country at once became the most interesting and imposing in the circle of civilized nations.— *Daniel Webster.*

LIBERTY.

SELECTIONS.

Is it nothing, then, to be free? Is it nothing that we are Republicans? Can anything be more striking and sublime than the idea of an Imperial Republic, spreading over an extent of territory more immense than the empire of the Caesars in the accumulated conquests of a thousand years, without prefects, or proconsuls, or publicans, founded in the maxims of common sense, employing within itself no arms but those of reason, and known to its subjects only by the blessings it bestows or perpetuates, yet capable of directing against a foreign foe all the energies of a military despotism, — a Republic in which men are completely insignificant, and principles and laws exercise throughout its vast dominion a peaceful and irresistible sway, blending in one divine harmony, such various habits and conflicting opinions; and mingling in our institutions the light of philosophy with all that is dazzling in the associations of heroic achievement and extended domination, and deep-seated and formidable power!— *Hugh S. Legare.*

A government founded upon anything except liberty and justice cannot and ought not to stand. All the wrecks on either side of the stream of time, all the wrecks of the great cities, and all the nations that have passed away — all are a warning that no nation founded upon injustice can stand. From the sand-enshrouded Egypt, from the marble wilderness of Athens, and from every fallen, crumbling stone of the once mighty Rome, comes a wail, as it were, the cry that no nation founded upon injustice can permanently stand.— *Robert G. Ingersoll.*

Liberty has been the battle-cry which has led to victory on a thousand battlefields; it wrung from King John the Magna Charta; it razed the Bastile to the ground; it peopled the solitudes of America with a hardy race of pilgrims; it led Washington and his faithful army through the perils and sufferings of a seven years' war. It has been the presiding genius which, age after age, in Greece, Rome, Switzerland, England, France, America, and in the South Seas, has molded constitutions, framed laws, and elaborated institutions, all seeking to secure to the individual the highest possible liberty.— *Thomas J. Morgan.*

Is true freedom but to break
Fetters for our own dear sake,
And with leathern hearts forget
That we owe mankind a debt?
No! True freedom is to share
All the chains our brothers wear,
And with heart and hand to be
Earnest to make others free!

They are slaves who fear to speak
For the fallen and the weak;
They are slaves who will not choose
Hatred, scoffing and abuse,
Rather than in silence shrink
From the truth they needs must think;
They are slaves who dare not be
In the right with two or three.

— *James Russell Lowell.*

All who stand beneath our banner are free. Ours is the only flag that has in reality written upon it " Liberty, Equality, Fraternity "— the three grandest words in all the languages of men. Liberty: give to every man the fruit of his own labor — the labor of his hand and of his brain. Fraternity: every man in the right is my brother. Equality: the rights of all are equal. No race, no color, no previous condition, can change the rights of men. The Declaration of Independence has at least been carried out in letter and in spirit. To-day, the black man looks upon his child and says: " The avenues of distinction are open to you — upon your brow may fall the civic wreath." We are celebrating the courage and wisdom of our fathers, and the glad shout of a free people, the anthem of a grand nation, commencing at the Atlantic, is following the sun to the Pacific, across a continent of happy homes.— *Robert G. Ingersoll.*

The land of Freedom! Sea and shore
  Are guarded now, as when
Her ebbing waves to victory bore
  Fair barks and gallant men:
O many a ship of prouder name
  May wave her starry fold,
Nor trail, with deeper line of fame,
  The paths they swept of old!

                      — *Oliver Wendell Holmes.*

O Freedom! Thou are not, as poets dream,
A fair young girl, with light and delicate limbs,
And wavy tresses gushing from the cap
With which the Roman master crowned his slave
When he took off the gyves. A bearded man,
Armed to the teeth, art thou; one mailed hand
Grasps the broad shield, and one the sword: thy brow,
Glorious in beauty though it be, is scarred
With tokens of old wars: Thy massive limbs
Are strong with struggling. Power at thee has launched
His bolts and with his lightnings smitten thee:
They could not quench the light thou hast from Heaven.

                      — *Alfred Tennyson.*

In relation to the principle that all men are created equal, let it be as nearly reached as we can. If we cannot give freedom to every creature, let us do nothing that will impose slavery upon any other creature. I leave you, hoping that the lamp of liberty will burn in your bosoms until there shall be no longer a doubt that all men are created free and equal.— *Abraham Lincoln.*

Hope of the world! Thou hast broken its chains,
Wear thy bright arms while a tyrant remains:
Stand for the right till the nations shall own
Freedom their sovereign, with law for her throne!

Freedom! Sweet Freedom! Our voices resound,
Queen by God's blessing, unsceptered, uncrowned!
Freedom! Sweet Freedom! Our pulses repeat,
Warm with her life blood, as long as they beat!

Fold the broad banner-stripes over her breast,
Crown her with star-jewels, Queen of the West!
Earth for her heritage, God for her friend,
She shall reign over us, world without end!

— Oliver Wendell Holmes.

SONG FOR INDEPENDENCE.

Hail to the planting of Liberty's Tree!
Hail to the charter declaring us free!
  Millions of voices are chanting its praises,
Millions of worshippers bend at its shrine,
  Wherever the sun of America blazes,
Wherever the stars of our bright banner shine.

Sing to the heroes who breasted the flood
That, swelling, rolled o'er them, a deluge of blood.
  Fearless they clung to the ark of the nation,
And dashed on 'mid lightning, and thunder, and blast,
  Till Peace, like the dove, brought her branch of salvation,
And Liberty's mount was their refuge at last.

Bright is the beautiful land of our birth,
The home of the homeless all over the earth.
  Oh! Let us ever, with fondest devotion,
The freedom our fathers bequeathed us watch o'er,
  Till the angel shall stand on the earth and the ocean,
And shout 'mid earth's ruins that Time is no more.

— Alfred B. Street.

THE UNION.

SELECTIONS.

I profess, sir, in my career hitherto, to have kept steadily in view the prosperity and honor of the whole country, and the preservation of our Federal Union. It is to that Union we owe our safety at home, and our consideration and dignity abroad. It is to that Union that we are chiefly indebted for whatever makes us most proud of our country. That Union we reached only by the discipline of our virtue in the severe school of adversity. It had its origin in the necessities of disordered finance, prostrate commerce and ruined credit. Under its benign influences, these great interests immediately awoke, as from the dead, and sprang forth with newness of life. Every year of its duration has teemed with fresh proof of its utility and its blessings, and although our country has stretched out, wider and wider, and our population spread farther and farther, they have not outrun its protection or its benefits. It has been to us all a copious fountain of national, social, and personal happiness.— *Daniel Webster*.

There are four things which I humbly conceive are essential to the well-being — I may even venture to say, to the existence — of the United States, as an independent power.

First. An indissoluble Union of the states under one Federal head.

Second. A sacred regard to public justice.

Third. The adoption of a proper peace establishment.

Fourth. The prevalence of that pacific and friendly disposition among the people of the United States which will induce them to forget their local prejudices and politics; to make those mutual concessions which are requisite to the general prosperity; and, in some instances, to sacrifice their individual advantages to the interest of the community.

These are the pillars on which the glorious fabric of our independence and national character must be supported. Liberty is the basis. And whoever would dare to sap the foundation, or overturn the structure, under whatever specious pretext ·he may attempt it, will merit the bitterest execration and the severest punishment which can be inflicted by his injured country.— *George Washington.*

While every part of our country feels an immediate and particular interest in Union, all the parts combined cannot fail to find, in the united mass of means and efforts, greater strength, greater resource, proportionably greater security from external danger, a less frequent interruption of their peace by foreign nations; and, what is of inestimable value, they must derive from the Union an exemption from those broils and wars between themselves which so frequently afflict neighboring countries not tied together by the same government, which their own rivalships alone would be sufficient to produce, but which opposite foreign alliances, attachments, and intrigues would stimulate and embitter. Hence, likewise, they will avoid the necessity of those overgrown military establishments which, under any form of government, are inauspicious to liberty, and which are to be regarded as particularly hostile to Republican Liberty. In this sense it is that your Union ought to be considered as a main prop of your liberty, and that the love of the one ought to endear to you the preservation of the other. — *George Washington.*

If Washington were now amongst us, and if he could draw around him the shades of the great public men of his own days — patriots and warriors, orators and statesmen — and were to address us in their presence, would he not say to us: " Ye men of this generation, I rejoice and thank God for being able to see that our labors and toils and sacrifices were not in vain. The fire of liberty burns brightly and steadily in your hearts, while duty and the law restrain it from bursting forth in wild and destructive conflagration. Cherish liberty as you love it, cherish its securities as you wish to preserve it. Maintain the Constitution which we labored so painfully to establish, and which has been to you such a source of inestimable blessings. Preserve the Union of the States, cemented as it was by our prayers, our tears, and our blood.

Be true to God, your country, and your duty. So shall that Almighty Power, which so graciously protected us, and which now protects you, shower its everlasting blessings upon you and your posterity."— *Daniel Webster.*

A nation may be said to consist of its territory, its people, and its laws. The territory is the only part which is of certain durability. "One generation passeth away, and another generation cometh, but the earth abideth forever." It is of the first importance to duly consider and estimate this ever-enduring part. That portion of the earth's surface which is owned and inhabited by the people of the United States is well adapted to be the home of one national family, and it is not well adapted for two or more. Its vast extent, and its variety of climate and productions, are of advantage in this age for one people, whatever they might have been in former ages. Steam, telegraphs, and intelligence have brought these to be an advantageous combination for one united people. There is no line, straight or crooked, suitable for a national boundary, upon which to divide. Trace through from East to West upon the line between the free and slave country, and we shall find a little more than one-third of its length are rivers, easy to be crossed and populated, or soon to be populated thickly upon both sides; while nearly all its remaining length are merely surveyor's lines, over which people may walk back and forth without any consciousness of their presence. No part of this line can be made any more difficult to pass by writing it down on paper or parchment as a national boundary.— *Abraham Lincoln.*

For my part, I have never believed in isothermal lines, air lines and water lines separating distinct races. I no more believe that that river yonder, dividing Indiana and Kentucky, marks off two distinct species than I believe that the great Hudson, flowing through the state of New York, marks off distinct species. Such theories only live in the fancy of morbid minds. We are all one people. Commercially, financially, morally, we are one people. Divide as we will into parties, we are one people.

    *   *   *   *   *   *   *

The silken folds that twine about us here, for all their soft and careless grace, are yet as strong as hooks of steel. They hold together a united people and a great nation. The South says to the North, as simply and as truly as was said three thousand years ago in that far away meadow by the side of the mystic sea: " Thy people shall be my people, and thy God, my God." — *Henry Watterson.*

My fellow countrymen of the North, we join you in setting apart this land as an enduring monument of peace, brotherhood, and perpetual union. I repeat the thought, with additional emphasis, with singleness of heart and of purpose, in the name of a common country, and of universal human liberty; and, by the blood of our fallen brothers, we unite in the solemn consecration of these hallowed hills, as a holy eternal pledge of fidelity to the life, freedom, and unity of this cherished Republic.— *John B. Gordon.*

What the sun is in the heavens, diffusing light and warmth, and, by its subtle influence, holding the planets in their orbits, and preserving the harmony of the universe, such is the sentiment of nationality in a people, diffusing life and protection in every direction, holding the faces of Americans always toward their homes, protecting the states in the exercise of their just powers, and preserving the harmony of all. We must have a Nation. It is a necessity of our political existence. We should cherish the idea that, while the states have their rights, sacred and inviolable, which we should guard with untiring vigilance, never permitting an encroachment upon them, and ever remembering that such encroachment is as much a violation of the Constitution of the United States as to encroach upon the rights of the general government, still bear in mind that the states are but subordinate parts of one great nation; that the nation is over all, even as God is over the universe.— *Oliver P. Morton.*

There is nothing more national in all this Republic than the spirit that saved the Union. The soldiers fought for the whole Union, and the spirit that animated us was the spirit of nationality against the spirit of sectionalism, and, in defending the truths for which we fought, we were national to the core and sectional in nothing. It was the spirit of sectionalism against which we fought, and the spirit of broad, united nationality which we defended, and will defend while we live * * * What could be more national as a material thing than the Mississippi River? We made that the river of one people, from Fort Benton, far up under the British line, down to the gulf; and every wave, every drop from the lakes at the far north goes singing of the Union all the way down till it joins the tropical ocean, and we made the song of the Union ring along its banks, and the people that inhabit its shores, one people, I trust, forever. The mountain chains that God made are one, and we made the people and the government that dwell on these mountains, in these valleys, — one, like the ocean, — one, like the ever-lasting hills, and one will we be with them forevermore.— *James A. Garfield*, Address at a Reunion.

The drama of the Revolution opened in New England, culminated in New York, and closed in Virginia. It was a happy fortune that the three colonies which represented the various territorial sections of the settled continent were each in turn the chief seat of war. The common sacrifice, the common struggle, the common triumph, tended to weld them locally, politically, and morally together. * * * The voice of Patrick Henry from the mountains answered that of James Otis by the sea. Paul Revere's lantern shone through the valley of the Hudson, and flashed along the cliffs of the Blue Ridge. The scattering volley of Lexington Green swelled to the triumphant thunder of Saratoga, and the reverberation of Burgoyne's falling arms in New York shook those of Cornwallis in Virginia from his hands. Doubts, jealousies, prejudices, were merged in one common devotion. The union of the colonies to secure liberty foretold the union of the states to maintain it, and wherever we stand on revolutionary fields, or inhale the sweetness of revolutionary memories, we tread the ground and breathe the air of invincible national union.— *George William Curtis*, Oration on Burgoyne's Surrender.

While the Union lasts, we have high, exciting, gratifying prospects spread out before us, for us and our children. Beyond that, I seek not to penetrate the veil. God grant that in my day, at least, that curtain may not rise! God grant that on my vision never may be opened what lies behind! When my eyes shall be turned to behold for the last time the sun in heaven, may I not see him shining on the broken and dishonored fragments of a once glorious Union; on states, dissevered, discordant, belligerent; on a land rent with civil feuds, or drenched, it may be, with fraternal blood! Let their last feeble and lingering glance rather behold the glorious ensign of the Republic, now known and honored throughout the earth, still full high advanced, its arms and trophies streaming in their original lustre, not a stripe erased or polluted, nor a single star obscured, bearing for its motto no such miserable interrogatory as — What is all this worth? — nor those other words of delusion and folly — Liberty first and Union afterwards — but everywhere, spread all over in characters of living light, blazing on all its ample folds, as they float over the sea and over the land, and in every wind under the whole heavens, that other sentiment, dear to every true American heart — Liberty and Union, now and forever, one and inseparable.— *Daniel Webster.*

We cannot escape history. We of this Congress and this administration will be remembered in spite of ourselves. No personal significance or insignificance can spare one or another of us. The fiery trial through which we pass will light us down in honor or dishonor to the latest generation. We say that we are for the Union. The world will not forget that we say this. We know how to save the Union. The world knows we do know how to save it. We — even we here — hold the power and bear the responsibility. In giving freedom to the slave, we assure freedom to the free — honorable alike in what we give and what we preserve. We shall nobly save or meanly lose the last hope of earth. Other means may succeed; this could not, cannot, fail. This way is plain, peaceful, generous, just — a way which, if followed, the world will forever applaud, and God must forever bless.— *Abraham Lincoln.*

The nation has been at war, not within its own shores, but with a foreign power, a war waged not for revenge or aggrandizement, but for our oppressed neighbors, for their freedom and amelioration. It was short, but decisive. It recorded a succession of significant victories on land and on sea. It gave new honors to American arms. It has brought new problems to the Republic, whose solution will tax the genius of our people. United we will meet and solve them, with honor to ourselves, and to the lasting benefit of all concerned. The war brought us together; its settlement will keep us together.

Reunited! Glorious realization! It expresses the thought of my mind, and the long deferred consummation of my heart's desire as I stand in this presence. It interprets the hearty demonstration here witnessed, and is the patriotic refrain of all sections and all lovers of the Republic.

Reunited, one country again and one country forever. Proclaim it from the press and pulpit; teach it in the schools; write it across the skies. The world sees and feels it. It cheers every heart, North and South, and brightens the life of every American home. Let nothing ever strain it again. At peace with all the world and with each other, what can stand in the pathway of our progress and prosperity?— *William McKinley.*

UNION AND LIBERTY.

Flag of the heroes who left us their glory,
   Borne through their battlefield's thunder and flame,
Blazoned in song and illumined in story,
   Wave o'er us all who inherit their fame!
      Up with our banner bright,
      Sprinkled with starry light,
   Spread its fair emblems from mountain to shore,
      While through the sounding sky
      Loud rings the Nation's cry,
   Union and Liberty! One Evermore!

Light of our firmament, guide of our Nation,
   Pride of her children, and honored afar,
Let the wide beams of thy full constellation
   Scatter each cloud that would darken a star!

*   *   *   *   *   *   *   *

Lord of the Universe! Shield us and guide us,
   Trusting Thee always, through shadow and sun!
Thou hast united us, who shall divide us?
   Keep us, O keep us, the MANY IN ONE.

             — *Oliver Wendell Holmes.*

CITIZENSHIP.

SELECTIONS.

Citizens by birth or choice, of a common country, that country has a right to concentrate your affections. The name of AMERICAN, which belongs to you in your national capacity, must always exalt the just pride of patriotism, more than any appellation derived from local discriminations. With slight shades of difference, you have the same religion, manners, habits, and political principles. You have, in a common cause, fought and triumphed together. The independence and liberty you possess are the work of joint counsels, and joint efforts, of common dangers, sufferings and successes.

    *   *   *   *   *   *   *

From the gallantry and fortitude of her citizens, under the auspices of Heaven, America has derived her independence. To their industry, and the natural advantages of the country, she is indebted for her prosperous situation. From their virtue, she may expect long to share the protection of a free and equal government, which their wisdom has established, and which experience justifies, as admirably adapted to our social wants and individual felicity.— *George Washington.*

The virtue, moderation, and patriotism which marked the steps of the American people, in framing, adopting, and thus far carrying into effect our present system of government, have excited the admiration of nations. It only now remains for us to act up to those principles which should characterize a free and enlightened people, that we may gain respect abroad, and insure happiness to ourselves and our posterity.— *George Washington.*

To complete the American character, it remains for the citizens of the United States to show to the world that the reproach heretofore cast on Republican governments, for their want of stability, is without foundation when that government is the deliberate choice of an enlightened people. And I am fully persuaded that every well-wisher to the happiness and prosperity of this country will evince, by his conduct, that we live under a government of laws, and that, while we preserve inviolate our national faith, we are desirous to live in amity with all mankind.— *George Washington.*

There can be no such thing, in the highest sense, as a home, unless you own it. There must be an incentive to plant trees, to beautify the grounds, to preserve and improve. It elevates a man to own a home. It gives a certain independence, a force of character, that is obtained in no other way. Homes make patriots. He who has sat by his own fireside, with wife and children, will defend it. Few men have been patriotic enough to shoulder a musket in defense of a boarding-house. The prosperity and glory of our country depend upon the number of people who are the owners of homes.

*   *   *   *   *   *   *

A man does not vote in this country simply because he is rich; he does not vote in this country simply because he has an education; he does not vote simply because he has talent or genius; we say that he votes because he is a man, and that he has his manhood to support; and we admit in this country that nothing can be more valuable to any human being than his manhood, and for that reason we put poverty on an equality with wealth. If you are a German, remember that this country is kinder to you than your fatherland,— no matter what country you came from, remember that this country is an asylum, and vote, as in your conscience you believe you ought to vote, to keep this flag in heaven. I beg every American to stand with that part of the country that believes in law, in freedom of speech, in an honest vote, in civilization, in progress, in human liberty, and in universal justice.— *Robert G. Ingersoll.*

It is the work of this generation to prove to the nineteenth century, in the face of Christendom, and for the race, the fact that the people do actually govern, and that what twenty millions of freemen

determine, shall be done.   The American Republic must live!   Popular commotion and partisan fury may dash their mad wars against it,
but they shall roll back shattered, spent.   Persecution shall not shake
it, fanaticism disturb it, nor revolutions change it.   But it shall stand
towering sublime, like the last mountain in the deluge, while the earth
rocks at its feet and the thunders peal over its head,— majestic, immu-
table, magnificent! — *Wendell Phillips.*

It is hard to believe that there is any necessity to warn Americans
that, when they seek to model themselves on the lines of other civiliza-
tions, they make themselves the butts of all right-thinking men; and
yet the necessity certainly exists to give this warning to many of our
citizens who pride themselves on their standing in the world of art
and letters, or, perchance, on what they would style their social leader-
ship in the community.   We Americans can only do our alloted task
well if we face it steadily and bravely, seeing, but not fearing, the
dangers.   Above all, we must stand shoulder to shoulder, not asking
as to the ancestry or creed of our comrades, but only demanding that
they be in very truth Americans, and that we all work together,—
heart, hand, and head,— for the honor and the greatness of our common country.— *Theodore Roosevelt.*

In the efforts of the people — of the people struggling for their
rights — moving, not in organized disciplined masses, but in their spontaneous action, man for man and heart for heart, there is something
glorious.   The people always conquer.   They always must conquer.
Armies may be defeated, kings may be overthrown, and new dynasties
be imposed, by foreign arms on an ignorant and slavish race, that care
not in what language the covenant of their subjugation runs, nor in
whose name the deed of their barter and sale is made out.   But the
people never invade; and, when they rise against the invader, are never
subdued.   If they are driven from the plains, they fly to the mountains.   Steep rocks and everlasting hills are their castles; the tangled,
pathless thicket their palisade, and nature, God, is their ally.   Now He
overwhelms the hosts of their enemies beneath His drifting mountains
of sand; now He buries them beneath a falling atmosphere of polar

snows; He lets loose His tempests on their fleets; He puts a folly into their counsels, a madness into the hearts of their leaders; and He never gave, and never will give, a final triumph over a virtuous and gallant people, resolved to be free.— *Edward Everett.*

The faith of our people in the stability and permanence of their institutions was like their faith in the eternal course of nature. Peace, liberty and personal security were blessings as common and universal as sunshine and showers and fruitful seasons; and all sprang from a single source, the principle declared in the Pilgrim Covenant of 1620, that all owed due submission and obedience to the lawfully expressed will of the majority. This is not one of the doctrines of our political system, it is the system itself. It is our political firmament, in which all other truths are set, as stars in the heaven. It is the encasing air, the breath of the Nation's life.— *James A. Garfield.*

Have you thought what the government has cost? Do you realize what free government means? Do you remember, as you have read the story of ages gone, how the barons met at Runnymede? Do you remember how they wrested a charter from the king? Do you remember how the Ironsides went into battle? Do you remember the psalm that rang out at the shock of the conflict? Do you remember Faneuil Hall, and Massachusetts, and John Hancock? Do you remember Carpenter's Hall and Benjamin Franklin? Do you remember Virginia and George Washington? Do you remember what the liberty we have has cost, and are you willing, because of fashion, because of ease, because of social enjoyment, are you willing to let the Republic get into the rapids simply because there are not strong men straining at the oars and keeping us back in the midstream of safety?— *Stewart L. Woodford.*

The supreme glory of our heroism in the Civil War was founded in the greatness of the common people. Do you tell me that they were unknown — that they commanded no battalions, determined no policies, sat in no military councils, rode at the head of no regiments? Be it so. All the more are they the fitting representatives of you and

24

me — the people.   Never in all history was there a war, whose aims, whose policy, whose sacrifices were so absolutely determined by the people, that great body of the unknown, in which, after all, lay the strength and power of the Republic.   When some one reproached Lincoln for the seeming hesitancy of his policy, he answered, " I stand for the people.   I am going just as fast and as far as I can feel them behind me."— *Henry C. Potter.*

I can most religiously aver, I have no wish that is incompatible with the dignity, happiness, and true interest of the people of this country.   My ardent desire is, and my aim has been, so far as depended upon the Executive Department, to comply strictly with all our engagement, foreign and domestic: but to keep the United States free from political connections with every other country, to see them independent of all, and under the influence of none.   In a word, I want an AMERICAN CHARACTER, that the powers of Europe may be convinced *we act for ourselves*, and not for others.   This, in my judgment, is the only way to be respected abroad, and happy at home.— *George Washington.*

There was never a time when we had a right to feel prouder of our country.   We take, every ten years, a census of our material advancement.   I wish we might take, once in a while, a census of brave deeds and brave thoughts; a census which would show the progress of the people of our Republic in heroism, in patriotism, in the instinct of honor, in the sense of duty.   I know that our history at this hour is full of good hope.

*   *   *   *   *   *   *

There never was a people who, as to the great subjects of public conduct, were actuated by a finer, by a profounder sense of duty and a clearer sense of justice than the people of the United States in this generation and at this hour.— *George F. Hoar.*

We shall never be successful over the dangers that confront us; we shall never achieve true greatness, nor reach the lofty ideal which the founders and preservers of our mighty Federal Republic have set before us, unless we are Americans in heart and soul, in spirit and purpose, keenly alive to the responsibility implied in the very name of American, and proud beyond measure of the glorious privilege of bearing it.— *Theodore Roosevelt.*

We know as well as any other class of American citizens where our duties belong. We will work for our country in time of peace and fight for it in time of war, if a time of war should ever come. When I say our country, I mean, of course, our adopted country. I mean the United States of America. After passing through the crucible of naturalization we are no longer Germans; we are Americans. Our attachment to America cannot be measured by the length of our residence here. We are Americans from the moment we touch the American shore until we are laid in American graves. We will fight for America whenever necessary. America, first, last, and all the time. America against Germany, America against the world; America, right or wrong; always America. We are Americans.— *Richard Guenther*, of Wisconsin, in a speech at the time of the Samoan trouble.

Men who wish to work for decent politics must work practically, and yet must not swerve from their devotion to a high ideal. They must actually do things, and not merely confine themselves to criticising those who do them. They must work disinterestedly, and appeal to the disinterested element in others, although they must also do work which will result in the material betterment of the community. They must act as Americans through and through, in spirit and hope and purpose, and, while being disinterested, unselfish and generous in their dealings with others, they must also show that they possess the essential manly virtues of energy, of resolution, and of indomitable personal courage.— *Theodore Roosevelt.*

Citizenship has its duties as well as its privileges. The first is that we give our energies and influence to the enactment of just, equal and beneficent laws. The second is like unto it: that we loyally reverence and obey the will of the majority, whether we are of the majority or not; the law throws the aegis of its protection over us all. There is an open avenue through the ballot-box for the modification or repeal of laws that are unjust or oppressive. To the law we bow with reverence. It is the one king that commands our allegiance.— *Benjamin Harrison.*

Constitutions do not make people; people make constitutions. Our constitution is great and admirable, because the men who made it were so and the people who ratified it and have lived under it were and are brave, intelligent, and lovers of liberty. There is a higher sanction and a surer protection to life and liberty, to the right of free speech and trial by jury, to justice and humanity, in the traditions, the beliefs, the habits of mind, and the character of the American people than any which can be afforded by any constitution, no matter how wisely drawn. If the American people were disposed to tyranny, injustice and oppression, a constitution would offer but a temporary barrier to their ambitions, and the reverence for the constitution, and for law and justice, grows out of the fact that the American people believe in freedom and humanity, in equal justice to all men and in equal rights before the law, and while they so believe the great doctrine of the Declaration of Independence and of the Constitution will never be in peril.— *Henry Cabot Lodge,* Speech on the adoption of the Spanish-American Treaty, United States Senate, January 24, 1899.

Let reverence of the law be breathed by every mother to the lisping babe that prattles on her lap; let it be taught in schools, seminaries, and colleges; let it be written in primers, spelling-books, and almanacs; let it be preached from pulpits, and proclaimed in legislative halls, and enforced in courts of justice; in short, let it become the political religion of the Nation.— *Abraham Lincoln.*

MANUAL OF PATRIOTISM.

QUOTATIONS

IN

PROSE AND POETRY

ON

OUR COUNTRY.

(373)

OUR COUNTRY.

QUOTATIONS.

The glorious Union is our world.— *Daniel S. Dickinson.*

Our Country — the strongest, richest, freest, happiest of the nations of the earth. — *George F. Hoar.*

> Valor's home and Freedom's lov'd retreat!
> — *William Leggett.*

One country, one Constitution, one destiny.— *Daniel Webster.*

The glorious Union our fathers gave us till time shall be no more.— *Reverdy Johnson.*

> Let all the ends thou aim'st at be thy Country's,
> Thy God's and Truth's.
> — *William Shakespeare.*

Never was a people so advantageously situated for working out the great problem of human liberty.— *Henry A. Boardman.*

The American Nation! Its men are as brave, energetic and dauntless as they are honest.— *Nicholas, Czar of Russia.*

> O land! of every land the best,
> O land! whose glory shall increase.
> — *Phoebe Cary.*

An indissoluble Union of indestructible States, one flag, one country, one destiny! — *Daniel Webster.*

I am an American; I know no country but America, and no locality in America that is not my country.— *Daniel Webster.*

> The blue arch above us is Liberty's dome,
> The green fields beneath us, Equality's home.
> — *Hezekiah Butterworth.*

The people's government; made for the people; made by the people; and answerable to the people.— *Daniel Webster.*

We are Americans, we will live Americans and we will die Americans.— *Daniel Webster.*

> Freedom's soul has only place
> For a free and fearless race.
> > — *John G. Whittier.*

Above all, we must stand shoulder to shoulder for the honor and the greatness of our country.— *Theodore Roosevelt.*

There never existed an example before of a free community spreading over such an extent of territory.— *John C. Calhoun.*

> Here began the kingdom not of kings, but men;
> Began the making of the world again.
> > — *John Boyle O'Reilly.*

Here the people govern.　Here they act by their immediate representatives.— *Alexander Hamilton.*

In our federal relations I know but one section, one union, one flag, one government.— *Daniel S. Dickinson.*

> We're bound by mutual ties,
> 　No hostile hands are ours,
> From where Maine's snowy mountains rise,
> 　To the fair land of flowers.
> > — *William L. Shoemaker.*

We are to constitute all together, North, South, East, West, one government. — *Hilary A. Herbert.*

The best son of his country is he who gives the best manhood to his country.— *Anon.*

> Hail, America, hail! the glory of lands!
> 　To thee high honors are given,
> Thy stars shall blaze till the moon veil her rays,
> 　And the sun lose his pathway in heaven.
> > — *Jonathan M. Sewell.*

The love of my country will be the ruling influence of my conduct.— *George Washington.*

One God, one country, one destiny.   This is the gospel of American nationality. — *Wendell Phillips.*

> Our country is a goodly land;
>   We'll keep her always whole and hale;
> We'll love her, live for her, or die;
>   To fall for her is not to fail.
>   — *Francis Lieber.*

Every good citizen makes his country's honor his own, and cherishes it not only as precious, but as sacred.— *Andrew Jackson.*

I know no North, no South, no East, no West to which I owe any allegiance.— *Henry Clay.*

> My country! ay, thy sons are proud,
>   True heirs of freedom's glorious dower,
> For never here has knee been bowed
>   In homage to a mortal power.
>   — *Mrs. Sarah J. Hale.*

Let every man that lives and owns himself an American take the side of true American principles.— *Henry Ward Beecher.*

The heritage of American youth is equal opportunities in a land of equal rights.— *William L. Wilson.*

> Columbia! First and fairest gem
> On Nature's brow — a diadem
> Whose lustre, bright as heavenly star,
> The light of Freedom sheds afar.
>   — *P. S. Gilmore.*

Every American should be proud of his whole country, rather than a part.— *William Tecumseh Sherman.*

We of this generation and nation, occupy the Gibraltar of the ages which commands the world's future.— *Josiah Strong.*

> The nation Thou hast blest
>   May well Thy love declare
> From foes and fears at rest,
>   Protected by Thy care.
>   — *Francis Scott Key.*

Territory is but the body of a nation. The people who inhabit its hills and its valleys are its soil, its spirit, its life.— *James A. Garfield.*

Of the whole sum of human life no small part is that which consists of a man's relations to his country and his feelings concerning it.— *William Ewart Gladstone.*

> Land of the West — beneath the heaven
> There's not a fairer, lovelier clime;
> Nor one to which was ever given
> A destiny more high, sublime.
> 　　　　　　　*— W. D. Gallagher.*

Without Union our independence and liberty would never have been achieved; without Union they cannot be maintained.— *Andrew Jackson.*

Liberty has a more extensive and durable foundation in the United States than it ever has had in any other age or country.— *George McDuffie.*

> O! make Thou us through centuries long,
> In peace secure, in justice strong;
> Around our gift of freedom draw
> The safeguards of Thy righteous law.
> 　　　　　　　*— John G. Whittier.*

Driven from every other corner of the earth, freedom of thought and the right of private judgment in matters of conscience direct their course to this happy country as their last asylum.— *Samuel Adams.*

The Fathers of the Republic, in their almost inspiration, saw clearly that a government to be enduring and free must be a Union, not of States, but of the people, and they fashioned their work accordingly.— *Roscoe Conkling.*

> Their country first, their glory and their pride,
> Land of their hopes, land where their fathers died,
> When in the right, they'll keep their honor bright,
> When in the wrong, they'll die to set it right.
> 　　　　　　　*— James T. Fields.*

May this immense Temple of Freedom ever stand a lesson to oppressors, an example to the oppressed, a sanctuary for the rights of mankind.— *Marquis de Lafayette.*

No words can depict, no pen can describe, the wonderful variety, richness, grandeur and beauty which the Almighty has stamped upon this, our favored land.— *John Sherman.*

> O Nation great, State linked to State, in bonds that none can break,
> From ocean unto ocean, from Gulf to northern lake!
> State linked to State, fate linked to fate, in mart and mint and mine,
> In rolling plain of golden grain, in toss of plumy pine.
>
> > *— Kate D. Sherwood.*

Now every man, woman and child is raised to the dignity of an American freeman, and that bright, triumphant banner of liberty now floats proudly over every foot of American soil.— *I. C. Parker.*

We are all one, and we will maintain our nation as it was handed down to us, the most priceless heritage that ever sons inherited.— *Gen. Nelson A. Miles, U. S. A.*

> * * * drifted past the storm of war
> To isles of peaceful calm,
> The lakes give greetings to the sea,
> The pine unto the palm.
>
> > *— Arthur Dyer.*

The worth of valor, the beauty of endurance, the grandeur of self-denial and the sacredness of honor — for all of these our flag is the symbol, our Union the flower, our Nation the synonym.— *Elbridge S. Brooks.*

The kindred blood which flows in the veins of American citizens, the mingled blood which they have shed in defense of their sacred rights, consecrate their Union. — *James Madison.*

> * * * our Country shall be
> Unshaken in strength and unsullied in name —
> And from the broad center all around to the sea
> Shall millions inherit her power and fame.
>
> > *— I. D. Van Dusee.*

Let us strive to aid and advance the liberty of the world by patriotic fidelity and devotion in upholding, illustrating and advocating our own free institutions.— *Robert C. Winthrop.*

Our very air is instinct with freedom. Every inhalation on American soil is fraught with American ideas. It is impossible for sane people to live in this country and not become Americans.— *Edmund J. Wolf.*

The breath of heaven is here!
One draught can make the slave and master one!
The grace of liberty softens year by year,
And in a richer flood the stream of life flows on.
                              — *Maurice Thompson.*

Let it be Patriotism first, last, and always; Patriotism in the history, in the reading lesson; in the general exercises; in the flags that adorn the school-room.— *Albert E. Winship.*

Our chief glory arises from the general welfare of our people, their contentment with their institutions, their enlightenment, and their general advancement in the virtues of Christian civilization— *John Adams Kasson.*

Daughter of Liberty! queen of the world!
Fairest of all earth's fair nations, arise!
Let thy bright banners and flags be unfurled;
Send thy glad voice to the uttermost skies!
                              — *Anon.*

We cannot more effectually labor for the good of all men, than by pledging heart, brain and hands to the service of keeping our country true to its mission, obedient to its idea.— *Thomas Starr King.*

We are One by the configuration of nature and by the strong impress of art. We are One by the memories of our fathers. We are One by the hopes of our children. We are One by our Constitution and our Union.— *Robert C. Winthrop.*

To her we owe
All that of happiness we know;
Justice, and Law's protecting care,
The rights of freemen everywhere.
                              — *W. W. Caldwell.*

The nation depends not on the wisdom of its senators, not on the vigilance of its police, not on the strong arm of its standing armies: but on the loyalty of a united people.— *Parke Godwin.*

We are a Republic whereof one man is as good as another before the law. Under such a form of government, it is of the greatest importance that all should be possessed of education and intelligence.— *Ulysses S. Grant.*

> We know no North, nor South, nor West;
> One Union binds us all;
> Its stars and stripes are o'er us flung —
> 'Neath them we'll stand or fall.
> — *Anon.*

That we live in the enjoyment of the fruits of our labors, that we live at all, perhaps, or live girt about by the blessings of civilization, we owe, under Providence, to our country. Let us prove ourselves true sons and daughters of such a mother.— *Epes Sargent.*

This is what I call the American idea of freedom — a government of all the people, by all the people, for all the people; of course a government of the principles of eternal justice — the unchanging law of God.— *Theodore Parker, D. D.*

> Oh the land of our Union! it sweetens the morn
> With the fragrance of orchards, the sunshine of corn:
> In its beautiful bosom the fountains are sure,
> And the gold of its furrows is wealth to the poor:
> And the children of exile as kindred may toil
> In the vineyards of freedom with sons of the soil.
> — *Anon.*

Freedom of religion, freedom of the press, and freedom of the person under the protection of the *habeas corpus*, these are the principles that have guided our steps through an age of revolution and reformation.— *Thomas Jefferson.*

Our country — whether bounded by the St. John's and the Sabine, or however otherwise bounded or described, and be the measurements more or less;— still our country, to be cherished in all our hearts, to be defended by all our hands.— *Robert C. Winthrop.*

> Father, whose mighty power
> Shields us through life's short hour,
> To Thee we pray,— bless us and keep us free;
> All that is past forgive:
> Teach us henceforth to live
> That through our country we may honor Thee.
> — *Marion Crawford.*

If this country is to reach the full development which we believe to be possible, it must be by maintaining in all its integrity the Constitution which our fathers framed, and in giving steadfast and uncalculating support to the Union which they formed.— *Hugh S. Thompson.*

God's mercy will still lead our country on.   On under the dearest flag that freemen ever bore.   On in the broad sunshine of liberty, equality, and justice.   On to the inspiring music of the Union.   On along the grand highway of the Nation's glory to the future of our country's hope.— *John M. Thurston.*

     Long as thine Art shall love true love,
      Long as thy Science truth shall know,
     Long as thy Eagle harms no Dove,
      Long as thy Law by law shall grow,
     Long as thy God is God above,
      Thy Brother every man below,
     So long dear Land of all my love
      Thy name shall shine, thy fame shall glow!
                  — *Sidney Lanier.*

THE NOBILITY OF LABOR.

PREFATORY NOTE.— In the life of the nation, true Patriotism and honest Labor are very closely allied. Then why not upon the printed page?

Only a few years ago, the State of New York recognized the cause of labor by making the first Monday in September of each year a legal holiday, called " Labor Day." On that day hundreds of thousands of the toilers of the great Empire State march in procession with flags flying and bands playing,— and then away for an afternoon of games and sports! And every on-looker feels not only that " the laborer is worthy of his hire," but of his holiday.

Moreover, the laborer is worthy not only of his hire and holiday, but of the best education for his children, and the best protection for himself and his family which the State can give! For without his faithful toil, the white Sails of Commerce would soon desert the seas; the Wheels of Trade would clog and stop — and the National Government itself stand still. There is no better patriot in the land than the strong-handed, true-hearted laborer.

SELECTIONS.

Honest labor wears a lovely face.
— *Thos. Dekker* (died 1641).

If all the year were playing holidays,
To sport would be as tedious as to work.

— *Shakspere.*

From toil he wins his spirits light,
From busy day the peaceful night;
Rich from the very want of wealth,
In Heaven's best treasures, peace and health.

— *Gray.*

As for bidding me not work, Molly might as well put the kettle on the fire, and say, " Now, don't boil!" — *Sir Walter Scott.*

(383)

FROM WHITTIER'S "SONGS OF LABOR."

Hark! roars the bellows, blast on blast,
   The sooty smithy jars,
And fire-sparks, rising far and fast,
   Are fading with the stars.
All day for us the smith shall stand
   Beside that flashing forge;
All day for us his heavy hand
   The groaning anvil scourge.

From far-off hills, the panting team
   For us is toiling near;
For us the raftsman down the stream
   Their island barges steer.
Rings out for us the axe-man's stroke
   In forests old and still,—
For us the century-circled oak
   Falls crashing down his hill.

              — From " The Ship-Builders."

Cheerly, on the axe of labor,
   Let the sunbeams dance,
Better than the flash of sabre
   Or the gleam of lance!
Strike! — with every blow is given
   Freer sun and sky,
And the long-hid earth to heaven
   Looks, with wondering eye.

              — From " The Lumbermen."

Rap, rap! upon the well-worn stone
   How falls the polished hammer!
Rap, rap! the measured sound has grown
   A quick and merry clamor.
Now shape the sole! now deftly curl
   The glossy vamp around it,
And bless the while the bright-eyed girl
   Whose gentle fingers bound it.

              — From " The Shoemakers."

Here we'll drop our lines, and gather
    Old Ocean's treasures in,
Where'er the mottled mackerel
    Turns up a steel-dark fin.
The sea's our field of harvest,
    Its scaly tribes our grain;
We'll reap the teeming waters
    As at home they reap the plain!

             — From " The Fishermen."

There wrought the busy harvesters; and many a creaking wain
Bore slowly to the long barn-floor its load of husk and grain;
Till broad and red, as when he rose, the sun sank down at last,
And, like a merry guest's farewell, the day in brightness passed.

             — From " The Huskers."

The gentleman, sir, has misconceived the spirit and tendency of Northern institutions. He is ignorant of Northern character. He has forgotten the history of his country. Preach insurrection to the Northern laborers! Who are the Northern laborers? The history of your country is *their* history. The renown of your country is *their* renown. The brightness of their doings is emblazoned on its every page. Blot from your annals the words and doings of *Northern laborers*, and the history of your country presents but a universal blank. Sir, who was he that disarmed the Thunderer, wrested from his grasp the bolts of Jove; calmed the troubled ocean; became the central sun of the philosophical system of his age, shedding his brightness and effulgence on the whole civilized world; whom the great and mighty of the earth delighted to honor; who participated in the achievement of your independence, prominently assisted in molding your free institutions, and the beneficial effects of whose wisdom will be felt to the last moment of "recorded time?" Who, sir, I ask, was he? A Northern laborer,— a Yankee tallow-chandler's son — a printer's runaway boy.—*Charles Naylor.*

And who let me ask the honorable gentleman, who was he that, in the days of our Revolution, led the Northern army,— yes, an army of Northern laborers,— and aided the chivalry of South Carolina in their defence against British aggression, drove the spoilers from their firesides, and redeemed her fair fields from foreign invaders? Who was he?

25

A Northern laborer, a Rhode Island blacksmith,— the gallant General Greene,— who left his hammer and his forge, and went forth conquering and to conquer in the battle for our independence! And will you preach insurrection to men like these? —*Naylor.*

Sir, our country is full of the achievements of Northern laborers. Where is Concord, and Lexington, and Princeton, and Trenton, and Saratoga, and Bunker Hill, but in the North? And what, sir, has shed an imperishable renown on the never-dying names of those hallowed spots, but the blood and the struggles, the high daring, and patriotism, and sublime courage, of Northern laborers? The whole North is an everlasting monument of the freedom, virtue, intelligence, and indomitable independence, of Northern laborers. Go, sir, go preach insurrection to men like these! — *Naylor.*

LABOR IS WORSHIP.

"Labor is worship!"—the robin is singing;
"Labor is worship!"—the wild bee is ringing:
Listen! that eloquent whisper up-springing
    Speaks to thy soul from out Nature's great heart.
From the dark cloud flows the life-giving shower;
From the rough sod blows the soft-breathing flower;
From the small insect, the rich coral bower;
Only man, in the plan, shrinks from his part.

Labor is life! 'Tis the still water faileth;
Idleness ever despaireth, bewaileth;
Keep the watch wound, for the dark rust assaileth;
    Flowers droop and die in the stillness of noon.
Labor is glory!—the flying cloud lightens;
Only the waving wing changes and brightens;
Idle hearts only the dark future frightens;
    Play the sweet keys, would'st thou keep them in tune!

Labor is health! Lo! the husbandman reaping,
How through his veins goes the life-current leaping!
How his strong arm, in its stalwart pride sweeping,
    True as a sunbeam, the swift sickle guides!
Work for some good, be it ever so slowly;
Cherish some flower, be it ever so lowly·
Labor! all labor is noble and holy;
    Let thy great deeds be thy prayer to thy God!
                    —*By Frances S. Osgood.*

THE WORK-SHOP AND THE CAMP.

The Camp has had its day of song:
  The sword, the bayonet, the plume,
Have crowded out of rhyme too long
  The plough, the anvil, and the loom!
O, not upon our tented fields
  Are Freedom's heroes bred alone;
The training of the Work-shop yields
  More heroes true than war has known!

Who drives the bolt, who shapes the steel,
  May, with a heart as valiant, smite,
As he who sees a foeman reel
  In blood before his blow of might!
Let Labor, then, look up and see
  His craft no pith of honor lacks;
The soldier's rifle yet shall be
  Less honored than the woodman's axe!

When the great obelisk, brought from Egypt in 1586, was erected in the square of St. Peter's in Rome, the tackle was all arranged for the delicate and perilous work. To make all safe and prevent the possibility of accident from any sudden cry or alarm, a papal edict had proclaimed death to any man who should utter a loud word, till the engineer had given the order that all risk was passed.

As the majestic monolith moved up, the populace closed in. The square was crowded with admiring eyes and beating hearts. Slowly that crystalization of Egyptian sweat rises on its base — five degrees, ten degrees, fifteen, twenty — there are signs of faltering. No matter — no voice — silence. It moves again — twenty-five, thirty, forty, forty-three — it stops! See! Those hempen cables which like faithful servants have obeyed the mathematician have suddenly received an order from God not to hold that base steady another instant on those terms. The obedient masons look at each other,— silent,— and then watch the threatening masses of stone. Among the crowd, silence,— silence everywhere, obedience to law,— and the sun shone on the stillness and despair.

Suddenly from out of the breathless throng rang a cry, clear as the archangel's trumpet,—"Wet the ropes!" The crowd turned to look. Tiptoe on a post, in a jacket of homespun, his eyes full of prophetic fire, stood *a workman of the people.* His words flashed like lightning and struck. From the engineer to his lowest assistant the cry had instant obedience. Water was dashed on the cables; they bit fiercely into the granite; the windlasses were manned once more, and the obelisk rose to its place and took its stand for centuries.—*Adapted.*

> What tho' on hamely fare we dine,
>   Wear hoddin gray, and a' that;
> Gie fools their silks, and knaves their wine,
>   A man's a man for a' that!
> For a' that, and a' that,
>   Their tinsel show, and a' that;
> The honest man, though e'er sae poor,
>   Is king o' men for a' that.

> Then let us pray that come it may —
>   As come it will for a' that —
> That sense and worth, o'er a' the earth,
>   May bear the gree, and a' that;
> For a' that, and a' that,
>   It's comin' yet, for a' that,
> That man to man, the warld o'er,
>   Shall brothers be for a' that!

> — *Robert Burns.*

Ashamed to toil, art thou? Ashamed of thy dingy work-shop and dusty labor-field; of thy hard hand, scarred with service more honorable than that of war; of thy soiled and weather-stained garments, on which mother Nature has embroidered, midst sun and rain, midst fire and steam, her own heraldic honors? Ashamed of these tokens and titles, and envious of the flaunting robes of imbecile idleness and vanity? It is treason to Nature,— it is impiety to Heaven,— it is breaking Heaven's great ordinance. Toil, I repeat — toil,— either of the brain, of the heart, or of the hand, is the only true manhood, the only true nobility! — *Orville Dewey.*

IMPORTANT DATES IN AMERICAN HISTORY.

It is believed that pupils may become interested in the study of American history by presenting for their study and investigation its important events on the anniversaries of their occurrence. Experienced teachers recognize the value of having at hand a few dates around which may be grouped a number of facts with sufficient accuracy to preserve that sequence of events so necessary to the study of history. What dates should be remembered is not particularly essential, and each pupil may largely be allowed to choose those which interest him personally or are in some way connected with his individual experiences.

The following arrangement of dates has been compiled for use in morning exercises in schools, in the belief that if used intelligently such exercises will materially aid the avowed purpose of this volume in stimulating an intelligent patriotism, through a knowledge of events that have been influential in shaping the development of our country to its present marvelous greatness and have added to its acknowledged prestige.

The references have, so far as possible, been chosen from works easily accessible, but they may always be supplemented to advantage by the alert and enterprising teacher. Either a class or a particular pupil chosen for the work should carefully study the history relating to the event which is the subject of a morning exercise, preparatory to its presentation, and should, under the direction of the teacher, provide short recitations or quotations supplementary to those given in connection with the several dates. Abundant material may be obtained from the excellent selections given in this volume.

It is suggested that pupils whose birthdays are the same as the anniversary of an event which is the subject of a morning exercise should be chosen to take part therein. It is also suggested that morning exercises should be limited to fifteen minutes.

In the arrangement, September has been placed first in order to correspond substantially with the opening of the schools of our State. As the dates in any given list must differ materially in importance, those of greater moment in the list presented have been printed in black-face type in order that they may be readily distinguished from others of minor importance but still of interest locally or in connection with other school work.

Believing that the faithful and efficient teaching force of the State will find much that is helpful in the material submitted, I unhesitatingly commit to their care the great interests which this particular work, as well as this entire volume, is intended to promote.

Charles R. Skinner

IMPORTANT DATES IN AMERICAN HISTORY.

September 1, 1675.— Attack on Hadley.

The Indians under Philip attacked Hadley. Most of the garrison were absent. Moreover it was a feast day, and the people were in the meeting-house when the alarm was given. The colonists were almost driven back when Goffe, the regicide, suddenly appeared, led the troops, repulsed the Indians, and as suddenly disappeared.

References:

Popular History of the United States.— Bryant.

September 2, 1864.— Capture of Atlanta.

General Sherman, by a series of masterly movements, compelled the Confederates to retreat, and after crossing the almost inaccessible country between Chattanooga and Atlanta, finally succeeded in capturing the important military center, Atlanta, the most important strategic point in possession of the Confederates in the southeast.

References:

Battles and Leaders of the Civil War.— Davis.
Bird's Eye View of Our Civil War.— Dodge.

September 3, 1783.— Treaty of peace signed at Paris. (This treaty marked the close of the Revolutionary War.)

References:

Popular History of the United States.— Bryant.
History of the United States, vol. X.— Bancroft.
Rise of the Republic of the United States.— Frothingham.

Appropriate Selections:

The Advantages and Disadvantages of the Revolution, from David Ramsay's History of the American Revolution.

September 5, 1774.— First Continental Congress.

The first Continental Congress met in Carpenter's Hall, Philadelphia, September 5, 1774. Every colony except Georgia was represented, and the delegates were the ablest politicians of the colonies. Its chief work was the adoption of a Declaration of Rights, and the establishment of the American Association.

References:

Rise of the Republic of the United States.— Frothingham.
American History Leaflets, No. 11.
History of the United States.— Hildreth.
The American Revolution.—Fiske.
History of the United States.— Bancroft.

Appropriate Selections:

" The Continental Congress and its Doings."— Edmund Olliver.
" The First American Congress."— Maxey.

Selection:

" When liberty is the prize, who would shun the warfare, who would stoop to waste a coward thought on life? We esteem no sacrifice too great, no conflict too severe, to redeem our inestimable rights and privileges. 'Tis for you, brethren, for ourselves, for our united posterity, we hazard all; and permit us humbly to hope that such a measure of vigilance, fortitude, and perseverance will still be afforded us that, by patiently suffering and nobly doing, we may eventually secure that more precious than Hesperian fruit, the golden apples of freedom. We see the hand of heaven in the rapid and wonderful union of the colonies; and that generous and universal emulation to prevent the sufferings of the people of this place gives a prelibation of the cup of deliverance. May unerring Wisdom dictate the measures to be recommended by the Congress; may a smiling God conduct this people through the thorny paths of difficulty and finally gladden our hearts with success."

September 5, 1887.— Labor Day first observed in the State of New York.

September 7, 1888.— Congress prohibited Chinese immigration.

September 8, 1565.— Founding of St. Augustine.

On the eighth of September, 1565, Don Pedro Menendez, a Spaniard, commenced to lay the foundation of St. Augustine, Florida, the oldest town in the United States.

References:

Popular History of the United States.— Bryant.
Narrative and Critical History of the United States.— Winsor.
Pioneers of France in the New World.— Parkman.
Discovery of America.— Fiske.

September 9, 1850.— California admitted to the Union.

September 10, 1813.— Battle of Lake Erie.

Perry, in command of the American ships, met a British fleet of six ships, and a hard-fought battle of four hours ensued. The result was a brilliant victory for the Americans; it established their naval supremacy on Lake Erie, Detroit was evacuated by the British, the Indians of Michigan were intimidated. Perry's motto for the day was Lawrence's dying words: " Don't give up the ship," and his message to Harrison after the victory, " We have met the enemy and they are ours."

References:

Popular History of the United States.— Anderson.
History of the Navy.— Maclay.
History of the Navy of the United States.— Cooper.
History of the Battle of Lake Erie.— Bancroft.

Appropriate Selections:

Selection from · The Second War between England and the United States. — Headley.

September 11, 1777.— Battle of Brandywine Creek.

At the landing of Howe's fleet at Chesapeake Bay, Washington marched to Brandywine to make a stand for Philadelphia, but superior numbers and stratagem gave the enemy the victory. While the Americans were being attacked from the front, a part of the British forces secretly fell upon them in the rear and routed them.

References:

The American Revolution.— Fiske.
Popular History of the United States.— Anderson.
Battles of the United States.— Dawson.
Popular History of the United States.— Bryant.
1776.— Lossing.

September 11, 1814.— Battle of Plattsburg and McDonough's victory.

A large British army advanced from Canada to attack Plattsburg, and at the same time their fleet, commanded by Commodore Donnie, began an attack upon the American fleet under Commodore McDonough, then lying in the bay of Plattsburg. Both land and naval contests were sharp and decisive. All the British vessels, with the exception of some galleys, were captured, while the army hastily retreated.

References:

History of the Navy.— Maclay.
Popular History of the United States.— Bryant.
Pictorial Field-Book of the War of 1812.— Lossing.
Battles of the United States.— Dawson.

September 13, 1759.— Taking of Quebec.

The great object of the campaign of 1759 was the reduction of Canada. General Wolfe was to lay siege to Quebec; Amherst was to reduce Ticonderoga and Crown Point, and then co-operate with Wolfe; and General Prideaux was to capture Niagara and Montreal and then join Amherst.

During July, Niagara surrendered, and Johnson, successor to Prideaux, instead of going to Montreal, made his way to Albany. The French abandoned both Ticonderoga and Crown Point without striking a blow, and Amherst went into winter quarters, failing Wolfe. With 8,000 men Wolfe ascended the St. Lawrence and landed his army on the isle of Orleans. On July 31st, he made a daring, through unsuccessful, attempt upon the French intrenchments at Montmorencie, near Quebec. Not discouraged by the disaster, the English continued the struggle, and finally effected a landing at night about two miles above the city, and, climbing the steep banks of the river, by daybreak on September 13th, stood on the Plains of Abraham, in battle array. This battle virtually decided the French and Indian war, and the supremacy of the English in America.

References:

Popular History of the United States.—Anderson.
. History of the United States.— Hildreth.
History of the United States.— Bancroft.

Appropriate Selections:

Taking of Quebec and Death of Wolfe.— Parkman.
Elegy in a Country Churchyard.— Gray.

September 13, 1814.— Bombardment of Fort McHenry, Baltimore.

After the burning of Washington, Ross started to attack Baltimore, but was slain on the way. His forces, checked for a time by the militia, prepared to co-operate with a fleet of sixteen vessels. But Fort McHenry hindered the advance of the fleet, and after a twenty-four hours' bombardment the British withdrew.

References:

History of the Navy.— Maclay.
Popular History of the United States.— Bryant.
Pictorial Field-Book of the War of 1812.— Lossing.
Battles of the United States.— Dawson.

Appropriate Selections:

The Star Spangled Banner.— Key.
The Flag of Washington.— F. W. Gillett.

September 14, 1807.— Fulton first ascended the Hudson by steam power.

This experiment was the beginning of the revolution in methods of navigation.

September 14, 1847.— Occupation of the City of Mexico.

The approaches to the City of Mexico were strongly guarded by batteries and troops, but by perseverance and daring all were overcome, and Santa Anna and his army fled.

September 14, 1847, "General Scott, at the head of the American troops, made a triumphal entry into the city."

References:

History of the Mexican War.— Mansfield.
Popular History of the United States.— Bryant.
Battles of the United States.— Dawson.
Our Country.— Lossing.
War with Mexico.— R. S. Ripley.

Appropriate Selections:

Selection from Mansfield's History of the Mexican War.

September 15, 1789.— James Fenimore Cooper born.

Selections from:

The Spy.
The Deerslayer.
The Pathfinder.

September 16, 1776.— Battle of Harlem Plains.

While Washington's army was in New York, after the retreat from Long Island, it was decided to fortify Harlem Heights. Here the Americans were attacked by a strong detachment of British, and after a severe skirmish, were victorious.

References:

The American Revolution.— Fiske.
Popular History of the United States.— Bryant.
Battles of the Revolution.— Carrington.
Battles of the United States.— Dawson.

September 16, 1823.— Francis Parkman born.

Selections from:

The Conspiracy of Pontiac.
France and England in North America — A Series of Historical Narratives.

September 17, 1787.— Adoption of the National Constitution at Philadelphia.

A stronger government than that provided for by the articles of confederation which had formerly held the colonies together, was found necessary, and a convention met at Philadelphia in May, 1787, to formulate a constitution.

References:

Critical Period of American History.— Fiske.
Popular History of the United States.— Bryant.
Rise of the Republic of the United States.— Frothingham.
1776.— Lossing.

Appropriate Selections:

The Building of the Ship.— Longfellow.
Insufficiency of the Confederation.— Hamilton.
See Dexter Smith, p. 318.

September 17, 1862.— Battle of Antietam.

Taking advantage of the weak condition of the Union army, the Confederates, under General Lee, marched towards Washington, but were confronted by the forces of Generals Bank and Pope. These generals were defeated, the latter in the second battle of Bull Run (August 29th and 30th); and Lee crossed the Potomac into Maryland. Meanwhile McClellan had been recalled from the James, and, having assumed the command of the army in Maryland, defeated Lee in the battle of South Mountain and in the greater conflict of Antietam (September 17). Lee at once withdrew across the Potomac, but McClellan made no pursuit and in November was superseded by Burnside.

References:

Battles and Leaders of the Civil War.— Davis.
Bird's Eye View of Our Civil War.— Dodge.

Appropriate Selections:

Barbara Frietchie.— Whittier.
The Conflict at Antietam.— Lossing.

September 18, 1793.— Cotton Gin invented by Eli Whitney.

References:

Popular History of the United States.— Bryant.

September 18, 1793. — President Washington laid the corner-stone of the National Capitol.

See " The Capitol," p. 51.

September 19, 1777.—First battle of Stillwater (Saratoga), or battle of Bemis Heights.

Under Arnold's and Kosciusko's direction, Gates had fortified Bemis Heights, a point which Burgoyne must cross on his way to Albany. The British, recognizing the necessity of pushing on, began the attack at once. The contest was ended by darkness, each side claiming the victory. Although the British remained on the field, their advance to Albany was stopped. The American loss equaled about half that of the British.

References:

The American Revolution.— Fiske.
Popular History of the United States.— Bryant.
History of the United States.— Hildreth.
1776.— Lossing.

Appropriate Selection:

The Right of the Line. See p. 20.

September 19, 1863. — Battle of Chickamauga.

In June, 1863, Rosecrans again undertook the task of capturing Chattanooga, but succeeded only so far as to compel Bragg to abandon the place. On September 19th, the Confederates under General Bragg suddenly attacked the Union forces under General Rosecrans at Chickamauga, and nearly routed them. But here, as at Murfreesboro, General George H. Thomas saved the day by holding the center of the Union position.

References:

Battles and Leaders of the Civil War.— Davis.
Bird's Eye View of Our Civil War.— Dodge.

Appropriate Selections:

Rosecrans and the Chickamauga Company — Major William J. Richards, in War Papers.

September 19, 1881.— Garfield died.   Arthur became President.

September 20, 1697.— **Peace of Ryswick, ending King William's war.**

September 20, 1703.— **Beginning of Queen Anne's war.**

September 22, 1780.— Meeting of Arnold and Andre.

References:

Popular History of the United States.— Anderson.

The American Revolution.— Fiske.

1776.— Lossing.

Popular History of the United States.— Bryant.

Diary of the American Revolution.— Moore.

The Treason of Arnold, by Jared Sparks in Half-Hours with American History, by Morris.

Appropriate Selections:

Execution of Major Andre, in Letter to Lawrens, by Alexander Hamilton, in Anderson's United States Reader.

Andre's Last Request.— Willis.

Benedict Arnold.— Garden. See Anderson's United States Reader.

" I was born in America, I lived there to the prime of my life; but alas, I can call no man in America my friend."— Arnold.

September 23, 1779.— Paul Jones' naval victory.

Paul Jones, with a small squadron, encountered two British frigates and a merchant fleet off the coast of Great Britain. Jones lashed his flagship, The Bon Homme Richard, to the British ship Serapis and one of the most desperate of sea-fights ensued, lasting from seven until ten, when the frigates struck their flags. It was the first naval victory won under the American flag.

References:

The American Revolution.— Fiske.

Popular History of the United States.— Bryant.

1776.— Lossing.

History of the Navy of the United States of America.— Cooper.

American History told by Contemporaries.— Hart.

Life of Paul Jones.— Mackenzie.

History of the Navy.— Maclay.

September 24, 1669.— Fort Orange surrendered to the English and was renamed Albany.

September 24, 1846.— Surrender of Monterey.

After a series of assaults by General Taylor's troops, Monterey capitulated, a city strong in natural defenses and furthermore garrisoned by ten thousand troops. The American force was far inferior.

References:

Battles of the United States.— Dawson.
Our Country.— Lossing.
War with Mexico.— R. S. Ripley.
History of the Mexican War.— Mansfield.

Appropriate Selections:

The Martyr of Monterey.— Rev. J. G. Lyons.
Monterey.— Charles F. Hoffman, p. 324.

September 24, 1869.— " Black Friday " in New York.

On the 24th of September, 1869, there was a terrific panic in the gold-room on Wall street, New York, when a few conspirators held nearly all the gold in this country, and would give it out only at ruinous prices. A telegram from the Secretary of the Treasury at Washington offering $4,000,000 of gold for sale made a great fall in the price, and relieved the financial situation. The business of the country suffered for months because of the effects of the panic.

References:

School History of the United States.— Lee.

September 25, 1513.— Discovery of the Pacific ocean by Balboa.

In 1513, Balboa, the governor of the Spanish Colony at the Isthmus of Darien, while crossing the isthmus, gained the summit of a mountain from which he discovered the Pacific Ocean. After falling on his knees and thanking God for the privilege of being the discoverer of this great ocean, he descended to the seashore and took possession of the whole coast in the name of the Spanish Crown.

References:

Discovery of America, vol. II.— Fiske.
America, vol. II.— Winsor

Appropriate Selections:
Discovery of Pacific Ocean.— Irving.

September 25, 1690.— First newspaper in America.

On September 25, 1690, there appeared in Boston the first newspaper in America, called " Public Occurrences," but the Legislature suppressed its publication after the first number.

References:

History of the United States.— E. E. Childs.

September 28, 1868.— Chinese Embassy.

In 1868 China sent to the United States the first embassy she had ever commissioned to any foreign nation.

October 3, 1800.— George Bancroft born.

A prominent historian.

October 4, 1777.— Battle of Germantown.

At sunrise on October 4th, Washington, with a large force, surprised the British at Germantown. "At first his success was complete, but a dense fog finally frustrated his plans, and, seeing that the day was lost, he ordered a retreat."

References:

Popular History of the United States.— Bryant.
Battles of the United States.— Dawson.
American Revolution.— Fiske.
1776.— Lossing.
History of the United States.— Bancroft.

October 5, 1813.— Battle of the Thames.

After Perry's victory on Lake Erie, American forces commanded by Harrison overtook the British and Indians commanded by Proctor and Tecumseh and defeated them. Tecumseh was slain and all that Hull had previously lost was was regained.

References:

Half-Hours with American History.— Morris.
Pictorial Field-Book of the War of 1812.— Lossing.
Popular History of the United States.— Bryant.
Battles of the United States.— Dawson.

October 7, 1765.— Stamp Act Congress.

As a result of the Stamp Act, delegates from all the colonies except Virginia, North Carolina, Georgia and New Hampshire, met at New York to decide upon some plan of opposition, and sent petitions to the king and commons. The unrepresented colonies also sent similar petitions.

References:

Rise of the Republic of the United States.— Frothingham.
Popular History of the United States, vol. III.— Bryant.
The American Revolution.— Fiske.
American History Told by Contemporaries, vol. II.— Hart.

Appropriate Selections:

It was in opposing the Stamp Act that Patrick Henry said, " Caesar had his Brutus; Charles I., his Cromwell; and George III.,"—" Treason, Treason! " cried his opponents. The orator paused, looked the speaker of the house calmly in the eyes and finished his sentence —" may profit by their example. If this be treason, make the most of it."

British Orations.— Adams.

October 7, 1777.— Battle of Saratoga.

Finding that he must either fight or surrender, Burgoyne attempted to cut his way through the American lines, but in spite of his determined exertions he was compelled to fall back. The battle of Saratoga is classed as one of the fifteen decisive battles of the world.

References:

American Revolution.— Fiske.
Battles of the United States.— Dawson.
Popular History of the United States.— Bryant.
'1776.— Lossing.
History of the United States.— Bancroft.

October 7, 1780.— Battle of King's Mountain.

The British under Ferguson were attacked and defeated at King's Mountain. The Americans ascended in three divisions on three sides, thus gradually entrapping the British, as the fourth side was too steep for retreat.

References:

The American Revolution.— Fiske.
Popular History of the United States.— Bryant.
1776.— Lossing.
King's Mountain and Its Heroes.— Draper.

October 7, 1826.— First Railroad in the United States.

A railroad was put into operation at Quincy, Mass., to transport granite about three miles to tide-water. Granite sleepers were used, upon which timbers were placed, and on these flat bars of iron were spiked. The cars were drawn by horses. This is commonly supposed to be the first railroad in America, but there is reported to have been an earlier one of unknown date in Pennsylvania.

References:

Popular History of the United States.— Bryant.
American Centenary.— Lossing.

26

October 9, 1779.— Abandonment of the Siege of Savannah.

General Lincoln, in command of the patriot forces of the South, with the help of the French fleet, tried to recover Savannah. After a three weeks' siege, an assault was made. The Americans were repulsed with heavy loss.

References:

Battles of the United States.— Dawson.
American Revolution.— Fiske.
Popular History of the United States.— Bryant.
1776.— Lossing.

Appropriate Selections:

Pulaski's Banner.— Longfellow.

October 12, 1492.— **Discovery of America.**

Christopher Columbus, the discoverer of America, was born in the city of Genoa, Italy. Believing the earth to be round, he concluded that by sailing westward he would reach India sooner than by the usual route by way of Egypt and the Red Sea. Genoa refused his applications for aid, as did also Portugal and England, but Spain finally came to his assistance. A little over four hundred years ago, on Friday, the third of August, Columbus sailed from the port of Palos, in Spain, and ten weeks later, on Friday, the 12th of October, 1492, he landed at San Salvador, one of the Bahamas.

References:

Students' History of the United States.— Channing.
History of the United States.— Bancroft.
History of the United States.— Hildreth.

Appropriate Selections:

Landing of Columbus.— From Irving's Life and Voyage of Columbus.
Landing of Columbus.— Robertson.
First Voyage of Columbus.— Joanna Bartle.
Character of Columbus.— Irving.
Chauncey M. Depew, p. 162.
Columbus Day, p. 157.

October 13, 1812.— Battle on Queenstown Heights.

References:

History of the Second War with England.— J. H. Headley.
Pictorial Field-Book of the War of 1812.— Lossing.
Popular History of the United States.— Bryant.
Battles of the United States.— Dawson.

October 16, 1859.— John Brown's Raid at Harper's Ferry.

John Brown took an active part in the Kansas troubles. An ardent abolitionist, he formed plans to liberate the slaves. Collecting a small, well-armed
force, he suddenly seized the arsenal at Harper's Ferry, Virginia, October 16,
1859. After a desperate resistance, he was captured, tried, and executed. The
event was of the utmost importance in the development of the Civil war.

References:

Life of John Brown.— F. B. Sanborn.
History of the United States.— Schouler.
Popular History of the United States.— Bryant.
History of the United States from the Compromise of 1850.— Rhodes.

Appropriate Selections:

The Battle-Cry of Freedom.

October 17, 1777.— Surrender of Burgoyne.

As a result of the Battle of Saratoga, Burgoyne was forced to surrender, for
he was hedged in without provisions by the patriot forces.

References:

American Revolution.— Fiske.
1776.— Lossing.
Half-Hours with American History.— Morris.
Popular History of the United States.— Bryant.

Appropriate Selections:

Surrender of Burgoyne.—Anderson's United States Reader.
Burgoyne's Surrender.— George William Curtis.

October 18, 1831.— Helen Fiske Hunt Jackson born.

Selections from:
Ramona.
A Century of Dishonor.

October 19, 1781.— Surrender of Cornwallis.

Cornwallis, shut up in Yorktown, attacked by sea and land, was compelled to
surrender. This virtually ended the Revolutionary war, although nearly two
years elapsed before the final treaty of Paris.

References:

The American Revolution.— Fiske.
Popular History of the United States.— Anderson.
Popular History of the United States.— Bryant.
1776.— Lossing.

Appropriate Selections:

Selection from Holmes' Annals of America.
Yorktown.— Whittier.
The Battle of Yorktown.— See p. 179.

October 22, 1776.— Execution of Nathan Hale.

References:

The Two Spies.— Lossing.
Popular History of the United States.— Bryant.
Popular History of the United States.— Anderson.
History of the United States.— Hildreth.

Appropriate Selections:

A Brave Man's Death.— Anonymous.
Nathan Hale.— Frances Miles Finch.
The Ballad of Nathan Hale.— Anonymous.
" I regret that I have but one life to give to my country."— Capt. Nathan Hale.

October 25, 1812.— The United States captured the Macedonian.

The frigate United States, Commodore Decatur, compelled the Macedonian
to surrender after a two-hours' action west of the Canary Islands.

References:

History of the Navy.— Maclay.
History of the Navy of the United States.— Cooper.
Pictorial Field-Book of the War of 1812.— Lossing.

October 28, 1776.— Battle of White Plains.

As Washington's forces on Harlem Heights were so strong, Howe determined
to gain his rear. But Washington, informed of Howe's movements, crossed the
Harlem River to meet him, and at White Plains a severe battle was fought. The
Americans were driven to the hills of North Castle, whither the British dared
not go.

References:

Battles of the United States.— Dawson.
Popular History of the United States.— Bryant.
American Revolution.— Fiske.
Battles of the American Revolution.— Carrington.
History of the United States.— Bancroft.

October 28, 1886.— Bartholdi's Statue of Liberty Enlightening the World, the gift of the French people, was formally unveiled in New York Harbor.

October 30, 1753.— French and Indian war.

The French having seized three British traders, and built forts on the land of the Ohio Company, an association formed under a royal grant to trade with the Indians, Governor Dinwiddie of the Virginia Colony selected George Washington, then about twenty-two, to carry a letter of remonstrance to the French commandant — the first public service of importance performed by Washington.

References:

History of the United States.— Anderson.
History of the United States.— Hildreth.
History of the United States.— Bancroft.
School History of the United States.— Lee.
America, vol. V.—Winsor.

Appropriate Selections:

Incidents of Washington's Journey.— Lossing.

October 31, 1864.— Nevada admitted to the Union.

November 1, 1683.— Original counties of New York established.

Albany, Dutchess, Kings, New York, Orange, Queens, Richmond, Suffolk, Ulster, and Westchester.

November 1, 1889.— Washington admitted to the Union.

November 2, 1889.— North Dakota admitted to the Union.
　　　　　　　　　　　South Dakota admitted to the Union.

November 3, 1794.— William Cullen Bryant born.

His "Thanatopsis," 1817, marks the first date in our true American poetry.

Selections:

Thanatopsis.
Forest Hymn.
Antiquity of Freedom.

November 7, 1811.— Battle of Tippecanoe.

In the troubles prior to the war of 1812, the British again excited the Indians to make war upon the American frontier. General Harrison took measures against them, and at Tippecanoe was treacherously attacked by the Prophet, a brother of the Indian leader. After one of the most desperate battles ever fought with the Indians, the Americans repulsed them with heavy losses.

References:

　　Battles of the United States.— Dawson.
　　Popular History of the United States.— Bryant.
　　Our Country.— Lossing.

November 7, 1814.— Seizure of Pensacola.

During the war of 1812, the Spaniards at Pensacola allowed the British to take possession of their forts and fit out expeditions against the United States. General Jackson, with 3,000 men, marched to Pensacola, seized the town, and forced the British to leave.

References:

　　Pictorial Field-Book of the War of 1812.— Lossing.
　　Popular History of the United States.— Bryant.

November 8, 1889.— Montana admitted to the Union.

November 11, 1778.— Massacre at Cherry Valley.

A party of Tories and Indians fell upon Cherry Valley, and killed or carried away captive many of the inhabitants.

References:

　　The American Revolution.— Fiske.
　　Popular History of the United States.— Bryant.
　　1776.— Lossing.
　　History of the United States.— Bancroft.

November 12, 1824.— Orleans county erected from territory of Genesee.

November 15, 1777.— **Articles of Confederation.**

The representatives of Congress entered into the Articles of Confederation, November 15, 1777. The Confederacy was to be "the United States of America;" each state was to retain its sovereignty and independence. The states were united for their common defence.

References:

　　American Revolution.— Fiske.
　　History of the United States.— Bancroft.
　　Popular History of the United States.— Bryant.
　　1776.— Lossing.

November 16, 1776.— Capture of Fort Washington by the British.

After the battle of White Plains, Howe sent a force of Hessians to attack Fort Washington. They captured it with a loss of 1,000 men while more than 2,000 American prisoners were taken.

References:

    The American Revolution.— Fiske.
    Battles of the American Revolution.— Carrington.
    Popular History of the United States.— Bryant.

November 19, 1863.— Dedication of the National Cemetery at Gettysburg.

One of the most interesting events of the year 1863 was the dedication of the National cemetery at Gettysburg. It took place in the presence of a vast concourse of visitors, and an oration was delivered by Edward Everett. The brief address of President Lincoln on that occasion was especially admired for the touching pathos of its sentiment and the simple beauty of its diction. Of all his utterances this is undoubtedly the most expressive of the purity and loftiness of his character.

Appropriate Selections:

    National Cemetery at Gettysburg — Address at National Cemetery at Gettysburg.— Edward Everett.
    Lincoln's Gettysburg address, p. 337.

November 23–25, 1863.— **Battle of Chattanooga.**

When Thomas took command of the army after the battle of Chickamauga, he was obliged to shelter his army in Chattanooga, where Bragg blockaded it. Meanwhile Grant with the combined armies west of the Alleghanies, Sherman's corps, and Hooker, with a detachment from the army of the Potomac, arrived at the scene of action. The Confederate center was carried by assault; Lookout Mountain was cleared in the " battle above the clouds; " all the strong Confederate positions were taken, and Bragg's army completely routed.

References:

    Battles and Leaders of the Civil War.— Davis.
    Bird's Eye View of Our Civil War.— Dodge.
    Popular History of the United States.— Anderson.

Appropriate Selections:

    Midnight on Missionary Ridge.— Captain A. C. Ford.
    Missionary Ridge.— Brevet Lieut.-Col. Martin L. Bundy.

November 24, 1832.— Nullification Act.

The cotton-growing states objected to the tariff of 1828, which was to encourage and protect the manufacture of certain articles in America by imposing a heavy duty upon imports. South Carolina openly opposed the law; a convention ordained that the tariff law was null and void, and that if the government should attempt to enforce, South Carolina would secede from the Union. Soon, however, quiet was restored by a compromise bill providing for the gradual reduction of the duties.

References:

United States.— Rhodes.
United States.— Schouler.
Half-Hours with American History.— Morris.
Select Documents of United States History.— Macdonald.

Appropriate Selections:

Johnston's Orations.— vol. IV.

November 25, 1783.— Evacuation Day.

On November 25, the British army left New York, while Washington and Governor Clinton took possession. It was a scene of public festivity.

References:

Popular History of the United States.— Bryant.
1776.— Lossing.
Critical Period of American History.— Fiske.

November 29, 1802.— Ohio admitted to the Union.

November 29, 1811.— Wendell Phillips born.

Selections from:

Toussaint l'Ouverture.
The Lost Arts.

December 2, 1823.— **Monroe Doctrine.**

Napoleon's triumph in Spain led to revolts in the Spanish Colonies in America; another so-called " Holy Alliance " had been suggested to consider aiding Spain to reduce the Colonies; and Russia had claimed part of the Pacific coast of North America. Finally Great Britain proposed that England and the United States should unite in a declaration against European intervention in America. The proposal was declined. In his annual message, Monroe stated the policy known as the Monroe Doctrine: " America for Americans."

References:

    Select Documents of United States History.— Macdonald.
    Popular History of the United States.— Bryant.
    Students' History of the United States.— Channing.

December 3, 1818.— Illinois admitted to the Union.

December 4, 1682.— Establishment of the Quaker colony in Pennsylvania.

    ¯Actuated by a desire to found a colony where civil and religious liberty might be enjoyed, and where the people might dwell together in peace, William Penn obtained from Charles II. a tract of land west of the Delaware and called it Pennsylvania. After several conferences with the Indians, he met them beneath the wide-spreading elm at a place now called Kensington, a part of Philadelphia, where he made his famous treaty of peace and friendship with the Redmen — a treaty " never sworn to and never broken."

References:

    School History of the United States.— Lee.
    Ha'f-Hours with American History.— Morris.
    History of the United States.— Hildreth.

Appropriate Selections:

    Penn's Treaty with the Indians, in Anderson's United States Reader.

December 4, 1783.— Washington took leave of his officers and gave up the active command of the American army.

References:

    Popular History of the United States.— Anderson.
    Popular History of the United States.— Bryant.
    Our Country.— Lossing.

Appropriate Selections:

    Washington's Address to the Officers of the Army.

December 10, 1817.— Mississippi admitted to the Union.

December 10, 1898.— **Treaty of peace signed between Spain and the United States.**

    The Commissioners of both governments met in Paris in October and exchanged their powers. The negotiations then begun, lasted until December 10, when the treaty was signed. The Americans did their work among hostile nations, in a way which added another triumph to the annals of American diplomacy.

References:

The War with Spain.— H. C. Lodge.

Appropriate Selections:

The Peace Conference and the Moral Aspect of War.— North American Review, October, 1899.

December 11, 1777.—Washington's army went into winter quarters at Valley Forge.

References:

Popular History of the United States.— Bryant.
The American Revolution.— Fiske.
History of the United States.—Bancroft.
1776.— Lossing.

Appropriate Selections:

Selections from the Life of General Greene.— Greene.
Selection from Irving's Life of Washington.

December 11, 1816.— Indiana admitted to the Union.

December 13, 1862.—Battle of Fredericksburg.

Led by General Burnside, their new commander, the Union army crossed the Rappahannock, the design being to march against Richmond by the route from Fredericksburg. Fredericksburg was taken December 13, but, after a disastrous attempt to carry the works behind the city, the river was recrossed. The horror of Fredericksburg led to Burnside's deposition from the command of the army of the Potomac.

References:

Battles and Leaders of the Civil War.— Davis.
Bird's Eye View of Our Civil War.— Dodge.

Appropriate Selections:

Wanted — a man.— E. C. Stedman.
Fredericksburg.— W. F. H., in Richard Grant White's Poetry of the War.

December 14, 1799.— Death of Washington.

References:

Popular History of the United States.— Anderson.
Popular History of the United States.— Bryant.
Our Country.— Lossing.

Appropriate Selections:

The Half-Masted Flag.— p. 25.

December 14, 1819.— Alabama admitted to the Union.

December 16, 1773.— **Boston tea-party.**

The East India Company sent several shiploads of tea to the Colonies. The colonists, however, refused to pay the tax, in spite of the extremely low price of the tea, and at Boston, December 16, 1773, a small band of men disguised as Indians, boarded the ships and threw the tea overboard. The action shows the strict adherence to principle which characterized the colonists.

References:

Popular History of the United States.— Bryant.
The American Revolution.— Fiske.
Rise of the Republic of the United States.— Frothingham.
American History Told by Contemporaries, vol. II.— Hart.

Appropriate Selections:

" It is not, Mr. Moderator, the spirit that vapors within these walls that must stand us in stead. The exertions of this day will call forth events which will make a very different spirit necessary for our salvation. Whoever supposes that shouts and hosannas will terminate the trials of the day entertains a childish fancy. We must be grossly ignorant of the importance and value of the prize for which we contend; we must be equally ignorant of the power of those who have combined against us; we must be blind to that malice, inveteracy, and insatiable revenge which actuates our enemies, public and private, abroad and in our bosom, to hope that we shall end this controversy without the sharpest conflicts,— to flatter ourselves that popular resolves, popular harangues, popular acclamations, and popular vapor will vanquish our foes. Let us consider the issue. Let us look to the end. Let us weigh and consider before we advance to those measures which must bring on the most trying and terrific struggle this country ever saw."— Josiah Quincy, Jr.

December 17, 1807.— John Greenleaf Whittier born.

See p. 152.

December 18, 1867.— **Abolition of slavery in the United States.**

A resolution of Congress, proposing an amendment to the Constitution, abolishing slavery, having been approved by three-fourths of the states, slavery was declared constitutionally abolished.

December 19, 1675.— Attack on the Narragansett Fort.

References:
Popular History of the United States.— Bryant.
Popular History of the United States.— Anderson.

Appropriate Selections:

  The Indian Hunter.— Longfellow.
  Death and Character of King Philip, from Irving's Sketch-Book.

December 20, 1860.— Secession of South Carolina.

  After an exciting canvass, in 1860, in which the slavery question was the
all-absorbing topic, the election resulted in favor of Abraham Lincoln, the can-
didate of the Republican party. When it became known that the party opposed
to the further extension of slavery had been successful, public meetings were
held in South Carolina to bring about a secession of that State from the Union;
and, on the 20th of December, 1860, an ordinance of secession was passed by a
state convention held in Charleston. Six days later, hostilities commenced
which led directly to the great Civil war.

References:

  Bird's Eye View of Our Civil War.— Dodge.
  Division and Reunion.— Wilson.
  Story of the Civil War.— Ropes.
  United States.— Rhodes.
  Confederate States.— Davis.

Appropriate Selections:

  In American Orations.— Johnston.
  Brother Jonathan's Lament for Sister Caroline.— O. W. Holmes.
  The Ordinance of Nullification.— Edward Everett.

December 21, 1864.— Occupation of Savannah.

  Having destroyed Atlanta, September 2, Sherman made his memorable march
through Georgia to the sea coast and occupied Savannah, Dec. 21, 1864.

References:

  Battles and Leaders of the Civil War.— Davis.
  Bird's Eye View of Our Civil War.— Dodge.
  Story of Our Civil War.— Ropes.
  Students' History of the United States.—Channing.
  Civil War in America.— Lossing.

Appropriate Selections:

  Sherman's March to the Sea — Wm. T. Sherman in Half-Hours with Ameri-
    can History.— Morris.

December 22, 1620.— Landing of Pilgrims.

  The first permanent settlement in New England was made at Plymouth by a
small band of pilgrims, dissenters from the Church of England, who fled from
their own country to find religious freedom.

References:

Popular History of the United States.— Anderson.
History of the United States.— Hildreth.
History of the United States.— Bancroft.

Appropriate Selections:

The Pilgrims.— Everett.
Landing of the Pilgrims.— Southey.
Settlement of Plymouth.— Palfrey, in History of New England.
The Pilgrim Fathers.— Pierpont.
The Landing of the Pilgrims.— p. 163.
John Boyle O'Reilly.— p. 167.
Landing of the Pilgrims.— p. 167

December 23, 1783.— Washington resigned his commission to Congress.

References:

Popular History of the United States.— Bryant.
Rise of the Republic of the United States.— Frothingham.
Critical Period of American History.— Fiske.

Appropriate Selections:

The closing scene from William Gordon's History of the Rise, Progress, and
Establishment of the Independence of the United States of America.
Selection from Ramsay's Life of Washington.

December 24, 1814.— **Treaty of Ghent.**

About a month after the defeat of the British at New Orleans, news came that
a treaty of peace had been signed at Ghent. " Peace! peace! peace! was the
deep, harmonious, universal anthem. The whole night, Broadway sang its song
of peace; and the next day, Sunday, all the churches sent up hymns of thanksgiving for the joyous tidings."

References:

Pictorial Field-Book of the War of 1812.— Lossing.
Popular History of the United States.— Bryant.

December 26, 1776.— **Battle of Trenton.**

The Americans were at this time gloomy and almost despairing of victory;
their army had met defeat, hardship, and discouragement. The British troops
were divided throughout New Jersey, a force of 1,200 being stationed at Trenton. On the night of the 25th, Washington himself led 2,400 trusted soldiers
to the attack. They crossed the river in a fearful storm; the next morning
marched nine miles to Trenton, through a driving storm, surprised and took the
city. " That victory turned the shadows of Death into the morning."

References:

The American Revolution.— Fiske.
Popular History of the United States.— Bryant.
History of the United States.— Bancroft.
Popular History of the United States.— Anderson.
1776.— Lossing.

Appropriate Selections:

Songs and Ballads of the Revolution.— Moore.
The Battle of Trenton.— Henry Cabot Lodge, p. 260.

December 28, 1835.— Second Seminole war.

As a result of the attempt to remove the Seminole Indians of Florida to lands
west of the Mississippi, war again broke out.   On December 28th, Osceola, the
chief, suddenly attacked a house where General Thompson was dining, and
killed five of the party.   The same day Major Dade, with over 100 men, was attacked, and all but four men were massacred.   The Americans could obtain no
decided victory.   Finally, Osceola appeared with a flag of truce, was captured,
and imprisoned.   Two months later, the Indians were defeated in a desperate
battle near Lake Okeechobee.

References:

Battles of the United States.— Dawson.
Popular History of the United States.— Bryant.
Our Country.— Lossing.

Appropriate Selections:

Osceola.— Lucy Hooper.

December 28, 1846.— Iowa admitted to the Union.

December 29, 1812.— **The Constitution captured the Java.**

After a two hours' fight the United States frigate Constitution, Commodore
Bainbridge, captured the Java off the coast of Brazil.

References:

History of the Navy.— Maclay.
History of the Navy of the United States.— Cooper.
Battles of the United States.— Dawson.
Pictorial Field-Book of the War of 1812.— Lossing.

December 29, 1845.— Texas admitted to the Union.

December 30, 1853.— **The Gadsden Treaty.**

The interests of the United States in a transportation route across the isthmus of Tehuantepec occasioned extensive diplomatic correspondence between the United States and Mexico. In addition, the running of the boundary line under the treaty of Guadalupe Hidalgo had been attended with difficulties. Both questions were dealt with in the Gadsden treaty, December 30, 1853. The area acquired from Mexico was 45,535 square miles.

References:

Select Documents of United States History.— Macdonald.

December 31, 1775.— **Attack on Quebec.**

After a long and hideous march through the wilderness in winter, Arnold reached the Plains of Abraham with only 550 of his 1,100 men. December 1st, Montgomery arrived with his force and took command. As their numbers were small and their field pieces few, a stormy night was selected for the attack. The advance was made in two divisions, under Montgomery and Arnold, but early in the conflict Montgomery was killed and Arnold wounded so that the command fell upon Morgan. In spite of his desperate resistance, he was overpowered by numbers and forced to surrender, for the town had been warned of the movement, and had received reinforcements.

References:

The American Revolution.— Fiske.
Popular History of the United States.— Bryant.
1776.— Lossing.
History of the United States.— Hildreth.

January 1, 1831.— First issue of The Liberator.

The Liberator, an abolitionist paper, was started by William Lloyd Garrison. It had an immense influence against slavery.

References:

Life of William Lloyd Garrison, by his sons.
Popular History of the United States.— Bryant.
Old South Leaflets, III., No. 1.
United States.— Schouler.

Appropriate Selections:

Selection from Old South Leaflets, No. 79.

January 1, 1863.— Emancipation proclamation.

On the first of January, 1863, President Lincoln issued his memorable proclamation, declaring free all the slaves within the borders of the States at war with the general government. By this measure, more than three millions of slaves were declared free. On the same day Galveston was taken; and the naval force before the place was captured, destroyed, or dispersed by the Confederates.

References:

Old South Leaflets; General Series, No. II.
Story of the Civil War.— Ropes.
Life of Lincoln.— Morse.

Appropriate Selections:

Boston Hymn.— R. W. Emerson.
Charles A. Dana.— p. 280.

January 1, 1879.— Resumption of specie payments.

During the Civil war, Government notes were greatly depreciated and gold became a marketable product. At the close of the war, however, the price gradually declined; and on the first of January, 1879, the government and the banks resumed specie payments, gold and silver once more coming into general use.

January 1, 1899.— Nassau county erected from territory of Queens.

January 2, 1776.— First Continental flag.

It was composed of thirteen stripes and the union of the crosses of St. George and St. Andrew.

References:

Popular History of the United States.— Bryant.
The American Revolution.— Fiske.
A Brief History of the Flag.— See p. 5.

January 3, 1777.— Battle of Princeton.

Washington's small force was confronted at Trenton by Cornwallis and a large army. As a battle seemed full of peril, Washington broke camp in the night, deceiving his enemy by keeping his camp-fires burning, and at sunrise met the British forces near Princeton. At first the Americans gave way, but Washington, with a select corps, routed the enemy. The British loss was about 400 men, while the American loss was not more than thirty.

References:

The American Revolution.— Fiske.
Popular History of the United States.— Bryant.
Popular History of the United States.— Anderson.
1776.— Lossing.
History of the United States.— Bancroft.

Appropriate Selections:

Washington at Princeton.— Miss C. F. Orne.

January 4, 1896.— Utah admitted to the Union.

January 8, 1815.— **Battle of New Orleans.**

Jackson, in command of the American troops at New Orleans, had raised a line of defense extending a mile in front of the forces, while the Mississippi was on his right flank, and a jungle on his left. The British under Pakenham made an advance, but volley after volley was poured upon them until they had to flee. Pakenham was slain and 2,000 of his men were killed, wounded, or taken prisoners. The Americans had seven killed and six wounded.

References:

Half-Hours with American History.— Morris.
Pictorial Field-Book of the War of 1812.— Lossing.
Popular History of the United States.— Bryant.

Appropriate Selections:

Dirge for a Soldier.
Battle of New Orleans.— Thomas Dunn English.
Selection from Paxton's Life of Andrew Jackson.

January 11, 1757.— Alexander Hamilton born.

A statesman and leader of the Revolutionary period, and during the formation of the Constitutional period.

Selection from:

The Federalist.

January 17, 1706.— Benjamin Franklin born.

Selections from:

His Autobiography.

27

January 17, 1781.— Battle of the Cowpens.

•At the Cowpens, the British under Tarleton attacked the Americans commanded by Morgan. After a severe battle, the British were completely routed, losing about eight hundred men, while the American loss was about eighty.

References:

Battles of the United States.— Dawson.
Popular History of the United States.— Bryant.
The American Revolution.— Fiske.
1776.— Lossing.

Appropriate Selections:

Selection from " Life of Nathaniel Greene."— George W. Greene.

January 18, 1782.— Daniel Webster born.

Selections from:

The Reply to Hayne.
Speech on the Fugitive Slave Law.

January 19, 1809.— Edgar Allen Poe born.

Selections:

The Raven.
The Bells.

January 26, 1837.— Michigan admitted to the Union.

January 27, 1789.— Ontario county erected from territory of Montgomery.

January 29, 1861.— Kansas admitted to the Union.

January 29, 1850.— **Compromise of 1850.**

The compromise measures proposed by Clay, January 29, 1850, consisted of four acts providing for " The organization of territorial governments for New Mexico and Utah without mention of slavery; the establishment of the boundary of Texas; the abolition of the slave-trade in the District of Columbia; and the surrender to their masters of slaves escaping to free states." The last measure was known as the Fugitive Slave Law.

References:

United States.— Rhodes.
The United States of America, 1765-1866.— Channing.
Popular History of the United States.— Bryant.
Select Documents of United States History.— Macdonald.
Johnston's Orations.

February 2, 1848.— Treaty of peace signed at Guadalupe Hidalgo (Close of the Mexican war.)

By the treaty with Mexico, February 2, 1848, all the territory north of the Rio Grande, New Mexico and California was ceded to the United States; $15,000,000 was to be paid for the acquired territory and debts due from Mexico to American citizens should be assumed by the United States.

References:

Popular History of the United States.— Bryant.
United States Reader.— Anderson.

February 5, 1823.— Yates county erected from territory of Ontario.

February 6, 1778.— Treaty between the United States and France.

The alliance with France therein made insured the final independence of the United States.

References:

The American Revolution.— Fiske.
American History Told by Contemporaries.— Hart.
Half-Hours with American History.— Morris.
1776.— Lossing.
Popular History of the United States.— Bryant.

February 7, 1791.— Rensselaer county erected from territory of Albany.
Saratoga county erected from territory of Albany.

February 8, 1690.— Schenectady destroyed.

The troubles between England and France led to war in the colonies between the English and French. On February 8, 1690, the first attack was made by the French and Indians. Albany was to be the place of attack, but the Indians chose Schenectady and the French followed. They quietly entered the town at midnight with no resistance, as the palisades were deserted, massacred many of the inhabitants and burned the town.

References:

Popular History of the United States.— Bryant.

February 8, 1860.— Organization of the Confederacy.

On the 8th of February, a congress, composed of delegates from all the seceding states, except Texas, met at Montgomery, and four days later organized a government by the adoption of a Provisional Constitution, assuming the title, Confederate States of America. On the 9th, this congress elected Jefferson Davis President of the Confederacy, and on the 18th, Texas being represented, he was duly inaugurated.

References:

Popular History of the United States.— Anderson.
School History of the United States.— Lee.
Bird's Eye View of Our Civil War.— Dodge.
Confederate States.— Davis.

Appropriate Selections:

Davis' Address.— Bennett, in Moore's Personal and Political Ballads.
Jefferson Davis.— Cornwall, in Moore's Personal and Political Ballads.

February 11, 1847.— Thomas Edison, the inventor of the phonograph, born.

February 12, 1809.— Abraham Lincoln born.

The Birthday of Abraham Lincoln.— p. 269.
Theodore Frelinghuysen.— p. 271
Ralph Waldo Emerson.— p. 274.

February 14, 1859.— Oregon admitted to the Union.

February 15, 1898.— Battle-ship Maine blown up in Havana Harbor.

In 1895 occurred one of the numerous insurrections in Cuba against Spanish rule. In a short time people were forced to recognize the fact that this time the Cubans were determined to win their liberty. Affairs went from bad to worse and the Spanish cruelties towards the Cubans, and finally towards the Americans in Havana, led to the United States sending the battleship "Maine" to Havana as a protection in case of further atrocities. Spain was unduly suspicious, and the effects of its corrupt system of government were shown in the blowing up of the Maine and the killing of two hundred and sixty-four men and two officers, in the fancied security of a friendly harbor.

References:

The War with Spain.— Henry Cabot Lodge.

Appropriate Selections:

The Maine. – p. 198.

February 16, 1791.— Herkimer county erected from territory of Montgomery.

Otsego county erected from territory of Montgomery.

Tioga county erected from territory of Montgomery.

February 16, 1807.—**Frigate Philadelphia destroyed at Tripoli by Decatur.**

The Tripolitans were accustomed to capture merchant ships of different nations, and make slaves of their crews. Even the tribute money no longer restrained them and different expeditions were sent against them. In one of these, Commodore Preble's frigate, Philadelphia, was captured and fitted up by the Tripolitans. Shortly afterwards, Stephen Decatur was sent to destroy the ship. At night he succeeded in entering the harbor unseen, boarding the Philadelphia, overcoming the Tripolitan guard, and destroying the vessel. A treaty of peace was made June 4, 1807.

Appropriate Selections:

See p. 237.

References:

History of the Navy.— Maclay.
History of the Navy of the United States.— Cooper.
Popular History of the United States.— Anderson.
Popular History of the United States.— Bryant.

February 17, 1865.— Evacuation of Charleston.

Sherman, having halted at Savannah only long enough to refit his army, was again in motion by February 1st. On the 17th he captured Columbia, compelling the Confederates by this achievement to evacuate Charleston.

References:

Story of the Civil War.— Ropes.
Battles and Leaders of the Civil War.— Davis
Bird's Eye View of Our Civil War.— Dodge.

February 22, 1732.— **George Washington born.**

See p. 243.

February 22, 1819.— Florida ceded to the United States.

When Jackson was sent to Florida to repress the Seminole Indians, he found that they were incited to hostilities by certain people there, and so invaded the country. Trouble with Spain was feared as a result, but all difficulties were finally settled by the treaty signed at Washington, February 22, 1819, when

Spain agreed to sell Florida to the United States for $5,000,000. Florida did not actually come into the possession of the United States, however, until two years later.

References:

    Narrative and Critical History of the United States.— Winsor.
    Students' History of the United States.— Channing.
    Popular History of the United States.— Bryant.

February 22, 1819.— James Russell Lowell born.
    See p. 153.

February 22, 1865.— Occupation of Wilmington.

The active operations of 1865 began with the reduction of Fort Fisher, the main defense of Wilmington, by General Terry, and Admiral Porter's fleet. Wilmington was occupied by the Federal troops a few days after the capture of the fort.

References:

    Story of the Civil War.— Ropes.
    Battles and Leaders of the Civil War.— Davis.
    Bird's Eye View of Our Civil War.— Dodge.

February 23, 1798.— Rockland county erected from territory of Orange.

February 23, 1821.— Livingston county erected from territory of Ontario and Genesee.
                       Monroe county erected from territory of Ontario and Genesee.

February 23, 1847.— Battle of Buena Vista.

With less than five thousand men, General Taylor was attacked at Buena Vista by a Mexican force nearly four times as large, under Santa Anna. After an all-day's determined contest, the Mexicans were driven in disorder from the field.

References:

    Half-Hours with American History.— Morris.
    Popular History of the United States.— Anderson.
    Popular History of the United States.— Bryant.
    Our Country.— Lossing.
    History of the Mexican War.— Mansfield.

Appropriate Selections:

    The Angels of Buena Vista.— Whittier.

February 25, 1868.— Impeachment of President Johnson.

In the summer of 1867, President Johnson requested the resignation of Secretary of War Stanton, who refused to resign. Johnson suspended him in accordance with the provisions of the Tenure-of-Office Act. When the Senate met it refused to agree with this suspension. The President then removed Stanton from the office and gave the portfolio to Thomas. In March, 1868, articles of impeachment were presented by the House at the bar of the Senate. The result of the trial was the acquittal of the President.

References:

Students' History of the United States.— Channing.

February 25, 1791.— First United States bank was chartered by Congress.

It went into operation with a capital of $10,000,000, the government subscribing $2,000,000, and individuals $8,000,000.

References:

Select Documents of United States History.— Macdonald.
Popular History of the United States.— Anderson.
Popular History of the United States.— Bryant.
School History of the United States.— Lee.

February 27, 1807.— Henry W. Longfellow born.
See p. 152.

March 1, 1799.— Essex county erected from territory of Clinton.

March 1, 1816.— Oswego county erected from territory of Onondaga.

March 1, 1867.— Nebraska admitted to the Union.

March 3. 1802.— St. Lawrence county erected from territory of Clinton.

March 3, 1845.— Florida admitted to the Union.

March 4, 1719.— Vermont admitted to the Union.

March 4, 1861.— First inauguration of President Lincoln.

References:

Life of Lincoln.— Morse.
Abraham Lincoln.— Hadley and Hay.
Lincoln.— Herndon.

Appropriate Selections:

Inauguration of Lincoln.— Greely, in American Conflict.
The Constitution and the People.— Lincoln, from his Inaugural Address.

March 4, 1885.— Letter postage reduced to two cents per ounce.

March 5, 1770.— Boston Massacre.

In a collision between the citizens of Boston and some of the British soldiers stationed there, three or four citizens were killed and others wounded. The event aroused the strongest feelings against British tyranny, although the soldiers probably fired into the mob only to preserve their lives.

References:

The American Revolution.— Fiske.
Students' History of the United States.— Channing.

Appropriate Selections:

The Boston Massacre.— Hawthorne.

March 7, 1788.— Clinton county erected from territory of Washington.

March 7, 1809.— Schenectady county erected from territory of Albany.

March 8, 1799.— Cayuga county erected from territory of Onondaga.

March 9, 1862.— **The Monitor and the Merrimac.**

The Merrimac, which had been sunk at Norfolk by the Union commander at the beginning of the war, had subsequently been raised by the Confederates, cut down almost to the water's edge, covered with a plating of railroad iron, and named the Virginia. On the 8th of March she steamed out from Norfolk to Hampton Roads, and destroyed the United States vessels Cumberland and Congress. During the night the Monitor, a newly invented floating battery, commanded by Lieutenant Worden, arrived from New York, and on the following day, the 9th, encountered the Virginia (Merrimac), and disabled her.

References:

Old South Leaflets, III., No. 3.
Battles and Leaders of the Civil War.— Davis.
Bird's Eye View of Our Civil War.— Dodge.
School History of the United States.— Lee.

Appropriate Selections:

The Merrimac and the Monitor.— Estvan.
The Cumberland.— Longfellow.
The Monitor and the Merrimac.— John W. Draper.

March 9, 1893.— Cleveland recalls Hawaiian annexation treaty.

Toward the close of Harrison's administration a revolution broke out in the Hawaiian Islands. The more intelligent inhabitants deposed Queen Liliuaka-lani, established a republican form of government, and then sent commissioners to the United States to propose annexation. A treaty was agreed upon, but, before the Senate had time to vote upon it, Harrison's administration came to a close and Grover Cleveland was elected President. One of the first acts of his administration was to withdraw the treaty from the Senate, and to announce the United States' protectorate to be at an end in Hawaii.

References:

History of the American Nation.— McLaughlin.
American Congress.— Moore.

March 10, 1797.— Delaware county erected from territory of Ulster and Otsego.

March 11, 1808.— Cattaraugus county erected from territory of Genesee.
Chautauqua county erected from territory of Genesee.
Franklin county erected from territory of Clinton.
Niagara county erected from territory of Genesee.

March 12, 1772.— Montgomery county (first known as Tryon county) erected from territory of Albany.
Washington county (first known as Charlotte county) erected from territory of Albany.

March 12, 1813.— Warren county erected from territory of Washington.

March 15, 1781.— Battle of Guilford Court House.

Greene, in command of the Americans, took up his position at Guilford Court House, where he was attacked by the British. Although the result was un-favorable to the Americans, it left Cornwallis in so disabled a condition that he was forced to retreat from the field of victory.

References:

Popular History of the United States.— Bryant.
1776.— Lossing.
American Revolution.— Fiske.

Appropriate Selections:

Selections from Life of Nathaniel Greene.— Greene.
Character of General Greene.— Alexander Hamilton, found in Anderson's United States Reader.

March 15, 1798.— Oneida county erected from territory of Herkimer.
Chenango county erected from territory of Tioga and
Herkimer.

March 15, 1820.— Maine admitted to the Union.

March 17, 1776.— British evacuated Boston.

After the fortifications of Dorchester Heights were completed, Howe, instead
of attacking the American forces, evacuated Boston. Washington was rewarded
with the first gold medal struck in the United States. " Hostibus Primo
Fugatis."

References:

Popular History of the United States.— Bryant.
America, vol. VI.— Winsor.
The American Revolution.— Fiske.
History of the Siege of Boston.— Frothingham.
History of the United States.— Hildreth.
Half-Hours with American History.— Morris.

March 18, 1796.— Steuben county erected from territory of Ontario.

March 21, 1806.— Madison county erected from territory of Chenango.

March 24, 1804.— Seneca county erected from territory of Cayuga.

March 25, 1800.— Greene county erected from territory of Albany and
Ulster.

March 27, 1809.— Sullivan county erected from territory of Ulster.

March 27, 1814.— Defeat of the Creek Indians.

The massacre at Fort Mimms aroused the country against the Indians, and
Generals Jackson and Coffee went into the country of the Creeks to avenge
the massacre. A thousand Indian warriors made a final and desperate stand at
the Horseshoe Bend of the Tallapoosa river, but were completely defeated by
Jackson's force of three thousand men.

References:

Pictorial Field-Book of the War of 1812.— Lossing.
Popular History of the United States.— Bryant.
Battles of the United States.— Dawson.

March 28, 1805.— Jefferson county erected from territory of Oneida.
Lewis county erected from territory of Oneida.

March 28, 1806.— Broome county erected from territory of Tioga.

March 28, 1814.— Surrender of the Essex.

> After a successful cruise of more than a year, Captain Porter was attacked in the harbor of Valparaiso by two British vessels and forced to surrender. The conflict was one of the most desperate of the war.

> *References:*

> History of the Navy.— Maclay.
> History of the Navy of the United States.— Cooper.
> Pictorial Field-Book of the War of 1812.— Lossing.
> Popular History of the United States.— Bryant.

March 29, 1836.— Chemung county erected from territory of Tioga.

March 30, 1802.— Genesee county erected from territory of Ontario.

March 30, 1820.-- **Missouri Compromise.**

> As the Northern people opposed any increase in the number of slave states they tried to prevent the admission of Misouri, with its constitution allowing slavery. After a long and violent discussion, the measure called the Missouri Compromise was adopted. Slavery should be prohibited in all the territory, except Missouri, lying north of the parallel 36° 30' and west of the Mississippi. Missouri was admitted August 10, 1821.

> *References:*

> History of the United States.— Schouler.
> Students' History of the United States.— Channing.
> Popular History of the United States.— Bryant.
> Johnston's Orations.

March 30, 1842.— John Fiske born.

> *Selections from:*

> American Political Ideas.
> The Critical Period in American History.

March 30, 1867.— Purchase of Alaska.

> In 1867, the Russian territory in America, now known as Alaska, was bought by the United States for a little over $7,200,000. It is a vast region, lying far north, but its climate is tempered by the warm Pacific current, and it has great tracts of fine cedar and other timber, valuable fisheries, furs, and important minerals.

> *References:*

> Men and Measures of Half a Century.— McCulloch.

March 30, 1870.— Fifteenth Amendment to the Constitution.

The Fifteenth Amendment to the Constitution, guaranteeing to *all citizens* of the United States the right of suffrage, without regard to race, color, or previous condition of servitude, was declared adopted March 30, 1870.

March 31, 1854.— Treaty with Japan.

Japan had always excluded all foreigners from her ports, but as the acquisition of California made commercial relations important, Commodore Perry was sent to open communications. At length a treaty was signed, permitting the United States to trade in two ports, and also the residence of American citizens and consuls at these ports. Thus America was among the first to obtain intercourse with Japan.

References:

Popular History of the United States.— Anderson.
Popular History of the United States.— Bryant.

April 2, 1792.— First United States mint.

By the act of Congress April 2, 1792, the first United States mint was established at Philadelphia for the purpose of national coinage.

References:

Dictionary of United States History.— Jameson.
Popular History of the United States.— Bryant.

April 2, 1743.— Thomas Jefferson born.

Selections:

Declaration of Independence.

April 2, 1821.— Erie county erected from territory of Niagara.

April 3, 1783.— Washington Irving born.

Selections from:

Knickerbocker History of the United States.
Life of Columbus.

April 3, 1822.— Edward Everett Hale born.

Selections from:

Franklin in France.
The Man without a Country.
My Double, and How He Undid Me.

April 3, 1865.— Occupation of Richmond.

On the 29th of March, 1865, commenced the final movement of the national forces which General Grant had gathered around Richmond. After ten days' marching and fighting, the Confederates were compelled to evacuate their defenses at both Petersburg and Richmond.

References:

> Story of the Civil War.— Ropes.
> Battles and Leaders of the Civil War.— Davis.
> Bird's Eye View of Our Civil War.— Dodge.

Appropriate Selections:

> Evacuation of Richmond.— Pollard.

April 4, 1786.— Columbia county erected from territory of Albany.

April 6, 1513.— Discovery of Florida.

In 1513 Ponce de Leon, searching, not for gold, like his countrymen, but for a fountain which the Indians declared would restore a man to perpetual youth, came upon another unknown coast. It was on Easter Sunday, in Spanish " El Pascua Florida," and the new land has borne the name of Florida ever since.

References:

> The Discovery of Florida.— Bancroft.
> Popular History of the United States.— Anderson.
> America, vol. II.— Winsor.

April 6, 1795.— Schoharie county erected from territory of Albany and Otsego.

April 6, 1862.— Battle of Shiloh.

On the morning of the 6th of April, General Grant's army, while encamped at Shiloh, was severely attacked by General A. S. Johnston's army. At nightfall the Union troops had been driven back to the river, where the gunboats aided them to keep the enemy in check. General Johnston was killed. The arrival of reinforcements under General Buell enabled Grant to assume the offensive on the following day, and the Confederates were driven towards Corinth. The forces engaged on both sides numbered more than 100,000 men. The losses on both sides were severe.

References:

> Battles and Leaders of the Civil War.— Davis.
> Bird's Eye View of Our Civil War.— Dodge.

Appropriate Selections:

The Battle of Shiloh.— William Swinton.

Shiloh.— Brig. Gen. George F. McGennis, in War Papers.

April 7, 1806.— Allegany county erected from territory of Genesee.

April 7, 1817.— Tompkins county erected from territory of Cayuga and Seneca.

April 8, 1808.— Cortland county erected from territory of Onondaga.

April 9, 1682.— Discovery of Louisiana.

In February, 1682, La Salle passed down the Illinois river, and on into the Mississippi, on an exploring expedition. The river he called St. Louis, and the vast region through which it flowed, Louisiana, in honor of the French King. On April 9, 1682, he planted a cross with the arms of France near the mouth of the river, and claimed all the territory drained by it and its tributaries for King Louis.

References:

Half-Hours with American History.— Morris.

History of the United States.— Hildreth.

April 9, 1865.— **Surrender of Lee at Appomattox.**

After the evacuation of Petersburg and Richmond, Lee withdrew his army and endeavored to escape by the valley of the Appomattox to the mountains. The retreating army was hotly pursued by the Union forces under Grant, and on the 9th, Lee, overtaken and surrounded, surrendered near Appomattox Court House.

Story of the Civil War.— Ropes.

Battles and Leaders of the Civil War.— Davis.

Bird's Eye View of Our Civil War.— Dodge.

Appropriate Selections:

Last March of Lee's Army.— Armstead L. Long, in Half-Hours with American History.— Morris.

April 11, 1794.— Edward Everett born.

Selection:

Apostrophe to La Fayette, at the close of Everett's address " On the Circumstances Favorable to the Progress of Literature."

April 11, 1823.— Wayne county erected from territory of Ontario and Seneca.

April 12, 1777.— Henry Clay born.

One of America's greatest orators.

April 12, 1816.— Hamilton county erected from territory of Montgomery.

April 14, 1861.— **Evacuation of Fort Sumter.**

Regarding their duty to the general government as secondary to the obligation they owed to their respective states, and in spite of the President's assurance that the new administration did not intend interfering with the constitutional rights of any of the states, the southern leaders organized an army under General Beauregard to reduce Fort Sumter. Accordingly, on the morning of April 12th, the first shot was fired on the fort. After a bombardment of thirty-four hours Anderson was compelled to evacuate. On the following Monday, as if with spontaneous protest against any dissolution of the Union, the flag of the Republic was raised throughout the free states.

References:

Popular History of the United States.— Anderson.
School History of the United States.— Lee.
Bird's Eye View of Our Civil War.— Dodge.
Story of the Civil War.— Ropes.

Appropriate Selections:

The Flag.— Horatio Woodman.
Fort Sumter's Bombardment.— Orville J. Victor, in Half-Hours with American History.— Morris.
The Flag of Fort Sumter.— Anonymous, in Moore's Personal and Political Ballads.
The 12th of April.— E. C. Stedman.

April 14, 1865.— **Assassination of Lincoln.**

Lincoln had served but a few weeks of his second term, when, less than one week after Lee's surrender, he was assassinated by a desperado acting in sympathy with the Confederate cause.

References:

Life of Lincoln.— Morse
Abraham Lincoln.— Nicolay and Hay.

Appropriate Selections:

My Captain.— Whitman, p. 291.

April 15, 1814.— John Lathrop Motley born.

Selections from:

The Rise and Fall of the Dutch Republic.

Merry Mount.

April 17, 1854.— Schuyler county erected from territory of Chemung, Steuben, and Tompkins.

April 18, 1838.— Fulton county erected from territory of Montgomery.

April 18, 1847.— Battle of Cerro Gordo.

The American forces under General Scott made a daring assault on the enemy at Cerro Gordo on the morning of April 18th, and before noon the Mexicans were defeated with a loss of one thousand men and their artillery.

References:

Popular History of the United States.— Bryant.

Our Country.— Lossing.

War with Mexico.— R. S. Ripley.

Story of the Mexican War — Mansfield.

Appropriate Selections :

The Bivouac of the Dead.—p. 28.

April 19, 1775.— Battle of Lexington.

On the night of the 18th of April, 1775, General Gage dispatched eight hundred troops under Colonel Smith and Major Pitcairn to destroy some military supplies which the Americans had collected at Concord, Massachusetts, about sixteen miles from Boston.

The patriots of Boston, suspecting such a movement, were on the alert. Signals had been pre-arranged by them, the alarm was given, and, when the British reached Lexington early in the morning of April 19th, they found about seventy of the militia drawn up under arms. Then was shed the first blood of the Revolution, the King's troops firing upon the American militia. At Concord some of the supplies were destroyed, but, the militia assembling, a skirmish took place in which several from both sides were killed. On their way back to Boston, the British were reinforced at Lexington; but during their retreat, as far as Charleston, the Americans pursued, keeping up a constant and destructive fire. The loss of the British during the day was over 200; that of the patriots about 90. The battle at Lexington was a signal for war.

References:

Siege of Boston.— Frothingham.
Battles of the United States.— Dawson.
Ballad History of the Revolution — Part I.— Moore.
One Hundred Years Ago.— E. E. Hale.
Field-Book of the Revolution.— Lossing.
American Monthly for April and July, 1875.— Potter.
History of American War.— Stedman.

Appropriate Selections:

Concord Hymn.— R. W. Emerson, p. 170.
Battle of Lexington.— O. W. Holmes.
Paul Revere's Ride.— Longfellow.
The Rising in 1776.— T. B. Read, p. 116.
The Revolutionary Alarm, p. 170.
George William Curtis, pp. 171, 172.

April 19, 1861.— First blood shed in civil war.

The news of the capture of Fort Sumter produced an almost uncontrollable excitement throughout the country, and the President's proclamation calling for troops was responded to at once by all the free states. A Massachusetts regiment, while on its way to defend the nation's capital, was attacked, April 19th, in Baltimore, by a mob of southern sympathizers. Two of the soldiers were killed and a number wounded.

References:

Bird's Eye View of Our Civil War.— Dodge.
Story of the Civil War.— Ropes.
United States.— Rhodes.
Popular History of the United States.— Anderson.

Appropriate Selections:

Apocalypse.— Clarence Butler.
The Massachusetts Line.— Robert Lowell.
Our Country's Call.— William C. Bryant.

April 20, 1898.— Declaration of war between United States and Spain.

The report on Cuban affairs having finally passed both Houses, April 18th, went at once to the President, who, on April 20th, signed the resolutions adopted — that Spanish rule must cease in Cuba. In fact, if not in terms, it was a declaration of war.

References:

The War with Spain.— Henry Cabot Lodge.

28

Appropriate Selections:

Selection I., p. 198.
The Stripes and the Stars, p. 308.

April 21, 1649.— Toleration act in Maryland.

The Toleration Act provided for the punishment of all disbelievers in God and for the punishment of those in any way interfering with any one's form of belief.

References:

Old Virginia and Her Neighbors.— Fiske.
A Short History of the English Colonies in America.— Lodge.

April 22, 1889.— Oklahoma opened to settlers.

April 25, 1862.— Capture of New Orleans.

In Louisiana the Union cause met with success of great importance. This was the capture of New Orleans on the 25th of April. The Union fleet, commanded by Farragut and Porter, ascended the Mississippi, bombarding and running past the Confederate forts. The city was reached, and General Butler, taking formal possession, placed it under martial law.

References:

New Orleans.— King.
Battles and Leaders of the Civil War.— Davis.

Appropriate Selections:

New Orleans Won Back.— Robert Lowell.
The Varuna.— George H. Baker.
Farragut on the Mississippi.— Joel P. Headley.
Admiral Farragut, p. 92.

April 26, 1777.— The Marquis de Lafayette, a wealthy young Frenchman of character and ability, sailed from Bordeaux to aid the Americans as a volunteer. He provided a ship and military stores at his own expense.

References:

The American Revolution.— Fiske.
American History told by Contemporaries.— Hart.
Popular History of the United States.— Bryant.
1776.— Lossing.

Appropriate Selections:

Lafayette Joins the Americans.— Sprague. Found in Anderson's Popular History of the United States.

April 26, 1846.— First blood shed in the Mexican war.

The annexation of Texas caused war between Mexico and the United States, as the United States claimed the Rio Grande river as the boundary line, while the Mexicans claimed the Nueces river. General Taylor was sent into Mexico to protect our interests; this the Mexicans regarded as an invasion of their rights. They attacked a small force near Matamoras and killed sixteen men, compelling the rest to surrender.

References:

Our Country.— Lossing.

April 26, 1865.— Surrender of Johnston's army.

After some time spent in elaborate negotiations between Sherman at his head-quarters, and Grant and President Johnson at Washington, terms were finally agreed upon, and Johnston surrendered on terms substantially the same as those accorded to Lee.

References:

Popular History of the United States.— Bryant.

Appropriate Selections:

The Conquered Banner.— Abram J. Ryan.

April 28, 1760.— Battle of Sellery. (Virtual close of the French and Indian war in America.)

De Levis, Montcalm's successor, made extensive preparations for the recovery of Quebec. He marched to Sellery, three miles above the city, and there, on the 20th of April, 1760, was fought one of the most desperate battles of the war. The French were obliged to retreat, Montreal capitulated, and the whole of Canada was surrendered to the English.

The war continued till 1763, when a treaty of peace was signed in Paris by which France ceded to Great Britain (February 10th) all her American posses-sions east of the Missouri and north of the Iberville river in Louisiana; at the same time, Spain ceded Florida to Great Britain. This finally determined that the dominant civilization of North America was to be English instead of French.

References:

Popular History of the United States.— Anderson.
History of the United States.— Hildreth.
History of the United States.— Bancroft.

Appropriate Selections:

State of the Colonies in 1765.— Grahame.

April 30, 1789.— **Inauguration of Washington at New York.**

References:

> Popular History of the United States.— Anderson. ·
> Popular History of the United States.— Bryant.
> 1776.— Lossing.
> Critical Period of American History.— Fiske.

Appropriate Selections:

> " Welcome, Mighty Chief, once more,
> Welcome to this grateful shore;
> Now no mercenary foe
> Aims again the fatal blow —
> Aims at thee, the fatal blow.

> " Virgins fair, and matrons grave,
> These thy conquering arm did save;
> Build for thee triumphal bowers,
> Strew, ye fair, his way with flowers,
> Strew your hero's way with flowers."

April 30, 1803.— **Louisiana purchased from France.**

> Price, $15,000,000.

References:

> United States Reader.— Anderson.
> Popular History of the United States.— Bryant.
> Our Country.— Lossing.

April 30, 1812.— Louisiana admitted to the Union.

May 1, 1541.— De Soto discovered the Mississippi river.

In 1539, Ferdinand De Soto, with a large force of men, landed on the coast of Florida, in a search for gold. The Spanish cruelties had made all the Indians hostile to them, and De Soto had to fight his way westward to the Mississippi river, which he reached May 1, 1541. He crossed the great river and proceeded some distance up the west bank, always disappointed in not finding gold. The party endured great hardships and De Soto himself died of a fever. His followers buried him in the Mississippi river, to secure his body from the savages, and after many days of suffering a few made their way back to Mexico.

References:

Discovery of America.— Fiske.
History of the United States, vol. I.— Bancroft.
Narrative and Critical History of the United States, vol. II.— Winsor.

Appropriate Selections:
Expedition of De Soto.— Parkman.

May 1, 1898.— **Battle of Manila Bay.**

During the night of April 30th, Admiral Dewey took the American fleet past the dreaded fort at the entrance to Manila Bay and then up the twenty-six miles through the narrow channel and over the Spanish mines to Manila, where, the next day, May 1st, the Americans completely destroyed the Spanish fleet. By the 3rd of May, the two forts at the entrance of the harbor had surrendered to Dewey, and Manila was blockaded by the Americans.

References:

The War with Spain.— Henry Cabot Lodge.

Appropriate Selections:
Dewey's Victory, p. 200.
Second Selection, p. 199.
Manila Bay, p. 238.

May 3d and 4th, 1863.— **Battle of Chancellorsville.**

General Hooker, toward the latter part of April, crossed the Rappahannock, and, encountering Lee at Chancellorsville, was disastrously defeated, losing more than 11,000 men. He then recrossed the river. In this battle the Confederate army lost its most brilliant general, Thomas J. Jackson, commonly known as "Stonewall" Jackson, who, towards the close of the action, was mortally wounded, it is said, by the fire of his own men, being, with his staff and escort, mistaken in the darkness for a company of the Union cavalry.

References:

Battles and Leaders of the Civil War.— Davis.
Bird's Eye View of our Civil War.— Dodge.
School History of the United States.— Lee.

Appropriate Selections:
The Wood of Chancellorsville.— Delia R. German in R. G. White's Collection, Poetry of the War.
Keenan's Charge.— G. P. Lathrop.

May 4, 1796.— William Hickling Prescott born.

Selections from:

    History of the Conquest of Mexico.
    History of the Conquest of Peru.

May 8, 1846.— Battle of Palo Alto.

    While returning from Point Isabel, General Taylor with a force of 2,300 men was attacked at Palo Alto by a Mexican force of 6,000 men. The Mexicans lost more than 500, while the American loss was 50.

References:

    Popular History of the United States.— Bryant.
    Battles of the United States.— Dawson.
    Our Country.— Lossing.
    History of the Mexican War.— Mansfield.

May 9, 1846.— Battle of Resaca de la Palma.

    At the battle of Resaca de la Palma the Mexican guns were holding the Americans well in check, when Captain May, at the head of his dragoons, charged with great fury and dispersed the gunners. The Mexicans were defeated with a severe loss.

References:

    War with Mexico.— R. S. Ripley.
    Popular History of the United States.— Bryant.
    Battles of the United States.— Dawson.
    History of the Mexican War.— Mansfield.

May 10, 1775.— Capture of Fort Ticonderoga.

    Early in the morning of the 10th of May, 1775, Ethan Allen, with the Green Mountains Boys, surprised and took Ticonderoga —"in the name of the Great Jehovah and the Continental Congress." It was the first incident of the war in which the Americans took the aggressive.

References:

    Popular History of the United States.— Bryant.
    Capture of Ticonderoga, in Narrative of His Own Captivity.— Allen. Found in Anderson's United States Reader.
    Battles of the United States, vol. I.— Dawson.
    Diary of the American Revolution.— Moore.
    History of the United States.— Hildreth.

Appropriate Selections:

    On General Ethan Allen.— General Hopkins.

May 10, 1775.— Second Continental Congress.

On May 10, 1775, delegates from each of the thirteen colonies assembled for the second continental Congress. They adopted decisive measures and appointed Washington commander-in-chief of the army.

References:

The American Revolution.— Fiske.
The Rise of the Republic of the United States.— Frothingham.
History of the United States of America.— Patton.

Appropriate Selections:

American History told by Contemporaries.— Hart. (The Necessity of Self-Defence.)

May 10, 1865.— Capture of Jefferson Davis at Irwinville, Ga.

References:

The Last Four Weeks of the War.— Hatcher.

May 10, 1876.— International exhibition opened at Philadelphia.

See p. 79.

Appropriate Selections:

Centennial Address.— W. M. Evarts.
Centennial Hymns.— Whittier.

May 12, 1776.— Surrender of Charleston to the British.

After a siege of forty days, General Lincoln, in command of the American troops, was forced to surrender to Clinton.

References:

The American Revolution.— Fiske.
Popular History of the United States.— Bryant.
1776.— Lossing.
Battles of the United States.— Dawson.

May 13, 1607.— First permanent English colony in America.

In 1606, King James I. divided the territory claimed by the English into North and South Virginia, granting the former to the Plymouth Company, the latter to the London Company. The first permanent settlement was made at Jamestown, in 1607, by an expedition sent out by the London Company, commanded by Captain Christopher Newport.

References:

   History of the United States.— Anderson.
   America, vol. III.— Winsor.
   Explorers.— Higginson.

Appropriate Selections:

   Settlement of Jamestown.— Grahame, in his Colonial History of the United
     States.
   Pocahontas.— Hemans.　From the poem entitled American Forest Girl.

May 14, 1841.— Wyoming county erected from territory of Genesee.

May 19, 1643.— New England Confederacy.

   May 19, 1643, the four colonies of Masachusetts, Plymouth, New Haven
and Connecticut entered into a league of confederacy "for unity, offence and
defence, mutual advice and assistance."

References:

   Colonial History of the United States.— Grahame.
   Popular History of the United States.— Bryant.
   New England.— Fiske.
   A Short History of the English Colonies.— Lodge.

May 23d and 24th, 1865. — Grand review.

   The last great scene of the Civil war was a grand military pageant in the city
of Washington, when the armies of the United States passed in review before
the chief officers of the Government, the Congress, and representatives of foreign powers.

   The Army of the Potomac was reviewed on the 23d of May, the Army of the
Mississippi on the following day.　Washington had a two-days' holiday and
everywhere in the city were greetings and displays suitable for the victorious
returning soldiers.

References:

   Popular History of the United States.— Bryant.

Appropriate Selections:

   Spring at the Capital.— E. A. Allen.
   Samuel Francis Smith.— p. 47.
   Sonnet on Disbanding the Army.— Col. David Humphreys.

May 24, 1819.—First ocean steamer.

About May 24, 1819, the Savannah crossed the Atlantic from Savannah, Ga., to Liverpool. Both sails and steam were used.

References:

Popular History of the United States.— Bryant.

May 25, 1637.— Pequod settlement.

Toward the close of 1635, difficulties with the Indians commenced. The Pequods, a warlike tribe in the southeastern part of Connecticut, having committed many acts of hostility, Hartford, Windsor, and Wethersfield united in declaring war against them. A force of colonists and friendly Indians proceeded against the Pequods, burned their forts and wigwams, killed more than 600 of their number, and completely broke them up as a tribe.

References:

History of the United States.— Hildreth.
Half-Hours with American History.— Morris.

May 25, 1803.— Ralph Waldo Emerson born.

Selections:

Hymn on the Dedication of the Concord Monument, p. 144.
From the Essay on History.
From the Essay on Heroism.

May 27, 1819.— Julia Ward Howe born.

Selections:

Battle Hymn of the Republic, p. 139.

May 27, 1844.— The first telegraph message.

The first telegraph line was established between New York and Baltimore by Professor Morse and was successfully operated May 27, 1844.

References:

Popular History of the United States.— Bryant.
P..pular History of the United States.— Anderson.

May 29, 1736.— Patrick Henry born.

Selections:

An Appeal to Arms (Address in the Convention of Virginia, September 28, 1775).

May 29, 1813.— Attack on Sackett's Harbor.

The British, learning that a large force had left Sackett's Harbor, sent a thousand men to attack the place. They were met by a small force, under General Brown, and repulsed.

References:

Pictorial Field-Book of the War of 1812.— Lossing.
Battles of the United States.— Dawson.
Popular History of the United States.— Bryant.

May 29, 1848.— Wisconsin admitted to the Union.

May 31, 1854.— **Kansas-Nebraska bill.**

In 1854 Kansas and Nebraska came into the Union under the rule of popular sovereignty, which left the question of slavery to the people of each territory. After a struggle of some months, the Kansas-Nebraska bill became a law. The Missouri Compromise was abrogated, and the question of slavery in the territories was adrift again, never to be got rid of except through the abolition of slavery itself by war.

References:

American History Leaflets, No. 17.
History of the United States.— Rhodes.
History of the United States.— Schouler.
Constitutional History of the United States.— Van Holst.
Life of Douglas.— Sheahan.
Life of Chase.— Schucker.

May 31, 1862.— **Battle of Fair Oaks.**

The few Union victories were counterbalanced by the ill success of McClellan, who had attempted to reach Richmond by the peninsula between the York and the James rivers. Having arrived within a short distance of the city, he was suddenly attacked at Fair Oaks, by the Confederates, when a bloody but indecisive conflict took place. A movement of McClellan's to change his base of operato the James river brought on a series of destructive battles, lasting through seven days (June 25 to July 1), the result of which was to leave the Union army in a weakened condition.

References:

Battles and Leaders of the Civil War.— Davis.
Bird's Eye View of Our Civil War.— Dodge.

Appropriate Selection:

American Volunteers, p. 222.

May 31, 1889.— Flood at Johnstown.

A broken dam in the Conemaugh Valley, Pennsylvania, flooded Johnstown, and destroyed 2,295 lives.

June 1, 1774.— **Boston port bill.**

England, enraged at the colonies' action in regard to the tea, passed the Port bill, closing Boston harbor to all commerce, and transferring the seat of government to Salem. The act aroused the greatest indignation of the colonists; they burned copies of it on scaffolds, and observed the day upon which it went into effect with fasting and prayer.

References:

Rise of the Republic of the United States.— Frothingham.
Popular History of the United States.— Bryant.
The American Revolution.— Fiske.
History of the United States.— Bancroft.

June 1, 1792.— Kentucky admitted to the Union.

June 1, 1796.— Tennessee admitted to the Union.

June 1, 1813.— **The Chesapeake and the Shannon.**

The American frigate Chesapeake, commanded by Captain Lawrence, was attacked by the British frigate Shannon, just outside Boston harbor. Soon some of the Chesapeake's rigging was cut so that a sail became loose and blew out, bringing the vessel into the wind. Then the rigging and anchor became so entangled that the ship had to remain exposed to the enemy's fire. As Lawrence, mortally wounded, was carried below, he cried, "Don't give up the ship." Finally the English sprang on board and pulled down the flag.

References:

History of the Navy.— Maclay.
History of the Navy of the United States.— Cooper.
Popular History of the United States.— Anderson.

June 3, 1898.— The Merrimac sunk in Santiago Harbor.

Lieutenant Richard P. Hobson, with seven selected volunteers, took the collier Merrimac into the channel of Santiago harbor, and there sunk her by means of torpedoes, as a temporary obstruction to the escape of the Spanish fleet. The deed was fraught with the greatest danger and required the most conspicuous bravery and daring.

References:

> The War with Spain.— Henry Cabot Lodge.
> With Sampson through the War.— Goode.

Appropriate Selections:

> Eight Volunteers, p. 233.

June 9, 1792.— John Howard Payne born.

> Actor and playwright.

Appropriate Selections:

> Home, Sweet Home, p. 39.

June 10, 1861.— Battle of Bethel.

> It can hardly be said that the national government made any offensive movement before the 24th of May. Then General Scott, commanding the Union army, sent troops into Virginia; and Arlington Heights, as well as the town of Alexandria, were occupied. Some days after, June 10th, a force was sent under General Butler to capture a body of Confederate troops posted at Little Bethel, a village on the north side of the James river. During the night, two of the Union regiments fired on each other by mistake; and the Confederates, thus made aware of their approach, escaped. The Union troops then pushed on, and were severely repulsed in an attack upon the Confederate works at Big Bethel.

References:

> Bird's Eye View of Our Civil War.— Dodge.
> Story of the Civil War.— Ropes.
> United States.— Rhodes.

Appropriate Selections:

> Bethel.— A. J. H. Duganne.
> Army Hymns.— O. W. Holmes.
> The Present Crisis.— J. R. Lowell.

June 12, 1812.— Putnam county erected from territory of Dutchess.

June 14, 1777.— Birth of the flag of the United States.

> Congress resolved, "That the flag of the thirteen united colonies be thirteen stripes, alternate red and white, and the union be thirteen stars, white in a blue field, representing a new constellation."

References:

History of the United States.— Hildreth.

Diary of the American Revolution.— Moore.

History of our Flag.— Rev. A. P. Putnam, in Anderson's United States Reader.

A Brief History of the Flag.— See p. 5.

Appropriate Selections:

The American Flag.— J. R. Drake, p. 303.

God Save the Flag.— O. W. Holmes.

Our National Banner.— W. M. Evarts.

The School House Stands by the Flag.— Hezekiah Butterworth, p. 45.

Selections 1 and 3, p. 15.

Our Flag, p. 9.

The Red, White and Blue, p. 19.

Selection, No. 6, p. 35.

June 14, 1812.— Harriet Beecher Stowe born.

Selections from:

Uncle Tom's Cabin.

June 15, 1772.— Benjamin Franklin drew electricity from the clouds and proved its identity with lightning.

References:

Autobiography of Benjamin Franklin.

June 15, 1836.— Arkansas admitted to the Union.

June 15, 1844.— Charles Goodyear patented the process of vulcanizing India rubber.

June 17, 1775.-- Siege of Boston began.

References:

The American Revolution.— Fiske.

Popular History of the United States.— Bryant.

June 17, 1775.— **Battle of Bunker Hill.**

On the evening of June 16th, Colonel Prescott was sent with a detachment of one thousand men to fortify Bunker Hill, but instead he fortified Breed's Hill, which was nearer Boston. The next morning the British commenced a cannonade upon the redoubt. This attack failed, and, later, General Howe, with three thousand men, was sent to dislodge the patriots. Twice the British approached within a few rods, each time to be repulsed with a heavy loss. Upon Clinton's arrival, the third charge was more successful, as the Americans had exhausted their ammunition, and were forced to retreat. The Americans lost General Warren. The determined and for a time successful resistance on the part of the Americans was so encouraging that it had all the effects of a triumph.

References:

    The American Revolution.— Fiske.
    Siege of Boston.— Frothingham.
    Harper's Monthly.— July, 1875.
    Popular History of the United States.— Bryant.

Appropriate Selections:

    Warren's Address.— John Pierpont.
    Grandmother's Story of Bunker Hill.— Holmes.
    Laying of the Corner-Stone of the Bunker Hill Monument.—Webster.
    Edward Everett, pp. 234-5.

June 18, 1778.— Evacuation of Philadelphia.

The loss of Burgoyne's army, the alliance with France, and the arrival of a French fleet under D'Estaing so alarmed the British that they left Philadelphia.

References:

    Popular History of the United States.— Bryant.
    The American Revolution.— Fiske.
    1776.— Lossing.
    History of the United States.— Hildreth.

Appropriate Selections:

    Battle of the Kegs.—Francis Hopkinson.

June 19, 1812.— **Declaration of war against Great Britain.**

The losses to commerce caused by the closing of the ports of England and France in their war, the right of search, the impressment of American seamen, and other insults to which England was subjecting the United States, led to the final declaration of war against Great Britain by the United States.

References:

    Popular History of the United States.— Bryant.
    Pictorial Field-Book of the War of 1812.— Lossing.

June 19, 1816.— West Virginia admitted to the Union.

June 19, 1864.— Alabama and Kearsarge.

The Confederates, by means of English-built privateers sailing under the Confederate flag, succeeded in destroying a large number of American merchantmen. Sumner, in the Alabama, pursued his career of destruction, luring vessels by hoisting the British flag; but the Alabama was at last met by the Kearsarge, Captain Winslow, and, after a short encounter, was sunk.

References:

The Navy during the Rebellion.— Boynton.
Battles and Leaders of the Civil War.— Davis.
Bird's Eye View of Our Civil War.— Dodge.
Story of the Civil War.— Ropes.

June 24, 1497.— Discovery of North America by John and Sebastian Cabot.

In 1497, about one year before Columbus discovered the continent, and two years previous to Amerigo's visit, John Cabot and his son Sebastian, while sailing under a commission from Henry VII. of England, discovered the coast of Labrador, and thus were the first to discover the mainland of America. In a second voyage, made by Sebastian Cabot, in 1498, the coast, from Labrador to Chesapeake Bay, was explored. These achievements of the Cabots, the discovery and explorations, proved of momentous importance, especially to England, as, by reason of them, that country based her claims to all the region from Labrador to Florida.

References:

America, vol. III.— Winsor.
Discovery of America, vol. II.— Fiske.
American History Leaflets.— No. 9.
Students' History of the United States.— Channing.

June 24, 1675.— First battle of King Philip's war.

After the death of Massasoit, the Indians became alarmed at the rapidly growing settlement of the whites, and so the New England tribes united to overthrow the colonists. The first attack was made by King Philip upon the people of Swanzey, as they were returning from church.

References:

Popular History of the United States.— Bryant.

June 24, 1795.— Jay's treaty ratified.

Difficulties had arisen with England because of violations of the treaty of 1783, so that a new treaty to dispose of them was negotiated by John Jay.

References:
   Popular History of the United States.— Bryant.
   History of the United States.— Hildreth.
   Our Country.— Lossing.

June 24, 1871.— Corner-stone of state capitol at Albany laid.

The ceremonies were under the direction of the Grand Lodge of Free and Accepted Masons of the State of New York. The first stone in the foundation was laid July 7, 1869.

June 28, 1776.— Attack on Fort Moultrie.

The people of Charleston, expecting an attack, had constructed a palmetto fort on Sullivan's Island, which was garrisoned by eight hundred men under Colonel Moultrie. On June 28th, the British fleet under Parker attacked it, the conflict lasting nine hours. Finally, however, Parker was forced to withdraw, with much shattered vessels. The fort was later named Moultrie in honor of the commander.

References:
   The American Revolution.— Fiske.
   Popular History of the United States.— Bryant.
   Popular History of the United States.— Anderson.
   1776.— Lossing.

June 28, 1778.— Battle of Monmouth.

The British army under Clinton, retreating from Philadelphia, was overtaken by Washington at Monmouth. Lee, leading the advance, was directed to make an attack, but instead, commanded a retreat. Upon Washington's arrival an advance was made. At nightfall there was no decisive result, and in the morning the British had fled.

References:
   Popular History of the United States.— Anderson.
   Popular History of the United States.— Bryant.
   The American Revolution.— Fiske.
   1776.— Lossing.

Appropriate Selections:
Selections from Irving's Life of Washington.

June 28, 1815.— Decatur in the bay of Algiers.

During the War of 1812, the Dey of Algiers, believing the United States unable to protect her commerce, broke the treaty and again resumed the practice of piracy against our ships. When peace with England was established, a fleet of ten ships, under Decatur, was sent to the Mediterranean. On the way he captured two Algerian vessels and, arriving in the bay of Algiers, June 28th, he forced the Dey to relinquish all American prisoners and all claim to a tribute from the United States.

References:

Popular History of the United States.— Anderson.
History of the Navy of the United States.— Cooper.
History of the Navy.— Maclay.
Popular History of the United States.— Bryant.

Appropriate Selections:

Selection from Cooper's History of the Navy of the United States. Death of Commodore Decatur.

July 1st, 2d, 3d, 1863.— Battle of Gettysburg.

On the 9th of June, Lee, whose army numbered nearly four hundred thousand men, began a northward movement. Hooker followed the invaders into Maryland, where (June 28th), his command was transferred to General Meade. At Gettysburg one of the most important conflicts of the war took place during the first three days of July. Lee was finally defeated, and, his army being reduced one-third, made a rapid retreat. The battle of Gettysburg is generally regarded as the greatest of the war. It was the turning point in the long conflict between the North and the South.

References:

Battles and Leaders of the Civil War.— Davis.
Bird's Eye View of Our Civil War.— Dodge.
Students' History of the United States.— Channing.
School History of the United States.— Lee.

Appropriate Selections:

Pickett's Charge at Gettysburg.— Comte de Paris, in Half-Hours with American History.— Morris.
National Cemetery at Gettysburg.
Gettysburg.— Captain Dudley H. Chase, U. S. A.
Bugles of Gettysburg, p. 219.
George William Curtis, p. 210.
Susan J. Adams, p. 210.
Henry C. Potter, p. 234

July 2, 1775.— Washington took command of the army at Cambridge.

References:

   The American Revolution.— Fiske.
   Popular History of the United States.— Bryant.
   Rise of the Republic of the United States.— Frothingham.
   Life of Washington.— Sparks.

Appropriate Selections:

   The Inconveniences of Militia.— General G. Washington, found in American History told by Contemporaries.— Hart.
   " Every exertion of my worthy colleagues and myself will be equally extended to the restoration of peace and harmony, as to the fatal but necessary operations of war."

July 2, 1881.— Assassination of Garfield.

   Garfield had been in office less than four months when he was shot by an assassin (Charles J. Guiteau), at the railroad station in Washington, as he was about to leave the capital for a summer trip to the east.

References:

   Life of James A. Garfield.— J. R. Gilmore.
   Students' History of the United States.— Channing.

July 3, 1890.— Idaho admitted to the Union.

July 3, 1898.— **Battle of Santiago.**

   On Sunday morning, July 3d, at half-past nine, the Spanish fleet started out of the harbor at Santiago with a rush, but the American fleet, always in readiness, closed in upon it and by half-past one every Spanish ship was a half-sunken wreck on the Cuban coast.

References:

   War with Spain.— Henry Cabot Lodge.
   With Sampson through the War.— Goode.

Appropriate Selections:

   The Men Behind the Guns, p. 224.

July 4, 1609.— **Discovery of Lake Champlain.**

   In 1608, Champlain planted on the St. Lawrence the post of Quebec. The next year, joining a party of Hurons and Algonquins in a war expedition against the Five Nations, he ascended the Sorel, and, first of white men, entered the lake which still bears his name. A series of explorations presently followed, whence arose the French claims to that vast tract of interior America, comprehended, along with Canada and Acadia, under its general name of New France.

References:

> Popular History of the United States.— Anderson.
> Discovery of America.— Fiske.

Appropriate Selections:

> Discovery of Lake Champlain.— Parkman.
> The American Indians, in History of the United States.— Hildreth.

July 4, 1776.— Declaration of Independence.

By the last of June the British had been repulsed from Charleston, and in the meantime, Congress, then in session at Philadelphia, was preparing to declare a separation of the political relations existing between Great Britain and the colonies. A resolution to that effect offered by Richard Henry Lee of Virginia, on the 7th of June, was passed by a large majority on the 2d of July. Two days after, Thomas Jefferson, of Virginia, in behalf of a committee of five members, presented a document which he had prepared; and, then, July 4, 1776, this document, the Declaration of Independence, was unanimously adopted by Congress.

Appropriate Selections:

> Independence Bell.— Anonymous, p. 111.
> Speech of John Adams.— Webster, p. 175.
> The Bell.— B. F. Taylor, p. 113.

July 4th and 5th, 1778.— Massacre in the Wyoming valley.

When the Wyoming valley was almost defenceless, as most of the able-bodied men had joined the patriot army, a band of Tories and Indians ravaged and desolated every settlement.

References:

> Popular History of the United States.— Bryant.
> American Revolution.— Fiske.
> 1776.— Lossing.
> Popular History of the United States.— Anderson.

July 4, 1804.— Nathaniel Hawthorne born.

Selections from:

> Mosses from an Old Manse.
> Snow Image.
> Twice-Told Tales.

July 4, 1817.— First spadeful of earth turned for the Erie canal.

July 4, 1817, the first spadeful of earth was turned for the Erie canal, and the canal, three hundred and sixty-three miles long, was completed in October, 1825. It was designed by De Witt Clinton, and cost $7,602,000. It has brought untold wealth to the state.

References:

Popular History of the United States.— Bryant.
Students' History of the United States.— Channing.
The United States.— Schouler.

July 4, 1826.— Death of Jefferson and Adams.

On the fiftieth anniversary of American independence, Thomas Jefferson and John Adams died. Both were members of the committee that framed the Declaration of Independence, both signed it, both were foreign ministers, vice-presidents, and presidents of the United States.

References:

Historic Americans.— Theodore Parker.
Popular History of the United States.— Bryant.
Popular History of the United States.— Anderson.

Appropriate Selections:

Oration on Adams and Jefferson.— Wert.
Selection from Life and Public Services of John Quincy Adams.— Seward.

July 4, 1828.— Driving of the first spike on the Baltimore and Ohio railroad.

Charles Carroll, the last survivor of the signers of the Declaration of Independence, drove the first spike for the Baltimore and Ohio railroad, the first in America to carry both passengers and freight.

References:

Students' History of the United States.— Channing.
Popular History of the United States.— Bryant.

July 4, 1863.— Capture of Vicksburg.

General Grant having gained a series of victories over the Confederate forces in the southwest, succeeded in taking Vicksburg, July 4th, after a daring and perilous siege of several months. Port Hudson having soon afterwards surrendered to General Banks, the Mississippi was completely opened.

References:

Battles and Leaders of the Civil War.— Davis.
Bird's Eye View of Our Civil War.— Dodge.
Story of the Civil War.— Ropes.

Appropriate Selections:

General Grant and the Civil War, p. 187.
Selecton IV, p. 222.
Hymn, for July 4, 1863.— George H. Baker.
The Fall of Vicksburg.— William Ross Wallace.
The Siege of Vicksburg.— Adam Badeau, in Morris' Half-Hours with American History.

July 5, 1814.— Battle of Chippewa.

General Brown met the British under General Riall at Chippewa, near Niagara Falls, where he won a brilliant victory.

References:

Pictorial Field-Book of the War of 1812.— Lossing.
Popular History of the United States.— Bryant.
Battles of the United States.— Dawson.

July 7, 1898.— Annexation of the Hawaiian Islands.

During the progress of the Spanish war the annexation of the Hawaiian Islands was finally consumated. A joint resolution was passed by Congress providing for the acquisition of the islands and for their temporary government. A group of twelve islands, with an area of 6,677 square miles and a population of about 100,000 persons, half of them native islanders, was thus made American territory.

References:

American Congress.— Moore.

July 9, 1755. — Braddock's defeat.

General Braddock, who had been sent to America as commander-in-chief of the royal forces, headed the expedition against Fort Duquesne. Disregarding the suggestions of Washington, his aide-de-camp, he fell into an ambush of French and Indians when within a few miles of the fort, and was defeated with great loss, he himself being mortally wounded.

References:

Popular History of the United States.— Anderson.
History of the United States.— Hildreth.
History of the United States.— Bancroft.

Appropriate Selections:

Defeat of Braddock.— Sparks.

July 10, 1890.— Wyoming admitted to the Union.

July 12, 1804.— Duel between Alexander Hamilton and Aaron Burr.

Alexander Hamilton and Aaron Burr met in a duel to settle a political quarrel, and Hamilton was killed.

References:

Popular History of the United States.— Bryant.
Our Country.— Lossing.
Students' History of the United States.— Channing.

Appropriate Selections:

Eulogy on Hamilton, from a discourse delivered in Albany by Dr. Nott,— found in Anderson's United States Reader.

July 15, 1779.— Storming of Stony Point.

The American forces, under General Anthony Wayne, forced their way into the fort from opposite directions, and meeting in the center, compelled the garrison to surrender. This stands out in high relief, as one of the most brilliant achievements of the war. The Americans had effected it without firing a musket.

References:

Popular History of the United States.— Bryant.
1776.— Lossing.
American Revolution.— Fiske.
History of the United States.— Bancroft.

July 17, 1898.— The Surrender of Santiago.

After several demands for the surrender of Santiago, General Shafter bombarded the place and forced the Spanish to yield, when Santiago passed into American hands.

References:

War with Spain.— H. C. Lodge.
In Cuba with Shafter.— J. D. Miley.

July 21, 1861.—Battle of Bull Run.

The Confederate army of about 100,000 men occupied a line through Virginia, from Harper's Ferry to Norfolk, their strongest position being between Washington and Richmond, at Manassas Junction. About the middle of July, an army under General McDowell marched to attack the Confederates. On the 18th, a conflict took place near Centerville and on the 21st, occurred the battle of Bull Run, a desperate conflict from which the Union forces, panic-stricken, fled in disorder towards Washington.

References:

Battles and Leaders of the Civil War.— Davis.
Bird's Eye View of Our Civil War.— Dodge.
Story of the Civil War.— Ropes.
United States.— Rhodes.
Popular History of the United States.— Anderson.
School History of the United States.— Lee.

Appropriate Selections:

On the Hill before Centerville.— George K. Baker.
The Run from Manassas Junction.— In R. G. White's Poetry of the War.

July 23, 1885.— Death of Ulysses S. Grant.

America lost her great military leader when General U. S. Grant died at Mount MacGregor, near Saratoga Springs.

July 24, 1819.— J. G. Holland born.

Selections from:

Life of Abraham Lincoln.
Lessons in Life.
Men of One Idea.

July 25, 1814.— Battle at Lundy's Lane.

The Americans under Brown were attacked at Lundy's Lane by Drummond, commanding a British force one-third larger than Brown's. The battle lasted from sunset to midnight, and was more death-dealing, in proportion to the numbers engaged, than any previously fought on the American continent. It ended without a decisive victory for either party.

References:

Half-Hours with American History.— Morris.
Pictorial Field-Book of the War of 1812.— Lossing.
Popular History of the United States.— Bryant.
Popular History of the United States.— Anderson.

July 27, 1898.— Porto Rico taken.

The British and German consuls, and several men representing the commercial interests of Ponce, acting under the authority of the Spanish commander, negotiated with the Americans for the surrender of that city. The American troops took formal possession, and the army held the city as a base from which they controlled the most important roads on the island.

References:

The War with Spain.— H. C. Lodge.

July 30, 1619.— First Legislative body in America.

On July 30, 1619, a legislative body met in a little wooden church at James-town. Each of the eleven local constituencies had two representatives, called burgesses, giving the name, the House of Burgesses. There was also an upper House called the Council; these with the Governor constituted a general assem-bly, whose functions were both legislative and judicial.

References:

Old Virginia and Her Neighbors.— Fiske.
Popular History of the United States.— Bryant.
A Short History of the English Colonies in America.— Lodge.
American History told by Contemporaries.— Hart.

August 1, 1876.— Colorado was admitted to the Union.

August 2, 1684.— Treaty with the Five Nations at Albany.

The Indians of the Five Nations made a treaty of peace with the English at a convention in Albany.

References:

Brief History of the Empire State.— Hendricks.
Popular History of the United States.— Bryant.

August 2, 1832.— Black Hawk defeated at Bad Axe river.

By a treaty of July 15, 1830, the Sac and Fox Indians ceded their land east of the Mississippi to the Americans. Black Hawk, a chief, refused to submit to the treaty, and began to massacre the whites. He was finally defeated by Gen-eral Atkinson at Bad Axe river.

References:

Popular History of the United States.— Bryant.
Battles of the United States.— Dawson.
School History of the United States.— Lee.
Our Country.— Lossing.

August 4, 1857.— The first telegraphic message passed from America to Europe.

The Atlantic telegraph was invented by Cyrus W. Field.

References:

Popular History of the United States.— Bryant.

August 6, 1777.— Battle of Oriskany and sortie from Fort Stanwix.

General Herkimer, on his way to relieve Fort Stanwix, fell into an ambuscade at Oriskany, was defeated, and mortally wounded. As Fort Stanwix was so hard pressed, Arnold was sent to its aid. Resorting to stratagem, he caused the desertion of the Indian allies, which left the British general, St. Leger, in such straits that he was obliged to decamp hurriedly, leaving much ammunition behind him. The retreat of St. Leger was of vital importance in deciding the fate of Burgoyne's army.

References:

Popular History of the United States.— Bryant.
Popular History of the United States.— Anderson.
The American Revolution.— Fiske.
See Selection 2, p. 21.

August 7, 1795.— Joseph Rodman Drake born.

Appropriate Selections:

The American Flag, p. 303.

August 7, 1807.— Trial trip of Fulton's steamboat, the Clermont.

References:

Popular History of the United States.— Anderson.
Popular History of the United States.— Bryant.

August 9, 1812.— The Constitution and the Guerrière.

An encounter between the American frigate Constitution, called "Old Ironsides," and the British frigate Guerrière, took place near the Gulf of St. Lawrence. The Guerrière opened fire, continuing nearly an hour before the Constitution answered with more than an occasional gun. Then drawing nearer, the Constitution poured in volleys with amazing rapidity and power. The Guerrière fought desperately, but at last was forced to strike her flag. Too injured to keep afloat, the ship was burned.

References:

History of the Navy.— Maclay.
History of the Navy of the United States.— Cooper.
Popular History of the United States.— Anderson.
Popular History of the United States.— Bryant.

Appropriate Selections:

"The first English frigate that ever struck its flag to an American ship-of-war had gone down to the bottom of the ocean. The sea never rolled over a vessel whose fate so startled the world. It disappeared forever, but it left its outline on the deep, never to be effaced until England and America shall be no more."

" Old Ironsides."— O. W. Holmes.

August 10, 1821.— Missouri admitted to the Union.

August 11, 1609.— **Discovery of the Hudson river.**

Almost contemporaneously with the first French exploration of Lake Champlain, another celebrated discoverer was penetrating from an opposite direction towards the same point. In 1609, Hendrick Hudson, in the employ of the Dutch East India Company, while searching for a north or northwest passage to India, discovered the river which bears his name.

References:

Discovery of America.— Fiske.
History of the United States.— Hildreth.

Appropriate Selections:

Voyage of the Half Moon.— Broadhead, in his History of New York.

August 12, 1898.— Signing of protocol with Spain.

Spanish defeats were confessed and a cessation of hostilities desired by the Spanish Government. Secretary of State Hay acceded to the request on certain essential conditions. The protocol was signed August 12, 1898, and hostilities ceased.

References:

The War with Spain.— H. C. Lodge.

August 13, 1898.— City of Manila taken.

General Merritt and Admiral Dewey, having demanded the surrender of Manila, ordered an attack on August 13. The combination of the land and sea forces was irresistible and the Spanish hoisted the white flag. A conference was held, the capitulation was signed, and the city surrendered. "And the empire which Magellan had found for Spain had passed away forever."

References:

War with Spain.— H. C. Lodge.

August 16, 1777.— **Battle of Bennington.**

Burgoyne, in need of supplies, sent Colonel Baum with a force of Hessians to Bennington to capture those of the Americans. General Stark, however, defeated the expedition.

References:

    Popular History of the United States.— Bryant.
    History of the United States.— Bancroft.
    American Revolution.— Fiske.

August 16, 1780.— **Battle of Camden.**

Gates, in command of the American forces, and Cornwallis, in command of the British, unexpectedly met at Sander's Creek. Overpowered by numbers, the American militia fled. The regulars, however, under the command of Baron de Kalb, offered the bravest resistance until de Kalb was mortally wounded.

References:

    Popular History of the United States.— Anderson.
    Popular History of the United States.— Bryant.
    The American Revolution.— Fiske.
    1776.— Lossing.

Appropriate Selections:

    The Old Continentals.— Guy Humphrey McMaster, p. 262.

August 16, 1812.— Surrender of Detroit.

Towards the beginning of the war, General Hull took his post at Detroit. He was soon followed by General Brock, commanding thirteen hundred British and Indians. The Americans were confident of winning the battle, about to take place, but instead of fighting, Hull surrendered at once, and by so doing lost Detroit and the whole territory of Michigan as well.

References:

    Pictorial Field-Book of the War of 1812.— Lossing.
    Popular History of the United States.— Bryant.
    Battles of the United States.— Dawson.

August 20, 1799.— Battle of Maumee.

The Indians north of the Ohio continued to show their dissatisfaction by many hostile acts, and were not subdued until General Wayne defeated them in a desperate battle on the Maumee River.

References:

    Popular History of the United States.— Bryant.
    Our Country.— Lossing.
    Battles of the United States.— Dawson.

August 24, 1814.— The city of Washington captured and partly burned.

Five thousand men under General Ross disembarked from a British squadron in the Chesapeake Bay, captured Washington, and set fire to the city. Until the last moment, the Americans could not determine whether Washington or Baltimore was to be attacked, consequently the force was divided, and the British met with little opposition.

References:

Popular History of the United States.— Bryant.
Popular History of the United States.— Anderson.
Pictorial Field-Book of the War of 1812.— Lossing.

August 25, 1839.— Francis Bret Harte born.

John Burns at Gettysburg.
Selection from East and West Poems.

August 27, 1664.— New Amsterdam called New York.

An English expedition, under Nichols, suddenly appeared in the harbor of New Amsterdam and forced the Dutch to surrender. The articles of capitulation were signed on the twenty-seventh of August, and the name was changed to New York, in honor of the Duke of York.

References:

History of the Empire State.— Hendricks.
Popular History of the United States.— Bryant.
Narrative and Critical History of America.— Winsor.
History of New York.— Roberts.
American History told by Contemporaries.— Hart.

August 27, 1776.— Battle of Long Island.

The British forces, under Howe, attacked the Americans at Long Island in three divisions, two in front, the third in the rear. Despite the brave fight of the patriots, they were forced to yield. The effects of the disaster were far-reaching; it decided the wavering to join the enemy; it gave form and direction to subsequent events; and it gave New York into the possession of the British.

References:

Half-Hours with American History.— Morris.
Popular History of the United States.— Bryant.
1776.— Lossing.

The American Revolution.— Fiske.
Battles of the United States.— Dawson.
Diary of the American Revolution.— Moore.

Appropriate Selections:
See p. 29, selection 4.

August 28, 1619.— First negro slaves in the colonies.

About August 28, 1619, a Dutch merchantman brought a shipload of twenty negroes to Virginia to be sold as slaves. A little over a year later the pilgrims landed in New England, and two antagonistic and opposing elements were then planted in America, that were destined to be in almost constant conflict until the question of slavery in the United States was settled forever by the great Civil war.

References:

Old Virginia and Her Neighbors.— Fiske.

August 29, 1779.— Battle of Chemung.

General Sullivan entered the region near the headwaters of the Susquehanna and Genesee rivers to punish the Indians for massacres. At Newtown, now Elmira, he gained a decisive victory in the battle of Chemung.

References:

American Revolution.— Fiske.
Battles of the United States.— Dawson.
Popular History of the United States.— Bryant.
General Sullivan's Indian Expedition, 1779.

August 29, 1809.— Oliver Wendell Holmes born.

Appropriate Selections:

Old Ironsides.
The Season's Masterpiece.

INDEX OF SUBJECTS.

A.

Admiral Dewey and the Spanish-American War, 197.
American Eagle, The, 130.
American Flag, The, 316.
Arsenal at Springfield, The, 127.

B.

Banner of the Stars, The, 15, 321.
Battle of Yorktown, The, 179.
Bell, The, 113.
Birthday of Abraham Lincoln, The, 269.
Birthday of Washington, The, 243.
Birthday Programs:
  Longfellow, 152.
  Whittier, 152.
  Holmes, 153.
  Lowell, 153.
Bivouac of the Dead, The, 28.
Black Regiment, The, 105.
Blue and the Gray, The, 146, 220.
Boy, Columbus, The, 161.
Brave at Home, The, 343.
Bugles of Gettysburg, 219.

C.

Camp, The, 61.
Capitol, The, 51.
Carmen Bellicosum, 262.
Centennial Hymn, 345.
Citizenship, 366.
Civic Creed for the Boys and Girls of the Great Republic, 35.
Columbia, the Gem of the Ocean, 313.
Columbus Day, 157.
Commemoration Ode, From the, 340.
Common School, The, 48.
Concord Hymn, 170, 222.
Constitution of the United States, The, 353.
Consulate, The, 85.
Contents, xv.

D.

Declaration of Independence, The, 351.
Dewey and the Spanish-American War, Admiral, 197.

Dewey's Victory, May 1, 1898, 200.
Dirge for a Soldier, 28.
Dove, The, 125.

E.

Eagle, The, 129, 133.
Eight Volunteers, 233.
E Pluribus Unum, 138.
Exposition Buildings, 75.

F.

Farragut, Admiral, 92.
Flag, A Brief History of the, 5.
Flag Day, 301.
Flag of Freedom, The, 65.
Flag of the Constellation, The, 18.
Flag that has Never Known Defeat, The, 10.
Flag, The, 313.
Fourth of July, The, 175.
Freedom, 101.
Free Schools Inspire Loyalty to Country, 50.

G.

General Grant and the Civil War, 187.
Grant, Ulysses Simpson, 189, 193.
Gray Forest Eagle, The, 133.

H.

Half-Masted Flag, The, 25.
Hats Off, 323.
His First and Last Surrender, 188.
Home, 41.
Home, The, 41.
Home, The Nation's Safeguard, The, 42.
Hospital, The, 69.
How Sleep the Brave, 25, 231.

I.

Incident, An, 71.
Incident of the French Camp, An, 61.
Independence Bell, July 4, 1776, 111.
In the Time of Strife, 230.
Introduction, v.

L.

Labor is Worship, 386.
Land, The, 87.
Landing of the Pilgrims, The, 163, 167.
Lexington and Concord, 169.
Liberty, 355.
Liberty Bell, The, 111.
Liberty Cap, The, 101.
Liberty's Latest Daughter, 178.
Lincoln, 296.
Lincoln, The Birthday of, 269.
Love of Country, 88.

M.

Maine, The, 198.
Manila Bay, 238.
Meditations of Columbia, 1876, The, 164.
Memorial Day, 205.
Men Behind the Guns, The, 224.
Monterey, 324.
My Country, 43.
My Country, 'Tis of Thee, 341.

N.

New Memorial Day, The, 225.
New York Day at the World's Fair, 76.
Nobility of Labor, The, 383.

O.

Observations on the Character of Columbus, 158.
O Captain, My Captain, 291.
Old Flag Forever, 10, 321.
Our Country, 375.
Our Country and Flag, 309.
Our Flag, 9.
Our Flag is There, 310.
Our Standing Army, 226.
Our State, 107.

P.

Palmetto and the Pine, The, 56.
Patriotic Pledges, 35.
Patriotic Poets, Birthday Programs:
Longfellow, 152.
Whittier, 152.
Holmes, 153.
Lowell, 153.
Patriotism, 331.
Patriot's Elysium, The, 340.
Phantom Army, The, 27.
Progress, 81.

R.

Red, White and Blue, The, 19.
Restored Union, The, 55.
Reveille, 66.
Revolutionary Alarm, The, 170.
Right of the Line, The, 20.
Rising in 1776, The, 116.

S.

Sailing of the Fleet, 200.
Salute the Flag, 321.
Saluting the Flag, 31.
Santa Filomena, 70.
School, The, 47.
School, Liberty's Safeguard, The, 47.
Sea, The, 91.
Shield, The, 135.
Ship of State, The, 91, 348.
Soldier Boy, The, 223.
Song for Independence, 358.
Song of the Camp, The, 64.
Song of the Flag, A, 30.
Songs of Labor, Selections from, 384.
Speech at Transfer of Flags, 36.
Stars in My Country's Sky — Are ye All There?, 137.
Stars, The, 11.
Star-Spangled Banner, The, 320.
Stripes and the Stars, The, 308.
Suggestions to Teachers, xi.
Sword, The, 115.

T.

Tableaux:
The Minute Man, 143.
Departure and Return of the States, 146.
The March of the Flags, 150.
The Army and Navy, 150.
Homage to Columbia, 151.
True Fame, 234.
True Patriot, The, 135.
Two Flags, The, 325.

U.

Uncover to the Flag, 32.
Unfurl Our Standards High, 94.
Union, The, 359.
Union and Liberty, 365.
Universal Education, 48.

V.

Vanquished, 194.
Vision of Liberty, The, 104.
Vision of the Stars, A, 16.

W.

Washington, George, 248.
Washington, The Birthday of, 243.

William Tell's Address to His Native Hills, 102.
Why They Called Him Leader, 195.
Women of the War, 71.
Work-shop and the Camp, The, 387.

Y.

Yorktown Lesson, The, 180.

INDEX OF SONGS AND MUSIC.

A.

America, 3.
American Flag, The, 303.
Angel of Peace, 121.

B.

Battle Hymn of the Republic, 139.
Breaking Waves Dashed High, The, 165.

C.

Camp Flag, The, 67.
Centennial Hymn, 79.
Columbus, 159.

D.

Dewey at Manila Bay, 203.

F.

Flag of the Free, 317.

G.

God Speed the Right, 265.
Good Comrade, The, 73.

H.

Heroes' Greeting, The, 217.
Home, Sweet Home, 39.

I.

Independence Day, 174.
In Memoriam, 227.

L.

Land of Washington, The, 181.
Laus Deo, 297.
Liberty Bell, The, 109.
Liberty Cap, The, 97.

M.

Man for Me, The, 289.
Many Flags in Many Lands, 83.
Memorial Day, Song for, 207.
My Country, 'Tis of Thee, 327.

O.

Ocean-Guarded Flag, The, 90.
Ode for Washington's Birthday, 255.
O Starry Flag of Union, Hail, 57.
Our Flag, 311.
Our Own Dear Land, 89.

R.

Red, White and Blue, The, 23.
Remembered, 239.

S.

Schoolhouse and the Flag, The, 45.
See, the Conquering Hero Comes, 191.
Song for Memorial Day, 207.
Star of Freedom, The, 53.
Star-Spangled Banner, The, 13.
Sword of Bunker Hill, The, 119.

T.

Three Cheers for the Olden Time, 173.

W.

Waving Flag, The, 33.
Where the Eagle Is King, 131.

INDEX OF AUTHORS.

A.

Adams, John, 246, 248.
Adams, Samuel, 378.
Adams, Susan J., 210.
American Naval Officer, 1812, 310.
Ames, Fisher, 334.
Andrew, Gov., 212, 270.
Arthur, Chester A., 183.
Atlantic Monthly, 209.

B.

Bailey, Lansing C., 233.
Ballard, H. C., 270.
Bancroft, George, 170.
Beck, Henry T., 302.
Beecher, Henry Ward, 189, 215, 305, 377.
Benjamin, Charles L., 10.
Bennett, H. H., 323.
Black, Frank S., 282.
Blaine, James G., 177.
Boardman, Henry A., 375.
Boker, George Henry, 28, 105.
Bradshaw, Wellesley, 219.
Bright, John, 272.
Brooks, Elbridge S., 379.
Brooks, James G., 244.
Brooks, Phillips, 273, 276.
Brown, John Mason, 209.
Browne, Francis F., 194.
Browning, Robert, 61.
Bryce, James, 244.
Bunner, H. C., 321.
Burns, Robert, 388.
Butterworth, Hezekiah, 260, 375.

C.

Caldwell, W. W., 380.
Calhoun, John C., 222, 354, 376.
Carroll, Archbishop John, 244.
Cary, Phœbe, 302, 375.
Castelar, Emilio, 272, 274.
Channing, William E., 250.
Chapin, E. A., 211.

Cheverton, E. C., 32.
Choate, Rufus, 247, 260.
Clay, Henry, 210, 377.
Cleveland, Grover, 247.
Coles, Abraham, 246.
Collins, William, 26, 231.
Conkling, Roscoe, 378.
Cooper, Peter, 271.
Corliss, C. P., 270.
Cowper, William, 135.
Cranch, Christopher P., 244.
Crawford, F. Marion, 315, 381.
Curtis, George William, 71, 145, 171, 210,
    214, 229, 230, 261, 334, 337, 347, 349, 363.
Cutler, George Washington, 138.

D.

Dale, H. W., 270.
Dana, Charles A., 273, 278, 279, 280, 353.
Dawes, Henry L., 270.
Deems, Charles F., 261.
De Kay, C., 194.
Dekker, Thomas, 383.
Dennison, Frederic, 302.
Depew, Chauncey M., 48, 162, 231, 274,
    285, 347.
Devens, Charles, 212.
Dewey, Orville, 336, 388.
Dickinson, Daniel S., 306, 375, 376.
Douglass, Frederick, 271.
Dowd, Emma C., 246.
Drake, J. Rodman, 316.
Draper, Andrew S., 277, 345.
Dwight, John Sullivan, 342.
Dwyer, J. Henry, 210.
Dyer, Arthur, 379.
Dyer, Sidney, 272.

E.

Edwards, Richard, 347.
Emerson, Ralph Waldo, 144, 170, 222, 274.
Everett, Edward, 167, 211, 234, 244, 246,
    251, 305, 335, 368.
Everett, Homer, 209.

F.

Field, David Dudley, 343.
Fields, James T., 378.
Finch, Francis Miles, 146, 220.
Fiske, John, 257.
Flower, Roswell P., 81.
Foote, Kate, 319.
Ford, Paul Leicester, 251.
Foster, Charles, 271.
Franklin, Benjamin, 244.
Frelinghuysen, Theodore, 271.
Frye, William P., 136.
Fuller, Melville, 247.
Furness, William E., 215.

G.

Gallagher, W. D., 378.
Garfield, James A., 271, 362, 369, 378.
G. A. R. Report, 331, 332.
Gilder, Richard Watson, 211.
Gilmore, P. S., 377.
Gladstone, William Ewart, 244, 378.
Godwin, Parke, 380.
Gordan, Cornelia M., 209.
Gordon, John B., 211, 362.
Gould, Hannah, 246.
Gould, Jennie, 302.
Grady, Henry W., 42, 52, 148, 234, 275, 348.
Grant, Ulysses S., 212, 213, 214, 222, 270,
    286, 380.
Gratton, Sir Henry, 244.
Gray, Asa, 270.
Gray, Thomas, 383.
Greeley, Adolphus, 15.
Green, John Richard, 244, 259.
Griffis, William E., 346.
Grimke, Thomas S., 333.
Grow, Galusha A., 326.
Guenther, Richard, 371.
Guizot, Francois, P. G., 244.

H.

Hale, Edward Everett, 246, 339.
Hale, Sarah J., 377.
Halpine, Charles G., 296.
Hamilton, Alexander, 245, 376.
Harper's Magazine, 211.
Harrison, Benjamin, 15, 307, 335, 371.
Harte, Bret, 27.
Herbert, Hilary A., 376.
Hesperian, 43.

H. E. W., Jr., 238.
Higginson, Thomas Wentworth, 209.
Hoar, George F., 246, 370, 375.
Hoffman, Charles F., 324.
Holmes, Oliver Wendell, 271, 302, 315, 357,
    365.
Howard, O. O., 270.
Howells, William Dean, 272.
Hunt, Helen, 215.

I.

Ingersoll, Robert G., 26, 102, 213, 287, 288,
    352, 355, 356, 367.
Ireland, Rt. Rev. John, 77.
Irving, Washington, 158, 246.

J.

Jackson, Andrew, 377, 378.
Janvier, Francis De Hass, 245.
Jay, John, 246.
Jefferson, Thomas, 248, 250, 381.
Johnson, Reverdy, 375.

K.

Kasson, John Adams, 380.
Kent, D. H., 212.
Key, Francis Scott, 320, 377.
King, Thomas Starr, 247, 340, 380.
Kiser, S. E., 223.
Knowles, J. Sheridan, 102.

L.

Lafayette, Marquis de, 378.
Lamartine, A. M. L. de, 245.
Lanier, Sidney, 164, 382.
Larcom, Lucy, 313.
Lasker, Raphael, 343.
Lecky, William E. H., 259.
Lee, Henry, 245.
Legare, Hugh S., 346, 355.
Leggett, William, 244, 375.
Lewis, Alonzo, 65.
Lieber, Francis, 377.
Lincoln, Abraham, 233, 244, 252, 307, 309,
    333, 337, 341, 351, 357, 361, 364, 372.
Lodge, Henry Cabot, 198, 245, 251, 260, 335,
    338, 372.
Longfellow, Henry Wadsworth, 70, 91, 127,
    348.
Lowe, Charles, 270.
Lowell, James Russell, 247, 276, 292, 340,
    356.

M.

Madison, James, 379.
Marion, Francis, 50.
Martin, G., 271.
Matthews, Stanley, 271.
McClellan, George B., 222.
McDowell, J., 344.
McDuffie, George, 378.
McElroy, Wm. H., 21, 81.
McKinley, William, 56, 198, 199, 224, 283, 284, 285, 286, 344, 364.
McMaster, Guy Humphrey, 262.
Meagher, Thomas Francis, 118, 346.
Merrill, Samuel P., 234.
Miles, Nelson A., 379.
Mitchell, George S., 209.
Montgomery, James, 340.
Morgan, Thomas J., 355.
Morton, Oliver P., 362.
Morris, Gouverneur, 245.
Moulton, Louise Chandler, 176.
Murphy, John A., 211.

N.

Naylor, Charles, 385, 386.
New, John C., 270.
Newman, John P., 282.
New York Tribune, 200.
Nicholas, Czar of Russia, 375.

O.

O'Connor, Joseph, 76.
O'Connor, Michael, 66.
O'Gorman, Richard, 177.
O'Hara, Theodore, 28, 216.
O'Reilly, John Boyle, 167, 376.
Orleans, Louis Philippe, Duc d', 272.
Osgood, Frances S., 386.
Outlook, The, 235.

P.

Paine, Albert Bigelow, 225.
Paine, Thomas, 244.
Palgrave, Francis T., 247.
Parker, I. C., 379.
Parker, Theodore, 252, 381.
Parkhurst, Charles H., 339.
Pease, T. C., 271.
Percival, James Gates, 129.
Peterson, Henry, 271.
Phillips, Charles, 253.
Phillips, Wendell, 272, 367, 377.

Pike, Manley H., 56.
Potter, Henry C., 234, 261, 294, 369.
Porter, Horace, 188, 248, 296.
Porter, M. S., 134.
Power, Thomas F., 210.
Pray, I. C., Jr., 316.
Proctor, Edna Dean, 308.
Putnam, George, 210.

R.

Ray, George W., 281.
Raymond, R. W., 15, 321.
Read, T. Buchanan, 18, 116, 315, 343.
Ripley, Mary A., 272.
Robbins, Asher, 249.
Robinson, Oscar D., 229, 347.
Robinson, William E., 309.
Rochambeau, Marquis de, 183.
Roche, James J., 245.
Rooney, John J., 224.
Roosevelt, Theodore, 92, 115, 224, 231, 276, 368, 370, 371, 376.
Rosenburg, C. G., 245.
Ross, Lawrence Sullivan, 219.

S.

Sangster, Margaret E., 9.
Sargent, Epes, 381.
Saxton, Charles T., 338.
Schurz, Carl, 247, 351.
Scott, Sir Walter, 88, 342, 383.
Scott, W. H., 36.
Seward, William H., 245.
Sewell, Jonathan M., 376.
Shakespeare, William, 302, 375, 383.
Shaw, Albert D., 322.
Shaw, David T., 313.
Shelley, Percy Bysshe, 245.
Sheridan, George A., 211.
Sheridan, Philip, 195.
Sherman, James S., 282.
Sherman, John, 379.
Sherman, William Tecumseh, 195, 210, 270, 271, 377.
Sherwood, Kate D., 379.
Sherwood, Kate M. B., 272.
Shoemaker, William L., 376.
Sigourney, Lydia Huntley, 137.
Simpson, Matthew, 271.
Skinner, Charles R., viii, 48, 49, 349.
Smith, Dexter, 314.

Smith, Samuel Francis, 47, 341.
Southey, Robert, 244.
Sparks, Jared, 252.
Spofford, Harriet Prescott, 319.
Stanton, Frank L., 10, 230, 321.
Stephens, Alexander H., 273, 293.
Stockton, Commodore, 236.
Stoddard, Richard Henry, 291.
Street, Alfred B., 133, 358.
Strong, Josiah, 377.
Stryker, M. Woolsey, 30.
Sumner, Charles, 126, 247, 250, 270, 306.
Sutton, George D., 10.
Swain, Charles, 41.
Swift, John L., 235.
Swing, David, 272, 293.

T.

Taylor, Bayard, 64, 178, 211.
Taylor, B. F., 113.
Tennyson, Alfred, 101, 133, 246, 357.
Thackeray, William Makepeace, 245.
Thompson, C. W., 130.
Thompson, Hugh S., 381.
Thompson, Maurice F., 209, 292, 295, 380.
Thurston, John H., 214.
Thurston, John M., 62, 280, 382.
Towle, Henry M., 259.
Trowbridge, John T., 272.
Twitchell, Joseph H., 209.

V.

Vandegrift, Margaret, 226.
Van Dusen, I. D., 379.

Vaughan, Virginia, 202.
Voorhees, Daniel W., 232.

W.

Waite, Morrison R., 270.
Ware, Henry, Jr., 104.
Warner, Charles Dudley, 75, 270.
Warren, Owen Grenliffe, 94.
Washington, George, 334, 359, 360, 366, 370, 377.
Washington, Mary, 245.
Washington Star, 294.
Waterbury, S. L., 15, 315.
Watterson, Henry, 55, 361.
Webster, Daniel, 52, 175, 177, 246, 249, 336, 352, 353, 354, 359, 360, 363, 375, 376.
Whitman, Walt, 291.
Whittier, John Greenleaf 107, 126, 273, 345, 376, 378, 384.
Willard, Frances E., 325.
Williams, Thomas, 302.
Wilson, John D., 200.
Wilson, William L., 377.
Winship, Albert E., 380.
Winter, William, 232.
Winthrop, Robert Charles, 149, 180, 257, 262, 305, 379, 380, 381.
Wise, George D., 287.
Wirt, William, 249.
W. K. W., xi, 16.
Wolf, Edmund J., 379.
Wood, Anson S., 236.
Woodford, Stewart L., 333, 369.

Printed in the USA
CPSIA information can be obtained
at www.ICGtesting.com
CBHW071903270524
9142CB00003B/47

9 781016 181600